Alienating Labour

International Studies in Social History

General Editor: Marcel van der Linden
International Institute of Social History, Amsterdam

ALIENATING LABOUR

Workers on the Road from Socialism to Capitalism in East Germany and Hungary

Eszter Bartha

berghahn
NEW YORK · OXFORD
www.berghahnbooks.com

First published in 2013 by
Berghahn Books
www.berghahnbooks.com

© 2013, 2024 Eszter Bartha
First paperback edition published in 2024

Library of Congress Cataloging–in–Publication Data

Bartha, Eszter.
  Alienating labour: workers on the road from socialism to capitalism in East
Germany and Hungary / Eszter Bartha.
      pages cm. -- (International studies in social history; volume 22)
  Includes bibliographical references.
  ISBN 978-1-78238-025-2 (hardback: alk. paper) -- ISBN 978-1-80073-759-4 (open access
ebook)
  1. Labor--Germany (East)--History. 2. Labor--Hungary--History. 3. Labor unions and
communism--Europe, Eastern--History. 4. Post-communism--Europe, Eastern. 5. Capitalism-
-Europe, Eastern. I. Title.
  HD8380.7.B37 2013
  331.0943'109049--dc23

                                                                                    2013006042

British Library Cataloguing in Publication Data

A catalogue record for this book is available from the British Library

ISBN 978-1-78238-025-2 hardback
ISBN 978-1-80539-124-1 paperback
ISBN 978-1-78238-026-9 epub
ISBN 978-1-80073-759-4 web pdf

https://doi.org/10.3167/9781782380252

CONTENTS

FIGURES AND TABLES

FIGURES

TABLES

ABBREVIATIONS

APO   (Abteilungsparteiorganisation): departmental party organization

AWU   (Arbeiterwohnunterkunft): workers' hostel

BPKK   (Bezirksparteikontrollkommission): district control committee of the party

FDJ   (Freie Deutsche Jugend): Free German Youth, the youth organization of the East German Communist party

GO   (Grundorganisation): base organization

IKL   (Industriekreisleitung): leadership of the party organization of the factory

IKPKK   (Industriekreis-Parteikontrollkommission): control committee of the party organization of the factory

IKPO   (Industriekreisparteiorganisation): the party organization of the factory

KISZ   (Kommunista Ifjúsági Szövetség): League of Communist Youth, the youth organization of the Hungarian Communist party

MMG   (Mosonmagyaróvári Mezőgazdasági Gépgyár): Mosonmagyaróvár Tractor Factory

MVG   (Magyar Vagon-és Gépgyár): Hungarian Wagon and Machine Factory

MSZMP   (Magyar Szocialista Munkáspárt): Hungarian Socialist Workers' Party

NES   New Economic System

SED   (Sozialistische Einheitspartei Deutschlands): Socialist Unity Party of Germany, the ruling party of the GDR

SZMT   (Szakszervezetek Megyei Tanácsa): County Council of the Trade Unions

VB   (végrehajtó bizottság): executive committee

VEB   (volkseigener Betrieb): state-owned enterprise

VGMK   (*vállalati gazdasági munkaközösség*): economic productive communities of the enterprise

ACKNOWLEDGEMENT

I am indebted to the János Bolyai Fellowship of the Hungarian Academy of Sciences, which enabled me to complete the manuscript.

WELFARE DICTATORSHIPS, THE WORKING CLASS AND SOCIALIST IDEOLOGY
A Theoretical and Methodological Outline

In the Hungarian 'hot' summer of 1989, when the newly formed parties had already agreed with the Hungarian Socialist Workers' Party (*Magyar Szocialista Munkáspárt* [MSZMP]), the ruling Communist Party of the country about the transformation of the political regime from the 'dictatorship of the proletariat' to parliamentary democracy and the holding of democratic parliamentary elections, many people in the countryside were still unaware of the forthcoming sweeping political and social changes.[1] Although the Hungarian democratic opposition was concentrated in the capital, there were, however, several signs across the country that displayed the crumbling legitimacy of the ruling communist regime. In the industrial town of Győr the recently launched oppositionist journal entitled *Tér-kép* (Map) put forward a provocative question to its audience: 'Would you call the capitalists back?' In an important industrial town and after many years of communist propaganda, it is less of a surprise that most of the respondents analysed the question from the perspective of the workers. The conclusion is, however, more surprising or at least detrimental to official socialism, which was the dominant legitimizing ideology of the regime,[2] because the majority of the respondents argued that workers would benefit more from a capitalist regime than they did from socialism:

> If one provides for the workers the same way as Zwack promised on TV, he can come tomorrow. Many Hungarians have been in the West and everybody can see the standard of living and social security there even if there is unemployment. I have read somewhere that the labour movement achieved real results precisely in the capitalist countries. And I don't think that the defence of the workers' interests would be only demagogy on behalf of the capitalists.[3]

That the above opinion was indeed widespread in the county of Győr-Sopron, whose centre was Győr, had been confirmed in an interview with Ede Horváth, the chief manager of Rába Hungarian Wagon and Machine Factory (*Rába Magyar Vagon-és Gépgyár*, Rába MVG), the largest factory in the county, which he gave to the same journal. In many aspects Horváth was an emblematic figure of the attacked regime. A former Stakhanovite, who started working in Rába as a turner, Horváth's life followed an exemplary communist career: after serving in different managerial positions in the 1950s, in 1963 he was appointed the chief manager of the Wagon Factory. Later he was also elected onto the Central Committee of MSZMP, a position that he held from 1970 until 1989.[4] He was also nicknamed the 'Red Baron': this was a reference not to his lifestyle – because contrary to the image of the 'idle and corrupt' cadre, which was widely criticized not only by the hardliners ('dogmatic' or 'orthodox' communists)[5] but also by the leftist critics of actually existing socialism, Horváth was a workaholic, who led a disciplined and modest life – but to his high power position in the party and the county. At the time of the interview he was increasingly attacked for his prominent political role. Horváth agreed to give an interview to the oppositionist journal with the purpose of defending himself against the charge that he held to be the most unjust and undeserved: he was accused of pursuing an 'anti-worker' policy. In the interview Horváth, who never denied his working-class origins and background, protested not only against this charge but he also sought to find an explanation for the 'pro-capitalist' feelings of the workers of his factory:

> At one time we tried to motivate the people with the slogan that the factory is yours, you are building it for yourself. This did not prove true. People are interested in two things: that they have honest work and they receive fair wages. If these two are fulfilled, they will regard their workplace, if not the factory, as their own. And then they will be satisfied and their political attitudes will reflect their content. We could not provide this, and we continuously darkened the political climate. This partly holds also for Rába. Despite the fact that we pay honest money in comparison to the national wages, we could not solve this problem completely. I said for a long time that we would pay a very heavy price for cheap labour. But I am not to blame for the fact that today there is a bad political climate for the regime in every Hungarian factory.[6]

The local drama was not yet finished. The trade union supported the workers' strike in the Mosonmagyaróvár Tractor Factory, which belonged to Rába – a protest act which would have been unthinkable at the heyday of communism, when the party held the trade unions under its firm control. The conflict eventually led to the resignation of the charismatic leader of the factory, who had been elected 'man of the year' in 1986, in acknowledgement of his managerial success: the enterprise council asked him to retire, to which he agreed on 18 December 1989.[7] In the political atmosphere of 1989 it was unlikely that he would have ever kept his position.[8]

The above documented local conflict was indicative of the crisis of actually existing socialism, which unfolded on a significantly larger scale in other East European countries, where the change of regimes was triggered not by parliamentary negotiations like in Hungary but by mass demonstrations and large, widespread and sometimes violent protests like in Czechoslovakia, East Germany, Poland and Romania.[9] The history of the collapse of communism in Eastern Europe has been narrated several times, from different disciplinary and methodological perspectives. The history of the workers under late socialism is, however, either underrepresented or, as in the Hungarian case, is outright missing from the otherwise vast literature on the demise of the East European socialist regimes.[10] The contention of this book is that a careful examination of the micro histories of two large factories, one located in Jena, East Germany (Zeiss) and the other in Győr, Hungary (Rába) offers novel insights into the nature and politics of these regimes as well as the causes of their rapid and apparently unexpected collapse – which has been confirmed by many contemporary observers and Western scholars of the former communist bloc.[11] In what follows I will elaborate three main themes, which are directly connected with the design and presentation of my research based on the two aforementioned factory case studies. Firstly, I will introduce and explain the terms 'welfare dictatorship' and the 'party's policy towards labour' in a historical context. Secondly, an attempt will be made to elaborate the claim of there being a relative lack of literature on the workers in the examined period as well as to designate the key themes of inquiry. Thirdly, I will justify the comparison of the two countries under examination – East Germany and Hungary – as well as reflect on the applied methodology.

After the Bolshevik revolution of 1917 when the 'impossible became possible' many people for a long time continued to believe that the new, socialist society would be capable of changing the basic needs of human beings, or at least the ways of satisfying these basic needs.[12] In an illuminating study Somlai shows how over-zealous party functionaries sought to realize the model of an ideal 'socialist family' and force people to a large, common household, where workers have their meals at their workplaces and they send their linen and dirty clothes to the socialist laundries ('where more clothes were spoilt and more were stolen than what were washed' – as Trotsky later ironically commented).[13] Kotkin depicts with a similar insight how the State attempted to raise 'the socialist man' in

Magnitogorsk, who has different, higher cultural and educational needs than an exploited wage worker, and he is motivated not by material incentives but he works unselfishly for the new, socialist regime.[14]

The pioneers could still believe in this naïve ideology; but time shortly showed that the universal liberation and emancipation of the working class, which the Marxist programme envisaged, was not realized in the Stalinist regime. A theoretically influential answer to Stalinism was given by Trotsky in his famous critique, *The Revolution Betrayed* (1937) that he wrote in exile.[15] The work was not only meant to be a fierce polemic against his victorious political rival, but the author had the more ambitious goal to understand the social roots of Stalinism which he linked with the 'degeneration' of the revolution. Trotsky concentrated on the issue of property, arguing that, contrary to the original Marxist programme, it was not the working class which took control of the means of production, but the Stalinist *nomenklatura*. The bureaucrats themselves were not proprietors, but their control of redistribution enabled them to appropriate surplus and reproduce social inequalities. Even though Trotsky used the term 'state capitalism', he claimed that the *nomenklatura* has not yet reached the stage to be called a new class. Only if they restored the old forms of private property relations could they be called proper capitalists, which, unless prevented by the Soviet people, would have meant the betrayal of the October revolution.[16]

Stalin, however, had a major advantage over his theoretically more trained and respected rival: he succeeded in finding an answer to the question of how to implement socialism in one country after the world revolution, in which Lenin and the Bolshevik leaders believed, had failed to materialize. Being conscious of the economic backwardness of Soviet Russia, Stalin gave priority to 'catching-up' development (the task of catching up economically with the advanced Western capitalist countries) over the original emancipating goals of Marxism.[17] The 'revolution from above', which Stalin led from 1929, combined a radical change of property relations (the prohibition of the private ownership of the means of production and labour) with a gigantic programme of extensive industrialization and collectivization, which demanded enormous social and human sacrifices but it quickly and drastically transformed a backward, predominantly agrarian country into a nation, which in the Second World War triumphed over the leading industrial and military power of Europe.[18] Some Western authors called the Great Patriotic War the 'acid test' of Stalinism.[19]

The victory over Nazi Germany enabled Stalin and the Soviet Union the export of the Stalinist regime, albeit it was only with the outbreak of the Cold War that Stalin demanded an exclusive communist influence within the East European bloc. The Stalinist programme of extensive industrialization and collectivization was adopted in all socialist countries, with the exception of Yugoslavia, which Stalin solemnly excommunicated from the communist bloc. The Stalinist experiment in Eastern Europe undoubtedly had important emancipatory achievements. The Hungarian sociologist Ferge wrote:

> We have done an honest survey of social inequalities in Hungary and at the end of the 1960s we could even state that poverty continued to exist in socialist Hungary. We, however, did not put another question, which at that time would have been viewed as flattering to the ruling regime: *why and how social inequalities – and with them, poverty – could have been decreasing so radically in comparison with prewar Hungary?* Even today we have no valid answer to this question.[20]

There were, however, important social differences among the working classes of Soviet Russia, East Germany and Hungary, who had to build a socialist regime, where the working class is the ruling class – as was widely propagated by the official Marxist–Leninist doctrine. In the political sphere, the 'dictatorship of the proletariat' was not attained by the working classes in East Germany or Hungary but it was forced upon them by their communist dictators, who enjoyed the confidence and support of the Soviet Union. Whatever myths the local party leaders created about the 'new socialist man', the Berlin working-class demonstration in 1953 and, even more radically, the Hungarian revolution and freedom fight of 1956 where the majority of freedom fighters came from the working class,[21] clearly demonstrated that many workers thought they had lived better in the past regime than under socialism. The widespread working-class protests in the East European countries proved the opposite of the communist propaganda, which celebrated the birth of a 'new, socialist hero': that people had the same needs in the socialist countries as under capitalism, and they wanted to consume not differently but in the same way as their counterparts in the Western, capitalist countries. After the Hungarian revolution of 1956, slogans such as 'socialist lifestyle' and 'socialist family' could only occur in the vocabulary of agit-prop[22] and in political jokes.[23]

János Kádár, the Hungarian party secretary, who reorganized the Communist Party after 1956 and changed its name to MSZMP,[24] was fully conscious of the political mood of the working class. After the violent suppression of the revolution, Kádár quickly became one of the most – if not the most – hated leaders in Eastern Europe.[25] He, however, succeeded in rebuilding the party as the main instrument of power and, more importantly, he won popularity by consolidating the economy and satisfying the most important material demands of the working class. This

was reflected in the 1958 resolution on the working class, which determined the party's new policy towards labour. Workers' wages significantly
increased, and further pay increases and a continuous improvement in the
standard of living was promised to the population – with the condition
that the working class would be the main beneficiary of the government's
new standard-of-living policy.[26] An ambitious state housing construction
programme started, with the main focus on Budapest, the capital city,
where workers' living conditions were particularly poor and inadequate,
and many lived in real misery in overcrowded cellar dwellings, which
lacked basic comfort (bathrooms and heating), or in workers' hostels
where conditions were often 'intolerable and unworthy of human beings'
– even in the wording of contemporary party reports.[27] The resolution
also put a great emphasis on the development and support of working-
class culture, community building and education: the education of a new
intelligentsia, who had working-class roots, was supported through the
provision of free and extra classes for working-class children and means
of positive discrimination (at the universities and colleges special quotas
were set for working-class children). The high leadership of the party was
determined to put the resolution into practice: national surveys had to be
conducted at regular intervals in order to ensure the implementation of
the policy towards labour.[28]

The term 'welfare dictatorship' derives from this new, consumption-
oriented policy of the party towards the working class, as well as from
the recognition that the workers' needs under socialism failed to develop
differently than under capitalism. Rainer argues that Kádár sought to win
over *all* segments of the population (at least those social strata who were
not directly opposed to socialism);[29] I, however, attempt to show that the
'workerist' ideology[30] that the party advocated was not only an integral
element of socialist propaganda (at least until the end of the 1970s) but it
reflected a social reality. The party held the large industrial working class
to be the main social basis of the regime; therefore, it concentrated its welfare policy on this group. Having failed with the project of creating a new,
socialist man and building a classless society as envisaged in the Marxist
programme, the party sought to offer material concessions to the working
class in exchange for their political support, or at least quiescence.

As the 1956 revolution showed, workers had not only economic but
also political demands. The demand for national independence and national self-determination was completed with the demand for a change of
political structure and enterprise management. As recent studies concluded, the revolutionary intelligentsia and the majority of the working class
did not want capitalism back; they supported a reformed, democratic socialism.[31] The role of the workers' councils in the revolution gave a fresh

impetus to the theoretical debates about workers' self-management.[32] In many places workers' councils continued to maintain control of the factories even after the defeat of the revolution, and the Kádár regime could consolidate its power only by satisfying a significant number of working-class demands.[33]

After the official dissolution of the workers' councils in 1957,[34] there were at least formal attempts to increase enterprise democracy. These councils had been formed as revolutionary organs to replace the so called 'shop triangle', which effectively secured the state and party control of the factories. The 'shop triangle' consisted of the state management, the party secretary and the secretary of the trade union committee. The secretary of the newly established communist youth organization (*Kommunista Ifjúsági Szövetség*, KISZ) was added to form the 'shop quadrangle', and instead of the workers' councils, enterprise councils were formed to increase the participation of the employees in management. Employees elected one-third of the members of the council and the trade union delegated the other two-thirds. The managers, the party secretary and the secretary of the KISZ were officially members of the council. The chairperson was the secretary of the trade union committee. The enterprise council had the right of oversight over issues of economic efficiency, it received reports on the management of the enterprise and decided the distribution of bonuses and the social and cultural funds. The managers were accountable to the enterprise council.

The reality of enterprise councils was, of course, distant from ideas of workers' self-management, and they were soon reduced to a formal role. Since they were regarded as institutions parallel to the trade union, they were eventually placed under the direct control of the trade union committees. The appointment (or replacement) of the managers was decided

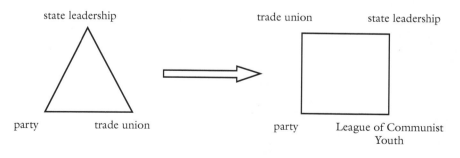

state leadership   trade union   state leadership

party   trade union   party   League of Communist Youth

1. Shop triangle   2. Shop quadrangle

Figure 0.1 Two models of enterprise management

by the central authorities[35] and not the trade union; thus, the criticism of the managers was often a theoretical right that few people exercised.[36] Although in the 1970s there was an academic debate about the scope and nature of enterprise democracy, state – and thus party – control of the factories remained unchallenged.[37]

After the revolution of 1956, the concept of workers' self-management was discussed only in narrow intellectual circles, and there is no evidence that these debates reached the workers themselves, nor did they become well known at the shop floor. The programmatic essay of George Lukács, *Demokratisierung heute und morgen* (1968)[38], in which he argued that the direct control of producers could establish a more democratic society without returning to capitalism, was published in Hungary only in 1988, when the restoration of private property relations was already on the political agenda. Socialist alternatives to Stalinist society were widely discussed and partly experimented with in Poland and Yugoslavia, but since they had even less influence on the two examined cases than the tradition of the workers' councils, the present chapter omits the introduction of these debates. While in Hungary the improvement of enterprise democracy appeared at least among the political slogans and was discussed even in the executive committee of the county, in the GDR there is no evidence of any criticism of the existing structure of enterprise management in the official discourse or on the shop floor. While dissident intellectuals voiced their criticism of 'actually existing' socialism, the party in both countries succeeded in confining any critical discussion to the academy (in 'liberal' periods), or critical intellectuals were silenced, persecuted, imprisoned or forced to emigrate.[39] In both cases it can be argued that even though there was an intellectual tradition of criticism of Stalinist society, the idea of self-management could not be embedded in the consciousness of the workers because the political regimes effectively prevented any public discussion of left-wing alternatives to their system.[40]

From the 1970s, Erich Honecker implemented the East German variant of the standard-of-living policy. Immediately after his takeover he increased the rate of growth of consumption. The new draft of the Five-Year Plan put increases in consumption at the head of the national tasks; this was the first time that a Five-Year Plan had put the rate of increase of consumption above that of investment. In 1971 Honecker announced that the main task of the Five-Year Plan was 'the further improvement of the material and cultural standard of living of the population on the basis of the rapid development of the socialist production, the increase of efficiency, the scientific-technical advance and the increase of labour productivity'.[41] In 1976 he felt confident enough to announce the ambitious programme of the 'unity of economic and social policy' (*die Einheit von*

Wirtschafts-und Sozialpolitik), which aimed to implement a socialist welfare programme suitable to beat the GDR's West German rival. Honecker promised 'a constant improvement of working and living conditions' to his people, which, according to his later critics, largely contributed to the growing indebtedness of the GDR. Even in the 1980s, when the GDR faced a deteriorating balance of foreign trade, Honecker consistently refused to increase the prices of consumer goods with the argument that the 'counter-revolutionary attempts' in the other socialist countries such as Poland all started with the increase of the prices.[42] The most important elements of his programme to which he remained loyal until the collapse of his regime were wage policy, state housing construction and support for families, with a special emphasis on working women.[43]

The term 'welfare dictatorship' is therefore appropriate to describe both regimes, which pursued a similar policy towards the working class. In order to pacify the workers and preserve the status quo in the power structure, both regimes were willing to give concessions to consumerism; and, moreover, they were constantly worried that left-wing critics would destroy the consensus, which they held to be the basis of their political rule. There is evidence from both countries that repression was used against left-wing critics of the system, which was occasionally harsher than the retribution they handed out for 'Western revisionism'. In Hungary for example, Miklós Haraszti, the author of *A Worker in a Workers' State* (1977), was also held to be a left-wing dissident and prosecuted on that basis.[44] In the GDR there was the case of Matthias Domaschk, a young worker from Jena, who joined a commune at the beginning of the 1980s. Because of his alternative looks, dress and political views he was placed under police supervision. After travelling to Berlin by train to visit his friends at the time of a party conference, he was arrested and subsequently he committed suicide in custody. There is an archive in Jena, which bears his name (*Thüringer Archiv für Zeitgeschichte, Matthias Domaschk*).

The thesis that the present book will demonstrate through an in-depth analysis of the party's policy towards labour and the local implementation and reception of this policy is that the welfare dictatorships were open to the right (towards consumerism) while they remained closed to the left, effectively blocking the public discussion of any leftism other than the official legitimizing ideology. Official socialism was, however, increasingly undermined by the wide gap between the practice of welfare dictatorships and the egalitarian socialist project.[45] It well describes the extent to which people became disappointed with 'actually existing' socialism in Hungary, and many workers thought that there was more social justice and a better life for them in a capitalist society than in a socialist one (as is shown by the answers to the question 'Would you call the capitalists back?'). East

German interview partners would repeatedly tell me that it was only after they started to live in capitalism that they believed the Marxist critique that they had learnt at school. Burawoy, who conducted fieldwork in Hungarian factories, among others the Lenin Steel Works, recorded that the workers persistently asked the American professor how much money a worker earns in the United States, while they forgot even to mention the proud achievements of the socialist regime such as free health care, education and highly subsidized cultural products (theatre, concerts, books, cinema), let alone the scale of social mobility after the Second World War, which was unparalleled in Hungary.[46] While welfare dictatorships did establish social peace, in the long run they paved the way for capitalism because they essentially failed to demonstrate a viable socialist alternative. After they could no longer increase the standard of living of the people, they lost popular support. As a result, by the time the authority of the communist parties collapsed, the majority of the workers did not see capitalism as a major enemy; and many expected that they would be better treated under capitalism than under socialism because they saw that the standard of living of the workers was higher in West Germany and Austria than in the GDR or Hungary. Western shops and supermarkets, which were full of goods, were better at convincing people of capitalism's apparent superiority over the bankrupt socialist economies.[47]

By turning the attention to the experience of the socialist working class, the book seeks to raise new questions, which examine the history of labour in the region from novel perspectives. In Hungary, like in other socialist countries, working-class histories were characterized by an ideological approach both under state socialism and after the collapse of communist regimes. The East European Communist parties everywhere claimed that the working class was the ruling class; the thesis that the struggle of the working class against capital triumphed under the leadership of the party became part and parcel of the official legitimizing ideology of the regime, and it became a recurring slogan of the official communist agitation and propaganda.[48] Thus, any researcher who came to a conclusion which contradicted this official socialism risked his or her academic career, at least behind the iron curtain. Even in the face of repression, however, internationally recognized studies were written on class and socialism in the 'merriest barrack' as Kádár's Hungary was nicknamed at the time. The Hungarian sociologist Kemény conducted fieldwork in various working-class communities. His research led him to the conclusion that the Hungarian working class, which was formed as a result of the extensive communist modernization project, was recruited predominantly from the peasantry, and many of them continued to preserve the original peasant culture and lifestyle. He also identified important factors in the stratification of the working class (origin, living place, skills, education, family size and the nature of work).[49] Kemény eventually came into conflict with the regime because of his research on poverty; his claim that poverty continued to exist in socialist Hungary triggered sharp political responses, and he was forced into emigration.

Ferge was one of the most distinguished scholars of the Marxist structuralist school, which obtained international reputation after the reinstitutionalization of Hungarian sociology.[50] Her research showed that the orthodox communist class distinction (two classes: workers and peasantry, and one stratum: intelligentsia) was not adequate for the structural description of socialist society. She distinguished between hierarchical occupation groups, which replaced the old and useless model.[51] One of her main achievements was the study of educational inequalities: she showed that after a brief postwar period characterized by educational mobility, cultural capital became again inheritable, and the children of intellectuals were more likely to enter higher education than the children of less educated social strata.[52]

The third school was that of industrial sociology. Rába was the focus of sociological research as a model factory under socialism. Makó and Héthy conducted a pioneering study of the plant in the early 1970s, which led to official discussions on the informal bargaining power of groups of workers who were highly skilled or who occupied other key positions in production. Makó and Héthy published their first report of the research in English in 1972. Héthy later studied other groups of workers in the construction industry to prove the thesis that workers who were indispensable for production because of their skills or their advantageous position in the production process could successfully represent their interests in wage disputes even against the enterprise management.[53]

The ideologically more rigid GDR tolerated far less deviance in this respect than Hungary. After a brief period of cultural liberalization, Honecker tightened the ideological grip of the party over the intellectual life of the GDR: the surveys of the Institute for Public Opinion Poll (*Institut für Meinungsforschung*) bear the label of 'strictly confidential' although the authors of the reports did their best to demonstrate the development of socialist consciousness in the GDR: in 1968, 65 per cent of the respondents thought that the GDR was more developed socially than West Germany, while in 1973, this ratio grew to 72 per cent. We have to add, though, that 20 per cent of the workers chose not to give an answer to the question of whether socialism would dominate future development.[54] The ideologically repressive climate continued to dominate Honecker's state: Eberhard Nemitz conducted a survey among East German trainees, in which he found that the majority of the respondents had a positive at-

titude towards socialism. The picture was not, however, altogether positive: the trainees criticized the supply of consumer goods, the prohibition of watching West German television channels and the propaganda
campaign of their government against West Germany. Nemitz eventually
published his study in West Germany, after his emigration.[55]

The Hungarian developments, however, indicated the beginning of a
reorientation from the legitimizing discourse, in which the working class
was constructed one-sidedly either as an oppressed or as a ruling class
towards new questions, which pointed beyond the Cold War ideologies
heavily propagated on both sides of the iron curtain. How did political
power function in the factory? How were party policies implemented at
local level and how did the workers respond to the party's policy towards
labour? How did they use official socialism to negotiate concessions with
the managers and the party? These questions could be best studied within
the realm of the factories.[56]

Inspired by Haraszti's ethnographic study of the everyday life of a socialist factory from the perspective of a worker, Michael Burawoy undertook similar fieldwork in the Hungarian Lenin Steel Works. From his
comparative studies in capitalist and postcolonialist countries he concluded that the despotism of early capitalism was replaced by hegemonic
despotism, where workers gave concessions to capital to preserve their
factories and workplace. His Hungarian fieldwork experience led him to
the conclusion that the socialist factory regimes also developed into hegemonic despotism. He distinguished between core and peripheral workers. The older, male, experienced and skilled workers constituted the first
group, who occupied key positions in the production process. They were
given better-paid jobs, and they were overrepresented among party and
trade union officials in comparison to other workers. Among the peripheral workers one could find the young and unskilled 'whose only hope
is to leave in search of a better job or to seek promotion to the core'.[57]
Burawoy was, however, optimistic at the time: he argued that once the
socialist workers get rid of the tutelage of the Communist Party, they
would be more likely to regain socialist consciousness and establish a self-
governing, socialist democracy than their capitalist counterparts.

The eventual and rapid collapse of communist regimes across the region
in 1989 discredited the legitimizing narratives of official working-class
histories; the events of the year disproved notions of a simple equivalence
between class position and class consciousness characterized of dominant
trends in Marxist thought. While, in 1989, there were some East European intellectuals who still argued for a democratic socialism based on
workers control, other groups, including many of the MSZMP reformers, were calling for a 'third way' between capitalism and socialism, and

some for the creation of a social democracy based on a mixed economy and strong trade unions, even though it was also widely expected that the working class would either resist any attempt to restore capitalism or even support a reformist collectivist alternative.[58] Of course, this expectation proved to be wrong, and there was little effective working-class resistance to the introduction of a capitalist economy. There was no country in Eastern Europe where workers supported any kind of democratic socialist alternative to the existing system.[59] Nor was the East European political and intellectual climate favourable for revisiting working-class histories after the change of regimes: all forms of class theory were regarded as utterly discredited, and the working class was often uncritically associated with the state socialist past, as intellectual elites invested in futures based on 'embourgeoisiement', which downplayed the social and political roles of industrial workers.

In recent years there has been a renewed interest in East European working-class histories but attention has focused on the era of early socialism during the 1940s and 1950s[60] – there is, consequently, almost no literature on the topic for the late Kádár era in Hungary, and there is relatively little for East Germany, and these studies rarely address the issue of how the workers related to the socialist state.[61] The present book is engaged with revisiting working-class histories from a perspective that has been largely ignored in the national literatures of both countries. It argues for a revisiting of issues of class, after these have been largely ignored for the past two decades. Since in the East European literature the concept of class itself developed ideologically, and with politically overloaded connotations in the later socialist years being associated almost exclusively with the legitimation of the party state, it is all the more difficult to bring it back in, however much the concept has been reworked.[62] Yet, the party-states' class-based legitimizing ideology concealed from the elites the social weaknesses of their system, for the workers did not defend the 'workers' states' in 1989. In part for this reason, the neglect of the working class carries another danger – that without a critical history of the relationship between the socialist system and industrial workers, the social roots of the rapid collapse of these regimes will remain largely unexplored.

My research uses two case studies, Carl Zeiss Jena in East Germany and Rába MVG in Győr, Hungary, to describe and analyse the party's policy towards labour in the factories and in the county (in Hungary) or the district (in the GDR) in order to interrogate three main questions: (1) How did the welfare dictatorships succeed in providing for lasting social peace in working-class communities? (2) What were the social roots of their rapid and unexpected collapse? and (3) To what extent could the essentially similar policy of the party towards labour level existing social and cultural differences between the East German and Hungarian working classes? The selection of the two factories was motivated by theoretical as well as practical considerations. The party regarded workers in large-scale industry as its central social basis, and it sought to focus labour policy around this group. The reorganization of enterprise management in the 1960s increased the concentration of the means of production. Giant industrial enterprises were formed, which had a monopoly over their given product. Technological improvement and product development also became the responsibility of the enterprise.[63] The policy of the party towards the working class was at its strongest in the large enterprises, which could offer cultural, recreational and sport facilities for their employees. In Hungary I selected Rába MVG, which was the largest industrial enterprise in the county of Győr-Sopron located in north-western Hungary, directly neighbouring Austria. I first conducted an interview project in the factory with the research question of how the workers experienced transformation and how they saw the two systems, socialism and capitalism, in comparison. The primary sources were life-history interviews conducted with twenty people who were still employed in the factory and twenty former workers of MVG. The practical consideration was the existence of an archive: Rába MVG had an enterprise party committee with a full-time party secretary, and the materials of the party organization were preserved in the county archives.

The Zeiss enterprise was selected after I had finished working in the Rába factory. It was important to find an ex-socialist-model factory, which had survived the change of regime and had a pre-socialist past. In the period of forced industrialization whole towns were built on heavy industry and cheaply imported fuels from the Soviet Union. Since these towns were obviously hit harder by restructuring, I decided to exclude this distorting factor. I also had to find a factory located outside of the capital in order to match the Hungarian factory. Peter Hübner called my attention to the Zeiss factory, which satisfied all of the above criteria. Apart from the party materials, which were located in the archive of the province, the enterprise maintained a factory archive. In addition, the district of Gera to which the factory belonged (today Thuringia) was one of the most developed parts of the GDR, just like Győr-Sopron county in Hungary. True, the two factories belonged to different industrial branches but my research aim was not to write enterprise histories but to examine the relationship between the workers and the party under late socialism. Since the workers of the Zeiss factory were part of the well-paid core of the industrial working class, their experience of socialism was comparable to that of the Rába employees.

The choice of the factory as the main locus of research links my work to a burgeoning literature, which seeks to revisit working-class histories 'in the field'.[64] This endeavour has a special relevance for the socialist working class. Hübner argues that the party concentrated its welfare policies on the factory; thus, it was not only the site of production but in many aspects that of reproduction as well (large enterprises such as Zeiss and Rába had their own polyclinics, nurseries, kindergartens, cultural centres, sport clubs, football teams, etc.).[65] The factory was thus central for the cultural life and self-identification of the workers as well as the main 'testing field' of the party's policy towards the working class.

While examining the functioning of welfare dictatorships on the shop floor, the present study will connect and explain the findings in a wider historical context by making creative use of what Burawoy called the extensive case method.[66] The first dimension of the extended case method is participant observation. Even though the book primarily relies on archival sources, it also uses life-history interviews conducted with workers and former workers of both factories. The second dimension is the establishment of a link between the macro and the micro levels. One way to think of the macro–micro link is to view the micro as an expression of the macro, discovering reification within the factory, commodification within the family, bureaucratization within the school. From the perspective of the extended case method, this link is established, however, not as a reference to an 'expressive' totality but to a 'structured' one in which the part is shaped by its relation to the whole, taking the nature of a dialectic relationship. This dimension is particularly important for the research presented in this book, since in order to compare the findings of the factory studies, which are located in different national contexts, it is essential to link the individual case studies to the labour policy of the state in both countries. The third dimension is the extension of the case study in time, a condition that is fulfilled in the research. The last dimension is the extension of theory: by showing workers' alienation from the socialist regime in large factories where state redistribution was at its strongest, the book argues that the social decline of the regime had started well before its political collapse.

Factory case studies enable us to examine the important issue of the party's varying degree of success of building legitimacy among the large industrial working class. Contrary to the totalitarian paradigm, which denied any legitimacy from the East European Communist parties,[67] Pittaway argues that the working class should be seen as a political actor, whose interests and demands the party had to take into consideration in order to secure its legitimacy and consolidate its political rule.[68] The success – and eventual failure – of the party's policy towards the working class can be best evaluated in large factories, which served both as a workplace and a unique social and cultural environment. By studying the party's policy towards working women in the GDR, Harsch develops the thesis that working women could and did use the egalitarian ideology that the party propagated to gain concessions in the sphere of private life and family.[69] Following this lead, this book will show how the party accommodated the material demands of industrial workers – or at least part of them – and how workers used socialist ideology to oppose the management and defend their social rights.

By focusing on factory histories, the present study joins critics of 'transitology' such as Burawoy, Hann and Verdery, who argued that anthropology could provide a necessary corrective to studies based on notions of 'transition'.[70] While in the East European mainstream historiographies it became fashionable to identify industrial workers with the socialist regime (and blame them for the failure to 'catch up' with the Western economies and standards-of-living), at the same time communism was also seen as the main reason for the historical economic backwardness of the region. Communist parties were therefore often depicted as if they had never had any welfare policies, or a policy towards the working class. Such claims are easily refutable. For the GDR Steiner[71] and for Hungary Földes[72] analysed the political history of indebtedness, which largely contributed to the economic collapse of these regimes. Kopstein pointed out the social constraints that led to increasing indebtedness: in order to preserve social peace, the party had to finance a generous welfare policy.[73] I go one step further to argue that even in the face of harsh economic realities, the party *had* to secure the political support of the large industrial working class and finance outdated industries in order to preserve a social compromise, which was the price of the consolidation of the regime's political power.[74] This compromise provided for the political silence of the working class and the 'appearance' of stability in both countries. This legitimacy was, however, essentially fragile because the compromise forced their weakly performing planned economies to compete with the economies of the most advanced capitalist countries, and in spite of all of the regime's socialist slogans, it spread a consumerist culture and materialistic mentality among the working class. Therefore, in the long run the compromise paved the way for 'more market' rather than a reformed socialist democracy.

This book is built on the assumption that the dynamic interplay between the party and the working class can only be understood in a concrete historical context and in a concrete setting – in our case, the factory. Apart from labour historians, who propose a novel approach to working-class histories, critics of the traditional 'heroic' narrative of working-class histories likewise argued that the factory should be taken more seriously as a social environment where labour relations are formulated.[75] While there are several examples of the comparison of big structures, it is less common to compare local case studies. I argue that in-depth case studies can offer better insights into the everyday life and thinking of working people than the grand narratives that tend to assume a pre-given pattern of the formation of class consciousness. Without being related to a bigger structure, there is, however, a danger that analysis is lost in a mass of description, and local case studies discover specificity in institutions that were not specific to the interrogated national variant of socialism.[76] Since comparison requires the case studies to be more *relational*, it can offer novel insights into national working-class histories. The second aspect where comparison can 'extend' the extended case method lies precisely in the establishment of a macro–micro link.[77] Cross-national comparisons inevitably call for a more systematic and structural approach to local case studies in order to make them comparable. They can therefore help to reinforce the second dimension of the extended case method, and extend the scope of generalization – which seems to be a common problem of single case studies.

The two countries – the GDR and Hungary – offer the best examples of a welfare dictatorship in the East European socialist region, which for a while succeeded in winning over the political support of the 'masses'. The Polish Communist Party was less successful in this respect; the rise of Solidarity can be explained precisely through the failure of the party to establish a similar compromise with the working class.[78] After the violent suppression of the Prague Spring in 1968, Husák also implemented a form of 'welfare dictatorship' to ensure the quiescence of workers; the rapid 'normalization' in Czechoslovakia and the lack of a movement similar to Solidarity can be partly explained through the relative success of this policy. In Romania, Ceaușescu introduced a national Stalinism and a neo-Stalinist export-oriented economic model in the 1980s that depressed workers' standards of living.

The comparison of two case studies cannot, of course, give a fully fledged typology of workers in all of the East European socialist systems, but it can provide us with useful insights into the relationship between the labour policies of the party and the absence of open working-class protest. The history of the welfare dictatorships follows common patterns – this *periodization* serves as the basis of the structure of the book. In the first part, I examine the reform era of the 1960s, which indicated the last time when the party entered into a real dialogue with the working class. The period of economic reform witnessed a real social debate, which divided the party in both countries, and increased its willingness to listen to workers' opinions. This was particularly remarkable in the GDR – in comparison with the later disappearance of criticism under Honecker. Workers voiced their dissatisfaction not only with the increasing social inequalities – a consequence of the economic reform – but also with the existing power structure in the factory and the effective exclusion of workers from decisions that concerned production. The first part will introduce workers' responses to the economic reform and in so doing reveal unexplored contradictions of the socialist system as well as demonstrate that the economic reforms in both countries were accompanied by a broader social dialogue. What rendered the reform period above all interesting in both countries was that it was the last time when elements of a real dialogue could be documented between the workers and the party. More importantly, workers accepted the party as a conversation partner and believed that it would be able to accomplish reform.

The reform period ended with the failure of dialogue in both countries: the party decided to buy the support – or at least the silence – of the people through the standard-of-living policy and the promise of catching up with Western levels of consumption. In the Hungarian case, the reform period ended with a retreat in economy (more radical reforms were planned to expand private or the so-called second economy) and a Pyrrhic victory of the hardliners or dogmatic communists in the field of ideology. In the GDR, Honecker came to power in 1971 after Ulbricht's economic reform failed, which forced the resignation of the first secretary. Ulbricht experimented with a different type of economic reform from that in Hungary, based on decentralization and the development of strategic sectors. His new economic system led, however, to mounting social discontent because of the increasing shortage of consumer goods. Honecker promised to 'correct' this policy and – in a marked parallel with the Hungarian standard-of-living policy – continuously to increase the welfare of his people. The second part focuses on the everyday functioning of this policy: housing policy, the building of working-class communities, education, culture, working women, the relationship between workers and managers, and workers' use of socialist ideology in defence of their social rights.

The consolidation of welfare dictatorships that is documented in the second part of the book was accompanied in both countries by the consequent suppression of any *leftist* attempt to reform socialism: the direct ownership of workers did not even come up in reform discussions. While in Poland an independent workers' movement started to develop in the late 1970s and blossomed during the sixteen months of Solidarity, in the GDR and Hungary 1953 and 1956 were the last moments of large-scale working-class resistance when workers articulated an alternative to the regime. Discussions of leftist alternatives were also suppressed on an everyday level; workers' self-management was never mentioned in information reports, or in other materials. True, the party's policy towards the working class promoted non-materialist values including community

building and support for workers' culture and education in both countries. These initiatives – including the socialist brigade movement – were
not, however, intended to increase worker control over the factories; in
actual fact, socialist collectivism of this kind was meant to compensate the
workers for their effective exclusion from political power.

The third part of the book is directly engaged with the relationship
between the party and the working class as well as with the limits of the
party's policy towards labour and the crisis of welfare dictatorships. The
orientation towards consumption was paralleled with a gradual change
in the rhetoric of the party: while the speeches of the East German party
leaders abounded in quotations from Marx and Lenin, real workers increasingly disappeared from the party documents. With the adoption of
the consumption-oriented policy the 'workerist' ideology of the party
increasingly lost its social content, which left people disillusioned.

The limits of this policy became visible in Hungary earlier than in the
GDR. This had an important impact on the relationship between the
workers and the party, which is documented at length in the third part of
the book that discusses issues of party-building, methods of recruitment,
agitation, party life and the party's evaluation on the shop floor. In Hungary the economic crisis of the late 1970s forced the government to seek
the financial support of the International Monetary Fund. In exchange
for credits, concessions had to be given: in the economy, liberalization
meant the expansion of the private (or informal) sector, which became
adjacent to state industry,[79] and in political life, a gradual softening of
the dictatorship (travelling, mitigation of censorship), which rendered
Hungary one of the most 'Western' socialist countries – also known as
'goulash communism' or 'the happiest barrack in the camp'. While many
workers used the opportunities of the private – or, as it was called, the
second economy – people's dissatisfaction increased because of widening
social inequalities.[80] Increasing interest in consumption and the increased
working hours, whether in the formal or informal economies, that were
needed to achieve a higher standard of living contributed to the decline
of socialist collectivism, and the increasing individualization of society.[81]

The GDR, by contrast, was always regarded as a socialist stronghold
on the border of the Eastern bloc where the Soviet military presence and
ideological control was much stronger than in Hungary. There was also
a more marked need to compete with the capitalist West directly. After
the collapse of Ulbricht's reform, Honecker combined central planning
with a significant extension of the welfare state. As the gap between the
East and West German standards of living continued to grow, repression
was used to a greater extent than in Hungary to prevent open criticism
that allowed the states publicly to maintain the fiction of the superiority

of the socialist system. Criticism was therefore targeted at the shortage of consumer goods – shortages that were generated more by the collectivist model prevalent in the GDR than by the reformist one found in Kádár's Hungary – and the economic gap between the GDR and West Germany. Even though the intelligentsia was believed to be privileged in comparison to the working class,[82] we cannot speak of widening social inequality in the GDR prior to 1989.[83] The comparison of party life in the third part shows how different models of socialist rule – one collectivist, the other reformist – influenced the workers' relationship with the party state.

One difference between the two models is clearly visible: even though the political crisis of the Kádár regime came in 1989, signs of decline were visible much earlier in Hungary. The failure of the standard-of-living policy meant, in essence, the exhaustion of the party's policy towards the working class. On the basis of the regularly collected information reports concerning the public mood of employees in Győr-Sopron county and Rába MVG, people became increasingly critical of the economic situation of the country and the standard-of-living policy from the second half of the 1970s. In the late Kádár era, mounting economic discontent gradually developed into overt criticism of the party and the political system.

In particular the second and third parts of the book make use of an in-depth archival research to depict the process of workers' alienation from the party at a local level. In the 1980s, the workers' alienation from the party could be documented in Hungary whereas the grass-roots members were silenced in the GDR: the party materials of the Honecker era are documents produced under the influence of official propaganda, and they tell us very little of workers' political ideas.[84] On the basis of the Hungarian materials it is, however, possible to trace growing awareness on an everyday level of the limits – and eventually the failure – of the standard-of-living policy, even among the party membership. The failure of the party's policy towards the working class also became evident in the GDR, where large-scale ideological control under Honecker – which was much stronger than in Hungary – prevented the open expression of mounting discontent among the population. It was only the mass flight of GDR citizens to the West in 1989 with the opening of the Hungarian borders that rendered the crisis of the welfare dictatorship in the GDR visible. In this respect, the more 'visible' social decline of the system in Hungary complements the picture of an East Germany engulfed in enforced silence about the tensions that lay under the surface.

After the failure of the state socialist project, the East European countries hoped to 'catch up' with the developed capitalist countries by adopting Western-style political institutions and market economies. The adoption of Western institutions facilitated new 'expectations of modernity'.[85] These expectations, as Bryant and Mokrzycki rightly argued, combined the aspiration to achieve Western levels of consumption with the maintenance of full employment, and some of the other social 'gains' of the state socialist years.[86] As it became clear that combining the market economy with the socialist welfare state was an illusion, the legitimacy of the 'transition' was called into question. This generated a search for new paradigms both at theoretical and at methodological levels.[87] The experience of transformation was economically less painful in East Germany than in Hungary because the former adopted the welfare system of West Germany, which mitigated the social costs of industrial restructuring. In Hungary the socialist welfare system was dismantled outright.[88] While it is recognized that collective memory of the previous regimes has been shaped by the experiences of postsocialist economic and social transformation, in the fourth part of the book the working-class memory of the Kádár and Honecker regimes is examined.

The fourth part directly confronts us with the question of how successful the welfare dictatorships were in levelling existing social and cultural differences between the East German and Hungarian working classes. Prior to the establishment of communist rule, Germany and Hungary stood at different stages of industrial development, the former being a leading industrial nation and the latter belonging to the East European semi-periphery of the European economy.[89] Despite different working-class traditions in the two countries,[90] socialist rule produced certain social responses that were common to both cases; near identical socialist institutions provided for similar experiences and sometimes even attitudes. The socialist brigade movement was, for instance, well remembered in both the East German and Hungarian interviews: workers would typically argue that 'back then' (under socialism) they had a more intensive community life than in the new, capitalist regime and the socialist brigades provided for a social space that they understood to be free of state control. In order to compare the memories of the Kádár and Honecker regime, we should, however, bear in mind that after the change of regimes, Hungary had a different experience of postsocialist transformation from East Germany, which was united with one of the most advanced capitalist economies. It is worth citing here a telling data, which should have warned the politicians and economists of the country of the illusory nature of 'catching-up development', which was heavily advocated after 1989: in 1974, only 6 per cent of the male workers of Zeiss did not finish a training school (three-year training after the compulsory primary school), while in 1975, a quarter of the total workforce of Rába did not finish primary school. Albeit the Communist Party in Hungary implemented several programmes to raise the educational level of the people, the (still) existing differences forecasted inevitable difficulties in the transition to a knowledge-based economy. While we can trace several similar patterns in the policies of welfare dictatorships, in particular in their policy towards labour, I use the East German and Hungarian case studies to identify differences in the formation and historical development of their working classes that determined both the possibilities and limits of the East European socialist regimes.

Notes

1. The change of regime in Hungary has been referred to as 'negotiated revolution' or 'constitutional revolution'. On the political history of the roundtable discussions (the negotiations among MSZMP and the new parties) see A. Bozóki (ed.). 2000. *A rendszerváltás forgatókönyve: kerekasztal-tárgyalások 1989-ben: alkotmányos forradalom: tanulmányok*, Budapest: Új Mandátum Könyvkiadó. For a study of the historical roots of the peaceful transition see R.L. Tőkés. 1996. *Hungary's Negotiated Revolution: Economic Reform, Social Change, and Political Succession, 1957–1990*, New York: Cambridge University Press. For a study on the democratic opposition in Hungary see: E. Csizmadia (ed.). 1995. *A magyar demokratikus ellenzék 1968–1988*, Budapest: TTwins.

2. In the era of Cold War it was a common practice in both the socialist and capitalist blocs to equate Marxism as a theory with the so called Marxism-Leninism, which – after Stalin's political victory and with his active assistance – became the official legitimizing ideology of the Communist Party. Krausz attempts to reconstruct the theoretical roots of the Stalinist reinterpretation of Marxist ideology: T. Krausz. 1996. *Szovjet thermidor: A sztálini fordulat szellemi előzményei 1917–1928*, Budapest: Napvilág Kiadó.

3. 'Visszahívná a kapitalistákat?', *Tér-kép*, 1 June 1989.

4. On the history of Rába see: Z. Tabiczky. 1977. *A Magyar Vagon- és Gépgyár története*, 2 vols, Győr: Rába; K. Bossányi. 1978. 'A versenyképesség stratégiája: Beszélgetés Horváth Edével, a Rába vezérigazgatójával', *Társadalmi Szemle* 33(11); K. Bossányi. 1986. 'Made in Rába', in I. Matkó (ed.), *Ipari közelképek*, Budapest: Ipari és Kereskedelmi Minisztérium Kiadása; L. Héthy and Cs. Makó. 1975. *Az automatizáció és a munkástudat*, Budapest: MTA Szociológiai Kutató Intézet Kiadványa. On the life of Horváth see: E. Horváth. 1990. *Én volnék a Vörös Báró?*, Pécs: Szikra Nyomda; A. Dusza. 2003. *A birodalom végnapjai: Így láttam Horváth Edét*, Győr: X-Meditor Kft.

5. For a discussion of the internal division within the Hungarian Communist Party see Gy. Földes. 1989. *Hatalom és mozgalom 1956–1989*. Budapest: Reform Könyvkiadó-Kossuth Könyvkiadó. Földes distinguishes between the 'orthodox' or 'dogmatic' communists, who were opposed to pro-market reforms and they wanted to maintain the status quo and the 'refomers', who called for the expansion of the market. For a study of the role of luxury in the Hungarian ruling elite see: Gy. Majtényi. 2009. *K-vonal. Uralmi elit és luxus a szocializmusban*, Budapest: Nyitott Könyvműhely.

6. 'Beszélgetés Horváth Edével, a Rába MVG vezérigazgatójával', *Tér-kép*, 1 June 1989.

7. Horváth tells the story from his perspective in Horváth, *Én volnék a Vörös Báró?*, 130–50. He argued that the managers sacrificed him in order to save themselves. The story of Horváth's removal is told from another perspective by András Dusza, the communication manager of the enterprise in Dusza, *A birodalom végnapjai*.

8. The evaluation of Ede Horváth is even today controversial. On 24 November 2003 the Rába sold its centrally located estate of 6.5 hectares to ECE-Einkaufs-Center-Győr. On this occasion many people recommended that Horváth should get a statute from the town (readers' letters were published in the local daily *Kisalföld*). In a public meeting of the

town on 9 January 2004 the mayor declared that because of the controversial judgment of his person, the town would rather consider a commemorative tablet. The overwhelming majority of the Rába workers and managers, who I interviewed between 2002 and 2004, recognized and respected Horváth's commitment to Rába and his work for the factory. His autocratic leadership style arose more controversies.

9. There is a very extensive literature on the collapse of state socialism in Eastern Europe. The comparative and historical aspects are, however, often neglected. For a good comparative study see: M. Pittaway. 2004. *Eastern Europe 1939–2000*, London: Hodder Arnold.

10. For a detailed discussion of the literature on workers in East-Central Europe after the change of regimes see: P. Heumos. 2010. 'Workers under Communist Rule: Research in the Former Socialist Countries of Eastern-Central and South-Eastern Europe and in the Federal Republic of Germany', *International Review of Social History* 55.

11. That the collapse of state socialism was unexpected has been confirmed by scholars such as Klaus von Beyme, who called 1989 a 'black Friday' for social sciences because of their failure to forecast this event. K. Beyme. 1996. *Transition to Democracy in Eastern Europe*, Houndmills: Macmillan. To be sure, convergence theory did predict that industrialization would bring about a gradual homogenization of social structures, leading to the overthrow of political regimes in the socialist countries. These regimes collapsed, however, not because they succeeded to catch up with the advanced capitalist countries but quite the contrary, because they failed to do so. For a detailed discussion of the main paradigms of the change of regimes see: E. Bartha. 2010. 'Transition, Transformation, "Postsocialism": Theorizing Systemic Change in Eastern Europe', in: K. Csaplár-Degovics, M. Mitrovits and Cs. Zahorán (eds), *After Twenty Years: Reasons and Consequences of the Transformation in Central and Eastern Europe*, Berlin: Osteuropa-Zentrum and Terra Recognita Foundation.

12. I cite here Stephen Kotkin, one of the best-known experts on Stalinism, who said at a conference organized at the Central European University, Budapest that after many years of research and the deatiled study of many Soviet archives, one can conclude that communists were indeed communists. See: S. Kotkin. 1995. *Magnetic Mountain: Stalinism as a Civilization*, Berkeley: University of California Press.

13. Cited in P. Somlai. 2008. *Társas és társadalmi. Válogatott tanulmányok*, Budapest: Napvilág Kiadó, 116.

14. The famous Soviet co-authors, Ilf and Petrov frequently made fun of this idealized socialist hero who, after working full time in the factory, volunteers for all kinds of social and cultural activities that the party propagates (studying in party school, working for the factory and wall newspapers, singing in choir and working in the trade union). The 'man of the movement' was a grateful source of contemporary Soviet humour.

15. The Trotskyist critique was, of course, not a single response to Stalinism. For a theoretical discussion of the internal division of the left see M. Linden. 2007. *Western Marxism and the Soviet Union: A Survey of Critical Theory and Debates since 1917*, Leiden: Brill.

16. Trotsky already predicted that the nomenklatura would not hesitate to privatize state property if they felt that their political power would be at risk. Krausz argues that this was exactly the case under perestroika, and this was the main reason why the Soviet economic elite abandoned Gorbachev, who represented this political programme and the reform of socialism, and committed itself to Yeltsin and the restoration of capitalism. T. Krausz. 2007. 'Perestroika and the Redistribution of Property in the Soviet Union: Political Perspectives and Historical Evidence', *Contemporary Politics* 13(1).

17. For a discussion of what this political change meant for the content of the official Marxist-Leninist doctrine, see T. Krausz. 1991. *Pártviták és történettudomány: Viták 'az orosz fejlődés' sajátosságairól, különös tekintettel az 1920-as évekre*, Budapest: Akadémiai Kiadó; Krausz, *Szovjet thermidor*.

18. See Deutscher's classical biography of Stalin: I. Deutscher. 1949. *Stalin: A Political Biography*, New York: Oxford University Press. See also Moshe Lewin's influential work on the

social history of Stalinism: M. Lewin. 1985. *The Making of the Soviet System: Essays in the Social History of Interwar Russia*, London: Methuen.

19. Geoffrey Roberts shows that contrary to the fabrication of the myth of the 'preventive war' (that Stalin sought to attack Nazi Germany – which was a recurring element in Goebbels' propaganda), in reality the Soviet dictator was conscious of the enormous risk of attacking the leading industrial and military power of Europe. He was therefore determined to preserve the peace with Hitler even though he knew his deeply rooted anti-communism. See: G. Roberts. 2006. *Stalin's Wars: From World War to Cold War, 1939–1953*, New Haven: Yale University Press. Roberts also shows that in the era of the Cold War there was a conscious attempt on behalf of the former Western allies to diminish the role of the Soviet Union in the defeat of Nazi Germany although it was the Red Army which defeated the Wehrmacht on land. See also: M. Geyer and S. Fitzpatrick. 2009. *Beyond Totalitarianism: Stalinism and Nazism Compared*, New York: Cambridge University Press. For the discussion of the Russian roots of the myth of the 'preventive war' see E. Bartha and T. Krausz (eds). 2011. *Háború és nemzeti önismeret: 70 éve támadta meg a náci Németország a Szovjetuniót*, Budapest: Komáromi Nyomda és Kiadó. Robert Thurston called the Second World War the 'acid test' of Stalinism. See: R. Thurston. 1996. *Life and Terror in Stalin's Russia*, New Haven: Yale University Press.

20. Zs. Ferge. 2010. *Társadalmi áramlatok és egyéni szerepek*, Budapest: Napvilág Kiadó, 71. Stress is mine.

21. M. Pittaway. 2006. 'A magyar forradalom új megközelítésben: az ipari munkásság, a szocializmus széthullása és rekonstrukciója, 1953–1958', *Eszmélet 72*.

22. Shortened form of agitation-propaganda.

23. Dissident intellectuals argued that 'socialist' functioned as a privative prefix: socialist market meant that there was no market, and socialist democracy meant that there was no democracy.

24. After the fusion of the Communist Party and the Social Democratic Party in 1948, the party was named Hungarian Workers' Party (Magyar Dolgozók Pártja). It was dissolved in 1956.

25. István Feitl documents what political preparations preceded the celebration of 1 May 1957 in Budapest because the party was still afraid of working-class protests and riots: I. Feitl. 2009. 'Új Budapest-politika felé', in I. Feitl (ed.). *Budapest az 1960-as években*, Budapest: Napvilág. Feitl also depicts how harsh measures were taken to secure the capital on 23 October 1957. Kádár expressed his surprise at the stillness of the city: 'Was this all that our enemies could do against us? Have they run out of strength?' he asked contemptuously the Central Committee. The political atmosphere of fear is also documented by Horváth, who recalls that the high party leaders in Győr-Sopron county carried guns even in 1957. Horváth, *Én volnék a Vörös Báró?*

26. On the 1958 resolution see A. Pető. 1992. *A munkások életkörülményei Magyarországon az 1950-es években*, Budapest: Eötvös University, manuscript. Földes gives a good analysis of the political background of the change of the party's policy towards labour. See: Földes, Gy. 1989. *Hatalom és mozgalom 1956–1989*, Budapest: Reform Könyvkiadó and Kossuth Könyvkiadó; Földes. 1993. 'A Kádár-rendszer és a munkásság', *Eszmélet 19*.

27. Kohut vividly depicts the misery of the workers' hostels in the light of contemporary documents: for instance, he recalls cases when people refused to use the common baths because their clothes were stolen while they were washing themselves. T. Kohut. 2008. '"Erkölcsi téren ma már a szállókon rend van". Mindennapi élet a szocialista korszak munkásszállásain', *Korall* 32(9). On the conditions of workers' hostels see also S. Horváth. 2012. *Két emelet boldogság. Mindennapi szociálpolitika Budapesten a Kádár-korszakban*, Budapest: Napvilág,

28. The reports on the conditions of the working class bore the designation of 'strictly confidential'. The national reports were prepared only in a couple of copies. Even in reports, which only Kádár and some top leaders could read, we can find sentences that in some large factories of Budapest workers said that their situation greatly improved but that they owed this to [the revolution of] 1956.

29. M.J. Rainer. 2011. *Bevezetés a kádárizmusba*, Budapest: L'Harmattan.
30. The term is used in M. Pittaway. 1998. 'Industrial Workers, Socialist Industrialisation and the State in Hungary, 1948–1958', Ph.D., University of Liverpool. Pittaway argues that the 'workerist ideology' of the party was central to the legitimation of the ruling communist regimes. In his book (Pittaway. 2012. *The Workers' State: Industrial Labour and the Making of Socialist Hungary, 1944–1958*, Pittsburgh: Pittsburgh University Press) he uses three case studies of different working-class environments to show how this legitimacy was undermined by the harsh measures that the Hungarian government took against the working class in the early 1950s to realize the military programme triggered by the Cold War and Stalin's fear of a Third World War.
31. See in particular: Pittaway, 'A magyar forradalom új megközelítésben'; C. Gati. 2006. *Failed Illusions: Moscow, Washington, Budapest and the 1956 Hungarian Revolt*, Stanford: Stanford University Press.
32. Bill Lomax was one of the chief Western advocates of the theory that the workers' councils represented the seeds of a new, democratic socialism. See: I. Kemény and B. Lomax (eds). 1986. *Magyar munkástanácsok 1956-ban: Dokumentumok*, Paris: Magyar Füzetek; B. Lomax. 1989. *Magyarország 1956*, Budapest: Aura. Recent authors, however, argue that the leadership of the workers' councils was dominated by intellectuals. For the debate see: E. Zs. Tóth. 1999. 'A Csepel Vas- és Fémművek munkástanácsainak története 1956–1957', *Múltunk* 4; I. Feitl. 2005. 'Parlamentarizmus és önigazgatás az 1956-os forradalomban', *Múltunk* 2; I. Feitl. 1989.'A magyar munkástanácsok és az önigazgatás 1956-ban', *Eszmélet* 2; T. Krausz. 2006. 'Az 1956-os munkástanácsokról', *Eszmélet* 72; L. Tütő. 2006. '1956 mint nyelvi probléma', *Eszmélet* 72.
33. Pittaway argues that the revolution found its social basis in the working class, which protested not only against their material pauperization but also against collectivization in the province since the overwhelming majority of the newly recruited workforce came from the peasantry. In addition, the wage policy of the early 1950s overthrew the traditional hierarchies based on skill, age and gender in the factories, and turned the more experienced, skilled core of the working class against the Stalinist regime. The author concludes that the consolidation of the Kádár regime was possible through the satisfaction of the most important working-class demands. Pittaway, 'A magyar forradalom új megközelítésben'.
34. Many leaders of the workers' councils were imprisoned or suffered other forms of persecution.
35. Officially, the managers were appointed by the relevant ministries, but the leading party organs had to approve of the appointments.
36. The formal role of the trade union in the enterprise management was criticized even in the executive committee of Győr-Sopron county (Győr Megyei Jogú Város Levéltára, GYML, X. 415/134/1, MSZMP Győr-Sopron Megyei Bizottsága. Pártbizottsági ülés jegyzőkönyve, napirendi anyagai. Az üzemi demokrácia helyzete, az egyszemélyi vezetés érvényesülése és a továbbfejlesztés feladatai. 1974. március 29).
37. In Hungary, Lajos Héthy and Csaba Makó wrote several studies on the functioning of interest representation and the often informal ways of successful bargaining. See: L. Héthy and Cs. Makó. 1972. *Munkásmagatartások és a gazdasági szervezet*, Budapest: Akadémiai Kiadó; L. Héthy and Cs. Makó. 1976. 'A munkások perspektívái és a szocialista vállalat', *Társadalmi Szemle* 31(1); L. Héthy and Cs. Makó. 1978. *Munkások, érdekek, érdekegyeztetés*, Budapest: Gondolat Kiadó; L. Héthy and Cs. Makó. 1972. 'Work Performance, Interests, Powers and Environment (The Case of Cyclical Slowdowns in a Hungarian Factory)', *The Sociological Review Monograph* 17; L. Héthy. 1977 'Bérvita az építkezésen (Az érdékérvényesítési képesség problémája)', *Valóság* 20(11). Concerning enterprise democracy see in particular: L. Héthy. 1980. *Az üzemi demokrácia és a munkások*, Budapest: Kossuth Kiadó; L. Héthy. 1983. *Vállalatirányítás és demokrácia. Az üzemi demokrácia szociológiai koncepciója és fejlesztésének lehetőségei szervezeti-társadalmi viszonyainkban*, Budapest: Közgazdasági és Jogi Könyvkiadó; Cs. Makó. 1979. 'Részvétel: a feladat átalakítása vagy a

hatalmi viszonyok átalakítása', *Valóság* 22(4). In the periodical *Társadalmi Szemle* there was also an extensive debate on how to realize enterprise democracy. See: A. Mód. 1974. 'Munkásismeretek, munkástörekvések, üzemi demokrácia (Kutatási tapasztalatok)', *Társadalmi Szemle* 29(11); I. Katona. 1976. 'Eszmecsere a párttagokkal', *Társadalmi Szemle* 31(2); L. Héthy. 1977. 'Hogyan látjuk ma az üzemi demokráciát?', *Társadalmi Szemle* 32(9); L. Héthy. 1979. 'A gazdasági munka pártirányítása és az érdekegyeztetés', *Társadalmi Szemle* 34(2); L. Héthy. 1978. 'Az üzemi demokrácia fejlesztésének útján (Az eszmecsere befejezéséhez)', *Társadalmi Szemle* 33(6); E. Sőtér. 1977. 'Gondolatok a szocialista brigádmozgalomról', *Társadalmi Szemle* 32(4); Cs. Makó. 1977. 'Az érdekegyeztetés és a cselekvési egység az üzemben. Az üzemi demokrácia fejlesztésének kérdéséhez', *Társadalmi Szemle* 32(5); L. Horváth. 1977. 'Üzemi demokrácia és vállalati stratégia', *Társadalmi Szemle* 32(9); Cs. Egerszegi. 1977. 'Termelési tanácskozás és üzemi demokrácia', *Társadalmi Szemle* 32(9); Gy. Akszentievics. 1977. 'Ki hogyan érdekelt az üzemi demokrácia gyakorlásában?', *Társadalmi Szemle* 32(10); Á. Simonyi. 1977. 'Munkásrészvétel üzemi bérezési döntésekben (Kutatói tapasztalatok a Magyar Vagon és Gépgyárban)', *Társadalmi Szemle* 32(10); Á. Simonyi. 1978. 'Munkahelyi demokrácia és nyilvánosság', *Társadalmi Szemle* 33(1); M. Búza. 1977. 'Az üzemi demokrácia érvényesítése: a gazdasági vezetők kötelessége', *Társadalmi Szemle* 32(9); J. Marosi. 1977. 'Nem csak a gazdasági vezetők dolga ...' *Társadalmi Szemle* 32(12); J. Fehér. 1977. 'Diósgyőri munkások az üzemi demokráciáról', *Társadalmi Szemle* 32(11); I. Ferenczi. 1977. 'Az üzemi demokrácia: fokozott társadalmi ellenőrzés', *Társadalmi Szemle* 32(12); P. Vitkovics. 1978. 'Az üzemi demokrácia és a pártszervezet munkája', *Társadalmi Szemle* 33(1); Gy. Marle. 1978. 'Az üzemi demokrácia és a termelés', *Társadalmi Szemle* 33(3); T. Folkmayer. 1978. 'Üzemi demokrácia és tervezés', *Társadalmi Szemle* 33(4); J. Andics and T. Rozgonyi. 1979. 'A vállalati konfliktusok és a hatékonyság', *Társadalmi Szemle* 34(5); Gy. Gergely. 1979. 'Hogyan látják a munkások üzemi gondjainkat és tennivalóinkat?', *Társadalmi Szemle* 34(9); J. Rózsa. 1978. 'Napjaink kérdése: az üzemi demokrácia', *Társadalmi Szemle* 33(2). It should be noted that Lajos Héthy and Csaba Makó conducted a study in Rába MVG about how automation influenced working-class consciousness. The research is discussed in: L. Héthy and Cs. Makó. 1972. 'Az automatizáció és az ipari munkások. Beszámoló egy nemzetközi kutatási program menetéről', *Szociológia* 2.

38. He wrote this work in 1968, but it was only published in 1985.

39. In the Hungarian case see: M. Haraszti. 1977. *A Worker in a Workers' State*, New York: Penguin; Gy. Bence and J. Kis [Mark Rakovski]. 1983. *A szovjet típusú társadalom marxista szemmel*, Paris: Magyar Füzetek; Gy. Bence, J. Kis and Gy. Márkus. 1992. *Hogyan lehetséges kritikai gazdaságtan?*, Budapest: T-Twins; Gy. Konrád and I. Szelényi. 1979. *The Intellectuals on the Road to Class Power*, New York: Harcourt Brace Jovanovich. Gy. Lukács. 1985. *Demokratisierung heute und morgen*, Budapest: Akadémiai Kiadó. In the German case see: R. Bahro. 1977. *Die Alternative: zur Kritik des realexistierenden Sozialismus*, Cologne: Europäische Verlaganstalt. It is worth pointing out that the East European intellectuals, who grew disappointed with 'actually existing' socialism, used the Marxist method to demonstrate that the regime had nothing to do with the socialism that Marx envisaged because the reproduction of inequalities and exploitation were central themes of their criticism of socialism. Thus, the oppositionist intellectuals formulated an essentially leftist criticism of 'actually existing' socialism. But I can also mention the example of Szelényi and Konrád's book *Az új lakótelepek szociológiai problémái* (The sociological problems of the new housing estates), which sharply criticizes the 'unjust' privileges of white-collar workers and the intelligentsia in the central allocation of flats – namely, that the latter could use string-pulling to obtain a flat quicker than the 'officially' positively discriminated workers (I. Szelényi and Gy. Konrád. 1969. *Az új lakótelepek szociológiai problémái*, Budapest: Akadémiai Kiadó). This research became the basis of the authors' famous book (*The Intellectuals on the Road to Class Power*) in which they develop the thesis that under mature socialism the ruling class

is not the bureaucracy but the intellectuals. Later, however, Szelényi self-critically revised this thesis and he argued that the resistance of the bureaucracy and the expansion of the second (private) economy prevented the formation of this new class: I. Szelényi. 1990. 'A kelet európai újosztály stratégia távlatai és korlátai: Az értelmiség útja az osztályhatalomhoz önkritikus felülvizsgálata', in I. Szelényi, *Új osztály, állam, politika*, Budapest: Európa. For other, influential left-wing criticisms of state socialism see: Casals [Pavel Campenau]. 1980. *The Syncretic Society*, White Plains, NY: M.E. Sharpe; M. Djilas. 1983. *The New Class: An Analysis of the Communist System*, San Diego: Harcourt Brace Jovanovich. See also: F. Parkin (ed.). 1974. *The Social Analysis of Class Structure*, London: Tavistock.

40. Workers' self-management as a possible alternative was not even mentioned in the interviews that I conducted with 40-40 workers in both factories between 2002 and 2004. When asked directly, the majority of the interview partners were unfamiliar with the concept.

41. Direktive des VIII. Parteitages der SED zum Fünfjahrplan für die Entwicklung der Volkswirtschaft der DDR 1971 bis 1975, in: Protokoll des VIII. Parteitages der SED, 2. volume, 322–27 and 380–91.

42. A. Steiner. 2004. *Von Plan zu Plan: eine Wirtschaftsgeschichte der DDR*, Munich: Dt. Vrl.-Anst., 190.

43. On Honecker's social policy see: B. Bouvier. 2002. *Die DDR- ein Sozialstaat? Sozialpolitik in der ära Honecker*, Bonn: Dietz. For contemporary studies on the Honecker era see R. Hürtgen and T. Reichel (eds). 2001. *Der Schein der Stabilität: DDR-Betriebsalltag in der Ära Honecker*, Berlin: Metropol-Verlag; Gert-Joachim Glaeßner (ed.). 1988. *Die DDR in der Ära Honecker*, Opladen: Westdeutscher Verlag; W. Weidenfeld and H. Zimmermann (eds). 1989. *Deutschland-Handbuch. Eine doppelte Bilanz 1949–1989*, Bonn: Landeszentrale für politische Bildung.

44. A further example, of a trial of left dissidents as early as 1971, is provided by L. Tütő. 1993. 'A szocialista ellenzékiség történetéből – az 1971-es Kemény-per', *Eszmélet* 5(3).

45. The existence of this gap is confirmed by M. Burawoy and J. Lukács. 1992. *The Radiant Past: Ideology and Reality in Hungary's Road to Capitalism*, Chicago and London: The University of Chicago Press; and E. Szalai.1986. *Beszélgetések a gazdasági reformról*, Budapest: Pénzügykutatási Intézet Kiadványai.

46. Burawoy, *The Radiant Past*.

47. There is an impressive literature on the demise of Honecker's state; see, for instance: J. Kopstein. 1997. *The Politics of Economic Decline in East Germany 1945–1989*, Chapel Hill, NC: University of North Carolina Press; M. Fulbrook. 1995. *Anatomy of a Dictatorship: Inside the GDR 1949–1989*, New York: Oxford University Press; C. Maier. 1997. *Dissolution: The Crisis of Communism and the End of East Germany*, Princeton: Princeton University Press; T. Lindenberger (ed.). 1990. *Herrschaft und Eigensinn in der Diktatur. Studien zur Gesellschaftsgeschichte der DDR*, Cologne: Böhlau; K. Jarausch and M. Sabrow (eds). 1999. *Der Weg in den Untergang. Der innere Zerfall der DDR*, Göttingen: Vandenhoeck und Ruprecht; H. Joas and M. Kohli (eds). 1993. *Der Zusammenbruch der DDR. Soziologische Analyse*, Frankfurt am Main: Suhrkamp Verlag. The working-class history of late socialism is, however, missing from the otherwise impressive literature. Fuller offers a sociological analysis of the lack of working-class action. She develops the thesis that the East German working class refrained from class action after the collapse of communist rule because they did not want to get involved in a struggle between the rival groups of intelligentsia as they viewed the change of regimes. My argument is different. See L. Fuller. 1999. *Where Was the Working Class?: Revolution in Eastern Germany*, Urbana, Chicago: University of Illinois Press.

48. The party itself was divided on the issue of how the ruling role of the working class could be realized with the 'advancement of the scientific-technological development'. Officially, however, the doctrine was not revised.

49. I. Kemény. 1972. 'A magyar munkásság rétegződése', *Szociológia* 1; I. Kemény. 1990. *Velünk nevelkedett a gép: Magyar munkások a hetvenes évek elején*, Budapest: Művelődéskutató In-

tézet. Kemény continued the work of Julius Rézler, who in the interwar period elaborated a strictly scientific method for the study of the large industrial working class. Rézler's survey includes the main characteristics of the settlements and the factories, the working-class society of manufacturing industry, working conditions, the social policy of the factories, the representation of labour interests, the scale and type of workers' organizations, housing conditions, family types and size, and the economic and cultural conditions of the working class. Rézler used this method to investigate the conditions of the working class of the brickyards, the sugar mills, the ironworks and the textile industry. His important work of this period bears the title *A magyar nagyipari munkásság kialakulása 1867–1914* (The formation of the large industrial working class in Hungary 1867–1914), and it belongs to the lasting achievements of the Hungarian sociology of the interwar period. Rézler, however, could not continue his work in Hungary: his friends warned him that he would be arrested and charged with espionage for his brother, who taught at Harvard University. After his immigration he lived and taught in the United States.

50. András Hegedüs, who was Prime Minister in 1956, played an important role in the reestablishment of sociological institutions. On the relationship between party policy and sociology see his memoirs: A. Hegedüs. 1989. *Élet egy eszme árnyékában*, Budapest: Bethlen Gábor Könyvkiadó. The education of Hungarian sociology owes much to the efforts of Tibor Huszár and his colleagues. Public opinion polls were considered to be a 'bourgeois' discipline. The 1960s, and the Western recognition of Kádár's Hungary (the United Nations decided to remove the retaliations from the agenda following the Hungarian amnesty for political prisoners of 1956) indicated a change in this respect: the first cohort of Hungarian academics travelled to the United States to learn how to conduct an opinion poll.

51. Zs. Ferge. 1979. *A Society in the Making: Hungarian Social and Societal Policy, 1945–1975*, Harmondsworth: Penguin. See also: Zs. Ferge. 1969. *Társadalmuk rétegződése: Elvek és tények*. Budapest: Közgazdasági és Jogi Könyvkiadó.

52. Zs. Ferge. 1976. *Az iskolarendszer és az iskolai tudás társadalmi meghatározottsága*, Budapest: Akadémiai Kiadó.

53. L. Héthy, 'Bérvita az építkezésen'.

54. Bundesarchiv (Archive of the Federal Republic of Germany), Stiftung Archiv der Parteien und Massenorganisationen der DDR, DY 30/IV/2.2.033, Institut für Meinungsforschung, 8 Januar 1976. On the relationship between the party and sociology in the GDR see: H. Laatz. 1990. *Klassenstruktur und soziales Verhalten. Zur Entstehung der empirischen Sozialstrukturforschung in der DDR*, Cologne: Verlag Wissenschaft und Politik.

55. E. Nemitz. 1988. *Junge Produktionsarbeiter und Lehrlinge in der DDR. Eine empirische Untersuchung über Jugendliche in volkseigenen Betrieben des Bauwesens*, Koblenz: Verlag Siegfried Bublies.

56. Conducting fieldwork in a factory was, of course, not easy. Burawoy negotiated his entry to Hungarian factories through well-connected sociologists. In the GDR, Lutz Niethammer and his colleagues conducted the first fieldwork – the results were published after the collapse of Honecker's regime: L. Niethammer, A. von Plato and D. Wierling. 1991. *Die volkseigene Erfahrung: eine Archäologie des Lebens in der Industrieprovinz der DDR*, Berlin: Rowohlt-Berlin-Verlag.

57. M. Burawoy. 1985. *The Politics of Production: Factory Regimes under Capitalism and Socialism*, London: Verso, 189.

58. In Hungary the idea of democratic socialism without the MSZMP was represented most completely by the Leftist Alternative Union (*Baloldali Alternatíva Egyesület*). After the political failure of its project, the intellectual heritage of this school was continued by the journal *Eszmélet* (Consciousness) launched in 1989. The internationally best-known intellectual of this circle is Tamás Krausz.

59. This concept had particularly strong theoretical roots in Hungary because of the work of George Lukács. Disappointed with Stalinist society and refusing to accept a capitalist res-

toration, Lukács wrote a famous essay (*Demokratisierung heute und morgen*) in the 1960s in which he sought to outline a third road. There is a sad irony in the fact that by the time this book was published in Hungary (1985), the reformers pressed for more rather than less capitalism.

60. For the GDR see: C. Kleßmann. 2007. *Arbeiter im Arbeiterstaat im "Arbeiterstaat" DDR: Deutsche Traditionen, sowjetisches Modell, westdeutsches Magnetfeld 1945 bis 1971*, Bonn: Dietz; P. Hübner. 1995. *Konsens, Konflikt und Kompromiß: Soziale Arbeiterinteressen und Sozialpolitik in der SBZ/DDR 1945–1970*, Berlin: Akademie Verlag. For other, more ethnographically oriented studies see: R. Bittner. 1998. *Kolonien des Eigensinns. Ethnographie einer ostdeutschen Industrieregion*, Frankfurt and New York: Campus Verlag; R. Bittner. 2000. 'Rund um die Uhr – ostdeutscher Arbeiteralltag im Kraftwerk Elbe', *Zeitschrift für Volkskunde* 96; R. Bittner. 2001. 'Der kleine Mann – Paradoxien und Ambivalenzen einer ostdeutschen Arbeiterfigur vor und nach der Wende' in Hürtgen, *Der Schein der Stabilität*; J. Richter, H. Förster and U. Lakemann. 1997. *Stalinstadt-Eisenhüttenstadt: von der Utopie zur Gegenwart: Wandel industrieller, regionaler und sozialer Strukturen in Eisenhüttenstadt*, Marburg: Schüren. There is also an orientation towards regional studies, see e.g. M. Vester, M. Hofmann and I. Zierke (eds). 1995. *Soziale Milieus in Ostdeutschland. Gesellschaftliche Strukturen zwischen Zerfall und Neubildung*, Cologne: Bund-Verlag; and on the study of gender, see D. Harsch. 2007. *Revenge of the Domestic: Women, the Family, and Communism in the German Democratic Republic*, Princeton: Princeton University Press; L. Ansorg. 1999. '"Ich hab immer von unten Druck gekriegt und von oben": Weibliche Leitungskader und Arbeiterinnen in einem DDR-Textilbetrieb. Eine Studie zum Innenleben der DDR-Industrie', *Archiv für Sozialgeschichte* 39; I. Merkel. 1990. *... und Du, Frau an der Werkbank:die DDR in der 50er Jahren*, Berlin: Elefanten Press; A. Schüler. 2001. *"Die Spinne": die Erfahrungsgeschichte weiblicher Industriearbeit im VEB Leipziger Baumwollspinnerei'*, Leipzig: Leipziger-Univ.-Verlag; F. Weil. 2000. *Herrschaftsanspruch und soziale Wirklichkeit: zwei sächsische Betriebe in der DDR während der Honecker Ära*, Cologne: Böhlau. Literature on the Honecker era mainly addresses particular aspects such as welfare policy (Bouvier, *Die DDR- ein Sozialstaat?*), consumption (I. Merkel. 1999. *Utopie und Bedürfnis: die Geschichte der Konsumkultur in der DDR*, Cologne: Böhlau) and historical consciousness (B. Faulenbach, A. Leo and K. Weberskirch. 1994. 'Die "Wende" 1989/90 aus der Sicht von Stahlarbeitern in Henningsdorf und Dortmund', *Jahrbuch Arbeit, Bildung, Kultur* 12; B. Faulenbach, A. Leo and K. Weberskirch. 2000. *Zweierlei Geschichte. Lebensgeschichte und Geschichtsbewusstsein von Arbeiternehmern in West -und Ostdeutschland*, Essen: Klartext-Verlag). For collected volumes see: R. Bessel and R. Jessen (eds). 1996. *Die Grenzen der Diktatur: Staat und Gesellschaft in der DDR*, Göttingen: Vandenhoeck & Ruprecht; P. Hübner and K. Tenfelde (eds). 1999. *Arbeiter in der SBZ – DDR*, Essen: Klartext-Verlag; P. Hübner, C. Kleßmann and K. Tenfelde (eds). 2005. *Arbeiter im Staatssozialismus: ideologischer Anspruch und soziale Wirklichkeit*, Cologne: Böhlau; Hürtgen, *Der Schein der Stabilität*; H. Kaelble, J. Kocka and H. Zwahr (eds). 1994. *Sozialgeschichte der DDR*, Stuttgart: Klett-Cotta. In the Hungarian case Mark Pittaway studied the relationship between the workers and the state in the era of Soviet-type industrialization, see: M. Pittaway, 'Industrial Workers'; M. Pittaway. 2002. 'The Reproduction of Hierarchy: Skill, Working-class Culture and the State in Early Socialist Hungary', *The Journal of Modern History* 74; M. Pittaway, *The Workers' State*. For a study of working-class youth,see: L. Kürti. 2002. *Youth and the State in Hungary: Capitalism, Communism and Class*, London: Pluto Press. The building of a socialist city is described in S. Horváth. 2004. *A kapu és a határ: mindennapi Sztálinváros*, Budapest: MTA Történettudományi Intézete. See also: S. Horváth. 2005. 'Remaking Working-class Life in Hungary's First Socialist City', *Journal of International Labor and Working-class History* 68. For studies of socialism and gender see: Éva Fodor. 2003. *Working Difference: Women's Working Lives in Hungary and Austria 1945–1995*, Durham, NC: Duke University Press;

E. Zs. Tóth. 2007. *'Puszi Kádár Jánosnak': Munkásnők élete a Kádár-korszakban mik- rotörténeti megközelítésben*, Budapest: Napvilág; E. Zs. Tóth. 2010. *Kádár leányai: Nők a szocialista időszakban*, Budapest: Nyitott Könyvműhely. For a collected volume on work- ing-class history see: S. Horváth, L. Pethő and E. Zs. Tóth (eds). 2003. *Munkástörténet – munkásantropológia*, Budapest: Napvilág Kiadó; S. Horváth (ed.). 2008. *Mindennapok Rákosi és Kádár korában*. Budapest: Nyitott Könyvműhely; Judit Sas studies the experience of the change of regime in the light of narrative interviews conducted at different time in- tervals: H. Sas Judit. 1995. *Szubjektív történelem 1980–1994*, Budapest: MTA Szociológiai Intézet. For a study of how the change of regimes impacted on her interviewees' lives see: H. Sas Judit. 2003. *Közelmúlt. Rendszerváltások, családtörténetek*, Budapest: Új Mandá- tum Kiadó.

61. For a thorough review of the East European literature see: Heumos, 'Workers under Com- munist Rule'. Class analysis is almost utterly missing from the post-1989 Hungarian litera- ture on the workers, with the exception of Pittaway and Kürti. The East German literature is more critical; however, issues of class also remain largely unexplored, and emphasis is given to special areas (welfare policy, the party's policy towards women, historical con- sciousness and consumption). The problem with this approach is that the point of refer- ence is West Germany and such – often unintended – comparisons often reproduce the East–West rivalry characteristic of the era of the Cold War.

62. For a challenging analysis see: D. Kalb. 1997. *Expanding Class: Power and Everyday Poli- tics in Industrial Communities, the Netherlands, 1850–1950*, Durham and London: Duke University Press.

63. For a good summary on the changes of the enterprise structure in Hungary see: I. Sch- weitzer. 1982. *A vállalatnagyság*, Budapest: Közgazdasági és Jogi Könyvkiadó, 36–61. For the discussion of the bargaining power of the large enterprises see: T. Laky. 1982. *Érdekviszonyok a vállalati döntésekben*, Budapest: Közgazdasági és Jogi Könyvkiadó; and E. Szalai. 1989. *Gazdasági mechanizmus, reformtörekvések és nagyvállalati érdekek*, Budapest: Közgazdasági és Jogi Könyvkiadó.

64. See, for instance, Kotkin, *Magnetic Mountain*; K.J. Murphy. 2005. *Revolution and Coun- terrevolution: Class Struggle in a Moscow Metal Factory*, New York: Berghahn Books; G. Akgöz. 2012. *Many Voices of a Turkish State Factory: Working at Bakırköy Cloth Factory, 1932–1950*, Ph.D., University of Amsterdam.

65. Hübner, *Konsens, Konflikt*.

66. The extensive case method is described in M. Burawoy (ed.). 2000. *Global Ethnography: Forces, Connections, and Imaginations in a Postmodern World*, Berkeley and Los Angeles: University of California Press, 1–38. The extensive case method heavily draws on the tra- dition of the Manchester School of Anthropology. On the latter see: T.M.S. Evans and D. Handelmann (eds). 2006. *The Manchester School: Practice and Ethnographic Praxis in Anthropology*, New York and Oxford: Berghahn Books.

67. For a good study of the close contacts between American governmental institutions and academic departments for Soviet and East European Studies see A. Gleason. 1995. *To- talitarianism: The Inner History of the Cold War*, New York: Oxford University Press. For a discussion of the Renaissance of totalitarian theory in postsocialist Eastern Europe see: E. Bartha: 'A preventív háború és a totalitarianizmus összefüggései: néhány megjegyzés a vitához az angolszász szakirodalom alapján', in: E. Bartha and T. Krausz (eds), *Háború és nemzeti önismeret*.

68. Pittaway, *The Workers' State*.

69. Harsch, *Revenge of the Domestic*.

70. See: M. Burawoy and K. Verdery (eds). 1999. *Uncertain Transition: Ethnographies of Change in the Postsocialist World*, Lanham: Rowman & Littlefield Publishers; C. Hann (ed.). 2002. *Postsocialism: Ideals, Ideologies and Practice in Eurasia*, London: Routledge.

71. Steiner, *Von Plan zu Plan*.

72. Gy. Földes. 1995. *Az eladósodás politikai története, 1957–1986*, Budapest: Gondolat.
73. Kopstein, *The Politics of Economic Decline*.
74. There is evidence that the Soviet leadership was informed of the slackening economic development: in 1979 governmental analysts conducted an extensive study of the state and perspectives of the Soviet economy under the leadership of V.A. Kirilin, the Deputy Prime Minister. The study concluded that with respect to the most important parameters there was an increasing gap between the Soviet Union and the countries using modern technology. The Kirilin report did not meet with the approval of the political leadership, and Kirilin was relieved of his post. Sz. Bíró argues that it was not the recognition of the economic problems that was missing from the central leadership but the political will to initiate structural reforms. See: Sz. Z. Bíró. 2003. 'Politikatörténeti vázlat a késői Szovjetunióról', in T. Krausz and Sz. Z. Bíró (eds), *Peresztrojka és tulajdonáthelyezés. Tanulmányok és dokumentumok a rendszerváltás történetéből a Szovjetunióban 1985–1991*, Budapest: Magyar Ruszisztikai Intézet.
75. While labour history in the East European countries was influenced directly by the political and ideological requirements, this 'traditional' paradigm – that Thomas Welskopp called the 'failed heroic history of the proletariat' – was present in the Western historiography as well. According to Welskopp's argument, in this traditional narrative the complex relationship between class position and class consciousness has been simplified to the triangle 'situation – consciousness – behaviour'. See: T. Welskopp. 1993. 'Von der verhinderten Heldengeschichte des Proletariats zur vergleichenden Sozialgeschichte der Arbeiterschaft – Perspektiven der Arbeitergeschichtsschreibung in den 1990er Jahren', *1999 Zeitschrift für Sozialgeschichte des 20. und 21. Jahrhunderts* 3. See also: T. Welskopp. 1996. 'Der Betrieb als soziales Handlungsfeld. Neuere Forschungsansätze in der Industrie- und Arbeitergeschichte', *Geschichte und Gesellschaft* 22. For a social history of the Hungarian revolution of 1956 see: Pittaway, *The Workers' State*.
76. This criticism is particularly valid for the East German literature, where the main point of reference is most frequently West Germany. While socialist institutions undoubtedly differed from those of West Germany, this alone does not prove the specificity of the Honecker regime. Further, this kind of comparison usually means a 'definition of absences' for the GDR since, when referred to West Germany, its institutions seem to be incomplete or they deviate from the structures understood as normative. It cannot be the intention here to reflect on the debates about the writing of the history of East Germany; from the extensive literature on the topic see: K.H. Jarausch. 1999. 'Die gescheiterte Gesellschaft. Überlegungen zu einer Sozialgeschichte der DDR', *Archiv für Sozialgeschichte* 39; C. Kleßmann (ed.). 2001. *The Divided Past: Rewriting Post-War German History*, New York: Berg Press; J. Kocka (ed.). 1993. *Historische DDR-Forschung: Aufsätze und Studien*, Berlin: Akademie Verlag; J. Kocka and M. Sabrow (eds). 1994. *Die DDR als Geschichte: Fragen-Hypothese-Perspektive*, Berlin: Akademie Verlag; S. Meuschel. 1993. 'Überlegungen zu einer Herrschafts- und Gesellschaftsgeschichte der DDR', *Geschichte und Gesellschaft* 19(1).
77. In his programmatic work Marcel van der Linden seeks to outline a new methodology for writing labour histories beyond borders. See: M. Linden. 2008. *Workers of the World: Essays toward a Global Labor History*, Leiden and Boston: Brill.
78. In addition, the party also lost the trust of the intelligentsia, which effectively prevented the creation of a compromise. From the rich literature on Solidarity see: D. Ost. 1990. *Solidarity and the Politics of Anti-politics: Opposition and Reform in Poland since 1968*, Philadelphia: Temple University Press; R. Laba. 1991. *The Roots of Solidarity: A Political Sociology of Poland's Working-class Democratization*, Princeton: Princeton University Press. For a contemporary study see: Alain Touraine et al. 1983. *Solidarity: The Analysis of a Social Movement, Poland 1980–1981*, Cambridge: Cambridge University Press.
79. Swain offers a thought-provoking analysis of the Hungarian attempt to integrate the private sector into the structure of planned economy. See: N. Swain. 1992. *Hungary: The Rise and Fall of Feasible Socialism*, London and New York: Verso.

80. Many economists believed at the time that the second economy contained the seeds of a new, capitalistic society and the small businesses that were set up in Hungary after 1982 could function well in a 'proper' market economy. Nonetheless, this assumption was much debated in the literature. See, for instance: Á. Róna-Tas. 1997. *The Great Surprise of the Small Transformation: The Demise of Communism and the Rise of the Private Sector in Hungary*, Ann Arbor: University of Michigan; R.I. Gábor and P. Galasi. 1981. *A „második" gazdaság: Tények és hipotézisek*, Budapest: Közgazdasági és Jogi Könyvkiadó; R.I. Gábor. 1994. 'Modernity or a New Kind of Duality? Second Thoughts about the Second Economy', in J.M. Kovács (ed.), *Transition to Capitalism? The Communist Legacy in Eastern Europe*, London: Transaction Publishers. According to the argument of Martha Lampland, capitalist relations in agriculture were established under socialism in Hungary. See: Martha Lampland. 1995. *The Object of Labor: Commodification in Socialist Hungary*, Chicago and London: University of Chicago Press.

81. For a similar argument see E. Szalai. 2004. 'Tulajdonviszonyok, társadalomszerkezet és munkásság', *Kritika* 33(9). Pittaway speaks of the privatization of the working class. See: M. Pittaway. 2005. 'Accommodation and the Limits of Economic Reform: Industrial Workers during the Making and Unmaking of Kádár's Hungary', in: Hübner, *Arbeiter im Staatssozialismus*.

82. For a discussion of the role of the intelligentsia in the East German society see: K. Belwe. 1989. 'Sozialstruktur und gesellschaftlicher Wandel in der DDR', in Weidenfeld, *Deutschland-Handbuch*; K. Belwe. 1990. *Entwicklung der Intelligenz innerhalb der Sozialstruktur der DDR in den Jahren 1978 bis 1989 – eine Literaturanalyse*, Bonn: Gesamtdeutsches Institut. For a counter-argument see G. Erbe. 1982. *Arbeiterklasse und Intelligenz in der DDR. Soziale Annäherung von Produktionsarbeiterschaft und wissenschaftlich-technischer Intelligenz im Industriebetrieb?*, Opladen: Westdeutscher Verlag.

83. J. Krejci. 1976. *Social Structure in Divided Germany*, London: Croom Helm. In his essay Johannes Weiß distinguishes between the high party leadership, the mid-level cadres, members of the old intelligentsia and Christian opposition, and the masses of workers and peasants. See: J. Weiß. 2003. 'Die namenlose Gesellschaft. Identitätsprobleme der Bevölkerung Ostdeutschlands', in: S. Beetz, U. Jacob and A. Sterbling (eds), *Soziologie über die Grenzen. Festschrift für Prof. Dr. Dr. h. c. Bálint Balla zum 75. Geburtstag*, Hamburg: Krämer. For a sociological analysis see also D. Pollack. 1998. 'Die konstitutive Widersprüchlichkeit der DDR oder war die DDR-Gesellschaft homogen?' *Geschichte und Gesellschaft* 24(1); Joas, *Der Zusammenbruch der DDR*.

84. The 'liberalism' of the Hungarian Communist Party was observed by the SED functionaries as well. In 1964 an East German delegation visited Hungary, and in the report they criticized the lax and too familiar working style of the Hungarian base party organizations, that 'there are not enough resolutions at the meetings', and that 'they had not seen enough posters and other forms of visual agitation in the factories and at the universities'. Bundesarchiv, Stiftung Archiv der Parteien und Massenorganisationen der DDR, DDR DY 30/IV A 2/5.

85. James Ferguson argued that what he called the expectations of modernity (see: J. Ferguson. 1999. *Expectations of Modernity: Myths and Meanings of Urban Life on the Zambian Copperbelt*, Berkeley and Los Angeles: University of California Press) – myths related to industrial development, and the expectation to catch up with the material welfare and levels of consumption of the developed capitalist 'core' countries (see Wallerstein's classical work, *The Modern World-System I: Capitalist Agriculture and the Origins of the European World-Economy in the Sixteenth Century*, New York: Academic Press, 1974) – persist longer in the periphery than in countries that are closer to the core.

86. C.G.A. Bryant and E. Mokrzycki. 1994. *The New Great Transformation? Change and Continuity in East Central Europe*, London: Routledge.

87. For an 'early' economic criticism of the neoliberal programme in Eastern Europe see: A.H. Amsden, J. Kochanowicz and L. Taylor. 1994. *The Market Meets its Match: Restructuring*

the Economies of Eastern Europe, Cambridge, MA: Harvard University Press; P. Gowan. 1995. 'Neo-liberal Theory and Practice for Eastern Europe', *New Left Review* 213; J. Pickles and A. Smith. 1998. *Theorising Transition: The Political Economy of Postcommunist Transformations*, London and New York: Routledge; J. Adam. 1999. *Social Costs of Transformation to a Market Economy in Postsocialist Countries*, London: Macmillan; H. Radice. 1998. 'A feltámadt kapitalizmus: Kelet-Közép-Európa a "globalizáció" fényében' in T. Krausz (ed.), *Rendszerváltás és társadalomkritika*, Budapest: Napvilág. For Hungary see also: L. Andor. 2010. *Eltévedt éllovas: Siker és kudarc a rendszerváltó gazdaságpolitikában*, Budapest: Napvilág Kiadó. Transitology has been widely criticized by authors with diverse theoretical backgrounds, from David Stark and László Bruszt to Michael Burawoy and Chris Hann.

88. To be more precise, while important elements of the socialist welfare system such as universal employment and the subsidization of food prices and utilities disappeared after 1989, social security provisions such as unemployment benefit were severely cut back after the Hungarian government accepted the Bokros-package (named after the Minister of Finance, Lajos Bokros) in 1995 in order to stabilize the state budget. For a discussion of the Polish case to which Hungary shows some similarity between 1990 and 1994 see: J. Kochanowicz. 1997. 'Incomplete Demise: Reflections on the Welfare State in Poland after Communism', *Social Research* 64(4). On welfare policy in postsocialist Hungary see: L. Haney. 2002. *Inventing the Needy: Gender and the Politics of Welfare in Hungary*, Berkeley: University of California Press. For a critical evaluation of the economic policy of the Hungarian Socialist Party see Andor, *Eltévedt éllovas*.

89. On the peripheral development of the Hungarian economy see I.T. Berend and Gy. Ránki. 1974. *Gazdaság és társadalom. Tanulmányok hazánk és Kelet-Európa XIX-XX. századi történetéről*, Budapest: Magvető; I.T. Berend and Gy. Ránki. 1985. *The Hungarian Economy in the 20th Century*, London: Croom Helm; Gy. Ránki. 1983. *Mozgásterek, kényszerpályák. Válogatott tanulmányok*, Budapest: Magvető.

90. The working-class formation and political mobilization of labour substantially differed in the two counties. In a challenging analysis Kenney shows how the rural backround of the newly formed Polish working class influenced their class activity under communist rule. See: P. Kenney. 1997. *Rebuilding Poland: Workers and Communists 1945–1950*, Ithaca, NY: Cornell University Press. On the working-class formation in Hungary see: Rézler, *A magyar nagyipari munkásosztály kialakulása*. See also: P.P. Tóth. 2011. *Válogatás Rézler Gyula 1932 és 1999 között megjelent írásaiból*, Budapest: Gondolat Kiadó. For a study on the political mobilization of labour in the interwar period see: P. Sipos. 1988. *Legális és illegális munkásmozgalom, 1919–1944*, Budapest: Gondolat. A collection of pre-war working-class ethnographies was published by Gy. Litván (ed.). 1974. *Magyar munkásszociográfiák 1888–1945*, Budapest: Kossuth Kiadó. There is much more extensive literature on working-class formation and political activity in Germany, see: J. Kocka. 1979, 'Stand –Klasse – Organisation. Strukturen sozialer Ungleichheit in Deutschland vom späten 18. bis zum frühen 20. Jahrhundert im Aufriß', in H.U. Wehler (ed.), *Klassen in der europäischen Sozialgeschichte*, Göttingen: Vandenhoeck & Ruprecht; J. Kocka. 1983. *Lohnarbeit und Klassenbildung. Arbeiter und Arbeiterbewegung in Deutschland 1800–1875*, Berlin and Bonn: Dietz Verlag; J. Kocka (ed.). 1983. *Europäische Arbeiterbewegungen im 19. Jahrhundert: Deutschland, Österreich, England, und Frankreich im Vergleich*, Göttingen: Vandenhoeck & Ruprecht; J. Kocka (ed.). 1994. *Von der Arbeiterbewegung zum modernen Sozialstaat: Festschrift für Gerhard A. Ritter zum 65. Geburtstag*, Munich: Saur; G.A. Ritter. 1976. *Arbeiterbewegung, Parteien und Parlamentarismus: Aufsätze zur Deutschen Sozial- und Verfassungsgeschichte des 19. und 20. Jahrhunderts*, Göttingen: Vandenhoeck & Ruprecht; G.A. Ritter. 1989. *Der Sozialstaat: Entstehung und Entwicklung im internationalen Vergleich*, Munich: Oldenbourg; G.A. Ritter (ed.). 1990. *Der Aufstieg der deutschen Arbeiterbewegung: Sozialdemokratie und Freie Gewerkschaften im Parteiensystem und Sozialmilieu des Kaiserreichs*,

Munich: Oldenbourg; G.A. Ritter and K. Tenfelde. 1992. *Arbeiter im Deutschen Kaiserreich 1871 bis 1914*, Bonn: Dietz; K. Tenfelde (ed.). 1991. *Arbeiter im 20. Jahrhundert*, Stuttgart: Klett-Cotta; T. Welskopp. 1994. *Arbeit und Macht im Hüttenwerk. Arbeits- und industrielle Beziehungen in der deutschen und amerikanischen Eisen- und Stahlindustrie von den 1860er bis zu den 1930er Jahren*, Bonn: Dietz. See also: I. Katznelson and A.R. Zolberg (eds). 1986. *Working-class Formation: Nineteenth-century Patterns in Western Europe and the United States*, Princeton: Princeton University Press. From the literature of the GDR see: J. Kuczynski. 1967. *Die Geschichte der Lage der Arbeiter unter dem Kapitalismus*, Berlin: Akademie Verlag. For a discussion of the German historiography see also: R.J. Evans. 1990. *Proletarians and Politics: Socialism, Protest and the Working Class in Germany before the First World War*, New York: St. Martin's Press. The working-class formation and political mobilization of workers substantially differed in the two counties. As Kemény pointed out, the Hungarian socialist working class had rural origins and many preserved the lifestyle and living place of the peasantry. Kemény, *Velünk nevelkedett a gép*.

CHAPTER 1

1968 AND THE WORKING CLASS
'What do we get out of Socialism?' The Reform of
Enterprise Management in East Germany and Hungary

In August 1968 the party committee of the district of Gera[1] received the
following report on the political mood of the population:

> The agitators' discussions brought to light several theoretical problems that
> revealed that people could not yet fully comprehend a number of fundamen-
> tals. This is supported by the following: First, expressions of doubt about the
> increasing strength of the socialist world system and the change of power rela-
> tions in favour of socialism at the global level; Second, inadequate knowledge
> of the complexity and intensification of the class struggle between socialism
> and imperialism; Third, comparisons between the principle of socialist inter-
> nationalism and the concept of bourgeois sovereignty.[2]

The analysis of the 'efficiency of our ideological work and people's understanding of the basic questions of our development' was even more
critical of the political climate of the working-class communities in
the district:

> In this respect the workers said that in the GDR other strata such as the ar-
> tisans, the self-employed, the private traders and part of the intelligentsia are
> privileged and they have a higher standard of living than the workers. Many
> workers put the straightforward question: *'what do we get out of socialism?' The
> workers have to be on overtime in order to decrease the losses that resulted from
> the wrong decisions of leading cadres. We frequently hear the argument (mainly
> from women): the decisive question is how we live today.*[3] People criticize poor
> provision with consumer goods, for instance, with children's clothes, women's
> clothes and women's underwear; poor supply of several food products; the
> prices of industrial products are too high; we export too much, for instance,
> we export of carpets while there are not any in our shops. Discontent is wide-

spread among the workers because there was a lot of overtime work (extra shifts, weekend work, etc.) in the second half of last year and this year, too. 'This won't solve the great tasks; it is always at the expense of the workers. How does the weekend work help us when we don't do anything during the week, or on Monday because there is no more material? We should stop talking about the five-day week and make a new law instead that one should work sixty hours in a week, and then the workers will do that.' 'We work overtime in order to fulfil the plans and the state leaders will spoil things again with their bad management. When the managers want us to do overtime, they come to the shop floor and talk with us; otherwise we hardly get any information from them. We get the allocated task from above, no one asks for our opinions.' 'If one wants to give a professional contribution, one needs to be familiar with the materials. We don't have time for that. We discuss the tasks of our brigades or departments but apart from this, we hardly discuss anything else.'[4]

The above text is a lot clumsier in the original wording; however, in comparison to the dry and standardized language of the East German party documents, it is refreshingly informative. In the party documents of the Honecker era we only occasionally encounter any criticism; the overwhelming majority of the surviving documents in the district are nothing else but reports of the (over) fulfilment of the plan, completed with the appraisal of the heroic struggle of the working class to accomplish the task and the positive evaluation of the international power relations – in favour of the Soviet Union, of course. It seems that the local party functionaries dared not take the responsibility for any deviance from the obligatory 'Marxist' praises, which were formulated in a difficult and often incomprehensible bureaucratic language in order to appeal to a broader public or evoke the attention of simple people.

The cited report from Gera, which was written in a very laborious style even in comparison to the original German language that has a preference for complicated sentences and eloquent compounds, represents a refreshingly honest report of the political mood of the population that the party carefully monitored. In spite of all efforts, the information reports written under Honecker are so identical in their content and wording, with reports of contented and loyal socialist citizens, that we can skip years and we still have the impression that we are reading the same documents. The unusually informative and surprisingly critical report bears the date of 2 August 1968. The year of 1968 was the heyday of the East German reform, which bore the somewhat euphemistic name of the New Economic System of Planning and Managing the People's Economy (*das Neue ökonomische System der Planung und Leitung*, NES), later renamed the Economic System of Socialism (*das Ökonomische System des Sozialismus*, ESS). I discuss this reform first, not only because the GDR was the first country in the communist bloc that announced an economic reform in the 1960s but also because Hungarian reformers adopted many of its elements although the latter had a more radical concept of private property relations.[5]

In the era of thaw initiated by Khrushchev, reform discussion started in the Soviet Union, which sought to increase the consumption levels of the population after the 'lean years' of Stalinism. In 1962, Liberman published an article in *Pravda* under the title 'Plan, profit, premium' in which he outlined a reform of enterprise management and the bonus system. He summarized his ideas in two slogans condemning the 'petty tutelage of centralized administration over the state-owned enterprises' and pointing out that 'what is useful for the society must be useful for every socialist factory and its employees'. By the first he meant that the financial autonomy of the individual enterprises should be increased; by the second he proposed to reward quality work rather than ever larger quantities as had been the practice under Stalinism.[6]

The Soviet reform discussion inspired economists across Eastern Europe to contemplate the reform of planned economy. Ulbricht did not only aspire to pioneer the reform process but he sought for a special German path in order to stress that Germans don't merely slavishly imitate the Soviet model but they are able to adapt it creatively to the local technical and social environment.[7] The reform, which Ulbricht announced at the Sixth Party Congress in December 1963, was also an attempt to improve the economic efficiency of the country, which even according to the officially published statistics displayed a negative trend: the national income increased by 11 per cent in 1958, 4.5 per cent in 1960 and 2.1 per cent in 1962; investments increased by 12 per cent in 1958 but only 2 per cent in 1962.[8] The reform sought to reorganize the enterprise structure, to increase the autonomy and financial responsibility of the enterprises, and to introduce more economic incentives and a more realistic price policy, mainly in order to improve the export performance of the country.

While Ulbricht used phrases resonant with Liberman's slogans, he maintained that the NES was a socialist system adapted to the specific needs and conditions of the GDR. The reform of the enterprise structure meant the creation of large state enterprises, the so-called 'socialist trusts', which were responsible for the production, improvement and research work within their profile.[9] The reform, like in Hungary, increased the legal, economic and financial autonomy of the enterprises; the NES delegated many of the chores of the material supply mechanism to subordinate bodies in the hierarchy. A basic tool of the material supply mechanism was the material balance, which checked whether a given production-cum-final-uses plan was consistent. The administration of these balances was, to a large extent, delegated to the enterprises. In 1963, nearly a quarter of all balances were balanced by the State Planning Commission (SPC) and the ministries.

In December 1965, encouraged by the positive experiences of the NES (observers even spoke of the 'red miracle'), Ulbricht announced the second phase of the reform, which continued decentralization. By 1966 the enterprises were responsible for nearly 90 per cent of the balances, and the delegation went further in 1967. Another part of devolution was to provide the enterprises with a much wider freedom of action within the assigned production targets. This was closely related to the functioning of the supply mechanism: for any material balance for which the top had no specific desire, neither limits for inputs nor detailed output targets had to appear in the plan. The 1967 plan included only products of strategic importance. In 1968, the heyday of the NES, enterprises received fewer directions on the composition of sales than before.[10]

Devolution was linked with the attempt to change the managerial approach and increase competition in the planned economy. Managers received funds from the centre that they could use relatively freely (e.g. for investment, research, innovation), and the enterprises could retain a significant part of the profit. The quantitative approach (the so-called ton- ideology) was replaced with qualitative criteria such as profit, cost, price, labour productivity, and the optimal use of materials. The managers received a free hand to decide about bonuses, and they were encouraged to make use of the economic incentives (which were euphemistically called *ökonomische Hebel*): in 1969–70 the centre regulated only the wage funds, and not the average wages of the workers. The industrial price reform, which attempted to adjust the prices to the social costs of labour, was completed in 1967. Reformers sought to ensure that profitability would determine the economic results of state-owned enterprises.

According to one of the most original analysts of the reform, Michael Keren, the year of 1968 meant not only the heyday of the NES but also the beginning of the end. Keren explains this apparent contradiction with the argument that devolution in a centralized system can work, if at all, only with reasonable reserves – that is with plans that are not too ambitious or taut. According to his analysis, this was precisely the case in the first period of the NES when the GDR economy achieved an annul growth rate of 5 per cent, which was a spectacular result in comparison with the provisos 'lean years'.[11] In 1968 priority planning was introduced, which indeed centralized the planning of certain sectors of the economy, considered to be crucial for export-driven growth. The taut and unbalanced plans of 1969 and 1970, which concentrated state resources on large investments and priority products, upset the fragile balance between central planning and devolution, on which the new economic system rested. Specific misfortunes hastened the fall of the reform: in the harsh winter of 1969 the shortage of electricity caused many breakdowns in production and arrears in contract fulfilment. Since structure-determining projects received high priority, even the low plan targets of consumer goods were not fulfilled.

Keren's main argument is that the economic upheaval in the last two years of the reform brought about the political fall of Ulbricht, who insisted on the maximal programme of the NES that he considered his life's work. As late as January 1971, in his last major economic address, Ulbricht still called for the concentration of the resources on priority products. Fearing a general social upheaval, the party leadership, however, refused to follow his economic programme. Tautness was given up when some 1970 plan targets were cut in September; at the same time it was decided to slacken the 1971–75 plan. A lower investment target was set, and priority was given to investments in electrical power and other intermediate sectors that had suffered neglect over the previous years. Ulbricht resigned two days before the publication of the plan.

Keren devoted less attention to social discontent, which, however, could have been a stronger motive for the party leadership than the economic upheaval. The Soviet intervention in Czechoslovakia undoubtedly weakened the position of the reformers, who had to do everything to distance the new economic system from the Czech reforms.[12] Another problem was that even though the reform started with a wage stop, the regime eventually agreed to increase the workers' wages in order to win them over to the NES.[13] Overtime work also increased the income of the working class, while there were not enough consumer goods in the shops. In this situation, Keren argues, the party could have generated inflation, but after the bloody riots that followed the increase of the prices announced in Poland on 12 December 1970, the GDR leadership did not dare to risk a similar course. They rather chose to abandon the maximal programme of the NES and the party secretary, who insisted on the maximal programme.

Decided upon in 1966 and implemented in 1968, Hungary's new economic mechanism (*új gazdasági mechanizmus*) emerged out of an extensive discussion among economists and a growing concern within the party leadership over poor export performance and the inefficient operation of state-owned industry during the mid-1960s.[14] Kádár was, however, more careful not to commit himself so openly to the reform as Honecker, and he preserved a 'centrist' position between the dogmatic or orthodox communists, who opposed the new economic mechanism and the reformers. Furthermore, the Hungarian reform was more ambitious and radical in its scope than the East German: while the GDR was the first to implement an economic reform inspired by Liberman's suggestions, the Hungarian economic reform, albeit adopted later, was targeted not only at decentralization but it granted more concessions to the market than did the new economic system of the GDR. The Hungarian economist János Kornai gave a theoretical criticism of over-centralization prior to Liberman.[15] In 1965 reform-minded economists outlined the *Criticism of our present economic management*, which argued, that the system of the allocation of the tasks to the ministries and enterprises was dysfunctional because the central planning apparatus could not have a clear picture of the production capacities and reserves of every enterprise, and the enterprises were not interested in increasing efficiency and the better satisfaction of consumers' demands.[16] Besides giving a sharp critique of the existing system of management, the document also pointed out the political dangers of the over-centralized economy:

> *The system of plan allocation has a negative impact on the consciousness of the people: on the one hand, they forget how to act autonomously, how to initiate things and to account for them and on the other hand, it confirms the politically harmful view that the higher leading bodies are responsible for every mistake and hardship.* Since we regulate everything centrally, it facilitates the wrong 'reflection' of reality that the increase of the standard of living is decided by the will of the central authorities.[17]

The document was also critical of the system of central pricing, observing that the prices largely and economically unreasonably differed from the social costs of labour.[18]

The reform increased the autonomy of the enterprises and the managers' authority to make tactical decisions. To stimulate the enterprises, the state allowed them to retain part of the profits, and the managers could decide the distribution of the bonuses. The state's proprietary rights were not, however, challenged; amongst others, the state retained the important right of appointing the management. Indirect control was established through prices and taxation of the enterprises, which eventually had a levelling effect. It was envisaged that there would be a limited competition among the enterprises that would improve the economic performance without restoring capitalist relations:

> An important feature of the new economic mechanism is that it enables the economic competition of the socialist enterprises and it urges them to compete in the market. This competition is, of course, limited. It is limited by the level of the development of the productive forces (concentration and specialization of production and distribution) and the socialist nature of our planned economy. This limited competition has, nevertheless, a special significance for

the development of enterprise initiative, the increase of efficiency, technical improvement and the satisfaction of buyers' needs.[19]

Even though the increase of enterprise autonomy was an important element of the reform, it was also linked with the reorganization of economic management. The structural transformation of the industry had been on the agenda since 1958 but the 'experimental' enterprise concentration was followed by a retreat, and it was only in 1962–64 that a new industrial structure emerged characterized by giant enterprises and an almost absolute lack of small companies. The grand-scale concentration of the means of production was expected to reduce bureaucracy and increase the authority and responsibility of the management. The enterprise was responsible for the determination of the social needs for the products within its profile (responsibility of planning) and the satisfaction of the demands (responsibility of supply), and it had to finance the technological improvement and the change of products.[20]

Although the reorganization of economic management increased the role of market incentives, Schweitzer had already indicated that the requirement to make profits often contradicted the responsibility of supply. The managers would typically argue that any product could be made profitable with more investment, and that if they stopped their production it would lead to shortage in the domestic economy.[21] String-pulling and political contacts were also frequently used to secure state subventions. The central allocation of the resources was thus subject to fierce criticism; profitable enterprises complained that the subventions were distributed at their expense.[22] Giant enterprises could at the same time represent significant bargaining power, and they could effectively prevent reform initiatives or the cuts of subventions. Szalai later showed that this was precisely the case and the state-owned large industry resisted any attempts at reorganization or the renegotiation of state subsidies.[23] It can be therefore argued that within the enterprise structure market incentives could only have a limited effect.

Within the framework of the new economic mechanism more radical reforms had been planned but the growing division of the party over reform and the Soviet intervention in Czechoslovakia resulted in a retreat. This, however, did not reverse the process, which indicated the real significance of the reform: the legal extension of the second or private economy (*második gazdaság*). Although the 1968 economic reform did not entail a concept of ownership, it made the development of industrial units within agricultural cooperatives possible, which did not carry out agricultural production, but industrial and service activities. The private economy within the framework of agriculture started to expand towards the industrial and service sectors, which influenced the competitive position of the state industrial and service companies in the domestic market significantly more than the very limited competition created by the private retailers and craftsmen. Although in the 1970s attacks against the agricultural subsidiary industries were renewed again and again, these became the ever-expanding bases of the development of the private sector.[24]

The 1960s indicated a reform era not only in economy but these turbulent years also opened up a debate within the party about the necessity and scale of reform. With the sharpening of political debates both the dogmatic or orthodox communists and the reformers felt compelled to turn to the 'masses' for support. Public opinion meant first and foremost the opinion of the large industrial working class, which the party held to be its main social basis. The following chapters describe how workers in the two counties responded to the economic reform: what kind of grievances they voiced in this respect, what other criticisms came up in the documents which related to the everyday life of the working class, and in what ways they required – or expected – the party to intervene in the reform process. I stress that in this period workers still believed in the possibility of a social dialogue and they accepted the party as the legitimate representative of their interests. This was the last, historically formative period in the relationship between the working class and the party when such trust can be documented. The Hungarian documents of the 1980s reflect disillusionment, distrust and the workers' increasing alienation from the party state. In 1989 the Communist parties could no longer mobilize the class that they represented in any East European countries. The reform era therefore has a distinguished role in the history of welfare dictatorships. Last but not least, the industrial reorganization of the 1960s indicated a landmark in the history of both factories. Given the nature of the sources, not every part could have been matched properly, of course, so, for instance, there is more data on the political mood of workers in Hungary, while labour policy for women or the housing policy of the factory is much better documented in East Germany. The difference in the political climate of the two countries is, however, reflected in the party materials: the Hungarian sources give a more critical and reliable picture of the relationship between the working class and the party than the East German reports written in a clumsy bureaucratic language with the compulsive and over-zealous intention to conform to official socialism. It is the main reason why the Hungarian case study is presented first.

Rába MVG and the Reform Process

The Hungarian Wagon and Machine Factory[25] which later became known as Rába MVG was founded in Győr, a commercial and administrative centre of western Hungary in 1896. Győr was a historically important town in the region: it was the seat of a diocese and also a county town. The Wagon Factory was established as part of the economic modernization of the Austro-Hungarian monarchy, which occurred during the last third of the nineteenth century. The production of carriages became a prosperous enterprise: the factory exported its products to Serbia, Bulgaria, Romania, Italy and Egypt, and it transported rolling stock to the London Underground and the Antwerp Tramways.[26] In 2001 the management located Rába products dating back to 1905 in South Africa.[27]

In 1939 the factory, which also started to produce buses, trucks and tractors in the interwar period, was officially declared an armaments factory, which entailed the development of plants important for war production. The new motor car factory was completed in 1943, and produced Botond cars,[28] Turán tanks and Rába Maros military trucks.[29] The personnel of the factory experienced a massive growth: in 1941 nearly five thousand blue-collar workers worked in Rába but by 1943 their number had doubled.[30]

In 1945 war losses to factory capacity were assessed at 70 per cent as against an average 36–40 per cent of the Hungarian machine industry as a whole. Summer production in 1945 amounted to about 10 per cent of that recorded earlier.[31] The rebuilding of the factory was all the more pressing since its products were indispensable for the rebuilding of the almost totally ruined railway network.[32] Simultaneously with the rebuilding of the factory ownership changed. In 1946 the government nationalized the largest enterprises in mining and heavy engineering, amongst them the Győr Wagon Works. After the first three-year plan reconstruction was successfully finished and the industrial production of 1949 had risen above that of the last pre-war year by 40 per cent, with 7,500 people now working in the factory.[33]

The first five-year plan (1950–1954) was a period of major change in the life of the factory. As a result of restructuring, the car plant and the machine-tool works were detached from the Wagon Factory in 1951. The equipment and production of the plants detached amounted to 50 per cent of the capacity of the enterprise.[34] At the same time the factory was granted significant sums to increase production. The production value of the factory surpassed that of the Ganz Wagon Works thus becoming the second largest machine manufacturing plant in the country. Exports rose, too: railway carriages, steam cranes, lift trucks, bridges and other steel structures were exported, mainly to the Soviet Union. The number of blue-collar workers rose from 4,861 to 6,239 during the plan period (without the detached plants) and the number of the factory personnel rose from 7,313 to 9,141.[35]

In 1963 a new chapter started in the history of the Wagon Factory. The Central Committee examined the situation of the machine industry in the country and concluded that the sector was outdated and labour productivity was low. In 1962 the Wagon Factory failed to fulfil the plan and it produced the greatest shortfall in the export plan.[36] A process of concentration started in the machine industry: in 1963 Ede Horváth was appointed the chief manager of the Wagon Factory.[37] With this the Industrial Tool Factory was officially reunited with the Wagon Factory. After a separation of thirteen years, the organizational unity of Rába was restored again by the beginning of the third five-year plan (1966–1970).

The enterprise started the third five-year plan under its traditional name (i.e. it was again called Hungarian Railway Carriage and Machine Works – MVG – from 1965)[38] and used the trademark 'Rába'. Horváth started a very ambitious project, which soon triggered a sharp conflict with the management of the Wagon Factory. He sought to modernize production by changing profile, by which he meant the decrease of the share of total production made up by rolling stock and the increase of engines and rear axles. The planned development was realized with the purchase of a licence to manufacture engines from the West German MAN firm. In the county the local power relations largely influenced the interpretation of the economic reform. The plan of Horváth, the manager of Rába, to change the production profile and buy a licence from a West German factory triggered a conflict between himself and the party functionaries. Ferenc Lombos, who was the first secretary of the county party committee between 1956 and 1966, was not indifferent to the Wagon Factory because he started working there. Lombos took the side of Horváth's opponents, who went as far as to attempt to relieve him of his post. According to Horváth's recollection, Jenő Fock, who later became the Prime Minister (1967–75), represented the Central Leadership at the special meeting of the executive committee in 1963, where Horváth was attacked.[39] Fock defended Horváth but only a temporary agreement was achieved. In 1965 the discord renewed when Lombos made attempts to intervene in the management of the enterprise which Horváth considered to be his exclusive authority. The situation became so tense that it was reported to the Central Leadership (*Központi Vezetőség*). After the party leadership investigated the case, both Lombos and Horváth received a strong reprimand. The ultimate winner was, however, Horváth, because in 1966 Lombos was replaced with László Pataki, who was in office until

1974. Lombos was left out of the Central Committee and Horváth also lost his membership (he was a deputy member and deputy membership was abolished). In 1970, however, Horváth was elected back into the Central Committee, where he kept his membership until the collapse of the regime.[40]

Horváth triumphed over the local party leaders and secured his position both nationally and in the county. According to all documents and memoirs he was a real workaholic, and the development of Rába was his only true and greatest passion. He accomplished the change of profile. Production of rolling stock gradually fell. In 1965 the total value of its finished products amounted to 3 billion HUF, with exports mounting up to 40 per cent. In that year Rába employed more than sixteen thousand people. The total volume of investment in that year amounted to 700 million HUF.[41] The new Rába plant producing engines was inaugurated on 17 June 1969 and it had the capacity to produce thirteen thousand engines and auxiliary parts. The biggest market for the engines was the Hungarian bus industry, producing over twelve thousand large buses a year at the Ikarus Factory in Budapest.[42] New plants joined the parent company – Sárvár and Ajka in 1967, the Foundry of Győr in 1968, the Red Star and the Mosonmagyaróvár Tractor Factories.[43] In 1975 Rába employed nearly twenty thousand people in its Győr plants (about fifteen thousand blue-collar workers).[44] Although its main export partner was the Soviet Union, the company also exported axles to the United States.[45]

In the national and local press the 'Rába miracle' received substantial media coverage. Rába was widely advertised as a socialist model factory, which worked well and made substantial profits.[46] The exports to the United States were understood as the Western recognition of the good quality of Rába products. In 1986 when economic reform was again on the political agenda, Ede Horváth was elected the man of the year in acknowledgement of his managerial success. The company enjoyed high prestige in Győr, where it was the largest employer. The enterprise built a huge stadium, sponsored the local football team called Rába ETO and launched many training and scholarship programmes. It also had a technical library, a cultural centre, a brass band, a chore, a dance group and a sports' club.[47]

The dissolution of the MSZMP[48] in October 1989 deprived Ede Horváth of political support. Members of the old political elite, who were held responsible for the economic troubles of the country, came under greater pressure. As a member of the Central Committee, Ede Horváth was an obvious target of attack. His conflict with the secretary of the trade union, Zoltán Kóh, exacerbated the situation and led to an abusive press campaign against him in the newly established independent newspapers.

Figure 1.1 Logo of Rába

The Mosonmagyaróvár plant demanded to be detached from Rába and the trade union organized a strike. Even though the enterprise council confirmed Horváth in his managerial post until 1992, the Győr court repealed this resolution. The enterprise council asked Horváth to retire, to which he agreed on 18 December 1989.

Downgrading the Working Class?
A Critique of the Economic Reform

In January 1977 the primary party organization of the Motor Factory of Rába MVG in Győr held a party meeting, where a mechanic made the following comment:

> Concerning the information reports, I can freely announce that on my side the political mood is not good. The previous speakers have mentioned the problem of revising the norms that affect blue-collar workers. We feel uneasy both about the revision of norms and the increase of prices. They nevertheless say that our mood is generally good. This cannot be said at all. The statistics show that everything is very good here. The increase of prices does not show me that the political mood is good. I don't experience a rising standard of living. When I pick up a newspaper, everything I read in it makes me angry. With respect to the utilization of working hours, even the psychologists of the capitalist countries have demonstrated that the human body needs a break during its eight working hours. So we cannot spend 480 minutes working. I think that they do not represent the workers' interests here. They always demand more work for less money. After the present revision of the norms I cannot earn my money even if I violate the technological regulations. I cannot understand where and in relation to what we can experience a rising standard of living. In spite of the increase of prices, they are decreasing our wages.[49]

The criticism received some consideration in the closing speech of the party secretary:

> The reasons why comrades are a bit passive have been explained in the discussion. I would like to point out that it is not right that the blue-collar workers have such a bad opinion of their white-collar counterparts and that this disagreement has been so often heard recently. Comrades should realize that we have equal need here of each and every employee. It is true that the money is not enough but it is the responsibility of the management that the wage is 8,000 Ft[50] for one job while it is only 2,000 Ft for another. The management should also provide better working conditions.[51]

In Rába MVG few records of grass-roots party meetings have survived, so it is difficult to tell how widespread criticism was in public forums. On the basis of the regularly collected information reports concerning the public mood of employees, reports of larger party meetings and other documents it can be, however, confirmed that in the era of the economic reform functionaries showed themselves to be more than ready to report about working-class grievances towards the higher political bodies. Many old communists thought that the economic reform would harm the social basis of the party and endanger the social consensus with the working class. In the provinces political leaders, anxious to retain their positions, undoubtedly had an interest in reinforcing anti-reformist feelings. This, apparently, succeeded only too well because debates over the reform brought to light real political concerns about the weakening of the position of the industrial working class; moreover, people used the opportunity to express a more deeply rooted social discontent with the ruling regime. In particular, workers addressed three issues critically: the increasing material inequalities between workers and managers, the high income of the peasantry and the lack of enterprise democracy. The first two criticisms were connected with the economic reform; the lack of control in the factory was, however, a criticism that was targeted at the established power relations of the socialist system.

In 1972 a survey was conducted on the conditions of the working class in the county. The survey found that material and social discontent was widespread among the working class.

> Significant masses of the working class (those who have low wages and big families) disapprove of the increase of prices, particularly that of clothing. They won't accept that it is not possible to improve their situation 'because of the interests of the people's economy'. The greater part of the working class does not hold workers to be a leading power, or to be proprietors, because the shortcomings that they experience in their workplaces confuse their

judgement. For instance, when nobody asks for their opinions and they have no say in production, enterprise democracy does not function and there are unreasonably high wage differentials between workers and managers. *In many places workers feel that they only have the right to work.*[52]

The last sentence of the report is highlighted because it nicely dovetails with the cited information report from Gera: workers cannot work continuously because of the bad supply of materials; they have to pay the price for the wrong decisions of the managers while the latter do not take into consideration the interests of working people; they have become detached from the masses, they have forgotten where they came from, they behave like the new rich, and the list of grievances can be continued. We can identify common sources of criticism: unprepared investments, bad management of work, the increase of material inequalities between workers and managers and the downgrading of the working class. It is also important to stress that these grievances were listed in an official report that was sent to the national leadership. The fact that sentences such as 'what do we get out of socialism' or 'workers feel that they only have the right to work' were included in the reports shows that the functionaries were well aware of the fact that workers did not believe in the official propaganda that the working class controlled the means of production. It is also important to note that functionaries showed an interest in working-class opinions and they took the criticism seriously with the expectation that the criticism would *influence* the party's policy towards labour and the fate of the economic reform.

According to a report of the political education of the party membership of the county many people questioned the leading role of the working class:

> A large part of the blue-collar workers and some intellectuals of working-class origin limit the term working class to blue-collar workers. They criticize their declining number in the leadership and wrongly conclude that the leading role of the working class is decreasing. They argue that with the change of economic management and the increase in technological requirements the working class lost its leading role and political leadership was taken over by the more educated economists, engineers, intellectuals and state officials. Some are even more pessimistic about the leading role of the working class in the future because they think that with scientific-technological development, society will be increasingly controlled by the economic and technical intelligentsia.

According to the report, many intellectuals look down on the working class: 'There are opinions among the intellectuals that the lack of education renders the working class unfit for leadership. This opinion can be also found among intellectuals who are members of the party.'[53]

The gulf between workers and managers was, however, deeper than the gulf between workers and intellectuals. Economic reform increased managerial rewards and reinforced the social distance between workers and managers. Trips to Western countries, luxurious offices and expensive cars suggested that it was primarily the managers who profited from the factories:

> The employees told us that they think little of protocol visits. A significant part of the party and state leadership and the members of the apparatus pay only hasty, administrative visits. They speak with the lower managers but they rarely see the employees. Mainly blue-collar workers complained that since the economic reform, managers had refused to deal with the problems of employees because they were too busy. There is a widespread – sometimes exaggerated – view in the working class that high incomes have rendered leaders too materialistic and that they live a petit-bourgeois life. (Signs of materialism can be found among workers too. Many of them undertake private work or they do odd jobs for artisans.)[54]

At party meetings workers also criticized the distinguished treatment of the leaders:

> In the Sopron Cotton Factory people said that at production conferences only workers are criticized, managers are not. They consider the wage differentials between workers and managers to be unjust, for instance in some party organizations in Sopron: the Wagon Factory,[55] etc. Managers who are relieved of their positions because of their mistakes will be given leading positions somewhere else. Why don't they send them back to the shop-floor?[56]

In theory, the enterprise council exercised control over the management, but in practice employees were afraid to criticize managers in public. The party organizations received many negative opinions about the functioning of enterprise democracy.

> A significant part of the party membership holds that people risk their livelihood with their criticism. It is only a formal requirement that the mistakes in the administration of the party, the state and the economy should be revealed to those competent to deal with them. In practice people won't exercise this right. They say that the party cannot protect the rightful critic from the consequences.[57]

Such comments suggest that there was a strong hierarchy within the factory, which rendered enterprise democracy largely formal. Although the party advocated an egalitarian ideology, in reality little effort was made to raise the political consciousness of the people.

In contrast to the Zeiss factory, which had a skilled, urban working class, in the personnel of Rába we find a significant group of workers, who commuted daily from the countryside to the factory and also farmed small plots of land next to their jobs in the factory. Interestingly, urban workers identified this group with the peasantry, whose growing wealth was also a frequent source of criticism next to the high managerial incomes. According to several information reports, urban workers charged the government with an outright pro-peasant policy, which threatened to undermine the worker–peasant alliance.

> Urban workers who are members of the party measured the worker–peasant alliance against the standard of living of the two classes. In some places people were biased against the peasants and they compared the low factory wages with the prosperity of the villages. We often heard the remark: 'It is always the working class that has had, and still has, to make sacrifices.' People thought that state subvention of agriculture only served the interests of the peasants. Even though in general they agreed with the improvement of the standard of living of the peasantry, they added that workers' power should do more for the working class.[58]

The secretary of the executive committee of the county also underlined that the better material opportunities of the peasants created tensions between the two classes:

> According to the five-year plan the wages of the working class and the peasantry should be equally increased. I don't think that this is the case now, or that we can ensure it in the future. Industrial wages increase by 3–4 per cent on average, but we cannot regulate the income of the peasantry. In our county the wages of the workers have increased by 4 per cent this year, while the income of the peasantry has increased by 16 per cent. This leads to increasing tension and workers say that we have a 'peasant' policy.[59]

Anti-peasant feelings were undoubtedly present in the party. Many party functionaries were biased against the villages, which they considered to be culturally backward and ideologically unreliable. The influence of the church was also strong in the villages, which was considered to be a sign of political unreliability. Religious people were often held to be members of the political opposition to the party.[60] According to a report on the conditions of the commuters of Rába MVG, it was difficult to engage them in social or party work because their agricultural activity took up all of their free time.[61] The bias of the functionaries that the working class was more politically developed than the peasantry was often manifest in the meetings of the executive committee. For instance, one member of the executive committee argued that backward political ideas came from the villages to the factory:

> The report states that political inconsistency and ideological wavering can also be found in the working class. I think you need to take a more differentiated approach and examine how things look within the working class: in the old guard, among the skilled workers, among the unskilled, the semi-skilled and the commuters. It would be good to know if the latter take home socialist ideas or bring in the backward views that negatively influence the political mood of the working class.[62]

The material prosperity of the 'backward' peasantry was therefore held to be politically unjust.

The conflict between the working class and the peasantry was, however, an artificial one. A study of social stratification in the county found that 'pure' working-class households constituted only 43 per cent of the population in the villages of the Győr district, while worker–peasant 'mixed' households amounted to 20 per cent. Pure peasant households amounted to 23 per cent in the district of Győr, 22 per cent in the district of Moson-magyaróvár, 24 per cent in the district of Sopron, and 31 and 40 per cent respectively in the districts of Kapuvár and Csorna. The ratio of the worker–peasant mixed households varied between 18 and 24 per cent in every district.[63] The prosperity of the villages mainly came from the double incomes earned in agriculture and industry: people worked in the factories of the nearby towns and they cultivated their household plots (*háztáji gazdaság*) in their free time. This was also frequently stressed in the party documents:

> The primary party organizations of MVG should deal more with the role of the household plots and the evaluation of the agricultural activity done there. You should explain to the workers that more and more working-class families have an income from subsidiary farming. Statistical surveys prove that there are less and less pure worker and pure peasant households in the county. The income of the overwhelming majority of the households comes from mixed sources because family members work in industrial, agricultural and intellectual workplaces.[64]

The aggregated information reports of the county, however, show that both workers and peasants thought that the other class lived better: 'In many places workers complained that the income of the peasantry was higher than that of the working class. The members of the party in the co-operative farms thought, on the contrary, that the working class received higher social benefits and they had better working conditions. They criticized the fact that, in this respect, the peasantry lagged behind.'[65]

Information reports show that urban workers often identified commuters as peasants. 'In the villages around industrial centres, the income of the peasantry is significantly higher than that of industrial workers. It is true but you should admit that they work more than eight hours. They make more money with more work. Urban workers do not have this opportunity. They have hobby gardens but it is not the same.'[66] It was widely believed that the peasantry had a higher income than the workers. According to information reports, urban workers discussed the sizes of houses people had built in the villages and wanted to know how they could afford them.[67] 'Many workers argue that the standard of living of the cooperative farmers is higher than that of the workers. They think that this is because they have more opportunity to work for themselves and they cultivate their private plots at the expense of the work of the collective.'[68] The conflict was, however, not between the workers and peasants but rather between two specific groups within the working class: the commuters and the urban workers. It is therefore misleading to speak of the 'peasant' policy of the government because fellow workers were also considered to be peasants.

The large group of commuters (they constituted 40 per cent of the workforce of Rába) indicates an important difference between the social composition of the East German and Hungarian working classes.[69] While there was a massive transfer of labour from agriculture to industry as a result of the grand-scale communist modernization programme, a large part of the newly recruited working class continued to preserve a rural residence. Although under Kádár there was a massive drive to reorganize farming into agricultural cooperatives, small-scale private farming was permitted. Many commuters were engaged in agricultural activity next to their jobs in industry, and preserved the culture of the peasantry. This group was often disadvantaged in the hierarchy of the factory: many worked as unskilled or semi-skilled workers, and their educational level was also lower than that of the urban workers.[70] It was also a recurring complaint that commuters 'have no time for party life'. Therefore we can safely conclude that the party organization of the factory was dominated by the urban working class, who had more opportunities to participate in adult learning and working-class social, cultural and community life than the commuters, who after finishing work in the factory, went back to their villages to farm their lands or raise animals. The significant size of the so-called 'worker-peasants' in Hungary shows that the economic backwardness of the country continued to provide for a different trajectory of the formation of the Hungarian working class than the more developed East Germany.

While there is evidence that the 'worker-peasants' were less interested in the political life of the factory and they also had less energy to demand more rights because they worked hard both in the factory and in their villages, in the more liberal atmosphere of the 1960s it was not only the income differences that were criticized – we can also read documents which addressed the contradictions of the established socialist system and the actual lack of working-class control over issues of production. The formality of enterprise democracy was criticized even within the executive committee. Even though the plan was discussed at production conferences, employees had no opportunity to influence decisions. As one report complained, in many places there was no preliminary information given to the employees, who consequently could not influence the managers' decisions that were announced at these meetings:

> So the majority will hear the account only once and won't be able to make substantial comments. It decreases the importance of the conferences that in many places the leaders announce the final plans and the already-decided facts to the collective. They won't discuss how they determined the objectives of the enterprise. The proportion of attendees who are prepared to speak is often below 10 per cent. People generally don't criticize their direct leaders. ... The managers are not responsible to the employees and this can render the leadership despotic. In the various democratic forums people refuse to evaluate the leadership and criticize their mistakes. The management often does not even ask the trade union.[71]

The weak influence of the trade union over management decisions was strongly criticized in the county executive committee, which shows how far criticism went in the period. The above contribution suggests, at any rate, that even though the trade unions were under the control of the party, trade union leaders were often very critical of the inability of the trade union to enforce interests. The sarcasm of the speaker also shows that this criticism was widely known:

> The various surveys show that 60–65 per cent of employees have no opportunity to influence the management of the enterprise. This makes one wonder how we are to realize enterprise democracy? The comrade who spoke before me asked if employees can influence the production conferences. They cannot, unfortunately. Let us take, for instance, awards of socialist distinctions such as 'eminent worker' and 'socialist brigade'. In our county, 5,225 people were awarded the title of 'eminent worker' and only 3,300 of them work in industry, including the technicians and engineers. Is it really workers who are winning these titles or are we trying to realize our own ideas? There is not even one case of a production conference where managers have introduced two or three alternatives enabling employees to really make a choice. You can ask to what extent leaders depend on employees today. I mean the management, the party leadership and the leadership of the trade union committee. For how

long can employees keep their positions? Does it depend on the employees themselves? No, it depends only on the higher leadership. If employees are not satisfied with the work of managers, it is in vain that they turn to the trade union committee because the trade union cannot call them back. But if a low-level manager dares to criticize his boss, he will get his notice the next day. You can say that the trade union has the right to criticize the managers. As long as we have a system of appointments and the party controls the appointment of the managers, this right only exists on paper. You cannot name one person in the county who has been rejected or appointed upon the recommendation of the trade union.[72]

The speaker was also bold enough to make fun of the system of democratic centralism: 'Last time when we discussed the internal management of the enterprises, it was said that it is useless to make a decision until we know the standpoint of the ministry. But if we know it, then why should we make a decision?'[73]

The above quotations illustrate well how far social dialogue went in this period – very probably against the intentions of the hardliners. Criticism reflected genuine discontent on the part of workers with their economic and political situation; it is remarkable, for instance, that party documents recognized that a large part of the working class did not hold workers to be socialist proprietors. Nor was the leading role of the working class – propagated by the party –reflected in the standard of living, particularly when the workers saw signs of prosperity among other social strata. Growing materialism reinforced internal divisions within the working class, too: for instance between commuters, who were often identified as peasants, and urban workers. In this competition the working class could rightfully feel disadvantaged because managers and their families, who could supplement their income in agriculture, were in a better position to accumulate wealth. Official socialism could not render people forget that their social status became increasingly determined by levels of consumption, which worked against the egalitarian ideology that the party propagated. The introduction of the reform, which advocated 'more market', in essence meant that the social position of people was increasingly determined by material means, which – in contrast to the official slogans of the party – downgraded the importance of the industrial working class. This paved the way for a deeply rooted working-class disillusionment with official socialism.

The Appearance of the New Rich

In the era of the economic reform, increasing material differentiation was one of the main targets of social criticism. The extravagant lifestyle of the new rich triggered envy: symbols of status like big houses and weekend cottages, trips to the West and Western consumer goods were among the most frequently condemned features of this lifestyle. Wealth became visible in society: people no longer sought to conceal their private property; on the contrary, good financial circumstances expressed the social status of people. According to information reports, people counted a large part of the *nomenklatura* among the new elite:

> We can conclude from the brigade inquiries that the number of anti-leader manifestations, particularly with respect to economic management, has increased within the party membership. People believe that the interests of the leaders and employees are distinct and even conflicting, even if they are members of the party. They also said that today our society is only theoretically divided into classes and strata; in practice, it is divided into the wealthy and the non-wealthy. Grass-roots members of the party argued that a new elite has emerged, whose income is much higher than that of an average employee. The majority of state leaders and enterprise managers and part of the petite bourgeoisie belong to the new elite.[74]

The party documents give abundant material for the criticism of the appearance of 'capitalist features', most notably materialism and individualism. The scramble for money was condemned as a petit-bourgeois attitude but the party organizations of the county all agreed that it was becoming more and more widespread and affected the whole of society.[75] The information reports similarly underlined that people were becoming more interested in material values:

> According to blue-collar workers, the petit-bourgeois mentality was widespread in the party leadership, where materialism and occasionally enrichment without work has gained ground. Factory workers who were members of the party sharply criticized the phenomenon that it is not work but the car, the plot and the weekend house that matter, and that a modest lifestyle is almost regarded as a social disgrace. Cunning, back doors and socialist connections play an ever-increasing role in the achievement of individual success. Collective solidarity has declined: people care less about the problems of others.[76]

'Petit-bourgeois' attitudes, however, also appeared in the working class: 'While working-class party members and collective farmers condemned petit-bourgeois egoism in others, they refused to see the same mistake in themselves. They did not consider it immoral to make things on the side or violate labour discipline.'[77]

The appearance of the new rich was a widely criticized social phenomenon, and even the executive committee and the party school discussed the question of how to fight against the 'petit-bourgeois' mentality. Even though no cure was found, it was clear that people observed the increasing prosperity of certain social strata and were angry that it did not belong to them. Party organizations argued that the economic reform increased social inequalities. 'People think that the increasing differentiation of income is the main source of mistakes (executive committee of Sopron). Many people think that the economic mechanism reinforces the capitalist view because the chief criterion is profit, and socialist humanism is lost.' It is also possible to read into this that the economic mechanism has given rise to more opportunity for fraud and unlawful profit-making. The party school of Sopron went even further, arguing that society has become immensely corrupt.[78] According to the reports, another manifestation of materialism was the declining interest of people in communal affairs and unpaid social work. The party committee of Sopron reported that people often ridiculed those who worked unselfishly for the collective. The party committee of Győr put it bluntly that socialist consciousness 'is not fashionable; whoever wants to live like that will often be isolated'.[79] According to many primary party organizations, 'unselfishness has disappeared and people are only willing to work for money. It is a social illness which has infected every social class. There are passionate debates about egoism everywhere, including the party membership.'[80] The reports also complained about the declining social activity of people, which they explained in relation to the fact that 'more and more people look for profitable occupations outside of the workplace instead of working for the collective'.[81] It was noted critically that some socialist brigades only worked for premiums.[82] The secretary of the county observed that managers were also chiefly interested in premiums: 'We criticize workers for doing private jobs but it is normal when managers first ask how much the premium is. They forget that it is their duty to do a decent job. We have got a thousand and one problems here.'[83] No wonder that the reports underlined that society had become more materialist: each social class charged the others with being interested only in money. Even though agitators spoke of the socialist mode of consumption, it was clear that consumer society did not work according to socialist principles.

The extravagant lifestyle of the new rich was also addressed critically in information reports. Conspicuous consumption was one of the chief characteristics of the 'petit-bourgeois' mentality, and conspicuous consumers were charged with ideological deviation and political disloyalty to the party. Students of the party school argued that it was not the petite bourgeoisie as a stratum that was dangerous, but embourgeoisement as an attitude:

> One of the most characteristic features of the petit-bourgeois attitude is the absence of sincerity. There are people who always follow the party line in public while they give their earnest opinion in private. This group spreads the wildest rumours and depicts an exaggerated picture of the difficulties. They glorify the West and underestimate our results, infecting the others with their defeatism.[84]

Although the party condemned the petit-bourgeois mentality, it had a rather conservative ethical code. Members of the party – particularly leaders – were expected to live an irreproachable family life. Adultery was condemned as a manifestation of petit-bourgeois conduct:

> We receive several warnings from the county that the benchmark of social rank is what kind of car, villa, weekend house and lover someone has. These manifestations of the petit-bourgeois lifestyle are all the more dangerous when it concerns party members, state, economic and social leaders because people generalize from the negative examples and they believe that the leaders today live like the gentry of the old world (party school of Sopron). In Győr people say that a society of the socialist gentry has been created. Employees criticize extravagance in the workplace, the luxurious equipment of offices, and frequent but unjustified foreign trips paid for from the budget of the people's economy.[85]

Informants would also draw attention to the fact that many members of the new rich in the county had religious connections, even if they were members of an atheist party, and they were charged with hypocrisy.

> 19.7 per cent of schoolchildren regularly attend Bible classes. The church even organizes beat-masses to win over youth. We have received information that the contacts of the Benedictine teachers and their former students (doctors, leading engineers) are legalized and regular features of the organ concerts of Pannonhalma. In recent years, participation in religious ceremonies has started to be fashionable, expressing membership of a wealthier, superior class. The negative example of the local elite (doctors, veterinary surgeons, non-party member leading engineers) is very harmful because people believe that for them everything is allowed.[86]

The appearance of the new rich did not only violate the principle of social equality but its members were also considered to be ideologically unreliable.

The 'struggle against a materialist mentality' was not very successful because the topic was also on the agenda of the party school in the following year. Attendees at the party school consequently distinguished between class position and mentalities. 'Students drew the right conclusion that it is not enough to consider only the class position of people; you can find a Marxist in the petite bourgeoisie and, conversely, it is also possible to find petit-bourgeois attitudes in the working class.'[87] The debates show that criticisms of these kinds of social phenomena persisted and that social differences kept on growing:

> Many students noted that our social system had also created its own 'aristocracy'. Managers and state leaders of working-class origin have become detached from the masses. There are leaders who look down on the collective, they believe themselves to be infallible and they behave haughtily towards their subordinates. Students also asked why leaders preferred trips to the West. The petit-bourgeois attitude becomes a problem when people reach a certain standard of living and start to ape the lifestyle of the 'upper class', imitating 'gentlemen'. Some leaders have family members who also do not know the limits and who dress and act very extravagantly. Students criticized the fact that 'socialist connections' mattered more than the true principles of the party.[88]

The indifference of society was also addressed in the discussion: 'The students see an increasing introversion in society. They explain it with the fact that the acquisition of material goods completely absorbs people, who retire from social work and the administration of public affairs. Some students argued that artists and sportsmen, who lived in very good material circumstances, had still decided to leave the country illegally.'[89] It was apparently ingrained in public consciousness that society had become more egoistic.

The image of the 'idle rich' also appeared in information reports. Like the complaint that managers' foreign trips and expensive offices produced no profit for the country but only enriched managers, people also condemned conspicuous consumption as harmful for the people's economy.

> The appearance of expensive furniture in shop windows, which is a capitalist export, was negatively received among the blue-collar workers. It is a general question which worker can afford to buy any of the products on display. According to the workers, the country should instead be buying industrial tools from the West, given that, in the first place, we have to be sparing with Western currency.[90]

Conspicuous consumption was confronted with the interest of the larger collective: the criticism that the rich lived well at the expense of the people's economy and produced no profit for the country, only for themselves, expressed a moral judgment of their egoism.

Even propaganda material suggests that the unequal distribution of wealth was already an accepted fact, and that the main objective was not to change this social reality but to demonstrate the moral superiority of non-materialistic values. Propaganda intended to render wealth less attractive in the eyes of the public, but even in this it was not really successful, since increasing wealth was an integral part of consumerism. It was characteristic of agitators, for instance, that they criticized the publication of the following article and not the social phenomenon that it described:

The employees were outraged by the article 'Living Room with Full Comforts and a Swimming Pool' published in *Lakáskultúra* (1973, no. 3). The value of the flat the article introduced is about 1,000,000 Ft. According to the author, a young couple built the flat and they saved the money for it. The workers can hardly believe this. They see no point in publishing such annoying articles.[91]

Parents also complained that local Roma were selling real Western jeans for double the price of what Hungarian jeans cost in the state store.[92] The material differences between families manifested themselves among their school-age children. Excessive consumption was condemned, but no one knew precisely what rendered consumption excessive. The creation of an egalitarian society was postponed to the distant future: the social message of propaganda was not to change property relations but rather to learn to live with existing inequalities.

Even the officially recognized literature expressed the social reality of 'embourgeoisement' and the essential hypocrisy of a society, which on the one hand propagated egalitarianism and the emancipation of the working class, and on the other hand became increasingly commercialized. A good example is the youth novel *Karambol* (Budapest, 1979) by Anna Dániel, which received the Gorkiy prize. The novel depicts a society which is socialist only in its state order, while more and more 'capitalist' elements appear that question the socialist set of values. This is manifest in the increasing social differences and the privileges that some of the young characters of the novel enjoy and others do not. The message of the book, however, is not to change the unequal world of the adults but to recognize the human emptiness of the world of the rich and to renounce materialistic values. In *Karambol* it is already remarkable that the moral superiority is the only consolation that society can offer to the poor heroes of the novel.

There was a great deal of complaint on the side of the functionaries that individualism negatively influenced party life. In Rába MVG an investigation of 1975 found that there were primary party organizations that had not held a party meeting for months. One speaker on the executive committee commented that it almost looked like punishment to participate in party meetings.[93] In the discussion of a report on exemplary communist conduct, one member of the executive committee of the county stated bluntly that one had to look for it with a magnifying glass. Although he did not relate it to the economic reform, his moral criticism keenly expressed the view of old party workers that the life of the movement was undermined by the spread of materialism and indifference:

We even experience passivity in the party. I don't want to argue about the 5 per cent,[94] but we can multiply it safely by five and even then we are too optimistic. No numbers can express the indifference to party work and political questions. When it comes to a political debate, party members just stand there open-mouthed and do not stand up to defend the party's standpoint. This question does not even come up in the factories and still we are all satisfied and declare that everything is all right.[95]

A survey of 1972 revealed, however, that even the party membership related critically to socialist propaganda, which was unable to respond to the new social environment. The representative sample included a thousand party members. Only a quarter (26.3 per cent) thought that the leading role of the working class meant that the working class had decision rights in the most important social and political issues, and even less (14.6 per cent) believed that the working class had a leading role in economy. A quarter failed to give a clear or relevant answer (18.1 per cent: schematic; 8.7 per cent: inadequate). According to the majority of the respondents, employees were left out of enterprise democracy: 40.7 per cent answered that enterprise democracy depended on the management, 26 per cent that it depended on the party and mass organizations and only one-fifth (21.1 per cent) that it depended on the political activity of employees. Half of the respondents (52.2 per cent) agreed with the statement that the employees had hardly any opportunity to influence the enterprise decisions that concerned them. Many respondents did not think that party membership played a decisive role in shaping political opinions: 92 per cent saw a difference between the thinking of Marxists and non-Marxists, but only 54.6 per cent thought that the difference was manifest in political ideas. Even though the party sought to sustain the moral respectability of its members, the respondents evidently did not connect human conduct with party membership: only 4.6 per cent saw a difference in moral attitudes and 3.3 per cent in the attitude to work between Marxists and non-Marxists.[96] Finally, the survey could not clarify concepts of socialism, which suggests the ideological uncertainty of the party membership:

> Some people seek a realized socialism where there is no conflict of interests, others think that socialism will be realized only in the distant future and there are also people who universalize economic interests. The result is either self-deception or unreasonable pessimism. People have a narrow understanding of socialist existence and consciousness, and tend to limit existence to purely materialistic issues. Part of the membership thinks in terms of rigid categories, drawing exaggerated conclusions from the surface phenomena.[97]

Given the closeness of prosperous, capitalist Austria, it was very difficult to argue that socialism offered a higher standard of living to its subjects than did capitalism. It is clear from information reports that Western consumer goods were regarded as symbols of status, and those who could travel frequently to the West were envied because they could acquire the desired products. The youth in particular were charged with 'excessive Occidentalism': party hardliners argued that Western lifestyles were seen as too attractive by young people, and that many young people – including working-class youth – were interested above all in money.[98] Tourists evidently returned with positive images of the West: in Győr informers found it important to report that people were less fascinated by Western lifestyles than had previously been the case.[99] Agitators pointed out that one should compare not only the wage difference between Austria and Hungary but also the cost of living – which indicated that people generally knew that the wages in the West were much higher. An information report from the Wagon Factory argued that the comparison of wages and prices 'only served the interests of the capitalist countries'.[100]

The 'fight against materialism' could not become successful because people became increasingly interested in consumption, and the party itself sought to gain popularity with the standard-of-living policy. A member of the executive committee, for instance, argued that the car, the weekend house and the trips were no luxuries.[101] The party fought against the 'petit-bourgeois' attitudes with words rather than with deeds. As criticisms show, in the eyes of the public a segment of the new rich was in fact closely connected with the system. It was difficult to expect exemplary communist conduct from grass-roots members when militant communism was replaced by a consumption-oriented policy and workers were increasingly integrated into a socialist middle class, which was essentially petit bourgeois in its nature. The increasing gap between official socialism and the reality of the Kádár regime rendered the political atmosphere hypocritical. The party succeeded in pacifying the working class; but in the long run, it had to pay a heavy price for the depoliticization of the workers, which was the price of their integration into the Kádár regime.

Ending a Social Dialogue

The materials of the reform era reveal a remarkably high level of concern among the party regarding the attitudes of the working class. It was in fact the last time the leading role of the working class was discussed by the party membership. According to information reports, the subject was also on the agenda of public meetings.

> Many speakers dealt with the issue of the leading role of the working class. We should influence the activity of the workers primarily with the demand of political consciousness and other factors. We need to increase the social rank of

physical work and introduce the perspective of a worker's career. The speakers recognized that it is important to engage the workers in the leadership of the party, state and social organizations but they underlined that it is an equally important political requirement to prepare them for the fulfilment of a given position and ensure their competence.[102]

The party evidently sought to renew the social settlement with labour and demonstrate that workers' welfare was central to its policy. The remarkable openness of the sources suggests that the party also attempted to improve its communication with the working class and to engage them in a real social dialogue.

The attempt at openness did not, however, last long and at the ideological level an outright re-dogmatization can be observed: from the mid-1970s the functionaries are recorded in the party materials as repeating the same old political slogans. The new first secretary of the county party committee, who assumed his duties in June 1974, introduced himself with a lengthy attack on private property, which displayed the widening gap between socialist propaganda and the reality of a consumer society:

> At the 9th Party Congress,[103] comrade Kádár said that communists seek to ensure that everybody has the same amount of food on his plate as they have. Some people are not interested in how much others have on their plates; only in what they have on their own. They separate their own interests from the interests of the community. The problem with private property is not that it increases, but that it becomes omnipotent – even if someone has acquired money by honest means. For instance, people build weekend houses not in order to rest in them, but in order to keep up with the Joneses. I visited one county and had a chat with a leading comrade. I noticed that he was not listening to me, but kept on looking out of the window. I asked him what he was thinking about. He said that he was worried it might rain, because he had sprayed insecticide on his plants. If it rained he would have to spray them again. Unfortunately we do find such phenomena.[104]

Party leaders of course had to represent the party line, but the secretary was apparently over-zealous and his speech showed little understanding of the economic policy of the party. Economic equality was obviously not on the agenda; the speech merely reflected that the secretary had no relevant message regarding the new social relations.

Similarly, the old political dogmas had no relevant message to offer the working class. One objective of the party-controlled media was to give a positive image of labour, but as the following contribution of an editor shows, propaganda was very much detached from the life of workers. The false image was more inclined to anger rather than win workers over to the cause, particularly given that they increasingly experienced a different social reality:

> When I received the report on the conditions of the working class in the county, I listened to a radio report. It was about why the workers of the Water Conservancy Directorate – drivers, cleaners and dam-keepers – decided to finish the seventh and eighth classes of primary school. These people won't get promoted, they probably won't get more money and they still decided to go to school because, as one of the drivers said – and I quote, 'it goes with our world-view that we yearn to study'. Mark the formulation: we yearn to study! You yearn for sweet fruit, tasty meat, fresh water or a nice landscape and – in the words of this driver – you yearn to study. A simple man has formulated this very fittingly and truly. Yes. Our strength and truth lie in rendering people able to yearn for everything that is beautiful and good. This is the point of the party resolution on public education and our repeated discussions of the conditions of the working class that is our topic today in the executive committee of the county. Because – and it is good to know this – the party is aware of the fact that the first and most important condition of the harmony of our social system, which is not contradicted by the dynamism of our development, is the general satisfaction of the working class; and a further condition is the stability of the worker-peasant alliance. We often declare that there is a good political climate and public mood in our country – and how very true it is![105]

The quotations reveal the basic contradictions of socialist propaganda. Functionaries typically considered workers to be too immature to understand their wider social context, and the ideological triumph of the hardliners reinforced this attitude. When enterprise democracy was again on the agenda, the strongest criticism was that not every party group had reconciled their opinions with the party steward.[106] Even in the official party documents there were comments that simple people were rarely expected to have anything to say about politics.

> All of our employees agreed – and this was also the opinion of the delegates – that until now there had not been such a well-organized and professionally excellent conference in our county, at which problems could be aired with such honesty. *It was a very surprising fact that simple workers gave their opinions on their work and also on the problems of the county and the country. It was even more surprising that several blue-collar workers contributed with such clever opinions.*[107]

The sentences in italics show that a certain bias against the 'simple workers' existed within the party apparatus.

This patronizing attitude effectively hindered communication between the party and the working class – all the more so when social experiences increasingly contradicted propaganda. Even though there were attempts to explain growing material inequalities between the social classes through the economic reform, the examined documents show that in public consciousness the increasing importance of private property was the product of a social process that had already begun. Apparent materialism was much criticized, but it influenced the behaviour of every social class. With respect to the response of labour one can, indeed, speak of two contradictory arguments. On the one hand, the fact that society had become more materialistic and the accumulation of wealth had gained an ever-increasing social significance was criticized. On the other hand, growing inequalities triggered the material discontent of the industrial working class because wages in state industry lagged behind the private sector. Consumerism gradually pushed unpaid social and political work into the background: people sought to be part of consumer society rather than social activists. The party could condemn materialism, but it did little to reverse this social process. Since part of the new rich belonged to the ruling elite of the system, the party lost the moral ground to attack the growth of private property.

Materialism and individualism were therefore not the products of the economic reform; the relatively liberal atmosphere of the reform era merely rendered visible ongoing social processes. Even party materials reflect the recognition that the new dividing lines in society could not be linked directly to the traditional classes. A good example is the perceived tension between workers and peasants. Many workers regarded commuters as peasants; thus, according to traditional interpretations, it was a conflict within the working class. Since employment in the private sector meant additional income, individualism also spread in the working class. Introduced surveys, too, support the argument that the traditional class categories failed to grasp the new social inequalities (e.g. a worker could also be a private entrepreneur or work in agriculture). The class category therefore became less important for the self-identification of people.

The individualization of society triggered many negative responses among people; in the light of the introduced sources, it was one of the most widely criticized social phenomena. This criticism may well have been reinforced by party functionaries, but it is remarkable that members of the party (and even its leaders) were charged with showing indifference to community work and party activities. Indeed, there were abundant complaints about the decline of the life of the movement and the devaluation of community work in the eyes of the people. According to party reports, people had become more egoistic and solidarity had declined; this was expressed in withdrawal from social work and communal activity.[108] The accumulation of wealth triggered the envy of other, less successful groups: the building of large houses in the villages outraged the public, but also motivated many to try to follow the example. This had a negative impact on community life because people worked more and had less time for social relations outside of the family. Hypocrisy had a detrimental effect on social moral perspectives within society; leaders who were themselves considered to be selfish and greedy could not expect their subordinates to resist the 'petit-bourgeois' mentality. The contrast between communist ideology and social reality created a crisis of values, which rendered many people disillusioned with that ideology.

The response of labour was surely not the only factor that stopped the economic reform, even though more radical steps were planned. Fearing a loss of popularity, in 1972 the government decided to increase the wages of industrial workers, and it unambiguously committed itself to the standard-of-living policy.[109] This meant that the party refused to consider the political criticisms of the industrial working class, choosing instead to offer material concessions in exchange for its silence. This manifested itself in the closing of social dialogue and ideological re-dogmatization.

The triumph of the hardliners proved illusory for two reasons. First, the standard-of-living policy was not in line with the economic realities of the country, and it led to overspending and growing indebtedness. Since the government unambiguously based its popularity on the increase of consumption, it automatically risked losing the support of the people with the failure of the standard-of-living policy. Second, and perhaps more importantly, the decision to end social dialogue reflected the party's failure to give a new basis for its communication with the people in a situation when the party was in urgent need of finding a new social message to address the working class. The old ideology was inevitably doomed to failure in this new social reality and the triumph of the hardliners meant precisely the return of the old political slogans.[110]

Carl Zeiss Jena in the New Economic System

The Carl Zeiss factory – or rather, the workers of the company – enjoyed a privileged position also among the industrial enterprises of pre-war Germany. The eponymous entrepreneur, Carl Zeiss, founded his precision-mechanical-optical workshop in Jena in 1846. Zeiss himself was well known for his pedantry, and he set his employees high standards of workmanship. The real fame of the enterprise was established, however, through his partnership with Ernst Abbe, a Jena physicist and philanthropist, and Otto Schott, a chemist specializing in high quality optical lenses. Zeiss was the only enterprise in the world that could manufacture microscopes according to catalogue and set characteristics. This established the success story of the enterprise: in 1875 the enterprise had 60 employees while by 1888 there were 327 in the factory. In 1889 the social-minded Abbe established the Carl Zeiss Foundation, which from 1891 became the sole proprietor of the enterprise. This form of ownership, which was at the time less typical, was combined with progressive social political measures and labour protection – for instance the regulation of the working hours, minimal wage, paid holiday, health care insurance, pension, severance pay and the legal representation of workers' interests in the factory. The generous social policy contributed not only to the success of the enterprise but it also facilitated the workers' identification with the factory that they could regard as their own from many aspects.[111]

During the Second World War, Zeiss was integrated in the armaments industry, and it suffered very heavy war losses. In March 1945, the enterprise employed 13,000 people, (around 70 per cent were Germans).[112] In 1945 the town of Jena was first taken by American troops, and when they marched out in order to handover control to the Soviets, they strongly encouraged the resettlement of scientists and professionals in the Western zone. The migrants did indeed found another Carl Zeiss factory in Oberkochen and a new Carl Zeiss Foundation in Heidenheim. The two firms could not reach an agreement about the use of the trademark, and after a long lawsuit, the matter was finally decided by a London court in 1971.[113] The rivalry of the two firms also symbolized the competition between the two German states in the period. Even though the Soviets ordered the dismantling of the factory, its rebuilding started in 1948 with a massive growth in the workforce: in 1950 the enterprise had around 10,000 employees while by 1954 their number had increased to 16,500.[114] The rebuilding – like in Hungary – went hand in hand with the change of ownership. The majority of the workers did not, however, greet the programme of nationalization and integration into the planned economy with unanimous enthusiasm precisely because of the former, generous social policy of the factory even though the party increased its propaganda to overcome their resistance.[115]

The East German economic reform and the reorganization of the enterprise structure opened up new perspectives for the town and the enterprise, which had already been renowned for its export performance. Ulbricht wanted to give the Zeiss factory a significant role in the new economic system, which manifested itself also in personnel policy. Ernst Gallerach, the deputy-in-chief of Zeiss, who was a loyal supporter of Ulbricht and his reform policy, regarded the implementation of the principles of the 'new economic system of planning and management' in the enterprise as his chief task. In 1966 Gallerach replaced Hugo Schrade, who was regarded as an 'old Zeissianer' (Zeiss employee), in the managerial post – according to some memoirs he indeed urged the retiring of the chief manager even though Schrade was aged sixty-five in 1965.[116] The enterprise was held to be one of strategic importance, not only because of its export output but also because it served as a 'laboratory' of the new system of planning and management. That said, already in 1964 a socialist working group was formed with the task of developing the principles of the application of the new system in the enterprise. Even more important was the task of elaborating a prognosis for the long-term (15–20 year) development of the Zeiss factory, which Gallerach presented at the Seventh Party Congress in 1967. The members of the working group received state awards for their work – according to later memoirs they spent many nights at their workplace in order to accomplish the task.[117] In April 1968 the Political Committee decided that the enterprise would be the centre of the research of the rationalization and automation technology in the GDR, and relevant production would be also concentrated in the town.[118] When Ulbricht visited Jena, he also promised to invest in the development of the town; he criticized the crumbling houses and declared that such conditions were unworthy of a town which hosted the internationally recognized Zeiss factory.[119]

The reform of the economic management thus initiated significant developments in the enterprise, for which Gallerach, who enjoyed Ulbricht's confidence, bore the main responsibility. In 1964 seven plants joined Zeiss, which thus became the leading enterprise of optical and precision instruments. In 1965 it received the right of foreign trade, first under the supervision of the Ministry of Foreign Affairs, but from 1968 the enterprise was solely responsible for its foreign trade. In 1967 the department of export–import was established, which from 1972 was accountable only to the chief manager. The research centre was officially opened in 1971, after two years of preparatory work. By 1975 the centre employed 4,741 people.[120] In 1980, this number was around 3,500 and 40 per cent of the employees had a university or a college degree.[121] The industrial and educational complex in Göschwitz was opened in 1970, where 2,100 trainees and 4,000 comprehensive school[122] students could be accommodated (there were also dormitories).[123] With that, Zeiss controlled supervision over the largest vocational training institution of the GDR.[124] The enterprise also played an important role in military research and development. Brezhnev's visit on 20 April 1967 is a clear sign of the Soviet interest in the enterprise.[125]

Despite these results, the reform of the economic management in the enterprise was not an unambiguous success story – on the contrary, in the light of the local sources, the chaos of the last years of the NES was strongly felt in the factory. The price reform had a very negative effect on the management of Zeiss because the costs of raw materials significantly increased while the prices of industrial products could not be increased accordingly because of political considerations. The increase of the prices put Zeiss in a difficult situation because they worked with very expensive materials: the price of raw diamond increased by 46 per cent, while a special opal glass cost 19.29 M instead of the previous 2.1 M.[126] The increase of energy prices, on which they likewise could not spare much, added to the financial difficulties of the enterprise: in 1964, the cost of energy increased by 1.6 million M, while the enterprise could only spare 125,000 M with rationalization.[127] In addition, there were huge arrears in export performance. The ambitious and taut plans of 1969 and 1970 worsened the situation of the factory to the extent that it could only avoid bankruptcy with significant state support.[128]

The evaluation of Gallerach's managerial achievement is ambiguous even in light of the above 'negative' facts, because several economic problems of the factory were connected with the structural contradictions of the reform. The reform itself was not consistent and foreign events (mainly in Czechoslovakia and Poland) largely influenced its outcome. Even though Gallerach was criticized by the central political bodies, it was not the economic problems of the factory but Ulbricht's political fall that decided his fate. It well characterizes the end of the reform that Gallerach received criticism not because of his economic performance but, quite the contrary, because 'he was too much absorbed in the economic tasks at the expense of political work'.[129] The report also charged the manager with liberalism, which was a clear sign of the dissatisfaction of the party leadership after the fall of the reform. Gallerach was relieved of his managerial post on 1 July 1971. His successor, Helmut Wunderlich, likewise proved himself too liberal to manage the ever-expanding enterprise, and he too had to leave the senior management in 1975. Contrary to his 'liberal' predecessors, the new manager, Wolfgang Biermann,[130] who was a candidate for the Political Bureau in 1966, was a supporter of the one-man management, and he ruthlessly removed the managers who he held to be politically unreliable or who dared to contradict him.[131] It is not accidental that no negative criticism of the manager manifested itself in the local sources until the fall of the Honecker regime.

With some justification it can be argued that the huge developmental projects started in the NES yielded fruit under Biermann. The workforce of the enterprise continued to grow because further plants joined Zeiss; the phase of concentration ended in 1985. In 1976 the Zeiss *Kombinat*[132] employed around 35,000 people, by 1980 it had risen to 42,000 and by 1985 it was 53,000. Out of this number, the workforce of VEB[133] Carl Zeiss amounted to 'only' 33,000 in 1985; of these, 26,000 had their workplaces in Jena while around 7,000 worked in the plants of Eisfeld, Gera, Lommatzsch, Saalfeld and Suhl.[134] The state housing projects that Honecker launched mitigated the great pressure on housing in Jena: the modern housing estates in Neulobeda and Winzerla were built in the period. While in 1968 fifty people refused to work in the factory because they did not get the promised flats,[135] 5,207 new state flats were handed over to the Zeiss employees between 1970 and 1974.[136] Zeiss, like Rába, offered various facilities and benefits to their employees: in order to enable full female employment, the factory ran nurseries and kindergartens for Zeiss employees, and operated sports clubs, a cultural centre, a football team, summer camps and a polyclinic.[137] The enterprise was not only the major employer of the town but it was also the main sponsor of cultural and sporting events. The Zeiss Planetarium, which was renovated and modernized in 1983–85, has attracted not only the local people but has become a favourite tourist spectacle.

Thanks to the ideological discipline and strict censorship, the political weakening of the regime was less observable in the GDR than in Hungary. In October 1989 the chief manager loyally reported of a handwritten pamphlet that was found on the staircase of one of the plants.[138] The 'transition' was so quick that a few months later the employees were informed that a warrant had been issued for the arrest of the manager, who was accused of fraud. The whereabouts of the chief manager were unknown.[139] The evaluation of Biermann's managerial achievement is ambiguous;[140] it was clear, however, that his prominent political role in the regime could not be forgotten.

Figure 1.2 Logo of VEB Carl Zeiss

Ideology and Management: The Lot of a Socialist Manager was not a Happy One

Since Carl Zeiss was in many aspects an 'experimental field' of the new economic system, and it was also an important export firm, it strongly felt the effects of the reform, many of which resulted from inconsistencies between the subsequent phases of the NES. The economic troubles, which affected the whole of the GDR in the last years of the NES, hit Zeiss particularly hard: the enterprise repeatedly could not fulfil the plans, there were huge arrears of orders, investments were not finished, and the enterprise accumulated huge debts. Even though many of these problems resulted from the structural inconsistencies of the NES, they undermined Gallerach's authority, who constantly received criticism from higher party organs in this period. In addition, in the light of the local sources, the middle management, who belonged to the old guard of Zeiss, also questioned the managing director's professional competence, who in response accused them of holding backward views and being attached to outdated methods.

This chapter examines the reception of the 'new system of management' among the managers and the workers of the enterprise in the last critical years of the NES. This period is all the more interesting because – contrary to the situation in Hungary, in which the ideological hardening of the early 1970s was followed by a relatively open discussion of economic and social problems during the 1980s – the sources of the Honecker era, at least in the light of the local (district and factory) party documents, tell us very little about everyday life and working-class attitudes. In this sense, Gallerach can be correctly termed a liberal for, while he tolerated attacks that undermined his managerial authority, the same could not be said of Biermann, whom nobody dared attack. The information report from Gera – which had an almost revolutionary tone in comparison with later sources – undoubtedly reflected internal party disputes, but it also revealed that at that time the local party organs were sincerely interested in working-class opinions about party policy, and they even attempted to engage them in a dialogue. Even more importantly, it seems that workers accepted the party as a conversation partner: it was evidently workers who made the quoted comments, and not party functionaries. The reform period was, however, the last time when the party demonstrated a genuine concern for its loss of working-class support. The Honecker regime did not even make an attempt to treat people as equal conversation partners: local party materials contented themselves with echoing official propaganda. The fall of Ulbricht's reform therefore ended the limited dialogue between the party and the East German workers.

In the light of the documents Gallerach tolerated criticism, and this ability served him well in the fierce ideological struggles over the NES in the

last, critical years of the reform. The internal division of the party is shown
by the relative abundance of surprisingly open criticisms in the documents,
which are sadly missing from the monotonous repetitions of ideological
phrases and over-bureaucratized language of the reports characteristic of
the Honecker era. Nor can we read such controversial accounts of Biermann's leadership and management as of the colourful conflicts between
Gallerach and the Zeiss managers. Even though many of the problems of
the enterprise were the product of structural economic problems beyond
Gallerach's control, the manager was frequently attacked, especially after
1968, when he had to reckon with both the weakening position of the
reformers and the economic problems that his enterprise caused to the
national economy, given its repeated under-fulfilment of its plan. In the
light of the documents, the middle management of the enterprise was
not enthusiastic about the ambitious investments and new methods. They
were, at any rate, discontented with the 'outsider' manager (contrary to
his predecessor, Gallerach was not an old Zeissianer), and they were ready
to see him as the chief scapegoat for the unreasonable projects and the
economic problems that resulted from the contradictions of reform. Gallerach was conscious of the conflict because, on his part, he frequently and
publicly criticized the old management of the enterprise for their failure
to understand and apply the principles of new economic management in
their fields. On the 'Day of the Socialist Leader' (*Tag des sozialistischen
Leiters*) – one year before he himself had to exercise self-criticism – Gallerach argued that the managers of VEB Carl Zeiss Jena had no reason
to be self-satisfied, let alone conceited: 'There are managers even among
our colleagues, who accustomed themselves to passivity, and they examine
every question of our development from the perspective of an observer.
We don't need observers and yes-men here, but we need active combat-
ants.'[141] It was perhaps an achievement of the NES that criticism could be
expressed in public, because otherwise it was not customary to trouble
people with problems, especially on an official holiday.

The conflict between Gallerach and the old guard among management
was, however, a very real one, as one month later the chief manager again
laid into the old-fashioned methods and the lack of initiative of much of
management in front of the factory party committee:

> Today's most important problem is the elimination of deficiencies in the or-
> ganization of production in our enterprise. I think that the greatest obstacle
> to this is self-satisfaction and managers' attachment to traditional, outdated
> methods. We need to pay more attention to the education of managers. In the
> factory I experience signs of resignation among part of the management. We
> need to treat this question as a political one. A manager needs socialist educa-
> tion, if he wants to educate others.[142]

East German leaders deployed a more militaristic rhetoric than the Hungarians even in the reform era; nevertheless, despite the rhetoric, the chief manager was not very successful in winning over the old guard to his new economic management style. More importantly, there was no sign that he had any effect on patterns of promotion, which suggests that managerial practice was more lenient than the rhetoric.

In the reform era even East German party jargon, which conformed to ideological requirements, sometimes turned into self-parody. Gallerach failed to give a more concrete description of how socialist managers had to be educated, but one year later when the problems of production again had to be discussed at a factory party leadership meeting, Gallerach's complaint suggested that he himself felt he should go on a shortened course:[143]

> Even comrade Gallerach said that he was disappointed with the results and he listed several examples in order to prove that the under-fulfilment of the plan was primarily due to political factors. 'There is no discipline in the instrument plant, the managers do what they want, they permanently disregard the plan, the direct production managers and shop managers are making their own plans (I can prove it with a number of concrete examples), of which the majority of the workers are not informed. In addition, shift work is unsolved, and the management of the plant has not dealt with the E-system[144] for a year.' Comrade Gallerach finished his speech with the argument that there were problems with the political stance of officials in the instrument plant, and they needed to be critically evaluated.[145]

The managing director attempted to shift responsibility (and work) to the party organization as far as was possible, which was diplomatically commented on by the first secretary of the party organization of the factory: 'We have to start from the present situation and consider how we can show ourselves worthy of the confidence of our comrade Walter Ulbricht. We have to educate our managers so that they become fully conscious of what is at stake. Since they are not hard enough on themselves, they cannot educate the collective in state discipline.'[146] Another member of the leadership pointed out that the socialist work contest lacked 'fighting spirit' because the evaluation of the results of January was published only in June.[147] It seems that not only production but officials also could not fulfil their plan targets.

However comical these reports may sound today, there were real production and financial problems in the background, for which both sides of the dispute blamed the other. Even though the enterprise attempted to depict a rosy picture of the situation, one did not need to read between the lines in order to find criticism. In 1968, for instance, it was reported that the enterprise 'largely' fulfilled the plan but the financial manager owed this more to the unselfish work and overtime of the employees, than to the management. That having been said, the report admitted that despite every effort, the enterprise could not fulfil the plan, which was explained primarily by the following reasons:

> It has been a problem for years that the methods of the direct production managers are outdated and they need a fundamental revision. It is alarming that in some fields the managers lacked a clear overview of the whole production process as late as in December. In 1968 there was a further decline in the quantity of production causing a loss of 20 million Marks. The results of plan fulfilment in December show that we can save a lot of money and reduce overtime with better organization of labour, so we must definitely improve cooperation between the different plants. In many places there are obstacles to the introduction of innovations; this is shown by the fact that the number of our instruments that bear the trademark Q has decreased from 338 to 301.

In addition, the report argued that employees had different attitudes to the fulfilment of the plan, and that the continuous overwork of the previous three months had tested the patience of workers; therefore their political mood was not good: 'On the one hand, there are those who are determined to fight for the plan; on the other hand, we can hear several doubts and complaints.' Concerning the mounting discontent among the workers, the report considered it necessary to mention that the management would increase the wages of those in the 4th to 7th wage groups and also those of the direct production managers in 1969.[148]

This, of course, did not mean the end of the affair. The management of the enterprise was compelled to give an explanation to the district party committee of the district for Zeiss's persistently poor plan fulfilment. The supervisory committee – not surprisingly – blamed middle management for the failure:

> The ideological reasons lie primarily in the missing political and professional qualifications and the weak fighting spirit of middle management, who fail to recognize their responsibility for the political education of the collective and they content themselves with the management of the technological-economic processes only. This is manifest in the deficiencies of socialist democracy, the lack of commitment in problem-solving, the adoption of a passive attitude and the toleration of mediocrity, self-satisfaction and conceit. Many employees think that they only have to wait and see. This attitude results from the failure of the management to put the resolutions of the party into practice creatively, because they have not yet fully understood our structural policy and they don't trust enough in the working ability of the Zeiss-collective.[149]

The factory party organization, was, however, opposed to further testing peoples' patience, because the report of the following month took the side of the employees, including management, stressing that they were doing everything they could to fulfil the plan (which implied that they could not be expected to work more without additional pay):

> We invested much in the improvement of political-ideological work in our enterprise, which helped our employees to better understand and apply the principle of the unity of politics and the economy. This manifested itself in the willingness of the workers to sacrifice their individual interests for the interests of the collective, and they did everything in order to realize the 1968 plan, as well as to fulfil the prerequisites for the successful realization of the 1969 plan. We could not, however, achieve this difficult goal, despite the outstanding performance of our employees. Even though we had good enterprise results, there are a huge number of unmet orders, the production of articles that are in demand, etc.[150]

The 'battle' was fought at the level of ideology, rather than at the front of production, and despite its military rhetoric, the party in fact took care not to anger the workers too much. The factory party leadership energetically objected to the polite hint that the Zeiss-collective was capable of higher performance; they immediately pointed out that people had already gone to their limits, and it was not their fault that the plan could not have been fulfilled. This situation did not change during the last years of Gallerach's management, and neither did the rhetoric of the party. In 1970, the following problems were singled out, which show that Gallerach was not in an enviable situation during this period:

> The main obstacle to the fulfilment of the 1970 plan is the continual production stoppages, and because of that we cannot fulfil the export plan in time. Today the VEB Carl Zeiss Jena is one of the largest debtors among the enterprises of the people's economy, which causes sensitive losses both to the people's economy of the republic and to other socialist countries. It is true that by 31 March 1970 we over-fulfilled industrial production by 4 million Marks but there are significant arrears of exports, and the enterprise cannot fulfil all of its orders by the given deadline. In sum, we have to conclude that our war plan, to make up arrears of the plan, has not been realized. Our political-ideological work, from the managing director down, is targeted at the following problems, which hinder the realization of the programme: the fight against outdated methods and the comfort of mediocrity; mistakes that are characteristic of many managers who are unable to identify themselves with the objectives. They explain everything by 'objective' difficulties and they always look for excuses for why a given task cannot be solved instead of pondering how they can mobilize every reserve for the solution of the problem, using purposeful information and education of the employees. Another problem is that some of the managers narrow-mindedly deal with their small fields only and they don't have an overview of the whole production process. Because of this, the individual plants often only shift the responsibility for the delay to each other.[151]

Since the consultation with the party organs was chiefly limited to the repetition of the same phrases, it is at best doubtful how it helped Gallerach in his fight to introduce the principles of the new economic management into the factory.

The above, 'friendly' reprimand was already a sign of the declining authority of the managing director, which was further undermined by the failure of the enterprise to execute a project for delivery to the Soviet Union by the deadline. The affair forced Gallerach to give a self-critical speech in front of the district party leadership:

> We have done significant damage to the Soviet Union because we could not find a satisfactory solution to the problem of the E-system. The GDR has always distinguished itself as a reliable partner of the Soviet Union. Our behaviour undermined this confidence, seriously threatening the reputation of the VEB Carl Zeiss Jena in the Soviet Union. We have to admit that we underestimated the difficulty of the task, we badly managed the project, and we failed to mobilize the resources of the VEB Carl Zeiss Jena in order to solve this problem.[152]

Gallerach and the first secretary of the factory party organization established a routine of diplomatically reporting bad news because the enterprise, as had already been predicted, failed to fulfil its 1970 plan:

> Even though the base organizations have their own action plans, in many places we lack clear analysis and a fighting spirit. We decided to fulfil the tasks by the end of the year. Meanwhile it clearly turned out that we cannot meet the export targets and cut production costs. The managers explain many problems through external factors and they talk much less of the tasks that need to be solved within the enterprise such as shift work, the improvement of labour productivity, etc. The common battle programme of the IKL[153] and the top management helped us to achieve good results in the plants where the managers themselves took the lead and they honestly informed the employees of our real situation. Despite the measures we introduced, we could not, however, fulfil 50 per cent of the annual plan in every field. We achieved 49.8 per cent in industrial production, 40.7 per cent in export, and the general enterprise result was 42.3 per cent. The export arrears amounted to 38.3 million Marks.[154]

The national leadership was concerned about Zeiss's poor performance. A report at the end of the year expressed even stronger criticism than before, blaming the entire management of the enterprise for the repeated failures. It is also remarkable that the report stressed the responsibility of the top personnel, particularly when we take into account the fact that Gallerach's mission was to reform the management of the enterprise according to the principles of the NES:

The export plan was not fulfilled mainly because of the mistakes of management. These mistakes are the following: deficiencies in the professional qualifications of management, and their Marxist–Leninist organizational work; failure to realize democratic centralism; chaos in management, lax discipline, a lenient, and sometimes careless working style; formalism in the management of the socialist labour competition. Efforts to improve labour organization have not yet ensured continuous production. It takes too much time to solve problems, even with the help of electronic data processing. The result is that production stoppages alone caused losses of 50 million Marks in the instrument plant. Why? The reasons are that they could not set the technical parameters that were negotiated with the Soviet partner; the central plants did not allow for sufficient capacity; there was not enough cooperation between the producers of the various optical components; we could not solve the material supply problems; the prefabricating and mounting plants performed very poorly (they under-fulfilled the plan by 550,000 hours). The labour plan was likewise not realized.

In respect of the workers, it was reported that the construction at Göschwitz and automation significantly improved working conditions, but despite that, some of the workers – mainly women – refused to work more shifts, 'which can be explained by objective reasons: there are not enough nurseries and kindergartens. Today we keep a record of 492 applications from women who would be willing to take up their work again in the enterprise if they could solve their child-care problems.'[155] The aspects of class struggle were not, however, forgotten even in this critical situation: the report stressed that all information was collected about the representation of the 'West German pseudo-enterprise' Oberkochen at the Bucharest international fair.[156]

Despite the enterprise's difficult situation, Gallerach might have received one more chance to 'prove himself worthy' of the trust of the central party leadership, had it not been for the weakening of Ulbricht's position, which strengthened the political attacks against him. At the beginning of 1971 the first secretary of the factory party organization sent a personal letter to the district party secretary, in which he criticized the political work of the managing director:

Today we have to face a number of ideological problems. In my judgement, the managers and colleagues of the departments of research, development and foreign trade even today do not understand that what we need here primarily is achievement and efficiency. The elections especially showed us that the employees do not have the fundamental information to engage with economic plans, and management were therefore unable to ensure that the VEB Carl Zeiss met the higher expectations that followed from the policy of the party.[157]

The district party secretary finished a speech he gave to the rest of the local party leadership in similar terms: 'we have a number of base organizations, which are busy with production tasks only, while they forget about
their actual task, the political leadership of the people'.[158] This – at least in
the light of the criticism that the chief manager received from the central
party leadership[159] – could have been addressed to Gallerach as well.

The economic results of the enterprise were not better in 1971 than in
the year before, so the first secretary of the IKL did not need to ponder
much over his report:

> Despite this positive development, we think that the factory – under the pres-
> ent conditions of efficiency and production capacity – cannot satisfy the de-
> mands of the people's economy of the GDR for scientific instruments. We
> simply cannot meet the demands of the country as stipulated by the party for
> the period between 1971 and 1974, despite the fact that we have increased
> production of industrial goods because we have to make up export arrears and
> have to fulfil our earlier obligations. Our big problem is labour shortage: in
> 1971 we need 1,708 full-time employees, mainly skilled workers and college
> graduates. The secretariat does everything in order to mobilize every reserve
> in the neighbourhood, to win over new people and to decrease the present 4
> per cent of fluctuation to 2 per cent. In addition, we are trying to make sett-
> ling in the city attractive for the newcomers. We would like the city council to
> open more nurseries and kindergartens so that the VEB Carl Zeiss can fully
> exploit the local workforce.[160]

Gallerach's eventual removal was decided at a higher political level than
the local party leadership because the enterprise belonged to the central
administration of state industry. At the beginning of 1970 the Central
Committee sent a commission to investigate the situation of the enterprise. Their report strongly criticized the managing director and it stated
that the VEB Carl Zeiss Jena failed to fulfil its obligations to the party and
the government, which vested the enterprise with tremendous responsibility.[161] Linguistic creativity was not one of the strengths of East German party jargon; the charge that economic tasks took precedence over
political work was part of the rhetoric of the generalized attack against
the reformers. It is worth adding that in this respect the criticism of the
district first secretary that he stated in public – namely, that several party
organizations 'neglected' the political education of employees – clearly
showed the conflicts within the party, because no other negative phenomena in party life was ever mentioned in his later speeches.

Despite the fact that when we compare Gallerach's statements with
the situation in Hungary, one may harbour doubts as to his liberalism,
his deeds often seem to contradict the military rhetoric, which shows that

the reform era in the GDR was characterized by tension. Firstly, it is remarkable that despite the repeated failures, criticisms and self-criticisms,
there was no change in the people managing, neither were such proposals
ever made in writing: the party organizations aimed to 're-educate' the
managers who lacked the necessary combative spirit, rather than remove
them. When the enterprise disappointed even its Soviet client, Gallerach
admitted the failure in a self-critical speech, but the affair had no serious
long-term consequences – the managing director was dismissed after Ulbricht's resignation and not because of his professional mistakes. A similar
point of tension could be seen in the complaint that the January results of
the socialist labour competition were published in June only; if something
like this could have happened under strict party discipline, then we have
to assume that this discipline was not that strict at all. While the rhetoric
of the party did not spare the management, the workers received totally
different treatment: no one blamed them for a shortfall in production –
on the contrary, the factory party organization took their side, increasing
workers' wages at a time when the Zeiss factory was at its least successful
in fulfilling the plan. If we compare this with the fact that the reform had
been originally launched with a wage freeze, we have to conclude that
the party was forced to give significant material concessions to workers.[162]

The reform era can therefore be regarded as a period of experimentation. Even though we cannot speak of political liberalization, it is remarkable that discontent among the workers – and sometimes even the rather
negative criticism of actually existing socialism – was sincerely reported to
higher bodies. The question of 'what do we get out of socialism?' and the
comments regarding the formal role of the workers in enterprise management (the lack of information about production plans and plan-related
tasks) were, at any rate, not linked to the economic reform, and they revealed that there was more substantial and deep-rooted criticism of state
socialism among the workers, than a concentration on their anger at shortages might suggest. It remains, of course, a theoretical question how far the
reform – had it been continued – would have addressed these criticisms,
or how far it would have engaged workers in decision making. It was, at
any rate, a merit of the reform era – particularly when compared to the
'consolidated' Honecker regime – that these questions at least emerged,
and there was a kind of dialogue between the party and the working class.

Planning the Impossible? An Investigation in the Instrument Plant

While the above part of this chapter examined the effects of reform on
the factory management, this next part is an attempt to examine working-
class attitudes during the period, using the minute books of an investiga-

tion conducted in the instrument plant. It has to be admitted that there is not much information about the everyday lives of workers in the party documents of the period: the materials of the *Konfliktkommission*[163] have been lost and letters of complaint[164] that survived in large numbers mainly addressed the housing problem of the employees or the latter asking the managing director to alleviate their unbearable living conditions. A large number of factory party organization documents are simply statistical reports; from the 1970s onwards, these materials were not even transferred to the provincial archive.

The surviving minute books of the 1969 investigation constitute a unique set of sources because, in complete contrast to other party materials from the period, they speak of the problems of the relationship between the party and the workers. The investigation was conducted by a commission that the party appointed to examine the situation in the instrument plant, which produced strikingly bad results. The managing director also criticized the poor performance of this plant in a speech in front of the factory party leadership.[165] The members of the commission visited several departments and they talked with many people in different positions, from managers to workers. The minute books obviously give no information about the conditions in which the conversations were held; it is, however, remarkable that workers and grass-roots party members furiously criticized their managers, whom they charged with incompetence and even with the deception of their superiors. It is interesting that, by comparison, contemporary party documents from Győr-Sopron county reported that the workers were afraid to criticize managers because they thought that the party could not protect even those who made justified criticism from managerial retribution. According to the minute books, workers in the instrument plant were not afraid to criticize their superiors and the deficiencies that they experienced in terms of the organization of labour – this was all the more remarkable because their criticism was targeted at precisely that system which tolerated such absurdities in the production. The inquiry in the turners' shop, for instance, concluded: 'The workers think that it is impossible to work properly under these conditions. The instructions are being changed from one day to the next, and they often completely contradict each other. The plan tasks do not at all correspond to the regular norms, which are always changed.'[166] Workers in the turners' shop had a low opinion of their party leaders:

The APO-leaders[167] and the party groups summon people to regular meetings where they say nice things to us, but nothing happens afterwards. Nobody feels the fighting atmosphere that they speak so much about. Neither are the meetings of the party groups of a particularly high standard. At these meetings officials and the state leaders speak only, workers never make any comments. The reasons lie in the fact that many comrades think here that nothing will change, everything will stay the same.[168]

What makes the comments especially interesting is that the workers told them to members of a commission that was created by the party. In East German party documents we hardly meet any sign of open criticism: such open formulations of the differences between officials and workers were unthinkable under the Honecker regime. The contrast between ideological language and the social experience of workers often resulted in intentional or accidental irony: the phrase – 'the reasons lie in the fact' – was one of the favourite expressions in party documents. A similar contrast can be found in some of Gallerach's statements: while he complained that there was no discipline in the instrument plant and the managers did what they wanted,[169] here it was the workers who revealed that the ideology of the regime had no basis on reality, and that the party meetings were no place for workers to express their opinions. If, however, this criticism was voiced at all in the presence of a party commission, we, nevertheless, have to assume that ideological discipline loosened during the reform era.

This argument is strengthened by the fact that the investigation detected several other 'ideological deficiencies', which reveal much of the tense relationship between the party and the workers, including the practice of simply thrusting party membership involuntarily on workers. They reported:

> We can experience serious ideological deficiencies in many respects; for example, we have permanent disputes with many comrades over the payment of party dues. Let's take, for instance, the case of comrade X, who has been employed as a turner in Zeiss for over a year. Already in January it turned out that he paid only 2.5 Marks instead of 11.85. In this month he should pay 17 Marks. The comrades tried to appeal to his better nature every day. In the beginning, he wanted to pay 3 Marks only and now he maintains he won't pay a penny. Even though he joined the party, he is free to terminate his membership whenever he wants to.[170]

Here we can also detect some – probably unintentional – irony, because people usually represented certain opinions in party documents. Much is revealed about ideological discipline by the fact that the worker did not budge on the question of paying party dues, despite daily exhortations to do so, and he even spoke of his intention to resign from the party. If the party group still considered it necessary to stress how much they invested in persuading comrade X (who had not paid the full party dues at the beginning of his membership), then it seems that the party had a greater need for workers than workers had for the party.

Workers' criticism of management was not only – or not primarily – targeted at the general lack of interest of the managers in workers' opinions, but workers directly addressed the perceived professional incompetence of their superiors. Turners, for example, argued that management had bought two turner's lathes, which had very high outputs, without asking the turners' shop if these machines could be used: 'One of the machines has been at a standstill ever since in the hardening shop, which is frequently discussed among the workers. They don't understand whether the management is completely incompetent or whether it is outright sabotage.'[171] One member of the party leadership of the base organization, who worked in the mill shop, commented that the machine cost a lot of hard currency, which was wasted, and because of the increased time spent with maintenance and production stoppages, the norms changed, too. He frequently criticized the managers for disregarding workers' opinions, and he even analysed the machines in his shop in support of his criticism.[172] Of course, it cannot be determined in retrospect how much the workers shared the opinion of the party leader, but he did have some support, as was shown by the results of the investigation in the other plants that there were problems with labour organization and the supply of material: 'There are always breaks in production because there is not enough material, chiefly casting, and they cannot arrange for the right piece on the machine at the right time.' While opponents of reform criticized managers for neglecting party work because they were allegedly too busy with economic tasks, the workers, on the contrary, thought their leaders were occupied too much with ideological work that they regarded as unproductive: 'People complain everywhere that leading officials, including the leaders of every social organization, can hardly be seen on the shop floor.'[173] Even though such criticism mitigated the social difference between worker and official, it revealed that the workers did not hold ideological work to be work at all.[174]

The situation of the East German managers, on whom political pressure was much higher than the workers, cannot be called enviable. According to the minute books, one economist (who was a member of the party) of the instrument plant apparently suffered from nerves, and while he talked with the members of the commission he could not hold back his tears. His testimony revealed that managers overlooked several irregularities in order to appease the workers:

> They do not keep 33 per cent of the technological working plans, and the norms are changed on 25 per cent of the wage sheets. In the grinding shop they keep to the official norms in three cases out of one hundred. The result is that the wages are rocketing, there are workers who bring home 1,400 Marks.

In the distribution department, they do not keep to 15 per cent of the official norms. The colleagues represent the opinion that an economist who comes from outside cannot understand their calculations, because he does not know their work. This is unambiguously an ideological problem. In this respect, comrade Z commented that this department is a state within the state.

At the same time the economist confirmed workers' statements that there were not enough professionals among the middle management:

They don't keep to the deadlines to deliver orders and fulfil contracts, and neither can they manage the supply of material properly. The instrument plant failed to solve the professional and political training of the middle management and therefore they are not in the position to be able to solve everyday tasks. Everything has to be decided from above, that's why everybody is overburdened at the top. My job is to patch up holes while new ones are created all the time.

In his testimony the economist also declared that 'the instrument plant has not fulfilled the plan for eight years and many colleagues doubt whether it is possible at all to meet their targets'. The management had given significant material concessions to the workers, for labour costs had just increased by 48 per cent.[175]

The conversation with the technical manager of the instrument plant fundamentally reinforced the information provided by the economist. The manager said that there was widespread scepticism among people. Workers did not understand why they had not fulfilled their plan for eight years running, despite constant overtime and weekend work. With respect to the rocketing wages, the manager commented that there were no concrete work plans in the grinding and mounting shops, and this explained high average wages. Direct production managers did not want conflict with the workers; consequently they always consented to informal wage rises. The technical manager added that the direct production managers did not have sufficient respect for the workers, because they frequently earned less than them.[176] He also complained about managers' workloads: according to his information every 'professional' manager spent at least 12 to 14 hours a day in the plant in order to cope with their daily tasks.[177] One member of the party leadership of the base organization mentioned concrete cases when direct production managers had not had the necessary qualifications, for example, in the grinding shop '35 per cent of the technological documents are false' and 'despite every instruction, the colleagues themselves write their own time sheets'.[178]

According to workers in the polishing workshop, the management acted hurriedly and inconsistently, and they kept on changing instructions.

The workers know that there are shortfalls in plan fulfilment, but they don't know of a common project, which would clearly tell everybody what they should do in order to work better. Therefore everybody wants only to finish his work as quickly as possible and they let the brigadier or the direct production manager do the calculations. The most important ideological obstacle is the extra shift, particularly because there are many women workers, who refuse to work in shifts because of their household duties. That's why we have no special programme for how the workshop can make up the shortfall.[179]

Furthermore, the brigadier of the brigade named after the 'Sixth Congress' did not attend party meetings, which the commission could not leave without comment: 'how can someone lead a brigade without party information?'[180] The brigadier listed the following problems in the workshop in his reply: 'poor supplies of materials; too much additional work; in the old times they produced for stores, which is not the case today; the brigade plan is too high; trainees without sufficient work experience were put on the job; the responsible managers come to the workshop only if they need extra shifts. All of these are factors that make it impossible for us to realize the plan.' In addition, the brigadier called attention to the fact that the 'Sixth Congress' brigade undertook eight hundred extra hours alongside the twelve hundred that they had already accomplished. He also spoke of his problems concerning party-work in the brigade: out of the eleven members of the brigade only two were members of the party, and when they asked three workers to be candidates, they refused, saying that party membership would mean too much extra work for them.[181] The investigation in the mill shop revealed similar phenomena: the workers complained that they could not work continuously because the components the plant had received were not of the right size, and the supply of material was inconsistent. According to the workers the managers underestimated the time needed for preparatory work; at the same time they naively revealed that they received higher pay themselves. Workers in the mill shop denounced the 'Sixth Congress' brigade as well: it turned out that they undertook weekend work instead of the second shift only because it was better paid by the enterprise. With respect to party life, the mill shop could not boast of better results than the 'Sixth Congress' brigade: their workers likewise did not hold regular party meetings. There were evidently more 'ideological problems': the meetings of the party leadership of the base organization were often not recorded and the campaign plan for the elections of 1969 was 'nowhere to be found'. According to the information of many grass-roots members the secretary of the base organization was hardly ever seen in the workshops: in the previous year he attended the mill shop only once even though he was invited many times to come.[182]

The employees criticized the results of the factory in other fields as well. Even though they worked a lot on the E-system, their effort did not bear fruit: 'The employees keep on asking whether their work makes sense if there is an ever-increasing deficit in respect of the plan.' The plant's technical manager laconically commented that Zeiss was promised fifty designers, who eventually did not come because the enterprise could not give them flats. The managers, he argued, could not be expected to maintain discipline if they did not have the means. He, for example, once cut the wages of three direct production managers because they did not fulfil the plan, but he refused to do it again because of his experiences with the Labour Court.[183] One party leader of the base organization of the plant also criticized bureaucracy; 'the contracts often travel 1 km between the various offices of the plant, and he knows of examples when contracts simply got lost during their trip. According to him, the various offices that are scattered around the area of the plant should be moved to one floor, which would already be an achievement.'[184]

The investigation also revealed that transferred goods had been falsely recorded in the accounts of the enterprise since 1959, and this practice was known to the entire party leadership of the plant. Thus, the goods were reported to be completed and transferred if little work or minor parts were missing that could have been completed before the 10th day of the following month. According to one of the managers, such manipulation was forgivable in every instrument plant. He explained the difficulties of production through the lack of technicians: while worldwide there were eight technicians to every one hundred workers, in the GDR there were only four per every hundred. In 1966, the plant only employed twenty technicians; by 1969 their number had increased by 70–80 per cent but there were still fifty designers missing, who did not come because of a lack of housing.[185] One member of the party leadership went as far as to argue that the political pressure from above forced the management of the plant into this manipulation:

The managers are expected to do everything and even more than they can in order to keep the red star burning. When we give our preliminary estimates for the plan, they frequently refuse to accept them and they demand 2–3 millions more. The managers have no choice but to consent to the plans even if the prerequisites are missing. According to comrade D the missing prerequisites are the responsibility of the central management. One example: the hardening shop was closed in the main plant half a year ago, while the new shop will open only now in the southern plant. The production of a number of plants, including the instrument plant, does, however, depend on the hardening shop and since we don't get the work pieces because the workshop is closed, we cannot complete our products. This is just one example out of many similar cases. According to comrade D this has nothing to do with planning; chaos is centrally organized and then the responsibility is shifted onto the individual plants.[186]

Another party leader evaluated the meetings of the party leadership similarly to the workers: 'A lot of talk without much being decided. There is
no point making comments, let alone criticize something, because the
state leaders are always right. Nothing will change here, the party leadership readily agrees to everything that the manager of the plant decides.'[187]
With respect to the relationship between the party and the factory it is
worth quoting the summary of comrade W, who singled out the following problems in the plant:

> Part of the workforce believes that socialism has been already realized and
> now people can have a rest, but they should get their rightful reward; *many
> colleagues work conscientiously because of their old loyalty to Zeiss, but not because
> of political consciousness or in the defence of a political standpoint on the basis
> of their class category;*[188] since the collective could not fulfil the plan for eight
> years, many of our colleagues have doubts about our economic policy – they
> think that the requirements are too high and it is impossible to fulfil the plan;
> many direct production managers are unfamiliar with the technical regulations
> and they can't keep discipline (bad norms, rocketing wages, etc.).[189]

Many negative comments can be explained through bad economic results
in the instrument plant, and it is likewise not surprising that while the workers blamed the management, the managers attempted to shift the responsibility onto the centre as far as they could. The conversations with people
in indifferent positions did, however, reinforce the two central arguments
of the chapter. The first argument is that the regime had a pronounced
policy towards the workers, which manifested itself not only in ideology
– there was, for instance, no attempt to shift the responsibility for failure
onto workers – but the managers offered several material concessions to the
workers, and they indeed overlooked 'minor' irregularities in wage calculation, which suggests that the bargaining position of the workers was not
at all bad in the plant. Production stoppages, which were the consequence
of raw material shortage, meant not only extra work but also extra money
for workers, because they received good pay for weekend work. Because
of shortages of technicians, managers undoubtedly needed the experienced skilled workers, and this probably explains why they overlooked the
subversion of the official wage system. It can be argued that even though
the workers could not participate meaningfully in the management of the
plant, they were more successful in persuading the management to recognize their economic demands. That is why the factory gave workers a pay
increase, even when the enterprise had very poor plan results.

The second argument is that the party was forced to give small political
concessions to workers – despite militant rhetoric and inflexible dogmatism – where worker party members did not pay party dues, or regular

party meetings were not held. The Zeiss enterprise was, of course, not a 'typical' communist factory: it was argued that because of the special social policy of the enterprise the majority of workers had been disappointed with the nationalization of their factory. The investigation in the instrument plant suggests that much of the distrust (or outright antipathy) of the workers towards the party persisted, and the factory party organization had to beg workers to join the party. Yet one cannot place too much weight on this, for the Zeiss factory was never a communist stronghold. Party membership was not necessarily advantageous for workers, and as the Hungarian party secretary maintained, it was not an existential question for them.[190] Frequently voiced criticism that state leaders were not interested in workers' opinions, at any rate, revealed that there was a pronounced difference between the workers and officials – or at least the workers regarded this difference as pronounced. It is worth stressing that such criticism or rather, *any* kind of criticism of the party could be detected very rarely in the East German party documents, and indeed they disappeared entirely with the consolidation of the Honecker regime. If people were not afraid to make these comments in front of members of a party commission, then the party was more responsive to criticism during the reform era than it became later. This is supported not only by the surprisingly open statements of grass-roots party members, but also that of the party leaders. The comment that the managers were expected to keep the red star burning at any price did not really demonstrate that the party was respected. Often older Zeissianers identified themselves more with the factory than with abstract categories like the working class in the way that official propaganda promoted it. If leaders voiced such heretical thoughts, then it seems that some signs of liberalization appeared within the party during this period, and people started to believe that they could express their opinions even in the rigid climate of the GDR.

The End of the Experiment

The over-ambitious taut plans of the last years of the reform undoubtedly increased shortages of consumer goods, and they deepened the divisions within the party. The opponents of reform referred not only to events in Czechoslovakia, but also to the mounting discontent of the population, which was reflected in information reports from the whole of the Gera district. In addition, the signs of liberalization within the party worried hardliners; at least the frequently repeated phrase that some party organizations and managers neglected the ideological leadership of collective and political work points in this direction. Workers' discontent was undoubtedly exploited to settle political differences, but the surprisingly

informative sources (as compared to those of the Honecker regime) suggest that during the period of economic experimentation the party indeed
sought to widen the boundaries of officially permitted discourse, instead
of relying exclusively on repression.

One reason why it is difficult to judge how open this discourse could
be is that, in comparison with the Hungarian sources, in the GDR the
party found it difficult to engage the 'masses' in a dialogue on any level
at all. Frightened of the prospect of economic chaos, the East German
leadership did not dare to take the risk of further experimentation while
Ulbricht insisted on the full implementation of the NES. His resignation
put an end to the East German reform attempt and – with Honecker's
takeover – the possibility of a meaningful social dialogue was closed off.
In the light of the rigid ideological dogmatism that became increasingly characteristic of the party from the 1970s onwards (where the party
leaders from year to year repeated the very same phrases – interspersed
with the 'compulsory' quotations from Marxist classics), it is illuminating to recall a meeting of the district party leadership, which was held to
consider resolutions from the Eighth Party Congress. The meeting was
attended by Professor Kurt Hager, a member of the Politbüro. In his
concluding speech the guest admitted the failure of the party's economic
policy, and he actually gave a critical evaluation of the situation that was
in sharp contrast to the usual triumphalist reports that abounded in East
German party materials. 'We cannot provide the population with a regular supply of drinks, bakery products and various industrial goods such
as electrical products, house wares, furniture, heaters, sewing machines,
baby carriages, and table wares', he admitted. He continued:

> We cannot satisfy the demand for these articles. I won't even mention the
> shoes now – the problem came up yesterday during a conversation and I think
> that you know much more about the topic in this district than I do. This
> means that the struggle that we continue in order to fulfil the plan targets for
> consumer goods' industries and services, so that we can provide the popula-
> tion a continuous supply of consumer goods, is the fundamental and decisive
> question of our work today. We have to provide for the stable and continuous
> supply of people with basic food products, fruits, greengrocery, daily con-
> sumer goods, children's clothes and spare parts; in short, we have to satisfy the
> needs of population, that is the main question and task that we have to face
> today. And, comrades, I consciously declare here, in front of the district party
> leadership, that the success of the Eighth Party Congress depends on how we
> can realize this task.

Despite his admission of increasing shortages of consumer goods, the professor made one more attempt to illustrate the advantages of decentraliza-

tion precisely using the example of shoes that he had already mentioned in his speech: 'In the Schäfer shoe factory of Erfurt, for instance, it is the responsibility of the management and the workers to decide what sort of shoes they produce and not that of the Ministry of Light Industry.' The rapid increase in consumption could not, however, be reconciled with Ulbricht's structural policy, which sought to increase investment first.

In the light of East German ideological discipline it is not surprising that no one spoke of the fall of the reform, or the resignation of Ulbricht – local sources carefully avoided these topics even later. In order to relax the mood, Professor Hager did, however, tell a story of one of his factory visits, which, even though it may be somewhat naïve ideologically, revealed that at that time the workers were very 'realistically' present in the policy of the party, while under the Honecker regime the 'working class' became only an abstract category of reference and a basis of legitimacy:

> Comrades, I visited a micro-electronics factory six or eight weeks ago, where I stood in the place of one of the workers and my back started aching. I asked the workers how they can work in this horrible draught, and besides, there was an awful noise in the workshop. And today I learn from the conversation with the comrades that they could not yet solve the problem in the factory! But comrades, this is a very serious problem, here we are building a modern factory, and in this plant there are mainly women workers, who mostly have to sit – am I right? – and the poor creatures have to sit in this horrible draught and noise during the whole day. I ask you, comrades: are there no technologists and engineers in this plant, who could solve this problem? Do we have to wait for a quarter of a year, or even more until it can be arranged? Surely, one can find enough reasons or explanations but I think that if we have such modern factories, where labour productivity is 100 per cent or even higher, we should provide for normal living and working conditions for the employees so that they don't contract rheumatism for the rest of their lives and instead they'll feel comfortable in their workplace.[191]

The story could be of course conscious propaganda, but even then it is striking that the highest party leadership considered it necessary to demonstrate that they had the workers' welfare at heart, and besides, the idea of emancipation also received a pronounced role in the professor's narrative. The story in fact illustrates exactly the opposite of the view that the party was never interested in the welfare of the working class: even at the highest party forums the leaders felt it important to demonstrate that they were conscious of the difficulties of a working-class life, and they did not forget 'where they had come from'. They also had to demonstrate that the emancipation of the working class did not disappear from the political agenda of the party, which shows that the goals of the old labour movement still meant a living tradition for the party leaders of the 1960s.

With the consolidation of the Honecker regime it was not only criticism that disappeared from the sources, but any debate of the role of the workers did, too. It is, at any rate, difficult to judge how far the party would have been responsive to further criticism and how they would have addressed problems that went beyond the shortage of consumer goods. Since increased criticism within the party was characteristic of the last years of the NES, it is difficult to tell to what extent there was a real chance for a process of radical renewal within the party. The SED was even less willing to renounce repression than the Hungarian MSZMP; and democratization would have been a precondition of any attempt to reformulate the political relationship between the party and the working class. It is, of course, a question of to what extent democratization was a viable alternative under the given historical conditions. The Hungarian example shows that even if democratic socialism was not an option, the building of socialism with a 'more human face' was possible, even in a country which was economically and socially more backward than the GDR. By comparing the achievement of Kádár and Honecker, the latter received a more negative judgement from the East German workers I interviewed. In the context and political realities of the Cold War and political dependence on the Soviet Union, the Hungarian party leadership – and Kádár personally – succeeded in bringing Hungary closer to the 'West' than the industrially more developed East Germany. And this was precisely how the East German workers remembered the two countries.

1968 and the Working Class: The East German and Hungarian Experience

The surviving East German and Hungarian documents do not enable a systematic comparison in every field – although a conscious attempt was made to reflect on the 'leniency' of the Hungarian party organizations, which the East German delegates criticized and the differences of a critical public that was still tolerated in the two countries. There were also important differences in the trajectories of the economic reform: the East German NES concentrated only on the reform of enterprise management and it sought to increase competition among state-owned enterprises, whereas the Hungarian reform-minded economists attempted to extend the private sector and they even considered a careful property reform. These differences determined the working-class reception of the reform in the two countries.

There were other, historically determined differences in the industrialization and working-class formation of the two countries. Innovation and the state support of research also ranked high among the Hungarian reform plans. Rába financed an innovation centre and a technical library, which were both nationally renowned, and there were even plans to upgrade the technical college of Győr to a university. This plan was eventually not realized; neither can we compare the research financed by the Wagon Factory with the great research centre and educated personnel of Zeiss (and in Jena we can also find the famous Friedrich Schiller University). Pre-war Germany was famous for its science and research universities, which received generous state support. Ulbricht's plan to base the future welfare of the East German people on the export achievements of the strategic sectors, where the GDR was supposed to be a world-leading exporter, was therefore compatible with the German tradition of industrial development.

The relative economic backwardness of Hungary could be also observed in the survival of the specific group of 'worker-peasants', who lived in the villages and participated in both industrial and agricultural activities. This group, as we have seen earlier in the section '*Downgrading the Working Class?*', were held to be part of the peasantry in the eyes of the urban working class. The 'worker-peasants' were also regarded as less educated and less interested in working-class culture, community and party life than urban workers. The low- and mid-level functionaries also thought that the 'village people' were politically backward, and influenced by the church. In the rural areas of Győr-Sopron county, peasants were traditionally hostile to communists, and the forced collectivization of the 1950s only worsened this relationship. It is therefore important to stress that the political culture of the 'worker-peasants' significantly differed from that of the urban working class.

This first part of the book has sought to give a picture 'from below' of how workers responded to the economic reform in the two countries. In both cases we can speak of ambiguous working-class reactions to the party's attempt to increase economic efficiency and introduce more incentives into the system. The reform divided the party, and both sides – the orthodox communists and the reformers – felt it necessary to raise popular support. The fact that the party sought to initiate a social dialogue and extend the scope of a critical public is of great importance. With the closing of the reform era, as we will see in the next parts of the book, the party no longer felt a need of a social dialogue – until the political collapse of the regime when the working class refused to accept the party as a conversation partner. After the 1960s, there was effectively no more dialogue between the party and the working class. In the GDR the political repression that was characteristic of the Honecker regime until the end of the state prevented any dialogue between workers and party functionaries, whereas in Hungary the process of 'petit bourgeoisement', which the party held to be the basis of the political compromise with the working class, increasingly constructed people as consumers and undermined the credibility of class ideology. Besides, the party leaders were themselves convinced that workers do not have a real need to have a say in politics; if they can earn extra money in the private sector, they would happily leave the important decisions to their leaders. The fact that in the 1960s critical working-class opinions were voiced in public forums should therefore be evaluated as an important result.

The social dialogue entailed the opportunity of bringing the party closer to the working class. Before discussing the results of this social dialogue, an attempt is made to compare the scale and content of working-class criticism in the GDR and Hungary. Workers in both countries went far in their criticism of the economic reform – certainly to the limit of the party's tolerance in the GDR where we can no longer meet such open criticism at public forums. The harsh criticism that was documented in the district was undoubtedly exploited by the hardliners, who opposed the economic reform. This partly explains the willingness of local party functionaries to report working-class criticism to the high party leadership. In the reform era the party leadership was more open to criticism than in Honecker's welfare dictatorship; furthermore, power relations and the relationship between the party and the working class was also more flexible.

The most important common characteristic of the two case studies is that the period of economic reform spoilt the 'established' political consensus, and even within the party there was a search for alternatives. As part of this political struggle, the party widened the social dialogue with the working class. Concerning the nature and content of working-class criticism of the economic reform, I single out three main similarities. Firstly, the working class widely responded to the dialogue that the party initiated: in the reform era workers accepted the party as a conversation partner and a respected political actor. It is important to stress that workers voiced remarkably open and harsh criticisms of the economic reform, which was implemented by the party in both countries, at public forums. This clearly shows that in the reform era the government took the social 'feedback' into consideration and the party took a sincere interest in the social dialogue with the working class.

In this period signs of 'liberalization' can also be observed in party life. This is obvious in the case of the GDR where the reform era was the last time when it was recognized in public that there were tensions in the relationship between the party and the working class. The report from Gera ('What do we get out of Socialism?') well reflects that party functionaries were conscious of the decrease of the party's appeal among the working

class, which influenced the politics of the party. In the light of the section
'*Planning the Impossible?*', the simplified view that the GDR was nothing else but a 'totalitarian' police state should be, at any rate, revisited.
Indeed, how far was terror and political control totalitarian when three
workers of the 'Sixth Congress' brigade could refuse party candidacy (in
spite of all agitation!), others did not pay party dues for months and managers openly told party functionaries that they were expected to keep the
red star burning? These examples do not really demonstrate that party
membership carried such a great prestige among workers and managers.
In Hungary we find a similar complaint from party functionaries: that
workers do not hold party membership to be an 'existential' issue for
them. The comment that Zeiss managers 'work conscientiously because
of their old loyalty to Zeiss, but not because of political consciousness
or in the defence of a political standpoint on the basis of their class category', at any rate refutes the argument that the East German state had a
'totalitarian' control over its citizens. In the Hungarian case we could also
observe a remarkably open criticism in party documents ('in many places
workers feel that they only have the right to work'). While open criticism
disappeared from the official documents in the GDR, in Hungary we
can also document greater self-censorship in the 1970s as a result of the
ideological triumph of the hardliners. This changed radically from the
early 1980s onwards, when the political climate became increasingly unfavourable for the regime, and more and more people criticized the party
and the politics of the government. In East Germany, political repression
prevented a similar documentation of the loss of the appeal of the party,
which seems to have surprised the party leaders of Gera district as well at
the time of the political crisis of Honecker's regime.

The second common characteristic is the fact that workers addressed
not only the social consequences of the economic reform that they held
to be harmful for the working class (increasing inequalities between managerial and working-class wages) but also the existing contradictions of
the socialist system. This criticism was, however, an essentially *left-wing*
criticism of actually existing socialism; the purpose of the critics was the
reform of a socialist system and not the restoration of capitalism. As I have
documented above, workers in both countries criticized unjust managerial privileges and increasing social and material inequalities, which we can
hardly interpret as longing for a capitalist regime, which produces not less
but more inequalities. The documented working-class criticisms rather
lead us to conclude that in this era workers were open to a democratic reform of socialism and that they believed in the possibility of the reform of
the socialist system and the party (because they participated in the social
dialogue in order to better the regime). In the reform era it was not only

the party that showed an openness to criticism but also workers declared themselves to be willing to accept the party as a conversation partner and a representative of their interests.

Thirdly, I list the most important common elements of the working-class criticism of the reform in the two countries. In both cases anti-reformist attitudes were manifest in working-class communities. East German workers protested against the economic incentives, which decreased average working-class wages; at the same time they also complained that other social strata (intellectuals, managers, self-employed) lived better under socialism than the working class. The Hungarian workers even more vehemently opposed the reform, which in their eyes benefited only the managers and the 'peasants'. Apart from this criticism, however, workers in both countries spoke of the formality of enterprise democracy and the actual powerlessness of the working class in the state-owned factories. In Hungary even trade union leaders criticized the weakness of the trade unions, and enterprise democracy was even discussed in the meeting of the executive committee of the county, where one report criticized that enterprise democracy depended on the management. In the GDR, party functionaries openly discussed that the party lost its appeal in certain social strata; further, we can also read such heretical statements in the minute books that working-class party members do not pay party dues (and their party organization overlooks it!) and the 'Sixth Congress' brigade only works overtime because they get extra money for it. In the reform era the East German party functionaries complained about the 'leniency' of party life (as the investigation discovered, the campaign plan for the elections of 1969 was 'nowhere to be found', and brigade leaders led their brigades without party information), and workers voiced their grievances more openly, even to functionaries. The statement that 'at these meetings officials and the state leaders speak only, workers never make any comments' indicates that the East German workers were as much critical of the 'working-class control' of the factories as the Hungarians.

We can, of course, also find differences between the two cases. The Hungarian reform sought to extend the private sector and their economists pressed for more radical market incentives than the East German reformers, who only intended to increase competition within the state sector. Therefore we can read abundant criticisms of the appearance of the new rich in the Hungarian documents, which shows that the Hungarian workers were more directly confronted with the increasing material inequalities than the East Germans. The increasing wealth of the 'worker-peasants' was also a frequent source of criticism in Hungary, along with the assumed political unreliability and cultural 'backwardness' of this group. The working class was never homogenous in Hungary; the reform, however, sharpened existing differences between the urban and rural groups, and rendered urban workers envious of the extra income of the 'peasantry'. The seeds of the 'petit-bourgeois' mentality had already penetrated the working class; or rather – and this is again an important difference between the two countries – for many Hungarian workers, especially those who were recruited from the landless, poor peasantry, this was the first time in their life when they could purchase durable consumer goods or move into flats which had bathrooms.

In spite of relative liberalization, the differences in the political climate of the two countries were manifest even in this period. In the GDR party discipline was more strictly observed and respected than in Hungary, even amidst the internal party debates. Zeiss failed to fulfil the plan for years; it caused great damage to the people's economy; there were huge arrears in export performance; it disappointed the Soviet partner; and in the final years of the NES the factory only avoided bankruptcy thanks to significant state support. The party functionaries, however, felt it important to demonstrate their ideological watchfulness even in this critical situation. In the documented conflicts between Gallerach and the Zeiss managers both sides insisted that they acted in line with the party (*parteimäßig*), and the failure to comply with the Soviet plans forced Gallerach to exercise self-criticism in front of the district party leadership. It is characteristic of this over-politicized climate that even in a situation which was so critical for Zeiss, the party secretary of the district received the assurance that all information was collected about the representation of the 'West German pseudo-enterprise' Oberkochen at the Bucharest international fair. This is only one example, but the second chapter ('Workers in the Welfare Dictatorships') introduces several other documents to show how ideology penetrated other areas of life, which had nothing to do with politics, and even worse, could not be solved by the citation of Marxist phrases. In the GDR there were political taboos even in the reform era; it was unthinkable to criticize enterprise democracy and the trade unions in public party forums, and neither could the party elite be criticized. In Hungary at the same time people counted a large part of the *nomenklatura* among the new elite, whose extravagant lifestyle and 'conspicuous' consumption was widely criticized as we have seen in the section '*The Appearance of the New Rich*'. In the GDR the party had just started to experiment with the extension of a critical public. Popular responses – and of course, other factors, along with the hardening of the Soviet line and the suppression of the Prague Spring – were, however, not very favourable for a successful social dialogue. The reformists retreated, Ulbricht resigned from his post and the party never again dared initiate a social dialogue with the class in whose name it exercised political power.

The dialogue also ended in failure in the more liberal Hungary. Let us be more precise: the balance of the 1960s depends on what we consider 'achievement' in the situation of the working class. The party gave important material concessions to the working class in both countries. In the GDR there was an increase in working-class wages (this was a significant concession if we take into consideration that the reform started with a wage stop!). In Hungary the government committed itself to a similar wage policy: in order to raise popular support, and 'level' the differences between the income of the industrial working class and other social strata, which benefited from the economic reform, the government increased working-class wages. Even more importantly, the party in both countries committed itself to the standard-of-living policy. The end of the reform era demonstrates that the working class had political significance in both cases because the government could not afford to risk any further decrease of the party's appeal among the working class. The records of the investigation in the instrument plant reveal that workers were in an informal bargaining position in the GDR, too, and they could exert formidable pressure on the management for material concessions: the Zeiss management had to increase working-class wages in a period when the enterprise could not fulfil the plan for years and could hardly avoid bankruptcy! The state guaranteed a workplace to everybody, so how could the functionaries threaten a worker who refused to pay party dues or terminated his party membership? That he would be a worker for the rest of his life? The sources suggest that many workers consciously tried to keep a distance from the party, and it should be stressed again that the party membership was not an existential question to them. It can thus be assumed that party membership did not always carry prestige among the workers. In this aspect one can indeed doubt the efficiency of the omnipotent East German state, especially as, in Zeiss, workers remained loyal to 'their' factory. The massive repression under the Honecker regime, while silencing any criticism, effectively prevented a dialogue even amongst the grass-roots membership, thereby demonstrating the party's refusal (and inability) to change.

Was the working class triumphant in this social dialogue? The balance is at best ambiguous. In the GDR the party retreated from the reform; and in Hungary there was a partial retreat, while the reform-minded economists abandoned more radical concepts of property reform. The government in both countries sought to win over the working class with a standard-of-living policy: working-class wages were increased and there was also a revival of certain elements of the old social democratic programme: housing construction, the support of working-class culture and education and community life (socialist brigades). The material concessions, however, only partially satisfied working-class demands. The social dialogue of the 1960s brought to the surface far-reaching social changes. The downgrading of the working class was an issue that had to be addressed, along with the question of how technical development – and in the Hungarian case, the extension of the private sector – would change the social role of the industrial working class. In the reform era these questions were discussed in front of a critical public.

In this respect, the closing of the social dialogue was a defeat both for the party and the industrial working class. The triumph of the hardliners meant the narrowing of a critical public and the canonization of official socialism as the hegemonic form of left-wing discourse in the East European countries. This effectively blocked the possibility of a dialogue between the party and the working class. In Hungary, for example, the ethnographic study of Miklós Haraszti did not go beyond the working-class criticism that could be documented in Rába in the 1960s: the author argued that workers were conscious of the lack of working-class control, and on their part, they attempted to cheat the managers in order to receive 'fair' wages. The show trial against the author indicated the end of the party's tolerance: the party leaders were more worried that a left-wing criticism would undermine the compromise embedded in the welfare dictatorships than they opposed market reforms. The disappearance of left-wing alternatives from the public rendered it impossible to find a new social message which was more in line with social reality. Besides, political repression silenced those who could come up with an alternative. The best examples are the East German information reports, which repeated the same slogans over the years as if the authors had been afraid that even a new wording could lead to trouble. Official socialism therefore became a hopelessly old-fashioned and outdated ideology, in which few people believed (including party functionaries), regardless of how frequently they cited Marx and Lenin. Not even in the more liberal Hungary did the regime tolerate the propagation of any leftism other than the official legitimizing ideology.

It can therefore be argued that the government's answer to the social criticism of the reform era (increasing consumption and refusal to address political demands) had, in the long run, contradictory results. While there were no working-class protests in Hungary, as in Poland, people recognized the increasing gap between the ideology of the party and social reality. Having failed to realize its egalitarian social programme, the system failed to represent convincingly the superiority of human values over materialism. Propaganda stressed the better quality of life under socialism, but was unable to tell people how they might experience this better quality of life. With the expansion of the market, the state could not control the income of significant social groups, and in the light of the new differences the creation of an egalitarian society seemed illusory. Like the mechanic who was angered by everything he read in the newspapers, people increasingly chose to disbelieve everything that the party said.

The retreat from the reform and the ideological victory of the hard-liners therefore ended an era in both countries. The party based its legitimacy on the welfare dictatorships, which are discussed in detail in the forthcoming parts of the book, and it refused to change the established power structure. With the exclusion of left-wing alternatives from the public, the party no longer sought for a dialogue with the working class. In this sense the end of the regime's social dialogue with the working class can indeed be considered symbolic.

Notes

1. In 1952 the former structure of provinces (Länder) was dissolved, and instead of them, districts were formed. Jena belonged to the district of Gera.
2. Thüringisches Staatsarchiv (ThStA) Rudolstadt, Bezirksparteiarchiv der SED Gera. Nr. IV B-2/9/1/550, Material zur Einschätzung der politischen-ideologischen Situation unter der Bevölkerung des Bezirkes Gera, 2 August 1968.
3. Stress is mine.
4. Material zur Einschätzung der politischen-ideologischen Situation unter der Bevölkerung des Bezirkes Gera, op. cit.
5. Even though the Hungarian reform of enterprise management has much in common with the GDR reform, there is very little contemporary literature on the NES, which shows that the ideological discipline effectively prevented communication within the socialist camp. After Ulbricht's fall the GDR sources do not even mention the reform. For literature on the NES see: M. Keren. 1978. 'The Rise and Fall of the New Economic System', in L.H. Legters (ed.), *The German Democratic Republic: A Developed Socialist Society*, Boulder, CO: Westview Press; G. Leptin. 1968. 'Das "Neue ökonomische System" Mitteldeutschlands' in K.C. Thalheim and H.H. Höhmann (eds), *Wirtschaftsreformen in Osteuropa*, Cologne: Verl. Wissenschaft und Politik; A. Steiner. 1990. 'Abkehr vom NÖS. Die wirtschaftlichen Entscheidungen 1967/68 – Ausgangspunkt der Krisenprozesse 1969/70?', in J. Cerny (ed.), *Brüche, Krisen, Wendepunkte: Neubefragungen von DDR-Geschichte*, Leipzig: Urania-Verl; A. Steiner. 1999. *Die DDR- Wirtschaftsreform der sechziger Jahre: Konflikt zwischen Effizienz- und Machtkalkül*, Berlin: Akademie Verlag. In Hungarian see: G. Manz. 1965. 'Tapasztalatok a népgazdasági tervezés és irányítás új rendszeréről az NDK-ban', *Közgazdasági Szemle* 12(2); F. Fejtő. 1991. *A népi demokráciák története*, 2. vol. Budapest: Magvető. On the 1960s in the GDR, see also H.G. Haupt (ed). 2004. *Aufbruch in die Zukunft: die 1960er Jahre zwischen Planungseuphorie und kulturellem Wandel: DDR, ČSSR und Bundesrepublik Deutschland im Vergleich*, Weilerswist: Velbrück-Wissenschaft.
6. On the impact of the Liberman discussion in the GDR see: Leptin: 'Das "Neue ökonomische System"'.
7. The criticism of the Stalinist economy appeared also in the GDR prior to Liberman. In 1957 Behrens and Benary published two articles in the journal *Wirtschaftswissenschaft* in which they argued that the product-money relations should be more fully exploited and the value principle should be given a greater role. At that time, however, both authors were forced to practise self-criticism and revise their theses. The affair is introduced in Leptin, 'Das "Neue ökonomische System"', 113–15.

8. Statistisches Jahrbuch der Deutschen Demokratischen Republik 1958 (Ost-Berlin, 1959), 272; Statistisches Jahrbuch der Deutschen Demokratischen Republik 1960/61 (Ost-Berlin, 1961), 302; Statistisches Jahrbuch der Deutschen Demokratischen Republik 1962 (Ost-Berlin, 1962), 282. Cited in Leptin: 'Das "Neue ökonomische System"', 112.
9. Schweitzer described a similar enterprise structure in Hungary without referring to the GDR experiences (Schweitzer, *A vállalatnagyság*).
10. Keren, 'The Rise and Fall of the New Economic System', 64–65.
11. There was even a talk of the 'red economic miracle'. Keren, 'The Rise and Fall of the New Economic System', 70.
12. From the 1968 second edition of Ulbricht's works a whole section was removed which contained the term self-regulation because it was considered too capitalist.
13. Hübner argues that in the defence of the Berlin wall, the party was more determined to resist the wage demands of the workers: they wanted to increase labour productivity without increasing the wages. The economic incentives however, enabled greater wage differentials, and the managers often had to fulfil the workers' demands (premiums, lower norms) if they wanted them to fulfil the plan. In 1967 the state made significant concessions to the lower-income groups: the minimal wage was increased from 220 to 300 marks. So the ratio between the minimal and average wages decreased from 1: 2.8 (1964) to 1: 2.2. See: Hübner, *Konsens, Konflikt*, 86–88.
14. On Hungary's new economic mechanism see: T. Bauer. 1975. 'A vállalatok ellentmondásos helyzete az új mechanizmusban', *Közgazdasági Szemle* 22(6); R. Nyers. 1968. *Gazdaságpolitikánk és a gazdasági mechanizmus reformja*, Budapest: Kossuth Kiadó; J.R. Pappné and L. Tüü. 1968. 'A kis-és középüzemek szerepéről', *Gazdaság* 2(2); I. Schweitzer, *A vállalatnagyság*; A. Bródy. 1983. 'A gazdasági mechanizmus bírálatának három hulláma', *Közgazdasági Szemle*, 30(7–8); T.I. Berend. 1990. *Hungarian Economic Reforms 1953–1988*, Cambridge: Cambridge University Press; Swain, *Hungary*.
15. J. Kornai. 1957. *A gazdasági vezetés túlzott központosítása*, Budapest: Közgazdasági és Jogi Könykiadó. For his famous criticism of the socialist economy see: J. Kornai. 1980. *A hiány*, Budapest: Közgazdasági és Jogi Könykiadó.
16. 'Jelenlegi gazdaságirányításunk kritikája', in: Az MSZMP Központi Bizottságának kiinduló irányelvei a gazdaságirányítási rendszer reformjára (18–20 November 1965). *A Magyar Szocialista Munkáspárt határozatai és dokumentumai 1963–1966*. 1978. Budapest: Kossuth Könyvkiadó, 237–47. For a similar criticism see: O. Šik. 1967. *Plan and Market under Socialism*, White Plains, NY: International Arts and Sciences Press. Šik described the interest trap of the command economy as an input–output game. The centre demanded the production of maximal output with the smallest possible input. The enterprise tried to get maximal investment and promised minimal output in exchange so that it could over-fulfil the plan and receive governmental awards and premiums.
17. 'Jelenlegi gazdaságirányításunk kritikája', 242. Stress is mine.
18. Ibid., 243.
19. Ibid., 318.
20. I. Schweitzer, *A vállalatnagyság*, 39–47.
21. Ibid., 47–54.
22. For a discussion of the relation between the giant enterprises and the central bodies see: Szalai, *Gazdasági mechanizmus*; É. Voszka. 1988. *Reform és átszervezés a 80-as években*. Budapest: Közgazdasági és Jogi Könyvkiadó.
23. E. Szalai, *Gazdasági mechanizmus*.
24. On the second economy see: Gábor, *A "második" gazdaság*. As opposed to sociologists, who thought that this private sector could be the 'training school' of real capitalism, the authors later pointed out that Hungary's second economy was subordinated to state-owned industry (namely, it received state orders). They were therefore sceptical about the prospects of the success of the second economy in a capitalist regime. Their thesis was verified after 1989; particularly in agriculture we can observe a sharp decline of small-scale farming.

25. The translation of the name of the factory is taken from the English summary of a book introducing the history of Rába (Z. Tabiczky, *A Magyar Vagon- és Gépgyár története*)

26. Z. Tabiczky, *A Magyar Vagon- és Gépgyár története*, 1.vol., 29–30.

27. Information from an interview with the communication manager of the enterprise.

28. The jeep Rába-Botond developed in 1936–37 was an independent design of the factory.

29. Z. Tabiczky, *A Magyar Vagon- és Gépgyár története*, 154–55.

30. Ibid., 156.

31. The total built-in area of the factory was 146,000 m²; buildings covering 45,000 m² were so badly damaged that they could not be restored. Z. Tabiczky, *A Magyar Vagon- és Gépgyár története*, 2. vol., 10.

32. 17 per cent of the total war damages was to the transport system, and the railway network suffered two thirds of the traffic damage. More than one third of the rails and 85 per cent of the combined bridges were destroyed. By the end of the war only around 10 per cent of the locomotives and 4 per cent of the carriages were in a usable state. Z. Tabiczky, *A Magyar Vagon- és Gépgyár története*, 9.

33. Z. Tabiczky, *A Magyar Vagon- és Gépgyár története*, 24–25.

34. The process was part of a central profile reorganization in the state industry. The car factory was independent only until 1952 when it was integrated into the Csepel Auto Factory. The Győr Screw Mill, the Foundry and the Industrial Tool Factory were also separated from the Wagon Factory. Ede Horváth was appointed chief manager of the Industrial Tool Factory. In 1953 another tool factory was also detached from the car factory. Z. Tabiczky, *A Magyar Vagon- és Gépgyár története*, 33.

35. Z. Tabiczky, *A Magyar Vagon- és Gépgyár története*, 44.

36. Ibid., 61.

37. Ede Horváth (1924, Szombathely-1998, Győr) came from a working-class family. He finished his training as a turner in the Rába factory and he also started working there before the Second World War. After the war, he established his career as a Stakhanovite and in 1950 he received the Kossuth Prize for his results in quick cutting. In 1953 he was appointed the manager of the Industrial Tool Factory of Győr. Between 1963 and 1989 he was the chief manager of Rába MVG. In 1980 he received a state prize for his results in the central developmental programme of the vehicle industry. In 1986 he was made an honorary citizen of Győr.

38. The Wagon Factory was officially reunited with the Industrial Tool Factory on 1 January 1964, under the name of Wilhelm Pieck Vehicle Industrial Works.

39. Horváth, *Én volnék a Vörös Báró?*, 29–32.

40. The conflict also had another personal dimension because the wife of Lombos was the chief human resource manager of the Wagon Factory and Horváth attacked the first secretary of the county through his wife, who allegedly misused her leading position in the factory and triggered the strong disapproval of the workers with her improper behaviour. The case is described in: J. Tischler. 2005. 'A "Győri csata" – 1965"', *Beszélő* 10(5). Tischler, however, does not mention the economic reasons of the conflict.

41. Z. Tabiczky, *A Magyar Vagon- és Gépgyár története*, 106–9.

42. Ibid., 109.

43. Ibid., 99.

44. GYML, X. 415/3/23, MSZMP Győr-Sopron Megyei Bizottsága. Pártbizottsági ülés jegyzőkönyve, napirendi anyagai. A Magyar Vagon-és Gépgyár vezérigazgatójának beszámolója a KB 1974. december 5.-i határozatáról a minőség, a takarékosság és a munkaerőhelyzetről 16, 1975. július 22.

45. The American export of Rába-axles started in 1974 with the Steiger company. In 1980 Rába signed a treaty with General Motors. In 1985 Rába had an export of $90 million to capitalist countries, and out of this sum the American export amounted to $54 million. Bossányi, 'Made in Rába', 35.

46. Bossányi, 'Made in Rába'; Bossányi, 'A versenyképesség stratégiája'; L. Horányi. 1976. 'Megalapozott teljesítménykövetelmények és a termelő kapacitás kihasználása (Beszélgetés a Magyar Vagon- és Gépgyárban)', *Társadalmi Szemle* 31(7).
47. Z. Tabiczky, *A Magyar Vagon- és Gépgyár története*, 76–84. There is also a photo documentation of the cultural and social institutions.
48. MSZMP was dissolved on 7 October 1989, at the last (14th) Party Congress.
49. GYML, X. 415/196/9, Magyar Szocialista Munkáspárt (MSZMP) Magyar Vagon-és Gépgyári Végrehajtó Bizottsága. Jegyzőkönyv a Motor Pártalapszervezet 1977. január 26.-i taggyűléséről, 4–5.
50. Forint (Ft) is the name of Hungarian currency.
51. Jegyzőkönyv a Motor Pártalapszervezet 1977. január 26.-i taggyűléséről, op. cit.
52. A munkásosztály helyzetéről szóló KB. és megyei pártszervek határozatai végrehajtásának főbb tapasztalatai, op. cit., 5. Stress is mine.
53. GYML, X. 415/122/6, MSZMP Győr-Sopron Megyei Bizottsága. Pártbizottsági ülés jegyzőkönyve, napirendi anyagai. Jelentés a párttagság ideológiai nevelésének eredményeiről, problémáiról, a feladatokról, 8. 1972. augusztus 15.
54. GYML, X. 415/117/7, MSZMP Győr-Sopron Megyei Bizottsága. Pártbizottsági ülés jegyzőkönyve, napirendi anyagai.a párt tömegkapcsolata, a pártszervezetek és tömegszervezetek, tömegmozgalmak politikai vitája, 7–8. 1971. augusztus 31.
55. The popular name of Rába MVG. It was established as the Hungarian Wagon and Machine Factory in 1896.
56. GYML, X. 415/122/5, MSZMP Győr-Sopron Megyei Bizottsága. Apparátus iratai. Összesítő jelentés a PB levelével és a KEB állásfoglalásával foglalkozó május havi taggyűlések főbb tapasztalatairól, 1972. június 6.
57. A párt tömegkapcsolata, a pártszervezetek és tömegszervezetek, tömegmozgalmak politikai vitája, op. cit., 9–10.
58. A munkásosztály helyzetéről szóló KB. és megyei pártszervek határozatai végrehajtásának főbb tapasztalatai, op. cit., 11–12.
59. GYML, X. 415/118/13, MSZMP Győr-Sopron Megyei Bizottsága. Pártbizottsági ülés jegyzőkönyve, napirendi anyagai. Feljegyzés 'A párt tömegkapcsolata, a pártszervezetek és tömegszervezetek, tömegmozgalmak politikai vitája' című vita anyagáról, 3. 1971. december 8.
60. GYML, X. 415/121/2, MSZMP Győr-Sopron Megyei Bizottsága. Pártbizottsági ülés jegyzőkönyve, napirendi anyagai. A kispolgári szemlélet és magatartás megnyilvánulásai, az ellenük való harc tapasztalatai és a további feladatok, 9-10. 1972. december 22.
61. GYML, X. 415/204/4/3, Magyar Szocialista Munkáspárt (MSZMP) Magyar Vagon-és Gépgyári Végrehajtó Bizottsága. Jegyzőkönyv a Vagongyári Párt V. B. üléséről. A vidékről bejáró dolgozóink helyzete. 1980. szeptember 12.
62. Jelentés a párttagság ideológiai nevelésének eredményeiről, problémáiról, a feladatokról, op. cit., 21.
63. GYML, X. 415/12/20, MSZMP Győr-Sopron Megyei Bizottsága. Apparátus iratai. Jelentés a megye társadalmi struktúrájának, az osztályviszonyok alakulásának helyzetéről, a változások fő irányáról, az ebből adódó politikai feladatokról. 3. sz. táblázat. A községi családok társadalmi rétegződése (1975. január 1.), 1977. július 19.
64. GYML, X. 415/118/13, MSZMP Győr-Sopron Megyei Bizottsága. Pártbizottsági ülés jegyzőkönyve, napirendi anyagai. Az életszínvonalpolitikánk értelmezése a gépipari nagyüzemek párttagsága körében. 1976. április 27.
65. GYML, X. 415/12/20, MSZMP Győr-Sopron Megyei Bizottsága. Apparátus iratai. Havi összefoglaló jelentések a kül- és belpolitikai eseményekről, a lakosság hangulatáról. 1975. február 7.- 1976. január 7. 1975. január havi információs jelentés.
66. GYML, X. 415/528/13, Magyar Szocialista Munkáspárt (MSZMP) Magyar Vagon-és Gépgyári Végrehajtó Bizottsága. Jegyzőkönyv a Szerszámgépgyár Egység Pártalapszervezetének 1983. februári taggyűléséről, 8.

67. Jelentés a megye társadalmi struktúrájának, az osztályviszonyok alakulásának helyzetéről, a változások fő irányáról, az ebből adódó politikai feladatokról, op. cit.
68. GYML, X. 415/198/22, Magyar Szocialista Munkáspárt (MSZMP) Magyar Vagon-és Gépgyári Végrehajtó Bizottsága. Információs jelentés a Hátsóhíd Gyáregységből, 1978. február.
69. On the commuters see: A. Bőhm and L. Pál. 1985. *Társadalmunk ingázói – az ingázók társadalma*. Budapest: Kossuth Kiadó; A. Bőhm and L. Pál. 1979. 'A bejáró munkások társadalmi-politikai magatartása', *Társadalmi Szemle* 34(10).
70. See: Kemény, *Velünk nevelkedett a gép*.
71. GYML, X. 415/134/1, MSZMP Győr-Sopron Megyei Bizottsága. Pártbizottsági ülés jegyzőkönyve, napirendi anyagai. Az üzemi demokrácia helyzete, az egyszemélyi vezetés érvényesülése és a továbbfejlesztés feladatai, 8-9. 1974. március 29.
72. Ibid., 5–6.
73. Ibid., 15.
74. Jelentés a párttagság ideológiai nevelésének eredményeiről, problémáiról, a feladatokról, op. cit., 13.
75. GYML, X. 415/123/8, MSZMP Győr-Sopron Megyei Bizottsága. Pártbizottsági ülés jegyzőkönyve, napirendi anyagai. A kispolgári szemlélet és magatartás elleni harc tapasztalatai, további feladatok, 6. 1972. október 24.
76. Jelentés a párttagság ideológiai nevelésének eredményeiről, problémáiról, a feladatokról, op. cit., 22–23.
77. Ibid., 23.
78. A kispolgári szemlélet és magatartás elleni harc tapasztalatai, további feladatok, op. cit., 5.
79. Ibid.
80. Ibid., 7.
81. Ibid., 9.
82. Ibid., 8.
83. GYML, X. 415/122/4, MSZMP Győr-Sopron Megyei Bizottsága. Pártbizottsági ülés jegyzőkönyve, napirendi anyagai. Jelentés Győr városban a pártszervezeti fegyelem, a kommunista munkamorál, magatartás, életmód helyzetéről, 18–19. 1972. április 11.
84. A kispolgári szemlélet és magatartás elleni harc tapasztalatai, további feladatok, op. cit., 9.
85. Ibid., 10.
86. A kispolgári szemlélet és magatartás megnyilvánulásai, az ellenük való harc tapasztalatai és a további feladatok, op. cit., 10.
87. GYML, X. 415/131/39, MSZMP Győr-Sopron Megyei Bizottsága. Apparátus iratai. Jelentés 'A kispolgárság és az ellene folyó harc feladatai' c. téma feldolgozásának tapasztalatairól, 2. 1973. április 6.
88. Ibid., 3.
89. Ibid., 4.
90. Havi összefoglaló jelentések a kül- és belpolitikai eseményekről, a lakosság hangulatáról, op. cit., 1975. július havi információs jelentés.
91. GYML, X. 415/132/54, MSZMP Győr-Sopron Megyei Bizottsága. Apparátus iratai. Információs jelentések a pártéletről, a lakosság hangulatáról, 1973. július havi információs jelentés Győr városából, 2.
92. Ibid., 4.
93. GYML, X. 415/4/31, MSZMP Győr-Sopron Megyei Bizottsága. Pártbizottsági ülés jegyzőkönyve, napirendi anyagai. A Győr városi V. B. jelentése az üzemi PB alapszervezeteket irányító tevékenységéről. 1975. november 26.
94. According to the report the passive members constitute 4–5 per cent of the total party membership that belongs under the party committee of Győr town (104 primary party organizations with 9,804 people).
95. Jelentés Győr városban a pártszervezeti fegyelem, a kommunista munkamorál, magatartás, életmód helyzetéről, op. cit., 19.

96. Jelentés a párttagság ideológiai nevelésének eredményeiről, problémáiról, a feladatokról, op. cit., Melléklet 1–5.
97. Ibid.,12.
98. GYML, X. 415/197/3, Magyar Szocialista Munkáspárt (MSZMP) Magyar Vagon-és Gépgyári Végrehajtó Bizottsága. Jegyzőkönyv a Vagongyári Párt V. B. üléséről. A munkásfiatalok között végzett nevelőmunka tapasztalatai és a további feladatok. 1978. szeptember 8.
99. GYML, X. 415/132/55, MSZMP Győr-Sopron Megyei Bizottsága. Apparátus iratai. Információs jelentések a pártéletről, a lakosság hangulatáról, 1973. szeptember havi információs jelentés Győr városából.
100. GYML, X. 415/211/33, Magyar Szocialista Munkáspárt (MSZMP) Magyar Vagon-és Gépgyári Végrehajtó Bizottsága. Információs jelentés a Jármű II. Pártalapszervezettől, 1982. április.
101. GYML, X. 415/134/2, MSZMP Győr-Sopron Megyei Bizottsága. Pártbizottsági ülés jegyzőkönyve, napirendi anyagai. Jelentés Győr-Sopron megye munkássága helyzetéről a KB 1974. márciusi állásfoglalása alapján, 7. 1974. október 9.
102. Havi összefoglaló jelentések a kül- és belpolitikai eseményekről, a lakosság hangulatáról, op. cit., 1975. január havi információs jelentés. A pártélet eseményei.
103. The 9th Party Congress was held between 28 November and 3 December 1966.
104. Az üzemi demokrácia helyzete, az egyszemélyi vezetés érvényesülése és a továbbfejlesztés feladatai, op. cit., 23.
105. Jelentés Győr-Sopron megye munkássága helyzetéről a KB 1974. márciusi állásfoglalása alapján, op. cit., 5.
106. GYML, X. 415/156/1, MSZMP Győr-Sopron Megyei Bizottsága. Pártbizottsági ülés jegyzőkönyve, napirendi anyagai. A munkahelyi demokrácia továbbfejlesztéséről hozott 1049. sz. MT-SZOT Elnökség együttes határozata beindításának és gyakorlati alkalmazásának 1983–84. évi tapasztalatai a Rába Magyar Vagon-és Gépgyár és a Győr megyei Állami Építőipari Vállalat területén. 1984. július 11.
107. Havi összefoglaló jelentések a kül- és belpolitikai eseményekről, a lakosság hangulatáról, op. cit., 1975. március havi információs jelentés. Stress is mine.
108. Szalai also argues that the individualization of the late Kádár period largely eroded working-class consciousness. Szalai, 'Tulajdonviszonyok'.
109. The official justification of the decision stated that the standard of living of the workers of the state-owned industry had not kept pace with the general improvement. 'Therefore the masses very much agree with the statement that when the standard of living of the people has been improving, it is not right that the workers of the state socialist industry lag behind.' (Közlemény az MSZMP Központi Bizottsága üléséről 1972. November 14–15. In: *A Magyar Szocialista Munkáspárt határozatai és dokumentumai 1971–1975*, Budapest, 1978, 382.) On the execution of the resolution in Győr-Sopron county see GYML, X. 415/128/1, MSZMP Győr-Sopron Megyei Bizottsága. Pártbizottsági ülés jegyzőkönyve, napirendi anyagai. A bérfejlesztés és a különböző bérezési formák bevezetésének hatása a dolgozók helyzetére és a munkaerőmozgásra (a KB november 14-15-i határozata alapján), 1988. február 23.
110. For a similar argument see: E. Bartha. 2005. 'The Disloyal "Ruling Class": The Conflict between Ideology and Experience in Hungary', in Hübner, *Arbeiter im Staatssozialismus*.
111. There is much literature on the history of the Zeiss factory, see e.g.: F. Auerbach. 1919. *Ernst Abbe: sein Leben und Wirken*, Leipzig: Akademische Verlag; F. Auerbach. 1925. *Das Zeisswerk und die Carl-Zeiss-Stiftung in Jena: ihre wissenschaftliche, technische und soziale Entwicklung und Bedeutung*, Jena: Fischer; M. Rohr. 1940. *Ernst Abbe*, Jena: Fischer; J. Pierstorff. 1905. *Ernst Abbe als Sozialpolitiker*, Munich: Allgemeine Zeitung; P.G. Esche. 1963. *Ernst Abbe*, Leipzig: Teubner; P.G. Esche. 1966. *Carl Zeiss: Leben und Werk*, Jena: Wartburg-Verl.; W. Schumann. 1962. *Carl Zeiss Jena, einst und jetzt*, Berlin: Rütten and Loening; H.A. William. 1967. *Carl Zeiss: 1816–1888*, Munich: Bruckmann; A. Hermann.

1992. *Carl Zeiss. Die abenteuerliche Geschichte einer deutschen Firma*, Munich: Piper; W. Mühlfriedel (ed.) 1996. *Carl Zeiss: Die Geschichte eines Unternehmens,* Weimar: Böhlau; K. Gerth. 2005. *Ernst Abbe: 1840–1905: Wissenschaftler, Unternehmer, Sozialreformer*, Jena: Bussert-Stadeler.

112. W. Mühlfriedel and E. Hellmuth. 2004. *Carl Zeiss in Jena 1945–1990*, Cologne: Weimar, Vienna: Böhlau, 8.

113. According to the London settlement, the Carl Zeiss JENA could use the trademark in almost every socialist country, in Syria, Kuwait and Lebanon. Zeiss Oberkochen could do the same in the member states of the European Community, with the exception of France, and in Austria and Greece. In several countries both companies were allowed to advertise and sell their products, with the exception of the former French colonies. Mühlfriedel, *Carl Zeiss*, 279.

114. Ibid. 115.

115. On the integration of the social policy see: Philipp Neumann. 2002. 'Betriebliche Sozial-politik im VEB Carl Zeiss Jena 1948 bis 1953', M.A., Jena: Friedrich-Schiller-Universität.

116. Mühlfriedel, *Carl Zeiss*, 199.

117. Ulbricht held economic prognoses so important that he himself undertook the leadership of the working group created within the Political Committee, which dealt with long-term (15–20 year) strategic planning. For a discussion of the development of prognosis in Carl Zeiss see: Philipp Neumann. 2000. '"… bisher nicht Gedachtes denken …": Zur Bedeu-tung der Prognostik im Neuen Ökonomischen System. Das Beispiel des VEB Carl Zeiss Jena', manuscript, Jena: Friedrich-Schiller-Universität.

118. The Political Committee's resolution of 26 April 1968 is quoted in: Mühlfriedel, *Carl Zeiss*, 206.

119. The first secretary visited the factory with his wife on 25 April 1968, on the occasion of the laying of the foundation stone of the building of 6/70. Mühlfriedel, *Carl Zeiss*, 205.

120. Ibid., 235.

121. Ibid., 44. Table, 375.

122. These schools gave a high-school leaving certificate as well as vocational training.

123. Mühlfriedel, *Carl Zeiss*, 222.

124. *40 Jahre in Volkes Hand: Aus der Chronik des Kombinates VEB Carl Zeiss JENA, Teil 1: 1948 bis 1970*. 1988. Jena: VEB Carl Zeiss, 91.

125. Mühlfriedel, *Carl Zeiss*, 204.

126. Ibid.,187.

127. Ibid., 186.

128. Ibid., 214–15.

129. Unternehmensarchiv der Carl Zeiss Jena GmbH, Jena (UACZ), VA Nr. 1231, Geschäfts-bericht des VEB Carl Zeiss JENA für das Jahr 1970, quoted in Mühlfriedel, *Carl Zeiss*, 215–16.

130. Wolfgang Biermann, who was the chief manager of Zeiss between 1975 and 1989, was also a member of the Central Committee of the SED (Sozialistische Einheitspartei Deutschlands, the name of the Communist Party in the GDR). Between 1965 and 1975, he was chief manager of the VEB 'Oktober 7' in Berlin, which produced large turner's lathes. Biermann was 48 years old when he was appointed as the chief manager of Zeiss (Mühlfriedel, *Carl Zeiss*, 284).

131. Ibid., 342–44.

132. The *Kombinat* encompassed every plant which joined Zeiss, although many of them re-tained their legal autonomy, for instance Jenaer Glaswerk, Feinmeß Dresden, Pentacon Dresden (Mühlfriedel, *Carl Zeiss*, 39. Table, 372).

133. VEB (Volkseigener Betrieb) state-owned enterprise.

134. Mühlfriedel, *Carl Zeiss*, 300.

135. ThStA, Rudolstadt, Bezirksparteiarchiv der SED Gera. Nr. IV B-4/13/079, Protokoll der IKL-Sitzung, 15. und 18. 8.1969.

136. *Gleichberechtigt. Die Entwicklung der Frauen und Mädchen im VEB Carl Zeiss Jena.* 1975. Weimar: VEB Carl Zeiss, 19.
137. UACZ, VA Nr. 1583, Rechenschaftsbericht der Direktor Kultur- und Sozialwesen, 3.3. 1976; also information from the interviews.
138. UACZ, VA Nr. 4722, Fallmeldung, 4.10.1989.
139. UACZ, VA Nr. 4743, 13.2.1990. According to the letter, he allegedly escaped to Munich.
140. See: Mühlfriedel, *Carl Zeiss*, 342–44. In the interviews the manager's image was likewise contradictory: while it was generally recognized that he had an autocratic leadership style, many workers held him to be a good patron, who fulfilled the justified demands (e.g. allocation of flats, transfer to other plants within the enterprise, etc.)
141. ThStA, Rudolstadt, Bezirksparteiarchiv der SED Gera. Nr. IV B-2/3/255, Informationsbericht des 1. Sekretärs der IKL (Industriekreisleitung) Zeiss, Tag des sozialistischen Leiters, 16 Oktober 1968.
142. ThStA, Rudolstadt, Bezirksparteiarchiv der SED Gera. Nr. IV B-2/3/255, Informationsbericht des 1. Sekretärs der IKL Zeiss, 12 November 1968.
143. Concerning the problems of management see: Hübner. 1999. 'Durch Planung zur Improvisation: Zur Geschichte des Leitungspersonals in der staatlichen Industrie der DDR', *Archiv für Sozialgeschichte* 39.
144. Electric data system.
145. ThStA Rudolstadt, Bezirksparteiarchiv der SED Gera, IV B-4/13/79, IKL-Sitzung, 15 and 18 August 1969.
146. Ibid.
147. ThStA, Rudolstadt, Bezirksparteiarchiv der SED Gera. Nr. IV B-4/13/79, Protokoll der IKL-Sitzung, 15 und 18 August 1969.
148. ThStA Rudolstadt, Bezirksparteiarchiv der SED Gera, IV B-2/3/269, Referat des ökonomischen Direktors des VEB Carl Zeiss Jena, 17 Januar 1969.
149. ThStA, Rudolstadt, Bezirksparteiarchiv der SED Gera. Nr. IV B-2/3/79, Protokoll der Sekretariatssitzung, Bericht der IKL VEB Carl Zeiss JENA über Probleme der politisch-ideologischen Arbeit und der Erziehung der Leiter bei der Gestaltung des ökonomischen Systems des Sozialismus als Ganzes, 30 Januar 1969.
150. ThStA, Rudolstadt, Bezirksparteiarchiv der SED Gera. Nr. IV B-2/3/84, Protokoll der Sekretariatssitzung, Bericht der IKL VEB Carl Zeiss JENA über Probleme der politisch-ideologischen Arbeit und der Erziehung der Leiter bei der Gestaltung des ökonomischen Systems des Sozialismus als Ganzes sowie Schlussfolgerungen für die Führungstätigkeit der IKL zur kontinuierlichen Erfüllung des Volkswirtschaftsplans 1969, 27 Februar 1969.
151. ThStA, Rudolstadt, Bezirksparteiarchiv der SED Gera. Nr. IV B-2/3/269, Informationsbericht des 1. Sekretärs der IKL Zeiss, 16 April 1970.
152. ThStA, Rudolstadt, Bezirksparteiarchiv der SED Gera. Nr. IV B-2/3/269, Kreisleitungssitzung, 22 Mai 1970.
153. IKL=Industriekreisleitung (the leadership of the party organization of the factory).
154. ThStA Rudolstadt, Bezirksparteiarchiv der SED Gera, IV B-2/3/150, Bericht des 1. Sekretärs der IKL Zeiss und des Generaldirektors des VEB Carl Zeiss über die Durchführung des Beschlusses des Politbüros vom 26.5.1970. zu Problemen des Planungs- und Leistungstätigkeit im Zusammenhang mit der Durchführung des Volkswirtschaftsplanes 1969/1970 im VEB Carl Zeiss, 1 Oktober 1970.
155. ThStA, Rudolstadt, Bezirksparteiarchiv der SED Gera. Nr. IV B-2/3/269, Informationsbericht des 1. Sekretärs der IKL Zeiss, 12 November 1970.
156. Ibid.
157. ThStA, Rudolstadt, Bezirksparteiarchiv der SED Gera. Nr. IV B-2/3/283, Persönlicher Brief des 1. Sekretärs der IKL/SED des VEB Carl Zeiss JENA an den 1. Sekretär der BL (Bezirksleitung), 17 Februar 1971.
158. ThStA, Rudolstadt, Bezirksparteiarchiv der SED Gera. Nr. IV B-2/1/19, Protokoll der Bezirksleitungssitzung, Auswertung der 15. Tagung des ZK der SED. 1 Februar 1971.

159. He was likewise criticized for his disregard of the leading role of the party and his negligence of political work. Unternehmensarchiv der Carl Zeiss Jena GmbH, Jena (UACZ), VA Nr. 1231, Geschäftsbericht des VEB Carl Zeiss JENA für das Jahr 1970, quoted in: Mühlfriedel, *Carl Zeiss*, 215–16.
160. ThStA, Rudolstadt, Bezirksparteiarchiv der SED Gera. Nr. IV B-2/3/283, Informationsbericht des 1. Sekretärs der IKL Zeiss, 10 März 1971.
161. Geschäftsbericht des VEB Carl Zeiss JENA für das Jahr 1970, op. cit.
162. On the wage policy of the GDR in the 1960s see: Hübner, *Konsens, Konflikt*, 77–88.
163. Commission that mediated labour conflicts in the GDR.
164. Correspondence between the authorities and ordinary citizens constitute a very interesting type of source that offers insights into the everyday life of people. See, for instance, the collection: I. Merkel (ed.). 2000. *'Wir sind noch nicht die Meckerecke der Nation': Briefe an das Fernsehen der DDR*, Berlin: Schwarzkopf and Schwarzkopf.
165. Protokoll der IKL-Sitzung, 15 und 18 August 1969, op. cit.
166. ThStA Rudolstadt, Bezirksparteiarchiv der SED Gera, IV B-4/13/79, Bericht, 19 September 1969.
167. Abteilungsparteiorganization.
168. Bericht, APO-Leitung, 19 September 1969.
169. Protokoll der IKL-Sitzung, 15 und 18 August 1969, op. cit.
170. ThStA, Rudolstadt, Bezirksparteiarchiv der SED Gera. Nr. IV B-4/13/79, Bericht der IKPKK (Industriekreis-Parteikontrollkommission), GDREH 1, 19 September 1969.
171. Ibid., Bericht (GDREH 1, Y, Abteilungsleiter).
172. Ibid., Bericht (Gen. R. és Gen T. GO-Leitungsmitglieder).
173. Ibid., Bericht (APO-Leitung).
174. Many interview partners said that the workers considered the functionaries to be idlers whom they had to provide for.
175. Bericht der IKPKK (Gen. Z, Ökonom), op. cit.
176. The party organization of the Rába factory also criticized the low wages of the direct production managers in the beginning of the 1970s.
177. Bericht der IKPKK (K, technischer Leiter der GB), op. cit.
178. Ibid., Bericht (Gen. N, GO-Leitung).
179. Ibid., Bericht (Gen. Q, PO).
180. Ibid., Bericht (Gen. L, Brigadier).
181. Ibid.
182. Ibid., Bericht (GFRÄS1).
183. Ibid., Bericht (K, technischer Leiter der GB).
184. Ibid., Bericht (Gen. A, Mitglied der GO-Leitung).
185. Ibid., Bericht (Gen. W).
186. Ibid., Bericht (Gen. D).
187. Ibid., Bericht (Gen. H).
188. Stress is mine.
189. Bericht der IKPKK (Gen. W), op. cit. Welche Probleme sieht der Betriebsleiter?
190. The East German party statistics is similar to the Hungarian in that the proportion of the workers was the highest (65–70 per cent) among those who were excluded from the party or had terminated their membership.
191. ThStA, Rudolstadt, Bezirksparteiarchiv der SED Gera. Nr. IV B-2/1/20, Protokoll der Bezirksleitungssitzung, Die sich aus den Beschlüssen de VIII. Parteitages ergebenden Schlussfolgerungen für die Arbeit der Bezirksparteiorganisationen, 19 Juli 1971.

CHAPTER 2

WORKERS IN THE WELFARE DICTATORSHIPS

After we have become acquainted with the rise of welfare dictatorships, the forthcoming chapter describes and compares the functioning of these dictatorships, which were based on a compromise between the party and the working class. The central thesis of the book is that having abandoned the harshness of the Stalinist strategy of modernization, the East German and Hungarian communist regimes turned themselves into welfare dictatorships that sought to win over the 'masses' with the promise of providing ever-increasing levels of consumption. This strategy achieved working-class acquiescence, but in the long run it proved to be detrimental for the regime because it shifted working-class political consciousness to the right and effectively excluded left-wing alternatives from the public sphere. This second part of the book seeks to rethink the relationship between the working class and the 'workers' state' in order to explain the apparent contradiction that while, on the surface, the rule of the communist parties seemed consolidated in the two countries, in 1989 the working class essentially refused to commit itself to any left-wing alternative, and readily accepted the restoration of capitalism.

The main thesis of this most meticulously documented and substantial part of the book is that the remarkable absence of independent working-class action at the time of the collapse of the authority of the communist parties can be explained through major contradictions between the economic and social policies of the governments on the one hand, and the communist ideology that they propagated on the other. I seek to illustrate that since the party in both countries saw an increase in consumption levels as the chief goal of the government and the main guarantor of social peace, workers also regarded emancipatory measures and projects as part of 'communist propaganda', which they refused to believe. The consumerist turn of the party therefore paved the way for the eclipse of left-wing alternatives in 1989.

The policies of the ruling communist parties towards the working class contained a number of contradictions. It can be argued that some elements of their policies actually did correspond to the project of building a socialist society that would offer an alternative model to capitalism. One example of such an element was the promotion of female emancipation and the establishment of full female employment, which was facilitated through a wide range of centrally provided child-care institutions such as nurseries, kindergartens, afternoon schools, organized holidays and summer camps for children.[1] These facilities were available at very low prices. Further examples include state investment in schools and teaching, with the aim of levelling differences in the educational and social background of parents and of providing equal educational opportunities; and community building at the workplace, supported in the form of the socialist brigade movement, which was supposed to be the basis for working-class education and cultivated entertainment.

However, while the above-listed elements could, indeed, be reconciled with the concept of a society based on workers' communities, there was a crucial contradiction between this programme and the reality of the power structure of the one-party state: namely, the party had no intention of renouncing its monopoly on power or of transferring much of its decision-making power to working-class communities. Therefore, the promotion of ideas of community within the workplace was not meant to prepare the workers for taking control of the means of production. Documentary evidence from brigade diaries, and the records of party meetings where the brigade leaders discussed their problems, as well as evidence from interviews I conducted with workers, show that the members of the brigades did indeed participate in an intensive community life. They went to theatres, cinemas and pubs together, they celebrated state festivals (in the GDR these were particularly numerous), they held common family parties, they helped each other with the repair of cars, renovating flats, and resolving personal problems such as an alcoholic partner or a divorce; but this sphere of social interaction was firmly separated from the sphere of power. It is telling that, in my interviews with former brigade leaders, when I asked if they were members of the party, most would answer no. For example, one respondent said: 'No, the party was not for me ... I was always a social-minded person, I liked being in company, organizing things ... of course, they [party members] tried to convince me to join, but I always said no ... not because I fundamentally disagreed with them, no ... the party was simply not for me'.[2] Some (even those who were in the party) openly admitted that fellow workers considered party members to be careerists, and this held back those who were indeed community-minded people.

This book distinguishes between the reformist and collectivist models of the welfare dictatorships. Even though there was a partial retreat from the initial, more radical programme of the Hungarian reform of 1968, the extension of the private sector continued in the 1980s, which influenced the existing social structure. While in Hungary reforms were concentrated on the decrease of state control of the economy, in Honecker's GDR the opposite can be observed: the state extended social provisions and promised to solve centrally even the housing of the citizens. Although the end of the reform era in Hungary witnessed a retreat from a more radical property reform, pro-market discussions remained on the agenda. When the government was forced to seek the financial support of the International Monetary Fund, further concessions had to be given to the market. Thus, after Hungary's new economic mechanism, the second major market reform came in 1982 when the government authorized the introduction of nine forms of small business. The reform allowed the formation of the so-called VGMKs (*vállalati gazdasági munkaközösség* = economic productive communities of the enterprise), which were in fact private enterprises using the infrastructure and personnel of the factory outside regular working hours. VGMKs often received contracts from their own factories. In the 1980s Hungary was already a socialist 'mixed' economy in so far as the second economy operated as a significant adjunct to the state sector.[3] Since salaries in the private economy were considerably higher than in the state sector, the expertise started to wander away to the private enterprises.

The second economy impacted on social stratification as well. In 1981 a national sociological survey led by Tamás Kolosi found that the private economy had the second largest impact on social stratification after occupation.[4] The interpretation of the Hungarian market reform was at the time subject to fierce political controversies. To overcome the resistance of the hardliners in the party, the reformers argued that it would 'correct' the inequalities of state redistribution. The reform did, in fact, increase social inequalities because people in higher state positions had better access to the private economy.[5]

Honecker came to power in the name of the consumption-oriented 'standard-of-living' policy, to which he remained loyal until the collapse of his regime. In the introduction I outlined the most important elements of his programme: pay increases, a generous welfare policy, a large-scale state housing construction programme and the support of working women. Keren argues that ever since Stalin combined taut, centralized planning with a high priority for investments, the economists believed that the reformers' mix was just the opposite: slack, decentralized and consumption-oriented. The Honecker regime, however, combined a slack, but centralized planning with an orientation towards consumption.[6] In the 1970s Honecker's state could boast of real results. Wages increased while prices were kept relatively stable. In 1971 the minimum wage was increased from 300 to 350 M, and in 1976 to 400 M. In 1977 the government decreased the unemployment insurance revenue of the workers. Even according to Western analysts the real income of the population significantly increased up to 1978.[7]

As a study of GDR wages shows, blue-collar workers earned relatively well as compared to other social strata.[8] In 1988 the average wage of a blue-collar worker was 1,110 M (gross) while that of a foreman was 1,370 M (gross). University or college graduates earned 15 per cent more on average than skilled workers. The difference among the various branches was also relatively little: 150 M per month. Shift bonuses could influence workers' wages by up to 30 per cent. The study found a smaller wage differential between the sexes in the GDR than in West Germany. In 1988 the average female income was 16 per cent lower than the male income in the GDR, while in West Germany the difference was nearly double.

The second main pillar of Honecker's social programme was the state housing programme, which aimed to solve the flat problem of every GDR citizen within twenty years, historically a very short period of time. The state promised to build, renovate or modernize 3.5 million flats, and provide every adult GDR citizen with comfortable and spacious housing (with own room for every adult family member). Young couples and shift workers principally enjoyed priority in the allocation of state flats. The housing programme was later criticized because it concentrated state resources on the building of the modern blocks of flats, and there was not enough capacity for the renovation of the old houses.[9] Despite this criticism, the social impact of the project should not be underestimated; the overwhelming majority of the surviving correspondence between the Zeiss employees and the enterprise addressed the issue of the allocation of the flats.[10]

The support of the working mothers was an important field of social policy because the regime aimed to enhance the participation of women in the labour market. This was mainly achieved through the extension of the state network of child-care institutions. In 1980, 60 per cent of the relevant age groups could be accommodated in the nurseries and 90 per cent in the kindergartens. The social policy package of 1972 gave various benefits for the working mothers: a 40-hour week for mothers with three children (or shift workers with two children), the increase of paid maternity leave, higher child benefits and more holidays. To encourage people to marry young, every couple who were below twenty-six and marrying for the first time received an interest-free loan of 5,000 M. The state also paid a maternity grant of 1,000 M after every baby. Single working mothers, who received no nursery places, were given paid leave. In 1976 the 40-hour week was extended to every mother with two or more children, paid maternity leave increased to twenty-six weeks, the mothers got one year paid leave after the second child and the paid holiday increased with the number of children. From 1986 every mother was entitled to a one-year paid leave after the first child, and in justified cases fathers could also take advantage of this opportunity. In 1987 the regime significantly increased child benefits: from 20 to 50 M after one child, from 50 to 100 M after two, and from 100 to 150 M after three children.[11]

The project of the socialist welfare state was, however, doomed to failure because the standard of living continued to be much higher in West Germany than in the GDR and the East German citizens compared themselves with their Western neighbours rather than with the socialist camp (where their standard of living was indeed high). While in Hungary the market reforms were accompanied by relative political liberalization, Honecker's standard-of-living policy was combined with repression, which closed the possibility of any dialogue between the workers and the party. The ideological discipline was reflected in the local party materials: while the Hungarian party materials inform us about the growing social discontent, the GDR sources remain silent about the troubles until the very end.[12] The mass flight of the population to the West when the Hungarian borders were opened revealed that the silence was the result of repression rather than a sign of people's consent to Honecker's policy. At that time, however, the party effectively lost social trust, and the brief attempt to reform the party and the system ended with the unification of Germany.

This second, heavily documented part of the book compares the working-class experience of the welfare dictatorships. The recognition that working-class demands did not differ substantially under capitalism and socialism triggered a consumerist turn in the party's policy towards the working class. Hungary was in a specific situation because of the legacy of the 1956 revolution; indeed, as we have seen, the spread of the 'petit-bourgeois' mentality and the formation of a socialist petit-bourgeois middle class (as one member of the executive committee of Győr county argued, 'a flat, the car, the weekend house and the trips were no luxuries') can be already observed in the 1960s. Nonetheless, a similar orientation towards consumerism can be traced also in the GDR, which experienced the rivalry with capitalism very directly because of its situation as one part of a divided Germany. While Walter Ulbricht built a wall to prevent the escape of the population to the Western 'consumer paradise', his successor Erich Honecker implemented the East German variant of the Hungarian policy regarding the standard of living in order to convince the people of the superiority of socialism. A social compromise was thus established between the party and the working class: people gave up their political demands, or at least refrained from open protest, in exchange for the state providing an uninterrupted and reasonable increase in the standard of living of the working people. The forthcoming sections seek to explore the possibilities and limits of the welfare dictatorships as well as demonstrate the essential fragility of the legitimacy based on the increase of consumption levels.

Labour Policy in Hungary

The Standard-of-Living Policy

In November 1972 the Central Committee drew a balance of Hungary's new economic mechanism introduced in 1968. In spite of the 'obligatory' appraisal of the many positive experiences of the reform, the committee considered it important to address the working-class criticism of the reform because the resolution, amongst others, stated that the standard of living of the workers in state enterprises had not kept pace with the general increase of the standard of living:

Figure 2.1 Motor Vehicle Unit of Rába

Therefore the masses very much agree with the statement that when the standard of living of the people improves, it is not right that workers in socialist industrial enterprises lag behind. It is also necessary to correct the uneven, sometimes unjust distribution of profit. Besides, workers complain that the increase of consumer goods puts a substantial burden on their families.[13]

The resolution shows that the party took into consideration the frequently declared criticism that the economic reform created income differences that were too high, and therefore unjust, while the managers and the peasantry prospered at the expense of the industrial working class. The increase in industrial wages was intended to strengthen the support of the regime among the working class. This measure indicated the main direction of the social policy of the party, which was called appropriately the standard-of-living policy. This policy promised the workers in state-owned enterprises that their standard of living would be increased in proportion to those in wealthier social strata, who benefited from the expanding private sector. The resolution received the extensive support of the working class, according to the executive committee of Győr county, which was probably not far from the actual reality.

In Győr-Sopron county a survey conducted in 1972 found the following inequalities in the distribution of income: the annual income of the peasantry was higher (19,060 Ft) than that of the average working-class and intellectual household (18,625 Ft). The average wage in a month amounted to 2,146 Ft in industry, 2,419 Ft in the construction industry, 2,538 Ft in the state farms, 2,593 Ft in transport and 2,271 Ft in the co-operative farms. Wages in light industry lagged behind significantly. The workers' wage levels did not keep pace with the top managers. The wages of the direct production managers also lagged behind, which created a problem of recruitment. Differentials between the skilled, semi-skilled and unskilled labour were low, which injured the pride of the skilled workers. The report also noted that there was a differential between men and women workers and that 'the principle of equal pay for equal work was not always effective'.[14]

There is remarkably little information about the wages in the materials of the party organization of Rába MVG, and aspects of the distribution of the annual bonuses were also not discussed; allegedly, the chief manager personally checked the lists every year.[15] Secrecy may well have been the policy of the enterprise. The wage increase of 1973 is therefore important because it is well documented and it gives a general picture of the distribution of wages in the industry of the county (see Table 2.1).

Table 2.1 Wage increase of industrial workers in the county in 1973 (Ft)

	1972	1973	Increasing	%
Heavy industry	2,256	2,510	254	11.25
Light industry	1,880	2,075	195	10.37
Food industry	1,994	2,236	242	12.17
Other industry	–	–		
Average	2,069	2,299	230	11.11

Source: GYML, X. 415/128/1, A bérfejlesztés és a különböző bérezési formák bevezetésének hatása a dolgozók helyzetére és a munkaerőmozgásra (a KB november 14–15.-i határozata alapján).

In the county sixty-one thousand workers and direct production managers received pay increases. Even though the pay increase was supposed to level wages in industry, statistics show that the party mainly aimed to win the support of the heavy industrial core of the working class. The pay increase was thus the highest in heavy industry. Table 2.2 shows how the standard-of-living policy was realized in the county.

Table 2.2 Wages of industrial workers in the county (Ft)

	1968	1970	1972	1973
Heavy industry	1,880	2,059	2,256	2,510
Light industry	1,568	1,735	1,880	2,075
Food industry	1,637	1,786	1,994	2,236
Other industry	–	–	–	–
Average	1,711	1,894	2,069	2,299

Source: GYML, X. 415/134/2, Jelentés Győr-Sopron megye munkássága helyzetéről a KB 1974. márciusi állásfoglalása alapján, 3. melléklet, Munkások havi átlagkeresete.

Even though there could be some unreliability in the statistical data, they still displayed basic trends. The pay increase favoured skilled workers; the direct production managers received only a bit more money than skilled workers. In heavy industry skilled workers got roughly twice as big an increase as their semi-skilled or unskilled counterparts. In light industry the semi-skilled and unskilled workers received nearly as big a pay increase as unskilled labour in heavy industry. It is remarkable that the pay increases for women were lower in every category than those for men, with the exception of ministry-run construction enterprises (we do not know how many women workers were employed in this industry). The wages of women workers lagged behind those of their male counterparts for two reasons. Firstly, heavy industry preserved its male dominance; women were mainly employed in the badly paid industrial branches like light industry. Secondly, the majority of women workers were unskilled: 35.8 per cent of the blue-collar workers in the county in 1973 were women but only 16.5 per cent of them were skilled workers.[16] The party held the large, skilled industrial working class to be its main social basis. Thus, well-paid jobs in industry were mainly 'male' jobs: in Rába 25 per cent of the workforce was female, but the majority worked as unskilled or semi-skilled workers, or in administration.[17] These data show that traditional gender hierarchies were preserved in industry. There are no separate data about men's and women's wages; but if one takes the differential between heavy and light industries, it is a reasonable assumption that men workers earned 25–30 per cent more than their female counterparts on average.[18]

A report of 1974 gave the following picture of the conditions of the working class of the county in statistical data: ninety-eight thousand workers were employed in state industry, and, together with retired workers, one hundred and thirty thousand people belonged to the working class. There were twenty-seven large enterprises, which had more than five hundred workers, and forty thousand people worked in the large industry. The number of commuters was estimated at thirty to thirty-five thousand. In the plan period,[19] the proportion of workers who earned 2,000–4,000 Ft a month increased from 43 to 60 per cent, while that of those who earned less than 2,000 Ft decreased from 56 to 40 per cent. According to the report, social benefits increased by one and a half times but the average income in big families was still less than 800 Ft per person. The average pension of retired workers amounted to 1,365 Ft. The overwhelming majority of the workers (94 per cent) had a 44-hour working week but there was much overtime. One quarter of party secretaries were blue-collar workers.[20]

Since the standard-of-living policy became the new social message of the party, it was important to know how people received this policy.[21] In 1976 there was a survey conducted of the party members in machine-manufacturing enterprises across the county. In six enterprises 1,013 people (almost half of them [471] from MVG) were asked to evaluate their material circumstances; 84 per cent of the respondents were men and 16 per cent were women. The distribution according to age group was the following: 21–30: 18 per cent, 31–41: 35 per cent, 41–50: 32 per cent, and 51–60: 12 per cent. Of these, 21 per cent had finished primary school, 26 per cent had a three-year vocational training certificate, 35 per cent had finished secondary school and 13 per cent had finished college or university; 35 per cent were skilled workers, 13 per cent semi-skilled and 3 per cent unskilled; and 49 per cent belonged to the 'other' category. (Blue-collar workers amounted to 53 per cent of the party membership in the machine manufacture of the county.)

The survey confirmed that workers in this sector were in a better financial situation than the working-class average. The respondents belonged to the old guard of the factories because 35 per cent had worked in the same enterprise for 20+ years, 18 per cent for 16–20 years, 21 per cent for 11–15 years, and 16 per cent for 6–10 years. The qualification of the respondents was clearly above the average: in 1972, one-third of the employees of Rába MVG did not finish primary school,[22] while in the sample it was only 5 per cent. The wages in the sample were also higher than the average wages in the county: almost half of the respondents (46.8 per cent) earned 3,100–4,000 Ft in a month, while only one-quarter of the industrial workers of the county fell into this category. In the county only about 40 per cent of the industrial workforce earned more than 3,000 Ft; but in the sample it was 66 per cent. In the sample, 16.5 per cent earned 4,100–5,000 Ft while in the industry of the county only 9.3 per cent fell into this category. Interestingly, there were reverse proportions at the top: in the sample 0.7 per cent earned more than 6,000 Ft while in the county the figure was 2.4 per cent. The difference can be explained through 'top' managerial wages; even though it should be noted that even these wages were only about twice as much as the average wages in the sample.

The record of continuous employment and relatively high wages enabled the respondents to live in good material circumstances – or at least at the level, which was at the time characteristic of the socialist middle class. Living conditions can certainly be described as good because the majority of the respondents were owner-occupiers. One-third of the respondents (31 per cent) lived in their own houses, one-quarter (24 per cent) in their own flats, one-third (30 per cent) were life-long tenants of state or council flats, 11 per cent lived at home as family members, and only 4 per cent rented a room. No one lived in workers' hostels. This means that the overwhelming majority had settled living conditions. The households of the respondents were well equipped with durable consumer goods: 93 per cent had a television, 94 per cent a radio, 91 per cent a washing machine, 69 per cent a spin drier, 87 per cent a fridge and 83 per cent a vacuum cleaner. One-quarter of the respondents (24 per cent) owned a motor bike and 26 per cent had a car; 22 per cent of the households possessed a record player.[23]

Even though the material conditions of the respondents were 'objectively' good, their subjective evaluation of the standard-of-living policy was less positive. Although almost everybody (99 per cent) agreed with the statement that the standard of living had increased, opinions differed as to the extent of the increase: 21 per cent of the respondents thought that there was a significant increase in the standard of living during the plan period, 64 per cent described it as average and 14 per cent said that the increase was insignificant. Two-thirds of the sample (68 per cent) described the supply of consumer goods as satisfactory, 31 per cent as not satisfactory and 1 per cent said that it was bad. The opinions on real wages differed from the opinions on the general standard of living: 33 per cent said that the pay increase had exceeded the increases in prices, 28 per cent thought that the pay increase balanced the higher prices, and according to 39 per cent pay did not keep pace with increasing prices – in Rába MVG, 44 per cent of the respondents agreed with this statement. The survey concluded that the population – even the party members – evaluated the increase of prices more negatively than 'was shown by the facts of economic policy. They spoke of the increase of prices even if they could satisfy their needs at a higher level and they bought more valuable products. They disregarded the improvement of the technical standard of the products and they evaluated only the prices.'[24]

People were only 'moderately' content with their wages: 75 per cent of the respondents described their wages as average (even though in reality they were higher than the average industrial wages in the county), 19 per cent thought that their wages were good and 6 per cent said that they were paid badly. The majority of people (57 per cent) were not content with the pace of the pay increase. Worker–peasant conflict was again manifest in the survey: according to two-thirds of the respondents (68 per cent) the peasantry had a higher income than the working class, and only 7 per cent said that the workers earned more than the peasants. The survey noted that according to the statistics the income of the peasantry was 10 per cent lower than that of the working class. During the discussion of the material, the representative of the Rába MVG argued that the workers regarded the commuters also as peasants: 'It is not the real peasants who live better but those who work in the factory and live in the countryside. According to the statistics the workers possess more land than the peasants. The survey reflects that the workers who live in the countryside also farm their land to increase their income.'[25] Worker–peasant conflict showed that the social integration of commuters into the working class had been a problematic process, and the commuters were still considered to be peasants in the eyes of urban workers.

The survey revealed some interesting psychological relationships between the skills, gender and the evaluation of wages. While the semi-skilled workers described the material situation of their families as good, the majority of the skilled workers said that it was average. The survey explained this difference through the almost equal wages of the two groups: skilled workers expected higher hourly wages than their semi-skilled counterparts and therefore they were more discontented with their wages. There was also a difference between the satisfaction of men and women: even though the majority of women earned less than the male average (2,100–2,500 Ft), they were more content with the financial situation of their families than the men. It is an interesting contradiction that while 99 per cent said that the standard of living had increased, more than half of the respondents were discontented with the pay increase. The survey stated that people evaluated the standard of living only according to the pay increase and they did not count the improvements in the communal infrastructure, schools, health service, roads and parks. Since the main social message of the party at the time was the standard-of-living policy, party members were unlikely to contradict assertions that the standard of living had increased. The detailed answers, however, show a more contested picture: it seems that people expected more from the standard-of-living policy than what it delivered. In the meeting of the executive committee the representative of the Rába MVG called attention to the psychologically harmful effect of the non-differentiating wage system:

> In our factory there are direct production managers who earn less than the blue-collar workers. It is no wonder that the workers often refuse to study or accept higher positions. What is the reason for this? One should investigate that the wage is disproportionate to the greater responsibility. The majority of the workers measure the standard of living with their wages, cars and weekend plots.[26]

To achieve all these things, people were willing to work more: nearly half of the respondents (48 per cent) said that they worked in their free time. At the same time many people saw little relation between the work performed and their wages: according to 22 per cent of the respondents the achievement rarely or never determined the wages (in Rába MVG 25 per cent gave this answer) and only 19 per cent thought that people were paid according to their work.[27] This, in general, shows that many people had doubts about the social value of labour.

As we have seen above, Ede Horváth, the chief manager of Rába, agreed with several elements of the economic reform; he was very conscious of the role of economic incentives and he was determined to use them in order to motivate people. With the growth of the production of Rába there was a massive increase of the workforce, particularly in the early 1970s. In this period the labour problems of the enterprise were also discussed in the executive committee:[28] Rába enticed many women workers from the textile factories in Győr, and it also opened new plants in other, smaller towns, which had little industry, like Sárvár and Kapuvár, where it was easier to recruit new workers. Despite these efforts, a production report of 1972 complained that there was a chronic shortage of labour in some professions such as metal cutting and at the smelters.[29] Another problem that the report singled out was the high fluctuation of labour: it was regarded as a good result that between 1969 and 1971 the percentage of employees who gave notice decreased from 29 to 19.2 per cent.[30] Shift work was likewise problematic because many employees continued to rely on agriculture so that the report proposed the pay of bonuses for different shifts in order to fully exploit machine capacity:

> Employees frequently refuse to work in two-three shifts referring to objective problems such as child care, lack of nursery or kindergarten places, long travelling times, etc., but it can be stated that the low differentials play a role in the refusal. The enterprises cannot give a shift bonus from their own funds. In our view it would be justified to pay a 10 per cent bonus for the afternoon and a 20–25 per cent bonus for the night shifts to motivate people. This should be solved centrally because today there is a high income from private farming, which definitely influences the willingness of the workers to work in different shifts.[31]

Ede Horváth also expressed his strong support for the economic incentives in a meeting of the executive committee:

> In my view the enterprise organization marks time nationally. We could not find a solution to fundamentally change the present system, which had been established in 1945. More or less this is where we stand today ... In my view there are two basic conditions of a modern enterprise organization. The first is to make people interested in higher achievement: the reward should be manifest not in a typed speech but people should get it in their pocket. I agree that there is surplus labour. It is an old problem. We have to say with self-criticism that we cannot do much. There is no material interest to get rid of unnecessary labour. If we could pay the wages of 2,000 people to 1,800, every economic unit, party organization and manager would be keen to solve this persistent, sensitive issue. The other thing is labour discipline. If we can't keep discipline, the best organizational concepts will be useless or even worsen the present situation.[32]

The delegate of the Wagon Factory supported Horváth's view of performance-based wage policies in the executive committee. He explained the problem of labour shortage in skilled professions through the low wage differentials:

> I point out the negative phenomena in the Wagon Factory that are related to the psychology of labour. Many employees leave because they are not satisfied with the wages and the professional development. The comrades here also

know that the fact that 40 per cent are unskilled workers is connected with a bad psychology: they received the highest wages and therefore complete unskilled brigades left the enterprises.[33]

The chairman of the county council of the trade unions (Szakszervezetek Győr-Sopron Megyei Tanácsa) also spoke of the positive effects of greater differentials:

> On behalf of the trade unions we recommend that it would be reasonable to introduce the wage volume management in other enterprises, too. For instance, since the wage volume management had been introduced in the foundry, we have had no labour problem. The workers are paid good money, they produce more with a smaller staff and there is no fluctuation. We should consider this and introduce it in other workplaces, too, particularly where there is a shortage of skilled labour. We should make people interested in working well. We should give a good estimate of the supply of skilled labour and make a proposal to the higher bodies.[34]

The chief manager put his ideas into practice wherever he could. The annual premium could amount to a substantial extra income;[35] allegedly, Horváth personally revised the list of annual premiums.[36] The regulation of premiums was also used to strengthen labour discipline because he introduced the practice of stopping workers who went off sick for more than five days a year, getting a premium. Quality could influence 30 per cent of the final wage, which Horváth defended with the argument that the wage cuts also improved the work of those who otherwise did not understand the significance of quality.[37] That having been said, he sought to pay competitive wages until he could, which he regarded as a prerequisite of high performance:

> In 1981 we will increase the wages of skilled workers by 17.2 per cent. But for this money we demand work. We need three shifts, piecework and quality! If someone cannot accept this, there is turnover. The executive committee should consider that there are problems on our side, too, and we cannot do much about them. We have to accept that if a worker gets more money somewhere else, he will want to go there.[38]

Mention must be made of a specific group, the direct production managers, whose low wages have been much criticized in the period. Allegedly, there were even cases when workers refused to be promoted with the argument that it does not pay to undertake more responsibility.[39] This, in fact, hindered the professional career of workers because the overwhelming majority of the lower management was recruited from the shop floor. In the Wagon Factory, 99 per cent of the foremen were recruited from the blue-collar workers.[40] The political reliability of the foremen was also important because they were usually entrusted with the organization and leading of the party cells. This involved more work, and therefore it was an important argument that the pay was not proportionate to responsibility. The interest of the party in the pay increase of the foremen was connected to the interest of the factory. According to a 1979 report, during a 'purge' of personnel in the Wagon Factory between 1974 and 1977, seventy-two foremen were removed from their posts because of professional incompetence. The rest of the lower managers were regarded to be professionally (88–90 per cent) and politically (75–80 per cent) competent.[41] The proof of professional competence was a high-school certificate, even though the report noted the difficulties of imposing this on older workers.[42] The executive committee of the party organization of the MVG also evaluated the competence of the managers. One speaker argued that a manager was politically competent if he could lead his team regardless of whether he organized anything else in the factory, while another thought that the most important was that the manager had a good relationship with those he managed.[43] They did not like that fact that many foremen were expected to drive trucks to ensure the supply of material even though it was part of their job description. The examination of eight plants of the Wagon Factory (Foundry, Auto, Rear Bridge, Blacksmith, Iron structure, Wagon, Motor, Vehicle) gave the following results. The average wages of the foremen in the eight plants varied between 5,100 and 5,400 Ft, while that of the managers stood at between 5,900 and 6,600 Ft. In the Motor Unit there were foremen who received 6,300 Ft and managers with a salary of 6,700 Ft. At the same time the average wage of the blue-collar workers was 4,000 Ft. According to the report there were only twenty-five to thirty workers in the enterprise who earned more than their superiors with overtime and working on Sundays.[44]

Counting with these wages the foremen earned 30 per cent more and the managers 60 per cent more than the blue-collar workers. The material recognition of the foremen, which 'the party and the government rendered a central question in 1970',[45] was therefore realized in the Wagon Factory. Other enterprises were in a less fortunate situation. In light industry, for instance, the basic wage of direct production managers was 4,800–5,000 Ft in 1984. One member of the executive committee of the county argued that blue-collar workers could earn the same money and therefore it was difficult to find managers.[46]

The manager's attempt to introduce a performance-based wage system in Rába evidently formed the consciousness of the employees. The representative of MVG in the executive committee, for instance, challenged a manager, who had boasted that the members of the VGMK in his factory

Table 2.3 Managerial wages in selected workshops of MVG (Ft) in 1979

Factory	Workers (No)	Direct production managers (No)	Factory managers (No)	Direct production managers/ workers	Wage of foremen	Wage of managers
Foundry	1,214	52	10	23	5,418	6,270
Auto	409	11	4	33	5,000	6,220
Gear	993	29	7	34	5,317	6,571
Forge-shop	473	20	5	24	5,215	6,220
Iron structure	578	20	5	29	5,305	6,340
Wagon	644	26	4	25	5,160	6,275
Motor	1,191	31	8	38	5,230	6,300
Vehicle	227	5	3	45	5,900	5,900

Source: GYML, X. 415/200/3, A közvetlen termelésirányítók helyzete, politikai-szakmai felkészültségük értékelése – az emberi kapcsolatokra gyakorolt hatásuk.

finished a weekly job in one weekend, with the question of what his employees had been doing during the week.[47] Stagnant real incomes, however, reinforced the voices of discontent. Even though in 1986 Horváth was made an honorary citizen of Győr and elected the man of the year, his titles did not compensate the Rába workers for the material recognition. Rába was presented in the national media as one of the most successful modern enterprises, which produced much revenue in Western currency for the country, but the workers thought that they profited little from this revenue.[48] In fact, when economic reform was placed again on the agenda, and the reform communist wing of the party started to leak information about the poor economic performance of the country in the second half of the 1980s, Rába workers believed that they were the losers of national economic policy:

> At the meeting of the commercial chamber, comrade Havasi spoke of the difficult economic situation that everybody knows. He explained why it is so difficult to realize the 3 per cent production growth. According to our employees Rába always produced more for the people's economy. If this is not the case in many other factories, the ones who have good results rightfully expect the government to intervene on their side. It is untenable that there are enterprises (and not so few), which produce losses[49] and they receive various favours (flexible working hours, VGMK, etc.). At the same time, the employ-

ees of factories like the Wagon Factory, where there is a strict economic order
and strong discipline, are at a disadvantage.[50]

The workers in the Industrial Tool Factory thought that the economic reg-
ulators had a contradictory effect because they indeed punished those who
worked well.[51] Many employees went as far as to relate the poor economic
performance of the country to the unfair redistribution of state revenues:

> The interview with the manager of our enterprise in *Népszabadság* had a very
> good reception. The employees fully agree with the statement that it is time to
> give more opportunities for the prospering enterprises because the capital in-
> vested in them produces greater profit. It cannot be in the interest of the people's
> economy to support the loss-making enterprises at the expense of the profitable
> ones. It is bad news for the employees who work decently that the various regula-
> tors will again prevent the recognition of the high achievements. The conference
> of the labour management stressed that the reward should be proportionate to
> the achievement. This is exactly the opinion of our employees, too.[52]

The consumption-oriented policy that Hungary's welfare dictatorship encouraged had, therefore, contradictory results. It successfully integrated
the working class into the system and in the mid-1970s, when the government could spend the most on the increase of the consumption levels
of the population, the surveys of the Research Center for Public Opinion
Poll of the Hungarian Radio and Television showed Kádár to be a very
popular leader – and we have to stress that the Hungarian political climate
was much less oppressive at the time than Honecker's dictatorship, so the
results of the surveys were more reliable.

The basis of this legitimacy was, however, essentially fragile. Even the
cited survey of 1976 revealed that the standard-of-living policy failed to satisfy people to the desired level as to convince them of the superiority of socialism, even when there was an effective increase in real wages. According
to national statistics the real wage increase was the greatest in 1970–75; in
the second half of the 1970s the real wages still increased but at a lower rate
because of the rapidly increasing prices.[53] Throughout the 1980s real wages
stagnated, and in 1988 they actually fell. But even in 1976 when the survey
was conducted, the majority of people achieved a higher standard of living
with more work, because the pay increase alone did not guarantee the desired level of consumption. Even this survey showed that the standard-of-
living policy was not the best political slogan; the actual counter-effect became manifest in the 1980s when people became more discontented with
their economic situation. In the 1970s the slogan that the oil crisis would
not creep into the socialist countries was much repeated; it did not improve
the credibility of the government when it still did. The quotations reveal

the process of how the political climate has been 'darkened' for the regime, what the manager also tried to explain in the quoted interview of the summer of 1989.[54] People regarded the financial restrictions that were necessitated by the economic situation of the country as unjust since they had not worked less than before. The warning of the reformer economists came true;[55] people thought that the government 'determined' the standard of living, and so when they started to live worse, their anger understandably turned against the political regime which had deceived them.

Working-Class Culture and Education

The revitalization of the educational project in the 1970s was supposed to benefit the working class as well as to render the cause of socialism attractive in the eyes of the people. The project sought to shape people's consciousness in two ways: first, by increasing the general level of education, and second, by providing for the cultivated entertainment of the people thereby increasing the level of general knowledge. The popularization of 'high culture' (theatre, concerts, ballet, art movies) was meant to demonstrate that workers were fully integrated into the socialist middle class.[56] At the same time the project carried the propagandistic message that intellectual values were more important than material ones, which was, unfortunately, contradicted by the social experience. There is also evidence from the interviews that although workers did participate in an intensive community life, people gave little credit to the socialist cultural propaganda, which advocated the superiority of intellectual values. The survey of 1976 shows that this was true also for part of the intelligentsia.

Increased educational performance on an individual level, of course, enhanced a person's employment prospects; evening courses were in fact offered in order to train working-class managers.[57] Education was important for ensuring their professional competence, which the county secretary formulated in a rather clumsy way:

> The other thing is the training of working-class managers. The resolution of the Central Committee attaches great significance to this. But there are excesses in the leadership. I have heard such opinions from some workplaces and enterprises that their workers will fill every leading position. Then why do we need to train ten thousand university graduates? We should not generalize but we always have to consider the concrete situation: if a worker is suitable for the job, we will choose him. But if we make a wrong choice and the new manager cannot bear the burden, we will put him in a very unpleasant situation. He has to go back to the shop floor and the workers will tease him and make fun of him. If we increase the number of working-class managers only statistically, we may discredit this noble political goal.[58]

Adult education was indeed supposed to strengthen political loyalty: selection to institutions of higher education depended on the recommendation of the party. With the increasing number of young university graduates, the importance of evening universities in individual mobility did,
however, decline.[59]

In the light of statistics there was also enough room for improvement
at the lower level of education, which the project strongly promoted. In
1974, about 37,000 skilled workers finished primary school or even had
secondary or other further education, but nearly 11,000 skilled workers
did not have basic education (the compulsory eight classes of primary
school). Between 1968 and 1973 there were 5,200 people who attended a primary school for adults (90 per cent were blue-collar workers);
and 8,500 trainees were admitted to the training schools of the county
in a year.[60] This working class was mainly of working-class origin itself;
80 per cent of the trainees came from working-class families.[61] The report noted that the proportion of students from working-class families
was very low in medical and language faculties at university.[62] The enterprises supported the education of their employees in economics and
engineering. Working-class children therefore had more chance of gain-
ing access to the technical intelligentsia, rather than to more traditional
intellectual occupations.

Another report from 1974 likewise painted a gloomy picture of the
state of public education. It was estimated that 40 per cent of the semi-
skilled workers and around two-thirds of the unskilled workers (33,000
people) in the county did not finish primary school. In the machine industry 25 per cent of the workforce did not have basic education. The
report noted that 24 per cent of the workers in the county commuted,
and travelling consumed much of the free time that they could have spent
cultivating their mind. It critically remarked that many social organizations neglected the cause of culture: 'The enterprises do not always support adequately the local cultural institutions, which could offer a basis
for the strengthening of the workers' collective and community life, and
the comprehensive development of workers' education.' Within the enterprises, the report stated, the socialist brigade movement provided an
organizational basis for workers' education. There were 2,585 socialist
brigades in the county, with around 32, 000 brigade members. The report, however, criticized the 'over-formality and often mechanic administration in the cultural initiatives of the brigades'. The general cultural
level of the population also received critical comments: 'We experienced
striking deficiencies in the economic, pedagogic and linguistic competence of the population; their development is essential for the further
expansion of enterprise democracy.'

The intellectual critics, however, contradicted themselves or they had too high expectations. The following data that they listed namely does not support the above negative picture: it was estimated that 25 per cent of the population regularly read books while around 40–45 per cent was reported to rarely read. The proportion of theatre audiences containing blue-collar workers was higher, and 10 per cent of workers regularly listened to classical music. 'Municipalities started organizing concerts but they suffer from a lack of experience. One major obstacle to popularizing classical music is that there are not enough town halls in our county – including Győr – that are suitable for concerts.' The report noted that even though fine arts improved, 'the decoration of the public squares left much to be desired'. The movement of amateur filmmakers 'was developed on a narrow basis but it was noticed nationally'. In 1972 there were 434 amateur artistic groups in the county, with 8,572 members; 6,000 of them were below thirty, which shows that it was primarily a youth-based movement. In 1973, the county had 90,315 television subscribers.[63]

Thanks to the massively propagated cultural programme,[64] there remains considerable information on the education of the Rába employees in Győr. In 1972 it was reported that out of the 17,000 employees of the MVG, 5,500 (32.3 per cent) did not have elementary education. Even the report noted that 'this number was strikingly high'.[65] Over the following five years this percentage decreased to a quarter of the total workforce (24.7 per cent). The educational statistics of the employees according to age group showed the general improvement of education (see Table 2.4).

The education of blue-collar workers was characterized by a similar generational pattern: the overwhelming majority of the workers without basic education were over thirty and there were many more workers in the age group below thirty who finished secondary school than in the age group over thirty. The educational difference between the older and younger generations was also considered in the appointment of managers: even though foremen had to have a high school certificate, it was noted that one could not expect this from older workers.[66] At the same time the acquisition of a college or university degree almost automatically meant promotion for the skilled workers: this is supported by the fact that amongst the blue-collar workers there were only fifteen college graduates (all of them in the age group below thirty).[67]

The MVG directly supported the education of young people. It supported its own training school and the trainees were employed in the enterprise during their training time. Between 1972 and 1976 the school admitted 350 children in a year on average, and around 75 per cent of the young skilled workers chose to stay with the enterprise. The choice was also motivated by the so-called social scholarships that the enterprise

Table 2.4 Education of workers according to their ages in MVG in 1977 (%)

Age Education	Under 20	20–30	30–50	Above 50	Total
University or College	–	6.6	3.4	2.7	3.9
High School	18. 5	27.7	17.1	14	20
Primary School	75	60.4	46.3	27. 5	51.4
Unfinished Primary School	6.5	5.3	33.2	55.8	24.7
Total	100	100	100	100	100

Source: GYML, X. 415/195/3, Jelentés a munkásmu″velo″dés tapasztalatairól, helyzetéro″l és szerepéro″l, fejlesztésének feladatairól a Magyar Vagon-és Gépgyárban, MVG összes dolgozójának iskolai végzettség szerinti megoszlása korcsoportonként.

offered to the trainees: they received a regular financial support during their three-year vocational training and they had to commit themselves to working in the enterprise for an equal period of time.[68] This type of scholarship was also offered to university and college students.[69] The enterprise evidently increased its support for training and education: in 1976 there were one hundred more trainees who received support than in 1972. While in 1972 the MVG spent 689,700 Ft on social scholarships, in 1976 it spent more than double, 1,751,000 Ft.[70]

Adult education, which was specifically targeted at the working class, likewise received support in the period. This was not limited to higher education; given the high number of employees without basic education, they were encouraged to finish primary school or do vocational training. The party organization of the factory listed two main problems in this respect: the first was that it was difficult to convince older people to study (and the majority of people without basic education belonged to the older generations) and the second was the problem of commuters. The party organization contacted the local village schools but only two of them answered declaring that they could not start the workers' primary school because people refused to go back to school.[71] The enterprise offered financial incentives, too: basic education was a prerequisite of vocational training within the enterprise, and those who received the skilled worker certificate received a pay increase of 10 per cent.[72] The attendance

Table 2.5 Education and qualification of blue-collar workers according to their age and gender in MVG in 1977 (person)

Education	Age	Skilled		Semi-skilled		Unskilled		Total	
		Men	Women	Men	Women	Men	Women	Men	Women
College	Under 30	15	–	–	–	–	–	15	–
	Above 30	–	–	–	–	–	–	–	–
High School	Under 30	754	56	78	102	5	1	837	159
	Above 30	444	22	57	25	6	2	509	49
Primary School	Under 30	2,633	96	824	479	166	150	3,623	725
	Above 30	2,539	88	946	778	99	201	3,584	1,067
Unfinished Primary School	Under 30	13	2	147	29	116	55	276	86
	Above 30	1,158	55	1,353	619	335	435	2,846	1,109

Source: GYML, X. 415/195/3, Jelentés a munkásmu"velo"dés tapasztalatairól, helyzetéro"l és szerepéro"l, fejlesztésének feladatairól a Magyar Vagon-és Gépgyárban, Fizikai dolgozók iskolai végzettsége.

of secondary school and university degree programmes was supported with paid study leave. Many socialist brigades committed themselves to increasing the education of the members, which aimed to strengthen the individual motivation. According to the report the interest of the employees in adult education was satisfactory, which can be supported with statistical data. Between 1972 and 1976, adult education in MVG had 3,999 participants: 387 men and 175 women finished primary school, 1,524 men and 741 women finished secondary school and 1,010 men and 162 women attended university or college courses.[73]

While much had been done to mobilize the collective for the educational project, there were also administrative means to enhance the participation. In December 1976 an educational committee was formed in the party organization of MVG to promote education and culture among the employees.[74] Whether it can be explained through the generally improving education or the support of the enterprise or both, statistics continued to improve throughout the 1970s (see Table 2.6).

Table 2.6 Development of the education of the workforce of Rába MVG (%)

	1975	1979
University or College	3.4	6.1
High School	18	23. 6
Primary School	54.6	52
Unfinished Primary School	24	18.3

GYML, X. 415/200/3, A közmu″velo″dés helyzete. Az MVG végrehajtó bizottságának jelentése az 1975-ös pártértekezlet után, 12, 1979. december 11.

The percentage of highly qualified workers increased. In 1979, 23 per cent of the employees were white-collar and 77 per cent were blue-collar workers; 25.2 per cent of the workforce were aged below thirty and 24.2 per cent were women.[75] Between 1975 and 1979 a total of 1,961 employees participated in technical training programmes, 410 skilled workers obtained further qualifications and 334 semi-skilled workers received the skilled worker certificate. Within the framework of production development, eleven courses were organized with 360 participants. In one year, thirty to forty university students received scholarships from the enterprise who then committed themselves to working in Rába MVG after graduation.[76]

Despite the improving statistics, even the reports admitted that there were two specific types of educational inequality that adult education could hardly reduce. The first was the education of the commuters. The commuters were less likely to participate in adult education than Győr residents because they had less free time and they depended on the public transport timetables:

> The ratio of the commuters is rather low in adult education. The reason is that they cannot reconcile the afternoon classes in the workers' primary school or secondary school with the schedule of public transport. Their trains and buses depart around 5 pm and if the commuters miss their buses and trains, they have to wait for the end of the afternoon shift. [77]

This inequality was also reflected in the statistics. Even though 39 per cent of the employees in Győr were commuters, in the 1978/79 academic year, of 25 Győr residents (90 per cent) and only 3 commuters

(10 per cent) obtained a university degree during work. In the same year 26 urban workers (90 per cent) and 3 commuters (10 per cent) obtained a degree from the workers' university. In the same year, 57 local residents (70 per cent) and 24 commuters (30 per cent) finished secondary school, and 12 Győr residents (70 per cent) and 5 commuters (30 per cent) finished workers' primary school. The low ratio of the commuters among the university graduates shows that they had fewer opportunities in the enterprise than the local residents. The training courses that were held in the enterprise more successfully engaged the commuters because they were adjusted to the schedule of their trains and buses, and 50 per cent of the participants in these courses were commuters.[78] A certain bias against the commuters, which was reflected in the worker–peasant conflict, persisted in the party organization of MVG. Commuters were allegedly interested in cultivating their plots rather than their minds: 'The agricultural activity of the commuters is a serious obstacle to their professional development. Husbandry, gardening and farming consume much of their time on a regular basis, which renders any intellectual activity impossible after work in the factory.'[79] Among the young skilled workers there was an equal proportion of local residents and commuters: in 1978, 56 commuters (59.6 per cent) and 38 local residents (40.4 per cent) started working in MVG, while in in the following year 39 commuters (55 per cent) and 32 Győr residents (45 per cent) took up work in the enterprise. The report, however, noted that in reality a much higher number of trainees came from the villages but they returned home after they finished training.[80]

The second specific problem was that of gender inequality. The educational statistics of MVG show that the education of women workers was in general lower than that of men. In 1977, there were 38 per cent of women workers who did not finish primary school, 56 per cent had only elementary education, and 6 per cent finished secondary school. At the same time, 29 per cent of male workers did not finish primary school, 59 per cent had basic education, 11.8 per cent finished secondary school and 8.2 per cent had a college or university degree. Within the group of skilled workers, the proportion of women who had a high school certificate was higher: 25.6 per cent of skilled women workers finished secondary school while this proportion was 16 per cent among the skilled men workers. The educational inequality between men and women could be clearly demonstrated in their participation in higher education: 8.5 per cent of the skilled men workers and 8.1 per cent of the semi-skilled men workers had a college or university degree, while the highest education of women workers was secondary school. The educational statistics of the total workforce of MVG reflected the same inequality: while 1.9 per cent of the women had a college or university degree, this ratio was more than double (4.6 per cent) among the men. At the enterprise level, the educational statistics were more balanced in the lower educational categories because the white-collar workers improved the statistics of women: 26 per cent of the women did not finish primary school, 52.1 per cent had basic education, and 28 per cent had a high school certificate, while 24.2 per cent of the men did not did not finish primary school, 52.1 per cent had basic education and 28 per cent had a high school certificate.[81] Adult education maintained a certain inequality at the university level: even though one-quarter of the employees were women, only 16 per cent studied in college or university during work between 1972 and 1976 (the ratio at the high school level was better because half of the adult students were women).[82] Since higher management was recruited from the university graduates, the lower ratio of women who finished college or university also meant lower career chances in the enterprise.

While statistics can tell us something of the improvement of education, they can hardly be used to describe the cultural life of the factory. Since no survey survived among the employees, apart from the later memoirs, one can only rely on a rather general report, which summarized some basic facts. In Rába (like in any other state-owned enterprise) the socialist brigades were regarded as the main basis of the cultural initiatives and undertakings.[83] The members of the brigade committed themselves to studying, obtaining a higher degree and participating in cultural events (attending theatre, concerts, artistic films, visiting museums, etc.); these cultural offerings counted towards the ranking of the brigades.[84] Whether it was motivated by genuine interest or the administrative measures, the number of regular theatregoers increased: 435 season tickets were sold in the enterprise in 1976, while in 1977 this increased to 585. The report noted that the enterprise established regular contacts with the artists of Kisfaludy theatre,[85] which helped to popularize the theatre among employees.[86] Three artistic groups functioned within the framework of the enterprise: a choir, a brass band and a dance group. In 1976, more than thirty thousand people saw the programmes of these groups. The workers' concerts were also reported to have had a positive reception.[87]

The most successful form of propagating general knowledge were the popular scientific lectures; not surprisingly, primarily the technical and economic subjects attracted employees, with 2,600–2,800 attending the lectures in eighty sections in a year. On 1 March 1977 a TIT-group (Tudományos Ismeretterjesztő Társulat = Scientific Association for the Propagation of General Knowledge) was formed in the enterprise, with twenty-two members.[88] The enterprise had a well-equipped technical and a trade union library (see Table 2.7).

Table 2.7 Main features of the libraries of MVG

	Trade union library	Technical library
Members No.	6,537	2,675
Brigade members No.	3,209	889
Visitors No.	52,323	12,676
Borrowed copies	160,690	29,487
Library stock	66,000	47,395

Source: GYML, X. 415/195/3, Jelentés a munkásmu″velo″dés tapasztalatairól, helyzetéro″l és szerepéro″l, fejlesztésének feladatairól a Magyar Vagon-és Gépgyárban, MVG könyvtárainak fo″bb jellemzo″i.

Nearly 40 per cent of the Rába employees were library members and the majority of them regularly attended the library. The members borrowed ten books in a year on average.[89] The libraries organized writer–reader meetings, which were attended by around six hundred employees in a year.[90] The larger cultural events took place in Ady Endre Community House, which hosted the various clubs, artistic groups and hobby groups. The report noted that the enterprise requested a new building for the organization of cultural programmes.[91]

In the light of the later memoirs the picture is more mixed. Many interviewers reported of positive experiences concerning community-building, where the members of the brigade did indeed support each other and the common cultural undertaking was regarded as real entertainment and not one more task that had to be fulfilled.[92] It was, however, admitted that not everybody was enthusiastic about the common cultural undertaking; even a contemporary report recognized that after one day of hard work, many people were happy to go home and spend time with their families rather than attend high cultural events. Despite the good intention of the party, the administrative measures were likely to have the opposite effect: in the eyes of many, the fulfilment of the cultural tasks was regarded as a constraint. Workers' education admittedly sought to increase the political consciousness of the people; it seems, however, that it missed its political goal. Even those who had positive experiences of brigade life stressed the loss of the community, while dismissing communist propaganda. Many pointed out that the members who failed to attend the events were also 'recorded' in the diary of the brigade, which reveals that (self-)deception had become part of the functioning of the system.

The revival of important elements of the old social democratic programme (support of working-class housing, culture, education and com-

munity-building) can be observed also in Honecker's GDR. The problem
with this project was not its content but rather the fact that the party was
unable to modernize its political and social programme. As we will see,
the shortage of flats and building materials remained a frequent source
of complaint in the GDR; facing competition with West Germany, it was
difficult to convince the working class of the superiority of socialism. The
support of working class culture and education was undoubtedly a positive socialist initiative; however, there is evidence from both countries
that educational mobility declined from the 1970s. The gap between ideology and social reality, should not, however, discredit the programme of
the support of working-class culture and education. Even though Rába
was a 'privileged' socialist factory, it did not have a homogenous working
class. Workers had different cultural needs: even if the whole brigade did
not attend the cultural events that they recorded, many could still participate in an 'affordable' cultural experience. There were brigades where
the community indeed gave motivation for people to study or learn lan-
guages. The party's effort to raise the education level of people should be
evaluated in the light of Hungarian statistics, which showed the relative
backwardness of the country in comparison to East Germany. The educational project of the party clearly improved the statistics of Rába MVG:
it decreased the percentage of people who did not finish primary school,
and enabled ambitious workers to obtain college or university degrees.
Those who had higher education were quickly promoted to white-collar
or managerial jobs. Both East German and Hungarian interviewees reported of such working-class careers.

Working-Class Housing and Commuting

The two most important fringe benefits were the support of housing and
public transport. With respect to the first, it is clear that Rába had far fewer flats to offer to the employees than the Zeiss enterprise, which could
distribute whole blocks of flats as a result of the state housing programme.
There is no survey of the housing conditions of the Rába employees but
there is indirect evidence that the housing conditions of at least the skilled
core of the working class corresponded to the standards of the socialist
middle class. The quoted survey of the evaluation of the standard of living among the membership of the machine-manufacturing enterprises in
the county involved 471 Rába workers (nearly half of the respondents).
The survey found that people had settled living conditions: the majority
of the respondents lived in their own houses or flats.[93] The high number
of commuters (39 per cent in the Győr factories) also improved living
conditions because building was cheaper in the villages:[94] it was often the

parents who gave the building plots, and young people could rely on the help of relatives and friends.[95]

The enterprise offered two specific types of help to employees. They could get tenancy in one of the flats that belonged to the enterprise; it was, however, a very limited opportunity because Rába only had ninety-three flats in Győr. Between 1971 and 1977, ten blue-collar and twenty-three white-collar workers could move to these flats.[96] The occupants were usually life tenants: in 1979, eighteen of the tenants of the enterprise flats no longer worked in the enterprise.[97] The second, more widespread form of support was the enterprise loan that Rába offered employees at preferential rates to buy flats. The support was not unconditional because the recipients had to sign a contract with the enterprise and agree to work there for a determined period of time.[98] Between 1970 and 1979, there were 1,093 employees who put in a claim for a flat, out of which the problems of 601 employees (392 blue-collar and 209 white-collar workers) were solved. In all, 447 people received a total of 22,465,000 Ft from the development funds and 170 employees received 2,122,000 Ft from the solidarity funds.[99] Between 1971 and 1977, no fewer than 148 blue-collar and 101 white-collar workers received enterprise loans to buy OTP-flats, and 131 blue-collar workers received support for housing cooperatives.[100]

The enterprise launched one workers' housing project in cooperation with the state construction company of Ipar street (Ipar=industry) in 1976. The project solved the flat problems of 120 people.[101] In the following years the enterprise had to rely on the city council for the provision of flats, which could help substantially fewer people a year. In 1979, for instance, the council offered only fourteen flats to the Rába employees.[102] A report of the flat committee of the enterprise did, however, stress that the employees had not experienced the 'severe flat problem that has become so fashionable today': between 1970 and 1979 the enterprise solved every second flat claim, and there was no flat claim put in for more than three to four years.[103]

Other criticisms emerged in the 1980s, which were mainly targeted at the unequal chances of young people to acquire the desired flats. Even a report on the social situation of youth in the county admitted that the social background increasingly mattered in the establishment of an independent household:

> The chance of youth to buy a flat is not uniformly negatively evaluated. We can summarize the opinions in the following ways: the young people in the big cities, who live from their wages, and whose parents have similar material circumstances – namely, they cannot count on the help of their parents and they have no extra income – are in the most difficult situation. The small towns give a better chance to youth: people can usually get flats in two to five years

(e.g. in Csorna). In the villages the cheaper ground plots, the extra income from farming, and friends' help improve the chances of youth to get settled.[104]

The party organization of MVG reported that the extra work to establish their own home was occupying working-class youth too much, and they often did not have time or energy for the social and party activities.[105] With the 'creeping in of the oil crisis' – as it was called – the government increased the price of petrol and utilities. The increase of the rents of the state flats found a particularly negative response among the population because the cheap housing was one propaganda slogan of the party:

> Out of the planned measures the increase of the state rents triggered loud debates among the employees. The responses, of course, depended on the involvement of people. Those who live in state flats are angry while some others would say that 'one has to pay the price of every service'. Many people think that the state flat is an achievement of the socialist society. We often used the cheap rents as an argument against the higher incomes in the capitalist countries.[106]

In 1984, workers said that a flat cost ten to fifteen times more than their annual income.[107] The problem was brought up in the information report of MVG in October 1985:

> The flat issue is the most important problem of today's youth. The topic came up in the preparation for the Thirteenth Party Congress but since then there has been no progress. On the contrary, the flat prices have increased. The great burden of saving for a flat deprives this age group of healthy education and entertainment.[108]

The flat problem was often used to explain the political indifference of youth: a report from the Mosonmagyaróvár plant, for instance, related the low level of interest of working-class youth in the communist organizations to the lack of material prospects.[109] Young people may not have seen as much future for themselves as their parents' generation did when they were young.

Interestingly, reports on the state of public transport allow for a similar line of argumentation. On the one hand, the enterprise did indeed give generous support for the public transport of the employees; on the other hand, informants reported an increasing discontent with the conditions of travelling as if it had expressed the bad political mood of the people for the regime. (Public transport constituted a separate topic of the information reports.) The overwhelming majority of the employees travelled by public transport, on trains or buses, to their workplaces, or they cycled.[110] From 1968 the employees could buy seasonal rail, bus or combined tickets at a discount in the enterprise (a combined ticket was valid for both the bus and the train). The percentage of reimbursement was higher for rail because the state covered 20 per cent of the fare, the enterprise covered 66 per cent and the employee had to pay only 14 per cent, while there was no state support for bus travel. The enterprise paid 40–60 per cent of the bus fares of an employee, depending on the distance.[111]

The travel allowance was, apparently, significant. In 1980, the enterprise supported the rail fares of 2,595 employees, the bus fares of 2,108 employees, and the combined tickets of 365 Rába workers.[112] This in practice meant that the support covered a significant part of the fares. The employees who travelled by train paid only 10 per cent of the fares (the enterprise paid a total of 523,932 Ft, while the employees paid 54,732 Ft) and those who travelled by bus paid around 50 per cent (the enterprise paid a total of 290,880 Ft, and the employees paid 324,811 Ft). Commuters comprised 39 per cent of the employees of the Győr plants. In 1979 the enterprise had twelve buses to solve the transport of the employees to the airport plant,[113] which employed 3,440 people (30 per cent of the total workforce in Győr). In the same year the enterprise ordered eight new buses to provide for the comfortable transportation of the employees.[114] According to the report, the same could not be said of the railway transport. There were many complaints that the workers' trains were overcrowded and dirty, and the carriages were old and damaged. Many wagons had no or poor heating and the windows could not be closed properly. The management complained that there were frequent delays in winter. In 1980, first quarter, 1,591 employees started work one hour late, causing a production loss of 810,000 Ft to the enterprise.[115]

The conditions of city transport may well have been poor throughout the period; criticism, however, became abundant in the 1980s. Information reports frequently addressed the problem of overcrowding as a source of everyday anger: 'It is not the first time that we criticize the poor standard of public transport from Adyváros to the airport plant. Why can't Volán[116] take into consideration that more people travel by bus in winter and increase the number of lines?' The informant added that 'people expect human travelling conditions for their money'.[117] After two years we can read the same criticism: 'Line 20[118] is extremely overcrowded in the morning hours. People complain that it is impossible to get on the bus at the Verseny ABC bus stop.[119] With the coming of the winter, this over-crowdedness can become intolerable.'[120]

One angry informant did indeed write a long report on the state of public transport, which reveals the general increase of frustration:

Civilized public transport has been neglected on 80 per cent of the bus lines for years. We don't speak of comfortable travelling because it is only a wish. But we would like to achieve tolerable conditions on the morning and afternoon workers' routes. Volán allegedly solved public transport between Ménfőcsanak and Győr, but all they did was to provide long-distance buses, which arrive so over-crowded in Csanak that people can't get on them. The passengers of the buses who pay 400–500 Ft for a season ticket also have a reason to be angry with the Csanak people who occupy their places when they go home from work. But what can they do if they only want to travel to Csanak, and they have no other option than to trample on the others and swallow their scolding and grumbling? This creates a very bad mood for work or the 'second shift' at home. It would be good if a town route was indeed a town route and not a compressed passenger carrier equipped with a town number! It is characteristic that in an interview with the managers of the Volán in Debrecen and Győr, the former said that they plan to buy new buses, while the Győr manager reassured his audience that they would solve the problem with a 'better organization' of city transport. Ever since then nothing has changed, only the passengers' anger has been mounting.[121]

This kind of irony manifested itself in other information reports. The forge shop ordered soda machines in the summer in order to provide the employees with cold drinks. The machines did indeed arrive but they remained in their packaging for a year. 'There was presumably a shortage of carbonic acid', an informant commented on the case with understandable irony.[122] Canteen food was another frequent source of ridicule:[123]

On Good Friday they probably fried stale meat because it tasted like the old leather shoe sole. In the canteen people wondered whether it was necessary to hurt the feelings of religious people by serving a meat dish. But during the meal it turned out that they hurt those who did not refrain from consuming meat on that day (although it turned bitter in the mouths of many people).'[124]

Another informant proposed that the kitchen drop the 'Győr' small roast from the menu because 'it destroys the reputation of the town'.[125] The canteen jokes sometimes had a political connotation similar to the comment on the shortage of carbonic acid – for instance, the observation that the 'overcooked pasta and tasteless meals cannot be explained through the increase in prices. These mistakes can be explained through the incompetence of the cooks'.[126]

The critical comments support the experience that Burawoy had among the furnacemen of the Lenin Steel Works.[127] People realized the gap between the promises and the actual results of the system, which no longer could consol them with a distant 'bright future' as had been done during the period of forced industrialization. In the light of the unprecedented scale of social mobility in postwar Hungary, the political and so-cial emancipation of the working class and peasantry that the Communist Party advocated could indeed be attractive catchwords in the 1950s and 1960s. However, as the information reports of the 1980s show, workers no longer believed that the regime could offer them a 'bright future': they openly made fun of the socialist propaganda and all of its prom-ises. Since informants were members of the party (and often low-level party functionaries), this criticism revealed that loyalty to the system had started to crumble.

'Community life was very different back then': The Socialist Brigade Movement

The role of socialist brigades is often misunderstood in the literature: they are linked with the Stakhanovite movement, which was primarily aimed at increasing production. There was a socialist work contest also between the brigades. In principle, the members of the brigades commit-ted themselves to accomplishing extra tasks in production and education. The accomplishment of the tasks was then evaluated and the best brigades received moral and material recognition (the title of excellent brigade, premium, etc.). The movement admittedly sought to increase competi-tion but at the same time it was aimed at community-building because so-cialist brigades were supposed to be the main basis of workers' education and culture. Members of the brigades were expected to meet regularly and to organize common programmes in order to keep their commit-ments. These programmes were recorded in the diary of the brigade.[128]

The surviving contemporary sources of brigade work in Rába tell us indeed little of what role the brigades actually played in the lives of workers.[129] In 1975 the Wagon Factory won 'the wandering red flag of Work', and it was given the title of 'Outstanding Enterprise'.[130] The avail-able party documents of MVG, however, suggest that the management had an ambivalent relationship with the brigade movement, particularly when the workers attempted to intervene in production decisions that the managers regarded as their own authority. The former Stakhanovite, Ede Horváth, was not very enthusiastic about production campaigns. At a meeting of the executive committee of Rába MVG he openly expressed his disapproval in front of the party leadership: 'Comrades, you have to compete on the sports field!' We should not, of course, forget that Hor-váth was a member of the Central Committee; the party secretary of the factory dared not contradict him publicly.

The management's ambivalent relationship with the brigade move-ment supports the argument that the brigades were first and foremost 'support groups', which offered space for social life and private contacts rather than production teams. We can even document conflicts between the brigadiers and the managers. Brigadiers often openly charged the management with hindering brigade work:

> As a former brigadier, I can tell that a collective can work even without special warning. Our brigade was formed nine years ago; since then sixteen people finished secondary school or college, almost everybody has his own library, and we made excursions across the country. The members of our brigade did not spend the premium on feasts but they used the money more reasonably. They knew each other's family problems. The former speaker brought up the issue of the contact with the management. We met the managers only if the task was very urgent. There was no regular contact. There was simply no opportunity to discuss the problems of the movement with the higher bodies. We could not speak about the problems that we had in production. It angered the management that we informed them of the problems in their field. We received answers that we are not competent in this, it is not our business. Or another case: there was a manager who declared in the evaluation form that there was no socialist brigade in his field.[131]

In a base-cell meeting a brigadier reported of a similar conflict with the management over the issue of authority:

> I do agree with the report and also with the refusal to evaluate the work of the party groups. In the axle and bridge production line political work is totally ignored at the level of the factory. I base this on the fact that one year after the formation of our brigade we had a meeting where they said that there is no brigade work even though I attended every brigade meeting. Then I resigned from my post because it was a great thing that we could form this brigade at all. The reasons why our brigade work was not better lie in the management and the trade union because it did not care about us. ... In my view, every worker has his own problem but he would not speak of it because it won't be solved anyway. I also had a tool problem; I was promised to get one and I did not get any. Why should we tell about our problems if they won't be solved anyway?[132]

The main tasks of socialist brigades triggered debates in the executive committee of the party organization of MVG. One speaker openly expressed his doubts about the comparability of brigades (and thus, about the validity of impressive statistics):

> As for me, I cannot agree with the following. The report states that there is excellent brigade work in some fields. I would like to examine this question. It is not easy to compare the work of a white-collar worker with that of a blue-

collar worker and similarly, it is disputable what we call excellent brigade work. We often have problems – when they request our figures, we declare that the organization of the socialist work contest is 55 per cent in our enterprise. What do the other 45 per cent do? If we compare individual work, we may find that many of those, who are not organized in brigades, also work well, or even better. Their work equally counts towards our results.[133]

Another speaker proposed that the brigades, whose members perform hard physical work, should be given a more lenient evaluation:

I think what we see here is only a search for solutions. They can't decide what the brigades should do. There are many documentaries of brigade life on TV. There is nothing in the films that we have not done. Or do we maybe set too high standards? We have to admit that it is difficult to realize the socialist work contest in our enterprise. We have to use different aspects of evaluation. There are brigades that keep a regular record of the fulfilled tasks – theatre, borrowing from the library – and there are others where people finish work and they are happy to go home to have a rest. They don't have time for the common meetings. We should understand that.[134]

Despite the positive figures of the socialist work contest, even the surviving sources suggest that brigade life was more important for community-building than for production.[135] In life-history interviews many former brigade members reported having participated in an intensive community life – an argument, which was also developed in the cited accounts of former brigadiers. The common leisure and sometimes even family programmes strengthened social contacts among colleagues, thus reinforcing cohesion and solidarity. Interview partners also reported of cases when these supportive social networks helped them (or others) through private hardships.

It was much better with the socialist brigades, we all knew each other. At that time they said that we have to pay attention to the others. On paper. But people also wanted to pay attention to the others. Because I remember that we went to see the babies of the colleagues, we went to the cinema, and what you can imagine, everywhere. To concerts ... and the community was at that time more united, we went to bowl, to play football; at that time we always went somewhere. Not because people undertook the tasks on paper. Ridiculous. But because they had a nice time together. And there were very few who wanted to be left out of this company.[136]

Many interview partners directly contrasted the old times, when communities at the workplace had been more important to the people, with the experience of the new, capitalist regime:

At that time it was possible to establish better communities in a workplace than today. I can say this as a brigadier. I invited them to this anglers' camp[137] a couple of times in a year. When the first was successful, they were likely to come again. They had an opportunity to get to know each other, and they were also interested in it. Now the same company – okay, not the same because three or four had already retired, but there are new people – so, ten years ago sixty to sixty-five came because many brought their families, too – last time it was only twenty-two. One has no time, the other is tired – only one had a really serious excuse, even though he still came in the afternoon. It is no longer fashionable today; perhaps people don't want to go to company because of their individual problems. But this also holds for our house. Eighty flats. When we moved in, I visited at least thirty-five flats on New Years' Eve. But people also came to us, we went from flat to flat together, we had a great time.[138]

The decline of community life was addressed in many other life-history interviews. People generally agreed that society had become more individualistic:

> That old community spirit, that brigade spirit that I represented, too – since I was the brigadier in this group – so it was possible to regularly bring together people; I invited them or we went to a restaurant, and we had a good chat. We don't have this today, people don't have time, even though we are not that many, everybody runs home after work, has other business.[139]

While many interview partners recalled community life with a sense of loss, brigades were not linked with communist ideology in the eyes of people. As one interview partner formulated, people had a nice time together and they cared little about the ideology. Other interview partners consciously distanced themselves from the propaganda of the regime, while maintaining that community life was different back then:

> In the past the collective was very different, for instance the socialist brigades, it is easy to say now that it was all communist propaganda, but I think, no, today you can't organize anything like that. I am not nostalgic, really not, because those times were also not very good, but it was different, people were related somehow differently. Now they don't care about others, it is a different age, a different style, everybody says, it was not so bad in the past, we were young, we used to go out, it was not bad at all. We went to the pub, to the wine-cellar, drinking, having barbecues, we also went to the library, there were eminent librarian members [laughs] so I was an eminent librarian member, too. I like reading very much, I wrote in the diary of the brigade, we had lectures, we planned socialism [laughs], it was not so bad, excursions with the brigade, cinemas, the collective was very different in the past. Okay there was a lot of Marxism, but we did not take it seriously, they could not fool us with everything.[140]

Both the life-history interviews and the local sources support the argument that the brigade movement did not increase workers' influence on production decisions and it did not improve their proprietary consciousness. It did improve community life but it failed to achieve its propagandistic goal because people were much more likely to identify themselves with their group (where everybody was in a more or less similar situation) than with the regime. It can be indeed argued that solidarity was often reinforced by the common feeling of powerlessness; in this sense it is worth pointing out the complaint of the brigadier, who spoke of his problem obtaining tools at work. It is likewise remarkable in the quoted sources that brigadiers would typically speak of 'us' and 'them' in relation with the workers and the management, which may be indicative of the weak influence of the brigadiers. This suggests that the brigade movement was regarded as a 'circus for the people' even by the party, and in the light of the life-history interviews, people actually understood the message. We do not, of course, know how much politics was discussed in brigade meetings but it can be assumed that this – and the growing economic difficulties – did not trigger a political climate that was favourable for the regime.

Opposing the Management

In principle, the party leadership of the county could intervene in the labour policy of the enterprise, and it could also influence indirectly the personnel policy through the party organization of Rába MVG. After the memorable conflict between the first secretary of the county and Ede Horváth, which ended with the defeat of the secretary, the leadership of the county, however, rarely attempted to intervene in the policies of the factory, which Horváth considered to be his territory. Horváth was, of course, himself a high-ranking official of the party because from 1970 he was a member of the Central Committee, a position that he kept until the dissolution of MSZMP in 1989. Some cases can still be documented, when the conflict between the manager and the employees did not remain within the gates of the factory but was reported to the leading county party organs. This section introduces three cases: an attempted strike in 1977; a series of dismissals in 1979; and the manager's regulation of paid holiday in 1986, which had a particularly negative reception in a political climate that called for more freedom. Given the strict managerial control, only few dared to oppose the manager in his heyday; the vehement objection to his autocratic leadership style manifest in the last case was inseparable from the political weakening of the regime and the attack against old hierarchies.

On 4 July 1977, in factory unit 28 of MVG, sixty-four workers stopped working for one and half hours because they did not agree with their wages. Ede Horváth talked to the workers, who finally agreed to return to work. The case was reported to the economics department of the party committee of the county, and an investigation followed (meanwhile there were two weeks of maintenance in MVG).[141] The investigation found that there was a coincidence of several factors that triggered the conflict. In 1977, MVG gave an average pay increase of 6 per cent but decided to increase the norms by 10 per cent.[142] The workers of the given unit received new work, where the wage-scales were low and they could not earn the average wages because they lacked the relevant experience. They complained to the company's labour department, but they received no answer. A further problem was that planned production value was increased from 6,335 million Ft to 6,760 million Ft in the first half year of 1977. To motivate the employees, MVG set a premium of a two-week wage for the units that could fulfil the increased target. The enterprise succeeded in fulfilling 95.4 per cent of the plan, and 44 per cent of the set premium (12.9 million Ft) was distributed among 7,671 employees (43 per cent of the total workforce). The managements and workers of the units that did not fulfil this plan did not receive this premium. In the Rear Suspension and Vehicle factories the managers failed to explain this situation to the workers, who thought that they had been deceived by the management.[143] According to the report a settlement was finally reached between the workers and the management: the wage-scales in the unit where the workers protested were revised, and it was promised to all employees who did not receive the set premium that if they succeeded in fulfilling the plan in the third quarter of the year, they would get both the promised one-week wage plus the two-week wage that had been denied to them. We do not know to what extent the stoppage influenced the decision; at any rate, the blue-collar personnel of MVG decreased by 222 people in that summer.[144]

According to the information reports the workers' discontent with wages frequently manifested itself in critical political comments:

It spoilt the mood of the unit that on 12 December the workers did not receive the high but rightful wages that the quality control had already signed. The workers say that the department of labour can revise the norms, strengthen the quality control, etc., but it cannot refuse to pay the wages for which they worked and the quality control signed. They are all members of the trade union and some of them are members of the party, too. They responded to this decision by refusing to pay the party dues and rejecting the papers to which they subscribed. People also discussed the communiqué of the meeting of the Central Committee. They consider the 4.5 per cent increase of the prices of consumer goods too high because incomes will increase only by 2 per cent, which means that in 1979 we will live worse than today. In sum: the mood of the workers of the unit is not good![145]

After half a year the mood of the workers was again reported to be bad:

Our workers are mainly concerned with recent events that negatively influenced their wages. This was for instance the increase of the norms – which was unreasonably high in some cases – and the increase in quality requirements. This can decrease wages by 30–40 per cent. According to the workers it should not be allowed that an experienced skilled worker, who has worked for many years, is paid 15–16 Ft for an hour! He cannot even buy his breakfast from this money. It is absurd that the wage of a crane operator is the same as that of a skilled worker, and a trolley driver sometimes earns more.[146]

Workers from the forge shop likewise complained that they could not buy a proper breakfast from their hourly wage:

In the past weeks our employees were mainly concerned with the change in prices. They agreed with some of the items but they found the increase in the price of meat to be definitely too much. They said that their hourly wage does not cover a normal breakfast and – as they say – one cannot do hard physical work while living on bread and jam.[147]

Horváth's decision to 'revise the personnel' triggered similarly negative political comments in 1979. The decision was not targeted at the blue-collar workers; Horváth sought to decrease the number of administrative staff. He ordered a check on the work duties of every employee, an evaluation of their work and then lay-offs of surplus labour. The city council had to find employment for those Rába workers who lost their jobs. The revision affected 1,318 employees: 170 retired, 124 were transferred from the administrative staff to production, 344 received new work in the enterprise, 98 people did not accept the offered position, 102 positions were closed, and 480 people were laid off.[148] Many regarded the measure as a result of the problems of the people's economy:

The employees talk a lot about our economic policy. They do not fully approve of the current actions of the people's economy. Perhaps they are a bit afraid of the open information about the situation of the people's economy. They do not understand, for instance, how it is possible that a dynamically developing enterprise like MVG dismisses people.[149]

The revision of the personnel likewise reinforced anti-manager attitudes:

> We need precise information because everybody asks our party members: what
> do you know, who will be dismissed? It cannot be the aim of our society to
> increase insecurity. We would also like to know what happens to the managers,
> who employed surplus labour. They also did a bad job.[150] The same people,
> who complained about the shortage of labour two or three months ago, sud-
> denly realize that on the contrary, there is a surplus of labour (not a surplus
> of the managers – only a surplus of the employees!).[151] Even though the blue-
> collar workers were little affected, their comments revealed that people per-
> ceived the political climate to be more insecure.

The regulation of paid holiday triggered more vehement protests in 1986
during which the employees did not refrain from expressing their opinions of one-man management. In order to improve the management of
labour, Horváth decided that the employees should take their holiday
once a year and they should inform management of the dates at the beginning of the year. Apart from the poor communication of the measure, the manager's regulation of paid holiday had very bad timing: the
economic prospects of the country deteriorated, and the call for political
reforms found a positive reception even among large parts of the party
membership.[152] In this atmosphere the 'senseless and heartless' regulation
and the manager's ignorance of enterprise democracy met with fierce opposition from the employees. Even the information report of the county
dealt with the issue:

> The decision of the manager of MVG to regulate paid holiday very negatively
> influenced the political mood of the town. People were angered by the ab-
> sence of democratic preparation, the disregard of the trade union and the rigid
> enforcement of the rules. Almost all of the base-cells in MVG brought up the
> issue. Many people gave back their trade union cards and refused to pay the
> trade union and party dues.[153]

The trade union estimated the decrease of dues to be 24–64 per cent in
April in the various production units and 20 per cent at the level of the
enterprise (3,800 employees refused to pay).[154] Another report warned
against provoking people in the unfavourable economic situation: 'In our
county the regulation of paid holiday met the disapproval of the majority
of the employees in MVG. Willingness to pay trade union dues declined.
The unfavourable economic situation led many people to question the
high number of awards on 1 May.'[155]

The base-cell reports formulated the problem even more sharply. The
regulation evidently turned the feelings of the workers against the man-

ager, who considered the interests of production more important than the interests of people. According to the report of the Rear Suspension Factory, the decision:

> triggered vehement protests and resistance, which has not subsided. People say that the management did not ask for their opinions before this significant decision. They consider it to be an anti-democratic step. Extremist opinions are expressed in the following ways: people speak of the weakness of the trade union and they criticize the managing director. They compare the declaration on the radio that the family comes first with the manager's decision that they consider to be inhuman. Fourteen members of the trade union gave back their membership cards as a sign of protest.[156]

Employees evidently thought that the manager's decision was an attack against the trade union and enterprise democracy:

> The topic of holiday still frequently comes up in the conversations. Particularly those people are angry who had to give back their holiday vouchers. They don't understand this unreasonably rigid attitude and that some people can just ignore the wish of the large majority. We cannot simply let it go, this decision torpedoes enterprise democracy! Everybody thinks now that although we have an enterprise council, collective decision-making plays no role in our enterprise even in cases which obviously violate the interest of employees. Our workers think that in the case of the holiday the interest of the individuals is not contradictory to the interest of the collective.[157]

With respect to the measure, the managerial censorship of *Rába*, the newspaper of the factory, was also strongly criticized:

> We cannot agree with the sanction against people who are on sick leave for more than five days, which is a typical regulation of the Wagon Factory. At the same time the *Rába* newspaper received a lot of criticism. This publication is not at all the newspaper of the workers. If it were theirs, it would report on the issues that really concern the workers. For instance: the period of notice or the decision about next year's holiday. Can't we recognize the socially damaging effects of these issues!?[158]

At the end of 1986 agitators in MVG reported that 'pessimism has spread, the mood of the employees has become tense, and there is a wide distrust of the measures of the government and the interest representation of the trade unions'.[159] The case of paid holiday ended with a compromise: in the beginning of the year a 'phantom holiday plan' was created and the managers overlooked the changes during the year.[160] The regulation thus only succeeded in reinforcing opposition to the manager and his leadership methods, without any practical use. The case is indicative not only of the changing political climate but also the manager's failure to recognize or respond to it. The incident ended similarly to how Burawoy depicted the scene of 'painting socialism' in the Lenin Steel Works. Everybody knew in the factory that it is only for keeping up appearances. Under the surface the regime was dismantling.

Labour Policy in the GDR

The 'Unity of the Economic and Social Policy'

While in Hungary the leading political slogan of the early 1970s was the standard-of-living policy, the GDR party leadership lived under the spell of the increase of the production of consumer goods. In the very same meeting where Professor Hager so passionately addressed the gaps in the supply of the population with daily consumer products, the first secretary of the party organization of the Zeiss factory could proudly announce that they already drew the 'right conclusions' from the resolutions of the Eighth Party Congress:

> In our political-ideological work we paid a special attention to the evaluation of the resolutions of the Eighth Party Congress, and thanks to this, we succeeded in winning the support of the management for the solution of the problem. Our employees made a pledge to work more, and therefore we could decide at the plenum of the IKL that our factory will increase the plan targets of consumer goods by 2 millions Marks already in this year. We undertake to produce 7,000 extra telescopes in 1971, and we will also increase the plan targets of cameras and lenses in order to provide for a better supply of the population with these articles, which are in high demand. We promise the party leadership that we will do our utmost together with every comrade and employee of the factory to realize the plan targets of 1971 and to concentrate our efforts on the tasks that follow from the resolutions of the Eighth Party Congress.[161]

Even though the party leaders promptly followed the party line, it is, of course, a question as to the extent the supply of the population with consumer goods did indeed improve in the early 1970s. Despite the fact that the reports were in general optimistic, there is some evidence that the 'fight' for the stable and continuous provision of the population with daily articles was indeed a difficult one. A report of 1974, for instance, called attention to the fact that 'despite the overall positive results of the fulfilment of consumer goods targets and the related improvement of the supply of people with these products as well as better services', there were still problems that the party leadership had to solve with consequent and purposeful work:

Figure 2.2 Work 1 of VEB Carl Zeiss Jena

Figure 2.3 Work 2 of VEB Carl Zeiss Jena

The demand for the 1,000 small things cannot be covered. There are not enough can openers, corkscrews, scissors, kettles and fittings needed for electric installation. We likewise can't satisfy the demand for television sets, tape recorders, wine, champagne, building materials, carpets, men's suits and women's coats, leather clothes, bath tubs, fire-proof glass and bulbs. People frequently criticize the public services in the towns, in particular the inadequate lightening of the streets.[162]

The list, at any rate, seemed to contradict the overall positive results, and the complaint about the inadequate lightening suggests that the shortage of electricity was still a problem at that time.

In 1976 the government could feel confident enough to announce further welfare measures (including a large-scale housing programme, which was expected to solve the problems of the population). The party leadership of the district likewise wasted no time in evaluating the resolutions of the Ninth Party Congress:

We have every reason to believe that socialism has decisively shaped the ideas and behaviour of our citizens. The general party line of the Ninth Party Congress with its resolutions that serve the interests and welfare of the working class and those of the whole population found an unambiguously positive reception among the working people, who passionately defend our political line. … As we all know, the state housing project is the core of our social political programme. Between 1976 and 1980, we will provide 20,000 citizens with new and comfortable flats so that every third family in the district can enjoy better living conditions. In addition, in 1980 the net income of the population will be twice as much as in 1960, and we promise to keep the same price level. We will introduce new basic wages for 70,000 employees in the district, and we will also increase the minimum wages. For these purposes we received 200 millions Marks. We have an additional 360 millions Marks for the improvement of the conditions of retired people. In order to fulfil the resolutions of the social political programme we will need 40 millions Marks for the support of the adult education of 18,000 working people. From 1 May 1977 we will introduce the 40-hour week for 54,000 employees of the district. During the Five-Year Plan we can support the extended weekend holidays and baby leave of working mothers with 60 million Marks. Besides, we have to mention that for the sixty social political measures that have come into force since the Eighth Party Congress we need an additional 36.3 million Marks. Comrades, all of these are grandiose objectives but they can be realized; and if we succeed in increasing labour productivity accordingly, we can even ponder over new social political measures in order to further improve the living and working conditions of the people.[163]

Even though the functionaries were not sparing of impressive figures when they praised the achievements of the social policy of the party, they were much less interested in the actual conditions of the working class in the district. It is, indeed, striking, particularly in the light of the omnipotent class-based ideology, how *little* labour-related topics were in fact discussed in the meetings of the party leadership of the district. Even on these occasions the party leaders mainly discussed 'purposeful' things, for instance, what kind of ideological work can improve the workers' willingness to undertake shift work or how to propagate full-time work among the women of the district. It seems that the 'improvement of the living and working conditions of the people' increasingly drove the real workers out of the vision of the functionaries, and working-class responses to the policy of the party were dissolved in the bureaucratic language of the official ideology.

In comparison with the Hungarian sources, there is remarkably little information on the working class of the district. In 1971 one document gives a figure of 303,000 for the total number of workers, employees and trainees in the district, out of which 186,000 were employed in industry, construction industry and traffic. The party had 89,000 members in the district out of which 77,000 attended party schools, which shows that the party paid much more attention to the ideological training of its members in the GDR than in Hungary.[164] Thanks to the overall efforts of the party to increase female employment, there are some more data about the working women in the district. Between 1970 and 1973 the percentage of women of working age employed increased from 73 per cent to 82.5 per cent, and in 1975 it reached 90 per cent in the district. Already at the end of 1972, 50.8 per cent of the employees of the district were women. A survey, which was conducted in forty-four selected enterprises of the district, found that 34.9 per cent of the female workers belonged to the skilled working class. In the Zeiss factory the proportion of the skilled female workforce was much higher, 49.3 per cent, but it was also high with 45.3 per cent in the Jenapharm factory and in the textile industry of the district.[165]

The problem of how to reconcile the family and household duties with those of a full-time job was discussed even in the meetings of the party leadership of the district. Women who were employed part-time were constantly encouraged to take full-time jobs; the women's commission of the Zeiss factory, for instance, loyally reported that in every half year they had a long ideological discussion with the part-time workers for this end.[166] The reports complained that even more ideological work was needed to persuade the working mothers to undertake shift work: in the Zeiss factory the shift nursery (which was opened also during nights) had to be transformed into a normal one because 'the discussions with mothers who had two or more small children led to the conclusion that the mothers are not ready to entrust a nursery with the night care of their offspring'.[167] The agitation for shift work, nevertheless, continued: according to a 1972 report, 15.8 per cent of the women workers of the district worked in a two-shift, and 6.7 per cent in three-shift, system. In this respect the report commented that the proportion of employees who ate in the canteens increased from 39.2 per cent to 43.2 per cent. Apart from the agitation and the extra money, other bonuses were also offered to make the shift work more attractive in the eyes of people: in the same year, 70 per cent of the holiday vouchers which were distributed in the district were given to workers, and those who did shift work had an advantage over the others. Thermal bath vouchers to other socialist countries were in the highest demand (in the trade union elections of 1972 the workers even criticized the low proportion of workers among the beneficiaries). The holiday commissions arranged with the child-care institutions about the accommodation of the children of the working mothers during the time of the holiday.[168]

Shift work gave another advantage, which in many cases (for instance in that of Zeiss) surely took precedence over the holiday vouchers in the eyes of people: namely, that shift workers were positively discriminated in the allocation of state flats. In the letters of complaint to the chief manager, shift workers never missed the opportunity to stress the priority of their claim, and from the replies it is evident that the flat problem of the shift workers was indeed more likely to be solved. This had a very practical reason: when a young family lived in a one-room flat with a baby, the parents could not get a normal sleep. Judged from the high number of complaints, people who lived in workers' hostels had the same problem because it often happened that the room- or flat-mates worked in different shifts. According to the report of the women's commission of the VEB Carl Zeiss, girls were more likely to give up their career in the factory than boys because of this problem:

> The young women workers who live in the workers' hostels complain a lot about the problems of cohabitation when their room-mates work in different shifts. The tension that comes from this situation increases their objection to shift work, and they often choose to leave the factory because of their living problems. We would like to ask for quick help from the leaders of the trade union and the responsible officials in the field of cultural and social policy. Every worker who we lose because of this problem is a great loss to us.[169]

Since the training opportunities of Zeiss were widely advertised across the GDR, the factory attracted trainees from many places, and it was interested in the settlement of the new workforce. Another report likewise stressed that girls were more likely to return to their homes if they encountered problems,[170] which suggests that despite the emancipatory rhetoric, traditional gender stereotypes continued to shape people's attitudes.

On these grounds, it is very difficult to say how working people did indeed respond to the labour policy of the party. While in Hungary a survey was conducted among the party membership of the county to learn how they evaluated the standard-of-living policy, we cannot find equivalent surveys among the materials of the party leadership of the district of Gera. It is clear from the quoted report of the evaluation of the resolutions of the Ninth Party Congress that the social political measures consumed enormous sums of money. A report of the Zeiss factory also commented that because of the extended holidays of the working mothers the enterprise lost twenty thousand working days, and the shortened working hours caused a loss of two thousand hours a week. The various benefits (child benefits, sickness benefits, the support of single mothers and maternity grants) cost the enterprise an additional 1 million Marks a year.[171] In the light of these sums, it is all the more remarkable that the party leadership was not interested in how the working people actually evaluated what had been done for them. There is some evidence, though, that people were not as enthusiastic about the socialist achievements as leaders claimed they were, and interestingly, it was mainly women who were more discontented with the conditions. In VEB Carl Zeiss Jena, many women complained that they arrived home so late that they could not manage the household:

> Even though we did much for the improvement of the living and working conditions, health care and labour protection, a number of the women employees have demands that we currently cannot satisfy. They complain that the rate of development is too slow, and they criticize the shopping opportunities and the opening hours. They say that there are not enough afternoon schools and holiday places for children and big families.[172]

It is remarkable that the supply of consumer goods was mostly criticized by women, which suggests that shopping remained more or less a women's job. This is also supported by the reasons why part-time women workers refused to undertake full-time jobs. The 'objective reasons' that were mentioned in a report of 1972 included the 'unsolved daily care of the children, the lack of places in the afternoon schools, and the poor supply of consumer goods'. In addition, there were 'ideological problems' with the division of labour within the family: 'many men are strongly opposed to the employment of their wives because they want to have a comfortable rest after work'.[173] This, at any rate, explains the apparent contradiction of why working women, who counted among the beneficiaries of the labour policy of the regime, were more likely to voice their discontent with the provision of the population; at the same time the criticism also revealed the boundaries of the 'unity of the economic and social policy'.

There were positive responses among the working women, of course, which were evidently exploited by the regime for the purposes of propaganda. At a district party meeting in 1972, the delegate of the Zeiss factory, who herself was a woman worker, gave the following speech:

> I work in the optic plant of the VEB Carl Zeiss Jena. I would like to tell you about the very positive reception of the social political measures of the Fifth Conference of our Central Committee among our colleagues. We were happy to hear of the outline of the social political programme. Our colleagues hold this programme to be the fulfilment of the resolutions of the Eighth Party Congress, and they fully comprehend that it pays to work diligently. I believe that we can all hold ourselves to be happy to live in this country, the GDR ... I myself come from a working-class family, where there were four children. If I compare now how difficult it was for my parents to secure the future of their children with that of our situation today, then I can only say that the current measures in the interest of the working mothers are fully in line with the essence of socialism. Of course, they did not fall into our laps. I regard myself as happy because my work also contributed to these results, and I believe that this gives a meaning to our lives. Many women and mothers think like me, and they are ready to do everything to the utmost of their power to prove themselves worthy of the resolutions of our party.[174]

Since the speech is full of phrases that were characteristic of the language of the functionaries (such as 'women ... ready to ... prove themselves worthy'), it is at best doubtful that it was written by the speaker only; further, the bureaucratic language renders it difficult to believe that it reflected the true feelings of people (even if the social political measures did undoubtedly find a positive reception among the women employees).

In this sense it can be argued that the disinterest of the party leaders in working-class opinions was symptomatic because the labour policy was 'subordinated' to the higher interest of the ideological struggle, and it was indeed held to be primarily a means of propaganda in the eyes of the functionaries. The chief aim of the labour policy was to appease the workers, not to emancipate them, and this difference was well reflected in the lack of the representation of the workers in the party materials. People evidently felt this, and they increasingly distanced themselves from the ideology of the party, which so blatantly held the workers a means of propaganda only. The propagandistic goals of labour policy were openly described in an information report of the first secretary of the party organization of the Zeiss factory, in which he reported about an interview for the Italian newspaper *L'Unita*, where comrade X, a 26-year-old worker was chosen to demonstrate that there is a new generation of well-paid, skilled young workers, who are fully conscious of their role in the building of their socialist state. The interview introduces how comrade X finished an evening school, and how he participates now in higher education. It describes the various social institutions of the factory such as the polyclinic, nurseries, kindergartens and canteens, and it argues that the real income of a worker in the GDR is actually higher than that of his West German counterpart. The interview concludes with the argument that the cause of the 'production miracle' of the GDR lies in the highly qualified personnel and the satisfaction of workers' needs, which was confirmed by every worker whom the author asked.[175]

Both cases – the speech of the woman delegate and the interview with the selected worker – show that communication between the party and the workers was effectively controlled by the party bureaucracy, and that the party did not trust the workers to formulate their opinions even if their responses would have been positive. This revealed that the reception of the labour policy among the workers had a propagandistic value only.

Managing Discontent

The sources well reflect the 'transition' from the naïve working-class ideology of the party under the NES to the bureaucratization of the communication between the workers and the party in the Honecker era. The documents of the late 1960s (and partly also those of the 1970s) demonstrated with real examples what the party could do for the improvement of the living and working conditions of the people (similarly to the quoted story of Professor Hager), and there were even reports of sporadic manifestations of workers' discontent. It is characteristic, however, how these complaints were managed: the party did not even consider ideological criticism if it came from workers, but it concentrated on their appeasement only. Therefore it may well have been a logical outcome that the reports of the 'mature' Honecker era contented themselves with the repetition of the general ideological slogans and the listing of production figures.

Since the party leadership evidently held the agitation of the workers for shift work to be an ideological task, it is not surprising that the conditions of the shift workers received special attention. In the Zeiss factory an investigation found that in many cases there were no responsible managers present on the afternoon and night shifts. The enterprise tried to explain away the bad report:

> A shift manager or a direct production manager is present on the second shift but it frequently happens that we can't put managers on the job during the

night shifts when only a few colleagues are working. For instance, at the time when the inspectors visited the plant, there were only ten colleagues who did night shift in the grindery of the instrument plant. They promptly received their tasks from the responsible manager of the second shift, and they could work without supervision. Reasoning: they are all experienced workers who can work on their own.

It was also reported that the inspectors were satisfied with the provision of the shift workers with food and drink: 'People in the afternoon and night shifts receive qualitatively nourishing, warm food, and the continuous supply of drinks is solved with the help of vending machines.'[176] It seems that the inspectors were indeed concerned about the well-being of the workers because it was suggested that the coffee in the vending machines should be freshly brewed for the night shift. Such small gestures could have expressed much better the essence of the labour policy of the party than any ideological phrases.

The women's commissions likewise had ideological tasks but the latter did not prevent them from reporting on the negative experiences that they had during visits to factories. A visit to a paper factory in 1976, for instance, concluded that even though the factory had a very good collective, the working conditions could hardly be described as satisfactory, and the state of the plant rightfully shocked the committee:

We learnt from the discussions that the whole brigade has achieved very good results in the improvement of quality and the increase of labour productivity. The colleagues have regular political discussions of the actual questions of our development, which help them clarify the ideological problems. We should add that the brigade won many times the title of the 'collective of socialist work', which is a recognition of their excellent work. Despite their tiring physical work and the not yet satisfactory wages, the women workers show a very positive attitude to their work and our development. Furthermore, the working conditions are not the best, for instance, an unfriendly hall and bad hygienic conditions (since it is mainly the colleagues who are cleaning the rooms). We were shocked at the sight when we walked through the plant and the paper hall. In our judgement, the hygienic equipments in these rooms are unworthy of human beings, and they recall the misery of the postwar years. The toilets and washbasins are dirty and broken. Furthermore, it seems that no one has had time for a proper clean since the machines were dismantled: waste has been piled up in the corner, in such a shocking condition that one is disgusted even to take a look. It is also a question of hygiene because it is a breeding place for vermin. We believe that even though the building of the factory is old and not modern, our concern about the people should – and indeed must – manifest itself also in the improvement of their working conditions so that they meet the socialist requirements.[177]

We do not know whether the visit had positive results (for instance, the ordering of a clean-up) or the dirty washbasins counted among the ideological problems that should have been discussed rather than solved. The report of the women's commission, however, does reflect something of the emancipatory objectives that could have been found in the professor's story as well, and it is also important to stress that the achievement of the women workers was highly praised even though it was admitted that they had to work under difficult conditions and for unsatisfactory wages. Their tolerance may well have been a sign of their political loyalty to the regime; and in the latter case it was indeed underlined that the collective demonstrated a political commitment. It is, however, remarkable that while both stories stressed the unselfishness of women, it turned out that sometimes even small things could not have been arranged for them in the factory, and they needed a wider public for their problems to be solved. It seems that it did not always pay to be tolerant.

People, however, had not always had the virtue of tolerance: at least in the early 1970s some cases were reported in which the workers gave clear signs of their discontent. These cases of protest all concerned disputes about the material rewards (wages or premiums), and their investigation suggested that the party sought agreement with the workers rather than to sharpen the conflict. This shows that the appeasement of workers was important, even in cases of open conflict. The workers of a Silbitz plant were so outraged by an unpaid bonus that they declared in front of the local party leaders that 'if we don't get our due, you will learn something tomorrow' – a reference to 17 June as the report commented. The reason of the conflict was that while the furnacemen received a loyalty premium of 750 Marks, the others were denied the payment of this premium. Similarly to the Hungarians, the East German workers expected the party to intervene on their side, and when it failed to do so they reacted with an understandable resentment: 'We don't need to organize any APO meeting because nobody comes anyway. I have not picked up the party literature because no one buys it any more. Out of the thirty-three comrades of the APO only three are willing to pay the party dues.' In the turners' shop, broken turner's chisels were found, and it was suspected that the workers vented their fury on the tools. The discussions with the workers led to the conclusion that the positive discrimination of the furnacemen 'hurt the professional pride of the skilled working class because the least qualified workers received the highest benefits'. It is remarkable that during the discussions the workers did not refrain from making direct political comments (such as the comment 'they won't talk with us but they put the Staatssicherheit on to us' or the reference to 17 June).[178] While no record of the resolution of the dispute exists, the party obviously demonstrated a readiness to negotiate with the workers (e.g. discussions). Further, the workers did not hesitate to openly show their disagreement with the party (and even make direct and very negative political comments). This suggests that they also knew how to put pressure on the party to recognize their rightful material demands.[179]

The distribution of the annual bonuses of 1972 in the metallurgic industry of the district was likewise not an easy task. It was calculated that the average bonus was 5–20 per cent higher than in 1971, and it amounted to 550–800 Marks. There were, however, big differences among the various plants, which were explained through the different calculations of the average wages in the individual plants, the different maximal values set by the enterprises, and the different recognition of overtime, shift work and the years of employment. The managers declared that the guidelines were too general and it depended on the plants how much they gave for the individual criteria. A foundry of Lobenstein, for instance, gave 120 Marks for the three-shift work while in the VEB Blawa Schleiz the shift workers received 300 Marks. The furnacemen caused further troubles for management because their loyalty supplement and shift bonus also counted towards the annual bonus. Since the enterprises received no more money, the bonus of the furnacemen could only be increased at the expense of the other employees. In some places such as the VEB Elektrobau Greiz, the management had to reduce the bonuses because of the higher material costs but they warned that the employees 'won't understand this measure'[180] because they had better results in 1972 than the year before. People may well have been discontented in other plants, too, because after the payment of bonuses, 'it was heard from many places that despite the fulfilment and even over-fulfilment of the plan, higher bonuses were paid in light industry and commerce than in metallurgy. In many plants the employees threatened to turn to the trade union.'[181] The comparison between the industries was probably not accidental, because metallurgy was held to be a stronghold of socialist industry. Such cases show that the workers also knew how to use 'political-ideological arguments' against the party in order to stress their demands.

The next case may well have been a good basis for capitalist propaganda because it was about a wage dispute with the workers of nationalized enterprises in 1973. Here the conflict was very simple even though the report tried to beat around the bush: the private enterprises paid more to the workers while the state wanted to pay 'in proportion to performance'. Many workers were not convinced by the political agitations: in VEB Stramo Greiz, five out of the seven people wanted to give notice reasoning that it would not pay them to commute if they received less money. With other employees the discussions led to 'decisive results'; the report, however, commented that one has to wait when people get the new wages, which render them fully conscious of the change. In addition, the leaders of the party and the trade union as well as the managers were requested to pay an 'increased political attention' to the new state enterprises, where the employees had to count with wage cuts.[182] It seems that the party also counted with the opportunity that in such cases the indignation of people could override their fear of political repression; besides, the case did not really demonstrate the advantage of socialism over capitalism.

The introduction of the new basic wages (which was, in general, favourable for the workers) in a Freital plant was likewise preceded by the party leaders giving several instructions to the local secretaries in order to avoid any disagreement with the workers:

> No question must be left unanswered! Everybody must feel that his word counts! No norm can be changed without justification. Our principle is: the same wage for the same achievement! You should stress the improvement of the working and living conditions and the support of working-class culture. Since the introduction of the new basic wages concerns one of the basic issues of labour, the party secretaries, trade union leaders and the chief manager are personally responsible for the whole process. The chairman of the central working group must be the chief manager so that he can solve every problem immediately. You should explain to the workers how the old norms relate to the new norms and how the new wages are calculated. The leading functionaries have to be present when the workers first receive the new wages so that they can answer any question that might come up. The workers must get a clear picture of the relationship between the old and new wages so that they realize that it is worth working under the new system.

The instructions show that it was as much in the interest of the party to avoid labour conflicts as in that of the workers; even though the new wage forms increased the average wages of blue-collar workers, the report argued that those who did not have the necessary qualifications should not be left out either: 'Unskilled workers had to be downgraded from the higher to the lower wage groups, which hurt their professional pride and self-respect. Therefore it would be better to change the job requirements with the help of science and technology or to organize training courses for the workers so that they can remain in their original wage groups.'[183] It seems more likely, however, that the decrease of the wages would have triggered protests, and the local party organization proposed this compromise so that there would be an unambiguously positive reception of the measure in the plant.

The above cases all illustrate the controversial relationship between the party and the workers: while the latter may well have 'agreed' not to intervene in politics, they expected the party to represent the interests of labour and arrange that the workers receive their rightful rewards – as one manager of the Zeiss factory formulated.[184] The manifestation of workers' discontent was harmful to the prestige of the party even in its mild forms (e.g. worker comrades terminating their party membership). Therefore, while the party strictly refused to engage in any political debates with the workers, it showed more readiness to fulfil their material demands (or at least to examine complaints of this kind). It is not surprising that the overwhelming majority of the letters of complaint addressed material needs. One can, for instance, mention here one case from the late 1960s: a worker asked for the help of the party leadership to get a Trabant before the usual waiting time on the grounds of his good production results and social work. He got the response that even though they could not help with the Trabant, he could immediately get a Zaporozhec.[185]

One, of course, does not know whether the above answer had the same comical effect at that time as it has today. It was already argued that during the era of the NES the 'party speech' sometimes turned out to be its own parody. Canteen food was an object of ridicule in the Hungarian factory, and it seems that it was not very popular among the workers of the Zeiss factory either, at least in 1968. The disagreement was described by the party secretary as the following:

> In recent time we have received an increasing number of complaints about the bad quality of food, particularly that of the dishes that can be freely selected from the menu. There are indeed objective difficulties: at present there is no skilled chef in the kitchen and we are short of thirty cooking assistants. It renders the situation more difficult that the kitchen staff get lower wages in our plant than in other similar factories. Last week the situation intensified and it culminated in a meeting of the party organization of O3 where the workers handed over a dish to the party secretary of propaganda/agitation with the following question: 'Can you eat this? Because we can't.' They also gave him a menu from 1959 in order to prove that at that time the selection was much better than today. I immediately took the initiative and I made constructive proposals for the improvement of canteen food in front of the responsible managers.[186]

It may well have been that the 'action' of the workers only demonstrated the simple fact that the bad food had nothing to do with ideology; the story, however, suggests that the party held the management of discontent to be its task even if it could offer nothing but ideology.

New Inequalities?

While in Hungary the declining social position of the working class received an ever-increasing emphasis in the information reports, it is not surprising that it was much less discussed in the East German sources, which preferred to stress the positive changes in this respect. In both cases it was discussed how the scientific-technical development of society would influence the social role of the working class. In Hungary a survey was conducted among the party membership of the county, which found that many members of the party were sceptical about the leading role of the working class in the future, because they thought that with scientific-technological development society was increasingly controlled by the economic and technical intelligentsia.[187] The party leadership of the East German district did not take the trouble to ask the membership (at least no surveys can be found among their documents). The concept of the technological development was, however, closely integrated into the political agenda (which is not surprising if we think of Ulbricht's scientific socialism). In a meeting of the party leadership of the district the second secretary of the district delivered a long speech in which he argued that the rapid technological development did indeed *strengthen* the social position of the working class:

> In the era of the scientific-technical revolution, which is characterized by the rapid growth of the forces of production, the masses of the working people are inseparably connected with the modern socialist industry. Therefore, the working class, the largest class of our state, which is the most closely linked with the building of the socialist system, will be increasingly recognized as a leading class, which performs both physical and intellectual work ... The bourgeois ideologists are trying to prove to us that the technological development renders the working class dependent on the intelligentsia. We as Marxists believe that the scientific-technical revolution can only be mastered by the people and for the people, and the future technological development can be successful only in so far as it supports and makes use of the ideas, knowledge and creativity of the working people.[188]

It is interesting that while the party documents tactfully avoided mentioning Ulbricht and his scientific system of socialism after the resignation of the first secretary, the faith in the technological development survived: at least, it was widely propagated that this development was the prerequisite for the further improvement of the living and working conditions of the people (see, for instance, the quoted interview in the Italian newspaper *L'Unita*).

The Hungarian materials in general show that according to people it was increasingly disadvantageous to belong to the working class (declining material conditions of the workers, the growing wealth in the private sector, etc.). In the case of the GDR there is some evidence that people wanted to remain nominal members of the working class at least, because of its advantages (e.g. in adult education or in the education of their children).[189] In 1975, for instance, the first secretary of the party organization of the Zeiss factory reported to the district party leaders that members of the party were discontented with the criteria of class qualification:

> In this aspect I would like to call your attention to two problems that were discussed among our comrades. The first problem is that of the workers who have obtained university or college degrees with systematic and purposeful work and now they are employed here as engineers. Our worker comrades don't understand how it can be that according to classification they no longer belong to the working class because they are 'over-qualified' for that. The other problem is that of the engineers who work in the production either as controllers or they manage the mounting of large scientific instruments. They don't understand why they are qualified as 'intelligentsia' even though they do the same job as the technicians, who count among the workers. Even though they accept the criteria of qualification, they don't understand them. We believe that some of these criteria should indeed be changed in order to provide for a realistic qualification that takes into consideration the type of work and the role of the workers in socialist production.[190]

It seems, however, that despite every effort of the government to increase the standard of living of the working people, even in the GDR people grumbled that there were strata which could afford a higher level of consumption than the working class. According to an information report of 1977, during the discussions with people it came up in the towns of Jena and Gera that even though there was a levelling between the classes, social differences, on the contrary, continued to grow (in incomes, education, leisure time, holidays).[191] The opening of Intershops (which sold goods for Western currency) and Exquisit shops (where the prices were considerably higher than in the normal shops) reinforced social criticism. The Zeiss employees, for instance, complained that in the GDR there were three classes: 1. those who had relatives in West Germany; 2. those who had incomes above the average and they could buy in the special shops; 3. 'normal' consumers. The employees added that the latter were in the worst situation because they could not buy what they wanted in the normal shops and they had to wait eight weeks or longer for the repair of their cars.[192] It seems that the Zeiss employees had ideologically less conformist opinions of the relationship with West Germany: it was, for instance, discussed among the employees that a worker received an unemployment benefit of 900 Marks in West Germany, which was more than the wages of many GDR workers. It was also raised that if the situation in West Germany is indeed so bad then why were there no revolutionary actions against the system. Concerning the Intershops, the employees commented that they supported the bourgeois ideology because the 'normal' workers, who do not have Western currency, were excluded from these shops. People did not understand why their money was of less value than Western currency.[193] The Exquisit shops were evidently considered to be the symbols of the new inequality in consumption: from the Zeiss factory it was repeatedly reported that the 'largest part of our comrades and employees believe that the spread of Exquisit shops only nourishes social differences and renders them more visible'.[194]

Even though much less negative criticism was reported from the GDR than from Hungary, the above reports show that the East German workers were not much more contented – at least relatively – with their level of consumption than their Hungarian counterparts. While in Hungary the private sector provided incomes that were above the average, in the GDR people counted those who had Western relatives or other contacts as being among the 'privileged' social strata. It was also raised in life-history interviews that parents who received Western currency from their relatives could buy the desired products that their children saw on television in the Intershops, and they were much envied by their less fortunate class-mates. While in Hungary the private sector 'influenced negatively the socialist consciousness of the workers' as the party secretary of the county formulated, in the GDR the Western standard of living, which was widely propagated also by the West German media, had the same effect. The East German state prohibited the watching of Western television channels (*Westfernsehen*), but behind the curtains people watched these channels in their homes. In addition, the opening of Exquisit and Intershops demonstrated that in spite of the egalitarian rhetoric of the party, there were differences among the consumers who could afford these shops and those who could not. Ironically, Honecker unintentionally assisted this process by putting the increase of consumption at the centre of his labour policy. When it turned out that the standard of living of the GDR could not surpass nor even catch up with that of West Germany, this labour policy rapidly lost credibility in the eyes of the people – together with Honecker's ideology.

From Hostels to Flats

Contrary to the Hungarian factory, where the reports uniformly claimed that the employees did not suffer from chronic housing shortages (largely a consequence of the high incidence of commuting), East German sources show that housing shortage was the principal social problem for Zeiss's employees. There were, of course, several factors that explain the huge pressure on housing: most importantly, the dynamic increase of the workforce; the need of the enterprise for expertise – a problem already in the late

1960s: the instrument plant, for instance, did not have enough designers because they could not give them flats;[195] the high number of new settlers, given that the training facilities of the enterprise as well as the educational institutions of the town attracted young people from across the GDR; and the centralized system of flat allocation.[196] Within the framework of state housing programmes, the Zeiss factory received a certain share of newly built housing estates, which were then distributed among the various plants of the factory. In addition, a percentage was reserved for the management in order to solve specific social policy and labour recruitment problems.[197] It should be added that the Zeiss factory was in an incomparably better situation with respect to the supply of flats than the Rába factory in Hungary. In 1976, Zeiss disposed of 11,321 flats and 3,342 places in workers' hostels in Jena.[198] There are no overall figures for the 1980s in the archive of the enterprise; but we know, for instance, that the optical precision instruments' division received 1,696 flats between 1972 and 1987,[199] which shows that the workplace played a key role in solving the housing problems of workers. This explains the much higher number of letters of complaint that addressed housing shortage in the GDR, when compared to Hungary.

Given the absence of overall statistical figures for the number of applicants and the average waiting time for a flat, one cannot draw definitive conclusions about the living conditions of the Zeiss employees from this type of source because the writers of the letters all complained of their miserable situation. It is possible, though, to identify some general patterns of how people acquired flats and also to identify some of the groups who were particularly dependent on this kind of state allowance. The new settlers undoubtedly constituted the most important group: as the cited reports stressed, Zeiss had an interest in winning over young people who had come from distant places for their training to settle in the town.[200]

The first accommodation that the enterprise could offer to young workers was a place in workers' hostels; as trainees, they were typically housed in dormitories. Here, younger single people usually shared a room, but there were also family hostels for married couples. Lodging in private houses was very rare. Since life in the workers' hostels meant the continuation of dormitory life – with common kitchens and bathrooms, and house-mates who often worked on different shifts – it is understandable that many young people tried to press the flat distribution committees and management to process their applications for a flat quickly. The issue arose in my life-history interviews: early marriages and the subsequent birth of a child were frequently motivated by the desire of young people for an independent household, as families with children had a much better chance to acquire a flat. Single people obviously stood at the bottom of the waiting lists.

The fact that practically everybody asked for a flat in the newly built housing estates that were under construction, increased the pressure on flat distribution committees and management still more. The enterprise distributed flats in old buildings too, but, as these were seen as undesirable, applicants frequently declined offers for such flats. Often they had no proper toilets, bathrooms, kitchens or central heating. In such cases, however, the applicants who stressed that they lived under miserable conditions risked an answer that their flat problem was not as urgent as they claimed it to be, and that they should wait patiently until their request for a modern, comfortable flat could be fulfilled. Flats were sometimes rejected on the grounds that they were too small for the needs of a family. It seems from the letters of complaint that many people chose to wait for a new and modern flat in their workers' hostels rather than to accept a flat in an old building. Reconstruction was difficult because of shortages of building materials, which explains the unambiguous preference for modern housing.

Although letters of complaint described individual problems, it is still worth introducing some of the cases, not only to give a picture of the living conditions of young East German workers who could not rely on parental help, but also to examine the communication between workers and official bodies. The letters depict a tense relationship: all the letters were requests, but every petitioner believed that they were entitled to a flat. Thus, the letters articulated demands of the state and management; they were not the requests of subordinates who felt themselves to be powerless. Some petitioners threatened to turn to Erich Honecker should they receive a negative answer to their application for a flat. The 'tense housing situation' – as it was called – brought some of the worst sides of human nature to the surface. Many were angered that their colleagues received flats earlier than they did, and they listed their names demanding an explanation. People were very inventive in pressing the factory for a shorter deadline, and there were persistent petitioners who wrote many letters of complaint. This, similarly to the cases introduced in the section entitled *Managing Discontent*, suggests that the government's policy of appeasement was a double-edged weapon: despite the oppressive ideological climate people could very assertively stand up for their social rights.

Because of the 'tense housing situation' in Jena, which was the favourite excuse of the officials who responded to such complaints, shared accommodation in the workers' hostels was an option that many people had to endure, regardless of whether they wanted it or not. Conditions in the hostels generated considerable criticism: the equipment and furniture was old and overused, cleaning was neglected and the common rooms were often filthy. The following letter well expresses the disappointment of young people who decided to take up work in the factory after they finished their training:

Having finished the 10th class of school, I trained to be a polisher in your factory. I learnt about this opportunity from the newspapers and TV. I could get no training in my home town and as I come from a big family (I have six siblings), I wanted to be independent. I lived in the factory dormitory until 9 July 1980 and then I received a place in the AWU.[201] Since then I have been living in a six-room flat with three colleagues. The 'bedrooms' are separated only with curtains from the common rooms, so I can't even close my door. The whole flat was in a very dirty state (garbage left by the former tenants, broken locks and damaged wardrobe doors). It took me days to make it fit to live in, and I have to live here because I can rarely travel home. I am very much disappointed with the living conditions that the factory offers to the young skilled workers because they do not meet our expectations. I would like to achieve good results but for good work one needs good living conditions that I unfortunately do not have here. For this reason I am asking for your support.[202]

Apart from the poor material conditions, the problems of cohabitation also rendered life difficult for young people who dreamt of an independent life and a home of their own. In this respect no gender difference can be observed: young men complained of the poor hygienic conditions of shared accommodation as much as young women. The following letter depicts a very unfavourable picture of life in the workers' hostels:

I started my training as a polisher in VEB Carl Zeiss Jena in 1980. During my training I lived in the Kurt Zier dormitory. I was born here in Jena and I lived for nine years in Kahla. After the divorce of my parents, I was sent to a children's home. I finished the 10th class of school there. If I include the time of my training, I have lived for more than eight years in shared accommodation (in twelve-, eight-, five- and four-bed rooms). After I finished my training, I was accommodated in the workers' hostel at Josef-Klose-Straße.[203] The conditions were so bad there that I considered giving my notice in. In my workplace you discussed my case and I was promised a flat in 1983. I have not, however, received this promise in writing. As I do not have a family home, the AWU is my main dwelling place where life is anything but easy for me. There is not enough room for my things: I have to store food in my wardrobe because the cupboards in the kitchen are invaded by cockroaches. The kitchen-cabinets cannot be locked properly because their doors are broken. Butter, cheese and drinks stand on the window ledge in my room. There are four of us living in the flat and we all work on two or three different shifts at once. Since the rooms are separated by paper walls, I cannot sleep when the others listen to music or they have visitors. The washbasin is often full of clothes so I can take a shower only very late at night. The hygienic conditions are poor and the flat is in a very shabby condition because of the frequently changing tenants. I like my work in the optic plant but I really need a place where I can have a rest after work. And this is indeed impossible in the AWU because of the reasons that I explained above. I do not expect a luxury home, just something that I can call my own.[204]

The answer is not known but there is some evidence that the social situation of the petitioner was considered because the sentence 'I lived for more than eight years in shared accommodation (in twelve-, eight-, five- and four-bed rooms)' was underlined with the comment that 'it is a really good argument!'.

Tenants also complained that they were too strictly controlled in the hostels. One petitioner attacked excessive supervision of hostel life by the police, a complaint directed to the managing director. The letter is cited because it shows how state repression turned workers who were in principle not at all opposed to the system of socialism against the regime:

I have been working as a locksmith for sixteen months in the VEB Carl Zeiss Jena. I live now in block 86/87 in the hope that I would eventually get a one-room flat where I could move in with my girlfriend, for whom I came here to work. I was told that I would get a flat after a year. Therefore I kept on waiting patiently even though life in the hostel cannot be described as pleasant. The toilets and washing facilities are in a very bad condition or they are altogether unfit for use. I put up with all the inconvenience and lack of comfort because at least my individual freedom was not limited. But for a few weeks members of the security personnel of the factory have been sitting at the entrance, and when one enters, one immediately gets the impression that it is a boarding school or a barracks. I feel an immediate attack on my personal freedom. The requirement to register guests annoys my girlfriend and friends who visit me here. At 10 P.M. every visitor has to leave the hostel and sometimes visits are denied in the absence of an identification card. This applies also to the weekends when we young people would like to spend more time together. Not even an extra ten minutes can be arranged with the security staff. *One is constantly controlled here as soon as one enters the hostel. The police also regularly patrol the neighbourhood, which makes one feel like a common criminal. Sometimes the policemen quietly creep from door to door, and they eavesdrop on people.*[205] I have come to Jena to build an independent life, which is impossible under these circumstances. Only a flat could give me prospects. I spend the whole year in Jena and I can only travel home for a couple of days, three times in a year. Therefore this small room with the many orders and prohibitions and a real jailer is, after all, my main residence. I think that 23-year-old people have a right to expect something better than this.[206]

The letter suggests that many people did not identify the whole system with the image of the 'police state' unless they consciously meant to provoke the authorities, which is highly unlikely if they wanted to solve their flat problem.

It is interesting to contrast the above letter that criticized excessive control, with another complaint concerning the supposedly deviant conduct of a room-mate. It may well have been that life in the hostels lacked comfort but, as the following letter shows, it was very difficult to terminate tenancy regardless of the unlawful conduct of the tenants:

I am a 26-year-old worker and I work on the three-shift system. I live in Neulobeda-West, block 10. My reason for writing is the following. At the beginning of this year a young man, Mr K, moved into our flat. He does not work in the VEB Carl Zeiss and he does not have a permanent job. He has, however, a hobby: he is a disc jockey. He stores his music equipment in the flat. He frequently comes home very late in the night with lots of other people who are very loud. The noise is really extreme, in particular at weekends. There are sometimes as many as ten strange people sleeping in the flat. They often help themselves to my food and drink from the fridge, and they leave the bath and the kitchen in a filthy state. I have worked for ten years in VEB Carl Zeiss Jena on the three-shift system, which is very tiring, especially when one can't sleep at home. I told the managers of the hostel about the problem but it seems that they either don't care or they can't help with this problem. Therefore I would like to ask for your help because this situation is getting on my nerves. I really need my rest so that I can concentrate on my work by the machine in the plant.[207]

In this case we know the reply: investigators found that Mr K had married a woman who also worked in the Zeiss factory, and they had received a one-room flat in a family hostel. The couple, however, broke up and Mr K was asked to relinquish the common flat, which he refused, arguing that he had nowhere to go. Then he received a room in the hostel of the petitioner. It turned out that Mr K was currently unemployed because he had resigned from Carl Zeiss declaring that he would earn his living by making music. Despite repeated warnings Mr K refused to change his lifestyle:

In March, after several complaints, the managers of the hostel went to his room (he lay in bed and he did not make any effort to get out of bed) and they demanded that he should look for alternative accommodation, a new job and should respect house rules while he lives in the hostel. He does not pay his rent on time, and he had to be warned many times to behave himself. In May 1983 he was again asked to leave, but he answered that he considered it unthinkable.[208]

The reply promised that there would be stricter enforcement of the house rules, but effectively management was as powerless in this case as the hostel: the letter repeated that Mr K was allowed to stay in the hostel for as long as he had no alternative accommodation. The case shows that despite the deeply repressive climate in the GDR, people not only defiantly asserted their rights but these rights (among others the right to housing) were indeed strictly protected by law.

Not much is known about the cleaning of hostels, but criticism of the dirty and untidy condition of common rooms suggests that like in almost every community it was very difficult to share the task equally among the tenants. The 'situation in the kitchen' sometimes declined to the point that the flats were invaded by cockroaches. In one case a single mother who lived with her one-year-old daughter in the AWU asked for urgent help because of the appearance of the insects. The inspectors, however, declared that one could not speak of invasion because they only found two living cockroaches (it was not mentioned how many of them perished). The case again points out the unintentionally comical effect of a party language that explained everything in terms of ideology. The inspectors, at any rate, held the woman to be responsible for the problem: when the cleaning staff had come, they could not spray insecticide in her flat because her kitchenette was full of food and dirty dishes. She was requested to 'contribute to the cleanliness of the hostel and to cooperate with the cleaning staff in the destruction of insects and germs in the future'.[209]

The letters reported also of cases where incompetence on the part of the staff rendered life difficult in the workers' hostels. The tenants of three houses of the Kernberge workers' hostel complained that their families had suffered for years from extreme cold in winter because of the laziness of those who stoked and fed the boilers:

> Life in our hostels is becoming more and more unbearable because there is not enough heating. The central heating has been replaced, but the staff of the hostel can only achieve a temperature of 15–18°C in the rooms. Heating stops for hours because the manager of the hostel has no control over his people. He just lets them do what they want; he has no authority. These are hard words but they are true. We believe that if we pay a rent of 1.2 Mark/m² (out of this 0.40 Mark/m² for heating), we have a right to the minimum temperature that is set by law. Because of the low temperature in the flats people always catch cold. The most vulnerable ones are the children. Although the stokers are paid to work from 8.00 A.M. to 16.00 P.M. at weekends, the heating only usually comes on at 10.30. The reason is simply a lack of discipline. Since we have suffered from this situation for four years, we ask you now to take the necessary steps.[210]

One can wonder what the chief manager of the factory (or his secretariat that dealt with the correspondence) had to do with the lazy stokers; the letter, however, is a further example that social and labour policies were inseparably intertwined.

There were, however, differences among the hostels in terms of the level of comfort and general standards. This is supported by the letter of a student who complained that he had received better accommodation as a skilled worker than as a student:

> Having finished my military service, I started working as a turner in the VEB Carl Zeiss where I worked until I was admitted to the engineering school of precision instruments of Carl Zeiss. Since my home is 300 km from Jena, I need an AWU-place here. I received a place in Jena-Kernberge but the conditions make me doubt whether my decision to study here was the right one. These are the problems: first, there are only common kitchens, baths, toilets, poor hygiene (lack of cleaning staff); second, I have very noisy accommodation in a four-bed room (with shift workers); third, there is no entertainment at weekends because I can rarely go home; fourth, there are no opportunities to store valuable objects. When I worked in the factory, I lived in a reasonable two-bed room in the Am Herrenberge hostel. The requirements of the engineering school are high and one needs peace to prepare for the classes. I had this peace in my old hostel, where I could have fulfilled my obligations at school. But the conditions in the Bernhard Kellermann Straße do not enable me to concentrate on my studies. I am asking for your support and an investigation into the circumstances that I describe above.[211]

The student did not get a positive reply, though: he was ordered to meet his homework obligations because other students lived under the same conditions. In order to prevent further damage, it was decided that the tenants should be financially responsible for the state of the rooms.

Because of the bad living conditions it was understandable that many people declined to show the flat distribution committee any respect. Angry letters survived from the mid-1970s that show that not even an expert could get a flat that had been promised to him in his work contract:

> I came to work at VEB Carl Zeiss Jena in 1972 when the enterprise promised me that my family would get adequate accommodation. It turned out that this 'adequate accommodation' consists of an AWU. My family had to stay in the house of my father-in-law and I was told to wait for one year. Now, after one and half years I still cannot get a flat because of 'objective conditions' and because my case is not urgent! Should you give me a negative answer, I have to assume that you approve of the fraud by which the factory bought me. How else can I regard the treatment I have been given, after one and half years of promises, only to declare now that my family can't move to Jena? Even my contract of employment guarantees adequate accommodation, which after so much waiting cannot be an AWU where I, a family father have to share a room with a strange colleague! If you can find no solution to my problem, I will be forced to turn to the Court of Labour.[212]

The answer was, however, negative despite the threat: the writer was informed that the factory was objectively unable to solve every social problem, and that adequate accommodation was in practice an AWU for many employees in the beginning. He was, however, reassured that his problem would be solved as soon as the 'objective conditions' enable it.[213]

Even members of the party wrote angry and disrespectful letters concerning their housing problems and the role of the factory in them. One example is the following letter:

> Last year I wrote some letters of complaint to which I received the answer that the flat distribution committee does everything it can to help my family. I am doing my military service now but I am forced to write a letter again because my wife had just the opposite experience. When she enquired about our application for a flat, the responsible colleague knew nothing of it and he found our application only after a long search. Then he sent her to another colleague, who told my wife that there were free flats adding that 'had you moved to an AWU two years ago, you would have lived under difficult conditions for one year and then you would have got a flat!' I was outraged to hear that such practices exist in VEB Carl Zeiss Jena and that the tenants of AWU are advantaged even though we live under similar conditions in one room of my parental house. Does this mean that there are double standards or that I am not important for my plant now that I am in the army? [214]

The letter was finished with the formula 'with socialist greetings' (*mit sozialistischem Gruß*), and the writer also referred to his community work and his good results in the factory. The answer was, however, negative: the writer was informed that the tenants of AWU were not advantaged, and that there were other, objective reasons why his problem could not be solved in that year:

> We had to solve urgent production tasks and therefore some plants received more flats. Further, a number of political emigrants from Chile had to be accommodated in the town. Therefore the failure to solve your flat problem does not mean that we do not treat our employees equally but it means that we have to consider first economic interests in order to be able to improve the situation of working people.[215]

The last sentence was probably meant to be an ideological reprimand from the party.

There were resolute petitioners who decided to fight for their rights: they wrote repeated complaints, they demanded information about the criteria for the allocation of flats and they pestered the flat distribution committee with their perpetual complaints. As the following letter shows, some of them were desperate (or tactical) enough to question the justice of the whole system:

> I have lived for five years in an AWU of the VEB Carl Zeiss. My daughter was born last year and since then three of us have been living in a room of 12 m². I think our situation needs no further description. Since we were on the priority list of our plant, we were supposed to get a new flat in 1980. To our great disappointment, instead of the promised new flat we received an offer of a totally miserable, sleazy, old, wet flat without a bath, toilet or functioning wiring. Under no circumstances would I move into this flat with a small baby. What has happened to the flats that our plant received? I was told that out of the 84 flats, 59 were allocated according to the decisions of the management, not by the flat distribution committee. Why do they make priority lists then if the managers allocate the flats anyway and it is connections that matter, not the situation of the family concerned? I cannot at all understand that there are couples without babies who spend only some weeks in the AWU and then they immediately get a flat. Where is justice here?[216]

After he received the flat list of his plant, the angry family man turned to the manager with a new complaint:

> I do not accept the reply to my former letter because my questions have been only partly or not at all answered. The list that I got confirms my main argument: flats are not allocated according to the social situation of people. Otherwise how can childless couples receive two-room flats while families with a child have to wait for years in the AWU? When I enquired about the concrete cases, the flat distribution committee was unable to justify these decisions. They referred to the 'summary of criteria' but they could not be concrete about them. I was told that the age of the child was not important. For us who are concerned, it is, however, a crucial question: how long do we have to live with our child under these miserable conditions? I expect a concrete answer to my question![217]

The reply was characterized by the authoritarianism of the managing director, even though it was most probably written by one of his administrators:

> In my answer to your repeated complaint I take the opportunity to explain to you once more the flat policy of the factory. According to the regulations of 1973 the factory has full responsibility for its employees with respect to housing. I have decided the following: first, every plant receives a flat contingent in each year; second, the managers of the plants are fully responsible to me in this question; third, there is a special contingent at my disposal so that I can personally solve special cadre problems or urgent social problems during the year. I am fully aware of my responsibility, and my decisions are in line with the

social political requirements of the Ninth Party Congress. I do not tolerate any deviation in this respect. My colleagues told you about the tense flat situation of the town. That's why it is all the more incomprehensible to me that you have refused two offers for old flats (a three-room flat in Mühlenstr. 41 and a two-room flat in Dornburger St. 131) because of the external toilet and the lack of a bath. I once more inform you that according to the urgency of your case your name will appear on the list of the next year. That said, I regard your complaint to be once and for all settled.[218]

The correspondence between the persistent petitioner and the chief manager does, in fact, prove the *opposite* of his argument: his social situation was, after all, taken into consideration. Further, the many checks in the system (flat distribution committees, priority lists, letters of complaint and the need to justify decisions) show that the social rights of people were, in fact, strongly protected, and that the applicants who were waiting for flats were all entitled to this benefit. It is, however, remarkable that the sharp criticisms of housing policy did not affect negatively the chances of the stubborn man: this suggests that petitioning also had the psychological function of venting passions, and the official bodies therefore tolerated the disrespectful language.

Unfortunately, there are very few accounts of the activities of flat distribution committees, but there is evidence that some people used the same disrespectful manner during the personal discussions of their flat problem. A certain Miss R, for instance, refused two offers for old flats and another two for AWU rooms because:

as she put it, the other tenants were 'dirty pigs'. However, because of the tense flat situation in Jena many young people and mothers with children live in AWU, and one cannot describe these people as this ... After the members of the flat committee discussed the problem with Miss R, she answered that 'it is bad enough that other colleagues accept everything and they don't dare to open their mouths'. She wanted to know whether we, the members of the flat committee, had ever lived under similar conditions. She put this question to a 64-year-old comrade, who grew up under capitalism. ... even though the members of the committee are trying to help Miss R, they are not ready to deal with her problem only. She received four acceptable offers in two years that she declined. She would like to have a dream flat that we cannot offer to her at the moment. She said that she would make a new complaint.[219]

It is quite remarkable that Miss R did not refrain from openly criticizing living conditions in the GDR in front of the flat committee. Despite the provocative conduct of Miss R, it was important for the committee to demonstrate that they did everything to help her. This again shows that the officials were expected to consider the social situation of people (even though the question of whether the 64-year-old comrade had ever lived in AWU was evidently held to be a negative political comment).

Some letters of complaint had, however, more serious consequences. Members of the party were evidently expected to show a higher level of conformity and, like in Hungary, to lead a 'decent' family life. The following case shows that the party attempted to intervene in the private lives of its members to defend the family:

> I live with my wife and my two children (a six-year-old son and a two-and-half-year-old daughter) in a two-room flat. I am attending a one-year course at party school, and I have to study a lot at home. My wife also studies. For this reason there are a lot of conflicts in our family. Since after the school I am supposed to be the party secretary of our group, and I am a candidate for higher education in engineering, I would like to ask you to give a positive reply to our application for a bigger flat.[220]

According to the report, during the discussion with comrade D it turned out that the letter was written and sent by his wife without his knowledge. The report commented that his family relations had been tense for one-and-half years because he spent most of his free time with a lover. During this time members of the party asked him many times to resolve his marital problems. Eventually, he declared that he would seek reconciliation with his wife and he would stay with his family. The report also confirmed that comrade D was a candidate for party secretary.[221] The case introduces a 'typical' career with the help of the party (party work, selection for education, responsible post) but it also reveals that the members of the party were expected to respect the moral code of the party.

While petitioners could freely complain of poor living conditions, the threat to leave the GDR was considered to be a political threat, all the more so because the following letter was addressed to the Council of Ministers of the GDR:

> My husband is a technologist in the optical precision instruments' plant of VEB Carl Zeiss Jena. I work as a nurse at the women's clinic of the Friedrich Schiller University. We have lived for seven years in a small furnished room of the nurses' hostel. Since my childhood I have had lived in poor conditions: when I was six, my parents got divorced and my mother and I got one room in a house. This room was wet with mould fungus on the walls. It took my mother ten years to get a bigger flat. When I came to Jena, I lived for three years in a dormitory, where I had only a bed and a shelf that I could call my home. In 1977 I received a room of 9 m² with sloping walls. Half a year later I got married and my husband moved in with me. We lived for three years in

this room where we could only sleep on a couch because there was no room for a bed. Then we got a room of 12 m² and we could finally have a double bed. Last year we had a baby so right now three of us have to live under these miserable conditions. The last offer that we received was a two-room AWU flat but I think that it is senseless to move from one AWU into another. I find it very unjust that after six years of waiting we can only get an AWU flat, and even this is too small. I hope that my family will get an adequate flat before the end of this year because I have no more strength to live in this state with my child.[222]

The petitioner also mentioned that she and her husband were both shop stewards in the trade union. The woman refused to appear in front of the committee because, according to her husband, she recognized that her letter contained incorrect and false statements. The husband himself did not know of the letter and he declared that he would have prevented its mailing:

He found the sentence 'I have no strength to live in this state with my child' particularly shocking, and he could not easily accept it. He maintained, though, that the sentence had no political message, and his wife did not think of leaving the GDR.[223] The chairperson of the committee and another member visited the woman in her home where they were personally convinced of the bad living conditions of the family. The colleagues made it clear to her that her letter had a political message, particularly if one took into account that she was active in the trade union as a shop steward. They concluded that she just wanted to underline the urgency of her case for which she does not blame our state.

It was, at any rate, stated that the letter was written because of an administrative mistake since the flat problem of the family had already been solved. In 1983 a single mother with a child received a three-room flat by mistake. This flat was then allocated to the family of the nurse while the single mother moved to a two-room flat. According to the report the problem was caused by the slow flow of information between the offices.[224] The case, however, reveals that it was also in the interests of officials to be attentive to the social problems of people.

While the cited documents reported many problems relating to the impact of the housing shortage on workers, including the primitive conditions of AWU and long waiting times for new flats, the letters, in fact, unambiguously prove that the social situation of the applicants was an important criterion for the allocation of flats. The comments in the letters suggest that those who were in a difficult situation could rely on the sympathy of administrators. There is evidence that the situation of single mothers received special consideration: a young woman turned to the chief manager with the complaint that she did not receive the one-room flat that the flat distribution committee had promised her, and the management of the hostel where she lived refused to store her furniture that she bought for the new flat:

> Two weeks ago colleague Mrs P invited me for a discussion with the management of the hostel. She did not let me speak or explain the situation and she was totally reluctant to help me. She told me: 'You can put your furniture on the street, that's your problem. By 30 September the room should be cleared'. It was not the first time that she spoke with me in this manner. I am no longer willing to deal with this colleague, and I really need a larger room for my furniture. I would like to ask for your support.[225]

The letter was marked with the comment 'Scandal!!!' The reply, unfortunately, has not survived but if the investigation proved the complaint to be true, Mrs P would have received a strong reprimand for her heartless words.

The following two cases are cited to show that letters of complaint could lead to real results if the recipient chose to decide that the social situation of the writer justified urgent help:

> I trained to be an electrician in VEB Carl Zeiss Jena, where I work now. I have had good results and I have never have received any reprimands. I live together with my parents even though I am already 27. We live in an old house (built in 1939), which consists of a living room, a bedroom, a children's room, a small room that can't be heated, a kitchen, a toilet and a bath in the cellar. The children's room has no heating either. Five years ago my son was born and our flat became too small because I also have a sister. In 1975 I applied for a two-room flat, and now, after four years of waiting, I received the answer that there are more urgent cases that take precedence over my problem. Now I ask you, Comrade Chief Manager, is not my case also urgent?!! My father treats me as a child in front of my son and he thinks that he is responsible for his education. I am deprived of my parental rights! I have to add that I have a fiancé who lives with us, so you can imagine the tense situation in our family. Now I ask you again, Comrade Chief Manager, is it not an urgent case?!![226]

The inquiry confirmed that the woman worker lived under difficult conditions and she received a positive reply to her letter: the chief manager promised that he would personally attend to her case.

The second case was that of a woman who lived with her daughter under similar conditions in the parental flat:

> I have a room of 8.5 m² in my parents' flat where I live with my daughter. My sister also lives with her child in the flat and she has an even smaller room than mine. She can't even put a children's bed in her room. A further problem is the common use of the kitchen and bath. Since we all start working at the

same time, I have to get up very early so that the others can use the bathroom in the morning. The flat distribution committee decided that my case was urgent after they visited our flat. Now I have learnt, however, that my name does not appear on the priority list. Since my fiancé works in the same plant and he has a room of 6 m², this complaint is our only opportunity to improve our situation and unite our family. For this reason I would like to ask you to find a speedy solution to end our misery. The flat committee can visit our flat at any time so that they can be convinced once more of our untenable situation.[227]

The woman was reassured that her case was regarded as socially urgent and that the chief manager would deal with the case personally.

Even though all of these cases describe individual situations and problems, they show how the system of the flat allocation functioned in practice. The largest group that was dependent on the factory for housing was either the new settlers, or those local people who could not rely on parental help. Often the latter were in a more difficult situation because, as the letters show, the family lived in cramped conditions in the parental home. Early marriages and the birth of children rendered the waiting time for a flat very difficult, as many generations had to occupy the same space. At the same time, however, a decision to have children at a particular time may have been motivated by the desire to obtain a new flat.[228] The social responsibilities of the enterprises towards its workers created a comprehensive work-based social security system, but it enabled a high degree of employer intervention into the private sphere. Letters of complaint addressed family problems such as divorce and adultery, and there were jealous spouses who used the opportunities such a system provided to denounce their partners to the workplace or to the party. Others asked for the help of management in order to expel a husband who drank heavily and engaged in drunken violence against family members from their home: solving one problem created another, for this employee needed a new home. The system of flat allocation rendered the factory to a large extent responsible for the social problems of their workforce. It helped to maintain a certain level of social justice (it was shown that the social situation of people received consideration in the factory), but it reinforced patterns of patriarchal dependence.

While the letters of complaint understandably focused on the negative aspects of community life, centralized mechanisms for distributing housing contributed to a strengthening of collective identities based around the workplace. Young people lived together in hostels, and the new housing estates ensured that Zeiss employees were not only colleagues, but also neighbours, given that the various plants received whole blocks of flats. In a similar fashion to Hungary, the intense community life in the GDR was recalled with a sense of loss in many life-history interviews:

In GDR era there was much greater solidarity among the colleagues. We met more frequently – also in the workplace – people went bowling, they organized garden parties or when the children first went to school, there were youth fêtes or the colleagues went together somewhere after work ... this is different now, people go to work, then they go home and they lock their doors ... with the neighbours it is not like it used to be. In the earlier time we had a housing community (*Hausgemeinschaft*) in these houses. We were all young people with mainly one or two children, we were all around 23–24 when we moved to our first flats, people sat together a lot, there were club nights organized, people had a good time together; it is different now, people don't do it any longer because everybody has his or her own problems and people withdraw from community life. People don't chat with their neighbours on the stairs; they say 'Good afternoon' to each other if they meet, and they close the door. I think that today people are much more stressed, they have to think about things that were natural in the GDR, everybody or almost everybody was treated equally, everybody had work and a stable income. Very few people had really big problems. I say again, people had work, every family could send the children to nursery or kindergarten – many things that used to be natural but today they are not. Today everybody is uninterested ... people don't care about their neighbours; they might hear that he is unemployed or she is now again at home but it is not their problem. Today people are concerned only about themselves.[229]

The living communities that were formed on newly built housing estates played an important role in social networks. Regular social contact and common activities in the neighbourhood were mentioned in many other interviews:

People used to organize parties, I mean here, in the garden in front of the house. Or there were small parties on Saturdays, people made a fire, they had a beer and they talked to each other. The neighbours helped each other, there was social work, they did something for the environment. Today a firm does this kind of work in the neighbourhood. I don't know why this has developed in this way. For instance, on Saturdays there were always three or four men in the yard, they repaired their cars, they had a chat. Today people don't repair their cars, they take them to a garage. Sometimes I think that it is difficult to make friends with new neighbours.[230]

According to many interview partners, the housing communities were part of a communal life that declined after the fall of the GDR:

Solidarity declined both at work and in private life. Take the collective of our house – there were forty-four flats in the house, families of similar age, we did a lot together, there were parties, we enjoyed ourselves. After '89 this has disappeared, people did not sit together, everybody stayed in the flats; it was not like as it was, more together, people organized children's parties in the houses, they were nice and they have disappeared, too. There were house parties twice a year but today people don't want to sit together and speak of their things, perhaps they are afraid that they give themselves away and that others take an advantage of them. Today people are afraid to share their ideas or problems with their friends, that's why they turn inside.[231]

Regardless of how one evaluates community in the GDR, the system of flat distribution undoubtedly reinforced a feeling of community and strengthened the relationship between workers and the factory. According to the official expectations, the flat generated feelings of gratitude from the population. Indeed people were most probably very happy when they could move into their first flats, particularly if they had had to live for years in various types of 'mass accommodation'. Yet 'dream flats' were not regarded as such forever by their new occupants. While community life in the GDR was seen positively after unification, their nostalgia did not spread to their view of the quality of housing:

I started work at Zeiss in May 1968 and by October I had already received a flat. Five months. At that time many people came to Jena because of the flats. That's a fact, there were many. There were factories like Zeiss in Jena, and the large chemical factories in Eisenhüttenstadt – I don't know if the name means anything to you – many young people moved there. You can see from here the houses … to the left. I moved afterwards because it was a two-room flat, you could get only a two-room flat if you did not have children. … My son is not married and he has a flat. I find this good. He is better off now than we were.[232]

The letters of complaint and life-history interviews suggest considerable discontent with housing in the GDR. While community was positively evaluated, state social policy was at best an ambiguous means of rallying the population behind the regime. Many people regarded the flats as fringe benefits rather than the realization of an egalitarian social programme. Furthermore, in the light of the letters connections continued to matter: experts enjoyed an advantage over the others and, since education (including adult education) was controlled by the party, the selection of the candidates for higher education (and thus, upward mobility) was largely dependent on their ideological reliability. The following letter is cited to show that there were people who felt that they were cast to the margins of the socialist social welfare state, despite waiting for years:

I have read the article about our social policy in the 30 January 1987 issue of *Volkswacht* with interest. The report argues that two-thirds of working-class families received new flats between 1971 and 1986 and that adult people have

at least 26 m² at their disposal. Further, 76 per cent of the flats are equipped
with baths or showers and 68 per cent have internal toilets; 42–45 per cent of
the new houses would be given to working-class people. I have to say that the
living conditions of my family (four people) are very different. We live in a flat
of 48 m² in an old building. We cannot use the largest room (11 m²) in winter
because it is wet and cold and it has no heating. So my eight-year-old daughter and my two-year-old son have to share a bedroom (10 m²). The flat has
neither a bath nor a shower and the toilet is in the common stairwell. There is
no drying room so we have to dry our washing in the flat. The building is in
a very bad state (the gutters are broken, the plaster falls off, and the windows
can't be closed properly). I received this flat in 1978 – I accepted it because I
lived with my baby in half a room in my parents' house. After my second marriage and the birth of my son, four of us lived in a flat that I received for two
people. My husband and I are both blue-collar workers and my husband works
on two shifts. I applied for a cooperative flat in 1971 but after sixteen years
of waiting I was told to file a new application. I have the impression that the
flat distribution committee consciously deceived me, so I just don't trust them
any more. Because of the circumstances that I described above, I consider this
complaint as my only opportunity to improve my living conditions. I would
like to ask for your support in this matter.[233]

The answer of the chief manager has not survived but the letter reinforces
the picture of a tense relationship between the workers and management
in which authoritarianism and social justice were often paradoxically combined.

The 'balance' of Honecker's great housing project is therefore, at
best, ambiguous. In the light of the interviews, housing communities
reinforced private contacts and solidarity among the workers, many of
whom knew each other already from the training school and the dormitories. Since they belonged to similar age groups, they shared several
family experiences: taking their children to nurseries and kindergartens,
family festivals and other common leisure programmes. There is no reason to doubt that many young couples were very happy to move to their
first homes – especially if they had to spend years in overcrowded AWUs
or the parental home, where couples often lived in one room with their
babies. Social rights, however, encompassed the right for 'appropriate'
housing and, as we have seen from the letters, East German workers did
not refrain from criticizing the management if they felt that these rights
were not respected. Honecker's welfare policy therefore led the GDR into
a similar debt trap as was the case with Hungary, because their planned
economies were ill equipped to compete with the market economies and
consumption levels of the advanced Western countries. And the Western
television channels and Western trips rendered this difference painfully
obvious, even in the eyes of the East German population. In Hungary we

can find abundant criticism of the increase of prices and the failure of the standard-of-living policy in the information reports of the 1980s. In the GDR, political repression provided for the quiescence of the population; the mass flight of the citizens in 1989 when Hungary opened its Western borders, however, demonstrated that East German youth no longer saw its future in the socialist system.

'Du und dein Werk'

Even though community building was an integral part of the labour policy of the factory – as we have seen with the example of housing – given the fact that the minute books of the meetings of the party leadership of the factory have not survived, there is very little documentation of the social activities that were undertaken for this purpose, including the socialist brigade movement. In 1973, when the Zeiss factory celebrated the 25th anniversary of the nationalization of the enterprise, the work plan of a special publication survived, which underlined that its main purpose was to stress workers' identification with the collective and the factory. The title of the publication was called characteristically 'Du und dein Werk' (You and your Plant). The most important aspects of the concept for the publication were the following:

> It should be, above all, introduced how under socialist conditions people – in particular the members of the leading working class – are trained to be socialist personalities with the help of their collective in the workplace. It is a process that cannot take place without conflicts because we have to overcome the biases and influences of bourgeois ideologies. In this respect you should describe the relevant, purposeful activities of the socialist brigades (the work pledges of the collectives) and the results of the socialist work contest. You should represent how the workers in partnership with the intelligentsia – under the leadership of the party – manifest themselves as socialist proprietors, producers and the possessors of power. The idea is not to give a historical outline of the past 25 years of the VEB Carl Zeiss Jena but to show that – as a result of a historically determined process – a landmark event took place 25 years ago that decisively determined the future of the Zeiss factory. In order to have an emotional effect, you should use the Du-form,[234] so you will directly address the reader and immediately engage him in the narrative so that he can commit to memory that his work serves the strengthening of the GDR and of the socialist world system, and thereby the defence of peace. And he is part of all of these with his work, with his initiative, with his collective, with his personality.[235]

The above text, albeit it was prepared for propagandistic purposes, expressed the main message of the community policy of VEB Carl Zeiss

Jena. The German language distinguishes between the formal ('Sie') and informal ('du') ways of addressing people. The use of 'du' shows that the party sought to eliminate the social distance between workers and managers, at least in interpersonal communication; hierarchical relations were supposed to be replaced with a homogenous working community. The state strongly supported working-class communities and community life. The German system was traditionally characterized by solid hierarchies and the separation of social classes. The party made great efforts to democratize the relationship between workers and managers. This was partly achieved through a levelling wage policy (it was a frequent complaint that foremen earned nearly the same money as skilled workers, especially if they were shift workers) and partly through a conscious decrease of social distance (workers lived in the same quarters as managers, they ate in the same canteens, there were common state festivals and equality was an important social message of the party). Workers gave credit to the emancipating policy of the party: the greater social equality of the old system was recalled in the interviews with a sense of loss.

In spite of the apt title of the chapter, the intensive community life of the factory that workers reported in the interviews has little archival documentation. The materials of the factory party organization are very scattered for this period so it is difficult to reconstruct the community life of the factory. A report of 1973 gave the following account of voluntary social work that was undertaken by the factory collective:

> Since the beginning of the year the number of brigades has increased from 598 to 664 in the plants of Jena (including Saalfeld). Out of them, 401 brigades participate now in the contest for the title of the 'Collective of Socialist Work' (*Kollektiv der sozialistischen Arbeit*) while at the beginning of the year there were only 389 participants. At the same time the number of brigades that won the title increased from 219 to 229. Currently, there are twenty schools with around 11,650 children who are patronized by our factory. Within the framework of this program 6,779 pupils participate in the training programmes of comprehensive schools and 445 pupils who are in the 11th and 12th classes are engaged in the scientific-political programmes of our institutions. More than 2,000 employees work in the eighty-two cultural groups of the factory. The political and cultural activities of our youth manifested itself particularly in preparation for the tenth world festival: there were 480 youth programmes with more than 20,000 participants. The high proportion of our youth who participated in 'Messe der Meister von Morgen'[236] (88 per cent), the socialist work contest and the discussion of the youth act show that young people are actively engaged in the solution of the problems. It expresses the increasing consciousness of responsibility that there were 2,100 meetings that discussed the plan of 1974 with the participation of 80 per cent of the members of the

brigades. Out of the 7,300 contributions there were 3,309 proposals for the improvement of working conditions, work culture and labour protection.

The report, however, concluded that despite these results, the tempo and the results of the process of socialist rationalization were still inadequate and more ideological work was needed to increase the number of shift workers.[237]

The cited documents suggest that memory of the special nature of Zeiss's history – that is the form of ownership and the generous social policy of the factory before the Second World War – survived as late as the beginning of the 1970s, and the functionaries considered it necessary to underline that the new, socialist system had established stronger bonds between the workers and the factory than did the capitalist system. Given the oppressive ideological climate and the lack of survey evidence it is difficult to determine to what extent this project was successful. The cited documents of the investigation of 1969 in the instrument plant, at any rate, suggest that the majority of the old guard of the factory kept a distance from the party and politics. With respect to the politics of factory identity and especially working-class engagement with official ideologies of socialist proprietary consciousness, it is worth recalling the comment of one of the managers that people work conscientiously because of their old loyalty to the factory, rather than because of their political commitment.[238] Beyond militant party language it is possible to detect the signs of the conflicts and attitudes of previous eras, for instance the admission that the nationalization of the enterprise was a contested process and that socialist rationalization did not have tangible results. Such comments reveal that despite the over-ideologized language, scepticism towards the campaigns of the party manifested itself among the employees.

The leadership of the district was also discontented with the political work of the party organization of the factory; at least at a meeting in 1978 the work with workers to improve socialist rationalization was met with a sharply hostile response:

> Certainly we all share the opinion that the concrete organization of the daily offensive work with the masses is of a remarkably low standard in the Zeiss factory. The much debated problems of the supply of consumer goods and the wide range of questions concerning foreign and domestic policies require that all of the employees should get a clear picture and they should be fully conscious of their personal responsibility for the ongoing development of the whole republic. You should explain to them that the increasing needs of the population that, as we all know, increases at a higher rate than our production, demand a high level of achievement from everybody.

The following contribution suggests that the whole town was regarded to be ideologically 'unreliable' – or more liberal – in the district: 'The IKL should pay more attention to concrete political work with the masses in the future. The criticism that this work needs to be more comprehensive and diverse concerns not only IKL but also the town of Jena, where there is much to be done in this respect because some problems cannot be solved through better economic propaganda alone.' The report of the IKL, not surprisingly, stressed the results of political work, amongst others the increase in the number of young workers who received awards for their quality work, the results of the innovation movement (*Neuererbewegung*) and the mass movement entitled 'Initiativpaß 30' in the optical instrument plant. Within the framework of the latter the employees undertook the task of sparing thirty working hours with the help of socialist rationalization.[239]

Although political campaigns (including the socialist brigade movement) were expected to lead to increases in production, even the above cited documents suggest that the campaigns mainly aimed to improve the relations between the party and the people.[240] This, at least, explains that the work with the masses – on the basis of the account – had few, if any, concrete results and neither were the methods of socialist rationalization more closely determined. Unfortunately, there are no overall figures regarding activity of socialist brigades in the factory. The 'Salvador Allende' brigade was the only brigade whose diary survived in the factory archive. It reinforces the argument that the brigades were more important for community building than for production. Amongst its work pledges there were general objectives listed such as fulfilment of the plan targets and the undertaking of special control tasks.[241] The brigade's cultural and social activities were very similar to those of their Hungarian counterparts: participation in adult education, movie programmes (visits to the Soviet film festival), bowling, the celebration of the International Women's Day, common excursions with the families of the members of the brigade, brigade evenings and the patronage of schoolchildren. The members of the 'Salvador Allende' brigade also committed themselves to studying the Soviet media, which suggests that more political work was expected from the socialist brigades in the GDR than in Hungary.[242] The accounts in the brigade diary recorded various aspects of community life: tours, excursions, nights at the cinema, visit to libraries, wine tasting, walking in the forest, a reading group, and the celebration of International Women's Day. The accompanying photographs showed that brigade life did not exist merely on paper, but that people did indeed participate in the common activities.

On the basis of contemporary sources it is very difficult to see to what extent the socialist project of community building was successful and how it shaped popular consciousness. Even though there is some evidence that the party could not win over the majority of the factory's old guard to its cause, this probably did not influence their attitude to the factory itself. In addition, with the rapid increase of the workforce from the late 1960s, the social composition of its personnel changed too: many young people came from distant towns and villages to be trained in Jena, and those who settled in the town grew up practically together with this new collective. The dormitories, the common training and the community life of the AWU inevitably established closer contacts among young people, and reinforced feelings of solidarity. Even though there is no documentation of their integration into the factory collective, the common fêtes, sporting events and socialist brigades undoubtedly played a role in the process. This type of socialization rendered people more responsive to the values of the community they had joined.

On the basis of life-history interviews, community building could be regarded as successful because the overwhelming majority of my interview partners stressed that there was a higher level of communality among colleagues and their neighbours during the Honecker era than under the capitalist system post-unification. In this context the positive values of the socialist brigades (solidarity and communality) were frequently contrasted with the individualism and egoism of the new system:

> This collective spirit that existed at the time of the GDR had a very different background. People helped each other because they had common problems to be solved. Today one speaks of team spirit but this team spirit is actually needed to achieve a goal. Not to solve problems but to achieve a goal. In the brigades it was not the goal that was important but collective social work, to have good results as a collective, for instance if someone did not have enough points, the others helped them and together they could achieve a good result. Today the system does not work like that. This is a pity because people had a greater sense of togetherness, in order to help each other. Today this help is not wanted. People are required to work together for the same goal but they are expected to work on their own and to achieve the maximum output.[243]

The majority of my interview partners felt a change in people's relation to their workplace and consequently that solidarity and human contacts among workmates declined.[244] They maintained that the communities that were built in the GDR had disappeared together with the socialist system:

> The collective was much better united in the time of the GDR. We went on excursions, held common festivals to celebrate Christmas in the workplace and other celebrations that we had at the time; we did many things together, we had many common trips and we had a rest. After work we always had a rest. But it is not the same now as it used to be. The collective is not what it used to be. I have work, I do my work – and the others? Earlier it was not like that. You can try but it no longer works. 'I work here, and what I do afterwards –

that's my business, that's my private life' – that's what many would tell you now. It hurts a bit, really. People need time to relax – it would be good if we had a little time for each other![245]

In this context the socialist brigades were linked with a higher level of solidarity that was held to be a positive feature of the previous system:

Today people are occupied with themselves. In the period of the GDR we had a community. Neighbours helped each other, we had common excursions with colleagues in the workplace, there were common activities ... There was a good climate in our plant, we regularly held brigade evenings, brigade parties. There were very many events organized amongst brigade members, among workmates, in the workshop, in the plant and in the whole factory – regular events. Workmates met privately, they mutually helped each other with various household jobs, for instance, repairing things or decorating the flat – that was totally normal. It was totally normal we helped each other. It is not like that today. It has been lost.[246]

Interview partners also told about cases when the brigades gave psychological support to their members:

Earlier there was a totally different feeling of solidarity between colleagues. Today it is more like a fight because people think that they cannot keep their jobs otherwise. It was different in the GDR era ... We had a colleague who had an alcohol problem and it was precisely this environment, her socialist brigade, that helped her to lead a normal life. After the *Wende* she became a real alcoholic.[247]

Like in the Hungarian case, community building in the GDR was a part of the labour policy of the regime that received strong institutional support. While the mutual assistance of workmates had its spontaneous aspects, the role of the brigade movement – organized from above – was recognized:

One has to admit that earlier everything was a bit more organized. Fêtes in the workshop, brigade parties ... such things ... and then everybody was there, and there were groups formed that understood each other well. And the framework was also very different then, there were 250 people in the workshop; when there was an excursion, they sometimes hired a whole ship. Workmates meet much less frequently now.[248]

There were interview partners who reported of a kind of nostalgia for the organizational framework of the brigade movement:

> We made work pledges, newspapers for the walls, sometimes it was a bit child-
> ish but ... we wrote in the brigade diary to record what we did together, there
> were reports, photos ... they have been all thrown away, these diaries; it is a
> pity – for instance, our boss whom we have now, he would be very happy if he
> could write such a diary now.[249]

In the light of my life-history interviews, the brigade movement left
mainly positive memories behind. It is, however, questionable as to the
extent the communities of the factory and the neighbourhood influenced
working-class political opinions and strengthened their loyalty to the regime. While many interview partners linked these communities with socialist values (solidarity, unselfishness, equality), they did not hold the
system itself to be socialist (none of the cited interview partners were
members of the party, and many had a negative opinion of the party and
the 'comrades'). As the following citation shows, community work and
participation in common activities had no relationship to the political
opinions of people:

> I was not a member of the party. I was pressured many times because my
> husband was a member, and they told me that if my husband is a member, I
> should be a candidate, too. Then I said to the woman, okay, convince your
> husband first that he should join and then I will join, too. I knew that he
> was not a member of the party. No one forced me. I know this is how they
> would tell it now – but it is not true. Neither were people forced to celebrate
> 1 May. Allegedly they checked the names of those who were not there but I
> have never seen any such lists ... At that time there was practical training for
> schoolchildren, one day a week, and I was persuaded to become a teaching
> assistant. I liked it very much, to organize the children, to find relevant tasks
> for them and to evaluate their work ... I enjoyed it very much. But I would
> not have gone to party meetings on every Monday.[250]

Surely there were people who could take advantage of their community
work, but for the majority these collectives offered no material advantages
and they were primarily appreciated as social spheres which were relatively independent of state control. Brigades were not, of course, organized
from below since the socialist brigade movement received strong support from the factory party organization. Independently of state support,
though, people could participate in the community life of the brigades
without identifying themselves with the party or the state ideology. In the
light of the interviews workers held the work and housing communities
to be social spaces free of state control. Private contacts formed on this
basis reinforced a common working-class consciousness in opposition to
the privileged cadres of the regime. Solidarity among workers was also

nourished by the oppressive ideological climate, omnipotent state control and the interdependence of people within the shadow economy of favours necessitated by goods' shortages. This kind of solidarity, however, helped to reinforce a critical attitude towards the regime and its privileged cadres.

Emancipated? Labour Policy for Women

Labour policy for women was a distinguished area of Honecker's welfare policy and the image of the emancipated, working East German women frequently appeared in the propaganda of the state as opposed to West German women, who were held to be confined to the household and the private sphere. Women's entrance to the labour market did not, however, mean full-scale emancipation; studies showed that household duties remained to be mainly the women's chore. In her book, where she analysed the women's policy of the East German state, Harsch shows how working women could exert pressure on the party to secure concessions in the sphere of private life and family.[251] The goal of this chapter is much more limited. In the light of the surviving documents from the women's commission in Zeiss, I seek to offer a case study of how women's policy functioned in a large factory such as Zeiss, and how far the party succeeded in emancipating women at the workplace. Since the sources do not enable the study of family life, statistical analysis will be limited to productive work.

Helping working women was a central aspect of the labour policy of the regime; it was so for two reasons.[252] First, the government sought to solve the problem of labour shortage by ensuring that women were integrated fully into the labour market. In addition to propaganda, this was encouraged by an extensive programme of state provision of child care: nurseries, kindergartens and afternoon schools. Places in these institutions were in principle offered to every family at highly subsidized prices. This kind of state support was meant not only to encourage female employment, but also to enable women to complete household chores. The second aim was to level the differences between the sexes in income, education and career opportunities (in fact, full female employment was an important element of the state's general egalitarianism). Thanks to the work of women's commissions,[253] whose task was to assist and control the realization of these goals in the enterprises, the situation of women workers in the Zeiss factory is better documented than that of their male counterparts (for instance, with respect to education).

Between 1960 and 1980 the proportion of women among the employees of the factory showed a slight increase: it was 37.8 per cent in 1960, increasing to 39.4 per cent in 1970, up again to 40.3 per cent in

1975, and then 43.5 per cent by 1980. The Zeiss plants located in Jena had a workforce that was 42 per cent female, and in some plants such as the optical plant women constituted a majority (60 per cent).[254] In the district the percentage of women of working age employed was 82.5 per cent in 1972,[255] and it increased to 90 per cent in 1975.[256] The town of Jena had a similarly high proportion of working women: 93 per cent of women were employed in 1976.[257] In the light of these figures we can speak of almost full female employment in the district and the town.

The factory made considerable efforts to provide conditions for full female employment. In 1976 in the town of Jena it maintained eight nurseries with 407 places, nine kindergartens with 856 places and two afternoon schools with 172 places.[258] The town could offer proportionally more places in nurseries than in the GDR as a whole (number of places per number of children) while the proportion of the kindergarten places lay a bit below the national average. Reports critically commented that there were not enough afternoon schools in the town. There are general figures with respect to the whole of the factory including plants outside Jena that show a slight growth in the capacity of the institutions for delivering child care in the second half of the 1970s: in 1976 the factory had 1,749 nursery and 2,762 kindergarten places, while in 1980 these numbers were 2,206 and 2,859 respectively. This improvement was demonstrated by the fact that, in 1980, only 141 women out of the employees of the factory (including all plants outside Jena) could not work because they could not get nursery or kindergarten places for their children,[259] whereas in 1970 nearly 500 women were in this situation in Jena alone.[260] It can be correctly claimed that the demand for child-care places could be almost fully satisfied. This was reflected also in the development of female employment.

Full female employment had, however, a negative side, too. Even though one cannot make general statements about how household work was divided within the family, the surviving documents suggest that shopping and provisioning were largely the task of women (for instance, in the information reports it was usually women who criticized the supply of consumer goods). This explains the high proportion of women among part-time workers: according to a 1973 report, out of the 2,347 part-time workers at the Zeiss factory 2,234 (95 per cent) were women. Around one-fifth of the female employees of the factory were part-time workers: their proportion was 19.5 per cent in 1973 and 20.8 per cent in 1980.[261] The proportion of part-time workers in 1973 was almost the same among the women workers: it was 18.1 per cent in 1980 (a slight decrease in comparison with the previous year, when it was 19.3 per cent as the report commented). During this period it was the task of the women's commissions to win over women for full-time employment:[262] even though the proportion of part-timers among female workers was lower than the national industrial average (25.8 per cent) in the Zeiss, they had regular discussions with part-time workers to this end. The report underlined that new part-time contracts could be given for a determined period of time only, and they had to be very well grounded. The following 'ideological obstacles' to full-time jobs came up from the women during the discussions: insufficient places in the afternoon schools, the issues around the supervision of children; an inadequate supply of consumer goods; household chores; the negative attitude of husbands; and financial calculations (the money was enough for the family budget).[263] This shows that in this case the interest of the state as an employer preceded the interests of working mothers, since many women would have preferred working part-time for as long as they had small children.

The political goal of fully integrating women into the workforce was high on the agenda of the women's commission, but improvement of the conditions of working women was also an integral part of this policy. In the optical plant of the Zeiss factory, 15 per cent of the women workers undertook shift work in 1976; the report of the commission added that the plant had one of the youngest staffs in the factory, with an average age of 23 (because of the mass recruitment of young skilled workers) and the mothers who had small children were not willing to work in shifts. The report also mentioned that the shift nursery had to be closed because mothers refused to leave their children there.[264] The women's commission paid special attention to the full use of working hours:

> Many women leave their workplace earlier reasoning that 'I have to pick up my children from the kindergarten or nursery on time because they are always the last'. An inquiry found that all of these institutions were open until 17.30 but parents usually picked up their children at 17.00. In the meantime we have arranged that all of the child care centres in Jena should be open until 18.00. Thus, women can spend more time in their workplace, they can participate in social life better than earlier, and they can also go shopping without being worried about their children.[265]

Despite their political commitment, the women's commissions did, however, represent the interests of working women sometimes even against management:

> *We can conclude from our work with big families that there are a number of ideological problems in the attitude of the managers and state leaders.*[266] In many cases the managers refused to recognize that working mothers carried the bulk of the responsibility for household chores and for homemaking beyond their work in the plant. These tasks were only rarely recognized and appreciated.

> Concerning the extension of shift work, it should be taken into consideration that it is not primarily mothers with small children who should be convinced to work in shifts.[267]

This comment shows that the commissions also acted as mediators between working women and the party and state leaders.

Even though, as the above comment also suggests, housework remained mainly the responsibility of women, in the life-history interviews the state network of child-care institutions and the extension of female employment were unambiguously positively evaluated. Most people regarded child care, the education system, health care, and full employment among the positive features of the socialist system. Full female employment was stressed among the differences between East and West Germany: many women interview partners mentioned that it was natural for them to work as opposed to the more traditional family model in West Germany: 'It was different here than in West Germany where so many women who are below fifty stay at home or they have other interests. No one wants to sit at home here. Those who grew up in work and have always worked as young people want to be active again, not to sit at home and play dominoes. I think that it is depressing to live like that.' In this context some interview partners consciously contrasted the family policy of East Germany with that of West Germany: 'In the old West Germany there were fixed gender roles. In our country never. I have never had any problems with housework. Equal rights – the whole marriage developed like that.'[268] In many life-history interviews, work was an integral part of women's lives; this was why the loss of a job was a particularly painful experience of the new system:

> When the children were small, I would have liked to work part-time, six hours in a day, but at that time it was not possible. I would have liked to spend more time with the children, I have had a bad conscience because I was too tired in the evening, I could not always pay attention ... The right to work, this is what I would like. I was unemployed for one and half years, I did not like it. That was not something for me. I was bored, one needs the stress of work somehow, the children have grown up, in the afternoon one can only wait for my husband to come home ... that was not self-realization. I wanted to do something on my own. I always went to the Office of Labour, I was looking for jobs, I wrote applications that were sent back in two weeks with a refusal and I was sometimes invited to interviews, three or four times. Once I received an interview for a date when I was on holiday, so my son went there, and they said that they want to see me because if the son is so attractive then the mother should be as well [laughs] – this rarely happens but this is how it was.[269]

The role of state-provided child care was a hotly debated issue in the two Germanies; many interview partners felt the need to defend socialist child care against the charge that they would be harmful to the education of their children:

> In my opinion our daughter only benefited from the nursery. My acquaintances from West Germany, well, they would say that in the socialist kindergartners children were educated collectively. But my daughter has become a more individual person who knows her strengths and weaknesses, and she learnt to live in a community, to adapt herself to other people. I think that child care did her only good, as it had a positive effect on the development of her personality. It is totally wrong to believe that mothers have to stay at home with their children for three years in the family home. Child care teaches the children how to live and behave themselves in a community, which is important for the co-existence of people and their social relations. My grandson also goes to nursery. I see no harm in it.[270]

Some interview partners consciously contrasted the Western image of socialist child-care institutions with their own experience:

> First we should get to know each other better. The West Germans likewise don't know much about us. Take childcare. Beautiful kindergartens, children played and they learnt nice songs, and they [the Western relatives of the speaker] thought that the children learnt communist songs only! They also exaggerated things the same way as it was done here.[271]

Child care was evaluated positively even by those who would have preferred working part-time when their children were small:

> Work was from 7.00 to 16.45. It was a long day, mainly for the children. I had to take them early to the nursery, to the city by tram, undress them, run to the workplace, work until the last minute, then back to the nursery, dress the children, pick them up, catch the tram – it was a long day. But I believe even now that the nursery and kindergarten did no harm to the children. In West Germany they believe that these institutions are bad for the children. I don't think so; they don't cause any harm whatsoever. But I think it would have been better if the mothers could have worked part-time.[272]

Others thought that they were in a better situation than young mothers are today:

> I have always worked full-time. I left at 6 in the morning, I took my son to the school, kindergarten or nursery and I picked him up at 5 in the evening. In the meantime I was working. But it was nice. There was stress but it was nice. Today

I can't imagine this stress and after all ... many young people who today have children say 'why should I have all that stress?' At that time I paid 20 Marks (Ostmark[273]) for the nursery and kindergarten places, today one pays 200–300 Euros. These are not comparable. Many would say: 'I rather stay at home, I don't do anything. I have enough money, I need ...' yes, many think like that.[274]

Apart from promoting full female employment, the party also sought to improve the career opportunities of women, the main means of which was through subsidizing education. This was of course linked with the egalitarian policies towards gender relations, as women belonged disproportionately to low-skilled groups. With respect to the training of women there was a clear improvement during the period immediately after the opening of the factory's comprehensive school. In 1966, of the female workforce of the VEB Carl Zeiss Jena, 31 per cent were unskilled, 45 per cent were semi-skilled, and 24 per cent were skilled workers.[275] By 1974, now 22 per cent of the women workers were unskilled, 22 per cent learnt other professions (dressmaker, etc.) and 49 per cent were skilled workers.[276] In the optical plant in 1976, skilled workers were 51.7 per cent of all female workers, university or college graduates 3.7 per cent, and semi-skilled and unskilled workforce 44.6 per cent.[277] Despite the marked improvement, the proportion of unskilled workers was still much higher among women than among men (in VEB Carl Zeiss Jena it was 6.4 per cent in 1974).[278] The proportion of skilled workers was also higher among male workers of the factory: it was 81 per cent in 1974.[279] According to the general figures of the factory (including the plants outside Jena) the proportion of unskilled workers among women was 17.2 per cent in 1980, which shows a slight decrease in comparison with previous years. The proportion of skilled women workers, however, increased to 68.6 per cent, which shows that the qualification level of the female workforce started to be comparable with that of their male counterparts.

The further education of women was supported by several means. Apart from the free education of selected candidates and paid study leave, in 1966 the factory organized special women's classes (*Frauensonderklasse*) in which working women could study during the regular working hours. These classes were very positively remembered by their participants (two of the interview partners attended classes of engineering economics and two of them trained to be designers):[280]

In 1979 I took up an engineering course, I trained to be an engineer-economist for four years. It was a special women's class, I don't know if you have heard of it. We were only women, we had class two days a week ... I liked it very much at that time, there were many of us in a similar situation, with small children, it was easier to help each other.[281]

Special women's classes were also organized to improve the qualifications of women: 511 women finished their vocational training in
these classes between 1966 and 1974.[282] There are no overall figures for
students in higher education but we know, for instance, that in 1976
ninety-nine women attended *Frauensonderklasse* in engineering economics.[283] In 1984, twenty women employees of the factory's research
centre[284] studied in classes specially laid on for women, and nine participated in adult education. In that year six other women started studying
in *Frauensonderklasse* and three in adult education.[285] These numbers
show that women's classes significantly helped the higher education
of women.

While with respect to vocational training the differences between the
men and women workers were significantly reduced, differences at the
top of the hierarchy proved more persistent. In 1972 only 16 per cent
of the employees of VEB Carl Zeiss Jena who had university or college
degrees were women, and their proportion was likewise low; 18 per cent
among those who finished comprehensive school and had a high-school
leaving certificate (*Fachschulkader*[286]).[287] According to the overall figures
of the factory, 6 per cent of the female workforce in 1976 had only the
Fachschulkader and 3.5 per cent were university or college graduates. In
1980 the proportions were 8.1 per cent and 5.2 per cent respectively,
which shows that the proportions of university or college graduates
among women workers nearly doubled over this period.[288] In 1984, of
the women employees of the research centre, 37 per cent belonged to the
above two groups and the figures show that the proportion of educated
women increased in the younger cohorts: of those between 40 and 60
years of age, the proportion of women was 13 per cent among those who
finished *Fachschule*, college or university, while in the age group between
25 and 45 it was 40 per cent.[289]

Table 2.8 gives an overall view of the development of the education of
women in the second half of the 1970s.

On the basis of the statistical evidence, the education of women improved much faster than the appointment of female managers. In 1972,
of the direct production managers of the VEB Carl Zeiss Jena, 7.1 per
cent were women,[290] and according to factory statistics the proportion
of direct production managers was still very low among women in 1976
(0.6 per cent) and in 1980 (0.9 per cent).[291] The proportion of women
was not much higher either among the managers or leading functionaries:
2,041 people had leading positions in the factory in 1976, and 10.6 per
cent were women, while in 1980 out of the 2,376 leaders and managers
12 per cent were women.[292] The critical comments of the reports suggest
that this was the field where it was the most difficult to implement the

Table 2.8 Development of the education and qualification of female employees in the Zeiss factory (in number and %)

	1976 Number	%	1980 Number	%
University, college	639	3.5	949	5.2
Fachshulkader	1,096	6	1,478	8.1
Direct production managers	110	0.6	164	0.9
Skilled workers (1+2 years)	12,137	66.5	12,514	68.6
Without qualification	4,270	23.4	3,138	17.2
Total	18,251	100	18,243	100

Source: UACZ, WB Nr. 487, Abrechnung der Frauenarbeit 1980 nach Schwerpunkten, Qualifikationsstruktur.

policy of equal rights and that misogynist attitudes continued to influence the selection of cadres: 'It contradicts the above development [the improvement of the education of women] that out of the 89 graduates of *Frauensonderklasse* (from 1970) only 12 (13.5 per cent) received mid-level or leading positions.'[293] But even a report in 1981 complained that there was not much progress with respect to the promotion of women leaders and managers in the factory:

> We cannot be satisfied at all with the rate of promotion of qualified women from the lowest to the highest levels. On the contrary, we have to say that there are huge shortcomings in this respect. The proportion of female brigadiers and direct production managers has almost totally stagnated for the past four years and the proportion of women among managers and leading cadres has even declined.[294]

It seems that of all the gender differences, career opportunities were the most difficult to level.[295]

The levelling policy was more successful with respect to the differential between male and female workers. The factory conducted several surveys to show that the principle of equal pay for equal work was realized in each individual plant. With respect to the overall figures, no abuses were reported in this respect: a detailed analysis of the wages of men and women

Table 2.9 Differential between men and women workers in VEB Carl Zeiss Jena in 1978 (monthly average wages)

	Wagegroup 4	Wagegroup 5	Wagegroup 6	Wagegroup 7	Wagegroup 8	Wagegroup 9	Wagegroup 10	Wagegroup 11	Wagegroup 12	Wagegroup 13
Average wage of female employees (M/month)	457	507	570	630	669	764	878	1,050	1,289	1,595
Average wage of male employees (M/month)	455	554	576	675	724	836	960	1,163	1,378	1,707
Difference in M/month	2	47	6	45	55	72	82	113	89	112

Source: UACZ, VA Nr. 03740, Analyse zur Entlohnung und Eingruppierung werktätiger Frauen im Vergleich zu werktätiger Männern, 12. Oktober 1978.

in 1978 found that there were very small differentials between men and women workers who belonged to the same wage groups (see Table 2.9).

A report of 1979 found that the average monthly wages of male workers were higher than those of women, but the principle of equal pay for equal work was not violated. The reason for the higher average wages of male workers was that their proportion was higher in the high wage groups while the majority of women belonged to the lower wage groups Of the employees in the lowest wage group 84 per cent were women, while in the highest wage groups their proportion was 5–10 per cent (see Table 2.10).[296]

Table 2.10 The distribution of men and women workers among the various wage groups in VEB Carl Zeiss Jena in 1978

	Wage group 3	Wage group 4	Wage group 5	Wage group 6	Wage group 7	Wage group 8
Number of female employees in the wage group	99	2062	4571	1375	289	46
% of female employees within the wage group	79.8	73.4	59.7	26.5	8.2	2.2
Number of male employees in the wage group	25	747	3,082	3,803	3,232	1,334
% of male employees within the wage group	20.2	26.4	40.3	73.4	91.8	96.7

Source: UACZ, VA Nr. 03740, Analyse zur Entlohnung und Eingruppierung werktätiger Frauen im Vergleich zu werktätiger Männern, 12. Oktober 1978.

There were other factors that negatively influenced the development of the average wages of women workers: the overwhelming majority of part-time workers were women, and the proportion of shift workers was higher among men (shift bonuses counted towards average wages). Besides, the report observed that there were 'typical' women's jobs that were badly paid such as secretaries and wages clerks (even though there was a handwritten comment asking 'Does it have to be like that? Are these jobs inferior?') The analysis of the wages therefore concluded that the higher average wages of men workers could be explained through their position in production and the women's greater responsibility for the household and the family.[297]

The above information, however fragmentary, reveals that the system did indeed do much to level the differences between the sexes in employment, education and income, partly for ideological reasons (competition with West Germany) and partly for economic reasons (labour shortage), but it also points out the contradictions that it could not solve, most notably the problem of how to reconcile the professional life of women with the family and household duties. The comments of the cited documents clearly show that in this respect, emancipation was a slow process, and in most cases women were expected to undertake the bulk of the housework. The state greatly facilitated full female employment both through propaganda and the provision of institutions of child care (nurseries, kindergartens, afternoon schools) at highly subsidized prices (which can be considered symbolic). True, shopping itself was a difficult task in an economy which continued to suffer from a shortage of consumer goods, in spite of all the heroic efforts of party functionaries. Zeiss was in this respect in a privileged position: when women workers complained about the shortage of women's underwear, the chief manager Biermann ordered a truck of the missing product, which could be purchased only by the Zeiss employees. The slow progress of the promotion of women leaders and managers likewise shows that misogynist biases were not easy to overcome.

While recognizing the failures of this policy, it should, however, also be emphasized that the majority of the interview partners thought that the socialist system did a lot for working mothers. All interviewees told me that work was an integral part of their life, and those who lost their jobs in the new system did everything that they could to find new employment, even if their husbands could support them. Men likewise said that it was 'natural' for them that their wives worked and the partners shared household duties. In this respect, the labour policy towards women was one of the few things that was unambiguously positively remembered and appreciated. In the light of the interviews, the GDR was indeed 'advanced' in this respect. Labour policy for women was also facilitated by the more advanced German industrial society – in the Hungarian case, the emancipating goals of the party were contradicted by the traditional gender roles characteristic of rural societies. As we have seen in the example of commuters, in Hungary large groups of workers preserved their rural residence, culture and mentality.

Comparing Welfare Dictatorships

With the end of the reform era of the 1960s a 'tacit' compromise was concluded between the party and the working class. The party in both countries concentrated on the increase of the standard of living of the people and the satisfaction of consumer needs in exchange for the political support – or at least quiescence – of the working class. State-driven technical development and an export-oriented economy were expected to provide for the material basis of the continuous increase of the consumption levels of the people. Ulbricht had a similar vision, but the politics of austerity that he employed and the decrease of consumer goods in favour of huge state investments in the so-called strategic sectors led to an economic and a political crisis. Frightened of the mounting discontent of the population, the party leadership decided to increase the plan targets for consumer goods while they lowered investment. Even though Honecker called this policy the 'unity of economic and social policy', in essence it was the same as Kádár's standard-of-living policy.

This second part of the book introduced and analysed the local functioning and reception of this policy in the two countries. In Hungary there was indeed a significant increase of the standard of living in the 1970s. Even in the 1960s, however, Hungary's reform policy relied more heavily on the private initiative than the East German reform. The example of commuters nicely demonstrates how workers participated in both the state and the private sectors (through *háztáji*) to increase their family income. Private initiative also played a more important role in the solution of housing in Hungary than in East Germany where the state could finance a grand-scale housing programme. The increase of the standard of living was therefore based on people drawing income both from the state and private sectors rather than pay increases in the state sector alone. The survey of 1976, which gave a picture of the conditions and opinions of the most privileged group of the working class in the county (concerning wages, housing conditions and education) highlighted some important relationships in this respect. Firstly, nearly half of the respondents said that they worked in their free time, which means that in order to live better, people had to work more. Secondly, the survey concluded that people were not 'fully' contented with the increase of the standard of living, even at a time when real wages increased at the highest rate in the examined period. This criticism could have been a warning for the party that legitimacy based on the satisfaction of consumer needs was essentially fragile. Thirdly, one-fifth of the respondents said the achievement rarely or never determined the wages (in Rába MVG, 25 per cent gave this answer) and only another one-fifth thought that people were paid according to their work.[298] This, in general, shows the declining social prestige of work in the 'workers' state' – even in the eyes of the working class.

After the failure of the East German reform and the mounting discontent of the population, which was documented in the first chapter of the book, the 'unity of economic and social policy' in the GDR aimed to increase the appeal of the party for the people. The satisfaction of consumer needs became the most important task of party functionaries – or if we want to keep to the language of the party, consumption policy became the main 'battlefield'. The party leadership of the district sent regular reports to the high party leadership in which they meticulously listed how they won the 'struggle' for the continuous and satisfactory supply of the people with consumer goods. At the beginning of the 1970s the struggle had uneven results, judged from the long list of products which could not be purchased in the local shops. Later there were shortages, mainly of such 'luxury' goods as coffee, bananas and women's underwear. The deepening crisis of the late 1980s was indicated by the expanding lists of shortage goods: judged from the party materials, there was a shortage of paper and indigo, but in the light of the life-history interviews even the purchase of nails met 'objective obstacles' in the language of the party.

The shortage of consumer goods was, however, not the only Achilles' heel of the Honcker regime. It was namely an important difference between the GDR and Hungary that while Hungarian reformers experimented with the expansion of the private sector, Honecker, on the contrary, sought to nationalize the (still) existing small private companies, and he wanted to satisfy consumer needs through a centralized system of state redistribution. The section entitled '*From Hostels to Flats*' showed that this system created much unnecessary frustration, discontent and grievances and many felt that their social rights were violated. Even less successful was the 'struggle' to provide for the continuous and satisfactory supply of the population with consumer goods. The information reports regularly listed – along with the compulsory, triumphant production records – that there was a shortage of x or y consumer goods, and even party members complained of the shortage of certain products – for example building materials or parts for cars. In addition, the GDR had to compete with one of the most advanced market economies of Europe, which widely advertised its 'consumption paradise'. Even though the GDR could boast of important results within the socialist camp (the East German working-class wages and housing conditions were significantly good, and the results of the social political programme, education and women's policy have been discussed above), the East German citizens compared their situation with the West German people, who did not have to wait for years for a car or use informal contacts to purchase 1 kg of bananas. This designated the limits of the standard-of-living policy.

In Hungary the failure of this consumption-oriented policy became visible earlier than in the GDR, where the repressive political climate concealed the true opinion of the people from the party. This was documented in the section entitled '*Opposing the Management*' where we could observe that with the failure of the standard-of-living policy informants started to openly criticize the programme of the government and the party. Canteen food, bad roads and overcrowded buses all provided topics for political jokes, which indicated the deterioration of the political mood of the people. The information reports of the 1970s can be characterized by an overall optimistic tone: people expect the party to correct the mistakes but they do not question the legitimacy of the ruling regime. The reports of the 1980s are abundant in negative criticisms, which reflect a general loss in the credibility of the party line and an increasing mistrust of the political power.

The party paid a heavy price for the 'tacit' compromise with the working class in both countries. The working class was integrated into the regime, which provided for political stability. However, despite the revival of elements of the old social democratic programme, the main social message of the party became the standard-of-living policy, which constructed workers as 'consumers' and reinforced material values and an essentially petit-bourgeois mentality.

This was reflected not only in the policy but also in the language of the party. In Hungary working-class topics were struck from the agenda of the party meetings. The information reports of the 1980s are abundant in criticisms that people who have access to the private sector have higher incomes than the workers of the state sector. Money became more important than class position. It is at best doubtful to what extent commuters possessed a working-class consciousness. The expansion of the private sector in the 1980s led to further divisions within the working class and a weakening of class consciousness. Although the East German collectivist model of the welfare dictatorships was more resistant to concessions to the market, the orientation towards consumption likewise led to the downgrading of the working class. From the second half of the 1970s, the party materials of the district essentially inform us only about the fulfilment of plan targets, production results and the celebration of the topical state holidays. Even though the speeches of the party leaders abounded in quotations from Marxist classics, the 'working class' was increasingly used as an abstract category; real workers disappeared not only from the party documents but also from the rhetoric of the party. It seems that with the new, consumption-oriented policy the working class lost its social reality even from the perspective of the party, and the idea of emancipating them received an ever-decreasing emphasis in the official ideology. The dogmatic speeches of the party leaders suggest that they did not even feel a need to address the workers as a class.

Interestingly, even though the party had a pronounced social policy towards labour, labour-related issues were discussed much less in the meetings of the party leadership of the East German district than that of the Hungarian county (if we disregard the continuous reports of the provision of the people with consumer goods). There was more scattered information about the working class of the former than about that of the latter. While in 1972 it could have happened that when the members of the old factory guard of a Silbitz plant did not get the premium, the workers threatened with a strike and even referred to 17 June[299] in front of the party members,[300] in later times the local party leaders saw no reason to disturb the peace of mind of their superiors. Judged from the sources, it seems that they themselves believed their own propaganda that the satisfaction of consumer needs rendered the people satisfied with the system. There is some sad irony in the fact that the most numerous sources of working-class lives are the surviving letters of complaint, which mainly addressed the accommodation problems of the writers (even though the housing conditions in the GDR were not at all bad when placed in comparative perspective); but it seems that despite its pronounced policy to labour, the regime preferred to communicate with the workers in the form of applications only.

Despite the egalitarian socialist rhetoric of the party, the standard-of-living policy in effect created new social inequalities and reinforced materialist values. In the Hungarian case already in the reform era working-class criticism was targeted at the increasing material inequalities, the gap between managerial and working-class wages and the prosperity of the 'peasantry'. The expansion of the private sector reinforced material inequalities between workers and entrepreneurs. In the light of contemporary surveys and literature, materialist values became more important than community life: the social rank of the people was increasingly determined by the quality of consumption.

The standard-of-living policy had contradictory results for the party even in the more egalitarian East German society. In spite of the results of the generous social policy, the visible gap between the full supermarkets of West Germany (which were widely advertised in the Western media) and the supply of the East German shops, where bananas and coffee were held to be 'luxury' products, failed to convince the East Germans of the superiority of socialism. It is unlikely that apart from the party functionaries anybody would have read the information reports, written in a heavily bureaucratic and clumsy language, with interest; but if a capitalist spy had done so, he would have surely been content to read that in the 'workers' state' people thought that those who had Western currency preceded 'normal' consumers, who stood at the bottom of the imagined social hierarchy.[301] The opening of Intershops and Exquisit shops rendered the differences among the consumers all the more visible. The new inequalities nourished social criticism and they did not help much to render the socialist ideology more appealing for the people.

An even more important consequence of the tacit compromise was the party's consistent refusal to tolerate any leftism other than the official legitimizing ideology. This in effect meant the persecution of any left-wing subcultures and communities which did not fit in with the socialist communities of the regime. In Jena the associations and housing communities of dissident young people were ruthlessly persecuted. One member of the *Jenaer Friedengemeinshcaft*, Matthias Domaschk, was arrested and committed suicide in custody. Other members of the group were forced to leave the GDR. In Hungary leftist critics of the regime also met harsh retaliations: there was a show trial against Haraszti because he painted a too-critical picture of the relationship between the workers and the state in his ethnographic study, and members of the so-called Budapest school, who had contacts with the New Left, were persecuted and forced into exile.

The tacit compromise therefore preserved an essentially patriarchal relationship between the party and the working class. The 'workerist' ideology of the party was not merely propaganda because the standard-of-living policy, the support of working-class housing, culture and education, the socialist brigade movement and the party's policy towards women that were discussed above did in fact serve the interests of the working class. And it cannot be denied that this was the field where the 'workers' state' had real emancipating achievements. In spite of the complaints, there were not really great differences between the working-class and managerial wages. In the GDR a shift worker earned more money than a young engineer or researcher, and the party committees of both factories held long debates about how to motivate skilled workers to become foremen, because the greater responsibility was not rewarded materially. Even though the expansion of the private sector in Hungary decreased the opportunity for the party to influence directly the incomes of the population, the large industrial working class remained a privileged group until the collapse of the Kádár regime.

Community-building and the support of working-class culture and education were elements of the progressive tradition of the old social democratic movement. However, while the original aim was to strengthen working-class consciousness and increase the political participation of people, the socialist brigade movement essentially depoliticized the workers in both countries. While people were encouraged to build com-

munities and spend their leisure time together, there was no political will
to involve these working-class communities in managerial decisions or
any other grass-roots political activity, as is documented by the conflicts
between the brigadiers and the managers. The socialist brigades had no
political role, and that is why people could regard them as communities
relatively free of state control.

Albeit working-class education continued a progressive tradition, we
have evidence from both countries that, with the expansion of higher education, workers' universities and adult learning lost their former significance. In Hungary, Ferge's studies showed that educational inequalities
increased in the 1960s and later when working-class quotas were abolished, the ratio of working-class children in higher education further declined.[302] But even the East German data show that educational mobility
declined in the Honecker regime and the children of the cadre elite were
positively discriminated in admission to higher education.[303] The support
of working-class culture therefore played a diminishing role in the social
mobility of the working class.

The emancipating programme of the party should not, however, be
altogether dismissed. The East German–Hungarian comparison well illustrates the relative educational backwardness of the Hungarian workforce. In the mid-1970s, a quarter of the Rába workers did not finish the
primary school – and Rába was a model factory in one of the most developed regions of the country and manufacturing industry received generous state support. At the same time only 6 per cent of the male workers
of Zeiss did not have a training certificate, and 80 per cent were skilled
workers. In Rába 65 per cent of the male workers were skilled workers
and 16 per cent did not finish primary school. Among the unskilled workers of the county this ratio was significantly higher: two-thirds of them
did not finish primary school. The library movement must be mentioned
as a positive initiative; this should, however, be evaluated along with the
information that the cultural committees found 'striking deficiencies' in
the linguistic competence of the population. It can, however, be listed
among the achievements of the library movement that 65–70 per cent of
the population of the county sometimes or often read books.

This chapter has introduced detailed statistics of the improvement of
education and community life. Even though community life was supported and organized from above, this social experience was uniformly
recalled with a sense of loss, both in the East German and Hungarian
interviews. The East German interview partners all said that solidarity was
stronger in the old regime than in the new one, and that colleagues could
expect more support from each other than under capitalism which was
characterized by fierce competition and more egoism.

The balance of the welfare dictatorships is therefore ambiguous. The skilled, large industrial working class became part of the socialist middle class. This was mainly reflected in the standard of living: we have seen that working-class wages were relatively high in comparison to other social strata in the examined period. Even though educational inequalities increased in the period, the state programme of 'educating the masses' sought to level cultural differences through cheap tickets to theatres and concerts, the popularization of libraries and free scientific lectures. Even if part of the cultural undertakings of the brigades remained on paper, many workers had positive memories of the subsidized forms of 'high culture'. The greater equality of the old regime was also positively recalled in the interviews. Postsocialist surveys likewise support the thesis that the welfare dictatorships had certain emancipating achievements: in both the GR and Hungary there was a relatively high ratio of people who identified themselves with the working class, while in West Germany the majority said that they belonged to the middle class.[304] It can therefore be argued that the socialist regime attempted to 'speed up' certain emancipating processes but the outcome of these efforts was contingent on the existing social structure. A good example of this is the party's policy towards women. Although the party sought to emancipate women in both countries, this policy was more successful in the industrially more developed GDR than in Hungary where the emancipating goals of the party were hindered by a more conservative attitude to gender roles.

Notes

1. It is a very much debated question, of course, to what extent the policy towards women that was followed in the socialist countries was eventually successful in emancipating women. For a challenging analysis of the GDR see Harsch, *Revenge of the Domestic*; for Hungary see Tóth, *Kádár leányai*.
2. Information from the interviews conducted with East German and Hungarian workers in 2003.
3. See: Szalai, *Beszélgetések a gazdasági reformról*.
4. T. Kolosi. 1987. *Tagolt társadalom: Struktúra, rétegződés, egyenlőtlenség Magyarországon*, Budapest: Gondolat.
5. Szelényi, *Új osztály, állam, politika*.
6. Keren, 'The Rise and Fall of the New Economic System', 79.
7. D. Cornelsen, 'Die Wirtschaft der DDR in der Honecker-Ära', in Glaeßner, *Die DDR in der Ära Honecker*, 357–70.
8. H. Stephan and E. Wiedemann. 1990. 'Lohnstruktur und Lohndifferenzierung in der DDR. Ergebnisse der Lohndatenerfassung vom September 1988', *Mittelungen aus der Arbeitsmarkt und Berufsforschung* 23. For a comparison between the incomes of blue-collar and white-collar households see: P. Krause and J. Schwarze. 1990. 'Die Einkommensstichprobe in Arbeiter- und Angestelltenhaushalten der DDR vom August 1988 – Erhebungskonzeption und Datenbankzugriff' Diskussionspapier No. 11. Berlin: Deutsches Institut für Wirtschaftsforschung. For East German working-class wages see also: M. Kaufmann.

1990. 'Arbeitseinkommen in der DDR', *Leistung und Lohn*, Nr. 223/224, Sonderheft DDR. For an analysis of household incomes see: K.-D. Bedau. 1993. 'Untersuchungen zur Einkommensverteilung und –umverteilung in der DDR 1988 nach Haushaltsgruppen und Einkommengrößenklassen auf der methodischen Grundlage der Verteilungsrechnung des Deutschen Instituts für Wirtschaftsforschung'. Beiträge zur Strukturforschung, Heft 143.

9. Bouvier, *Die DDR - ein Sozialstaat?*, 180–93.
10. In 1976 the enterprise disposed of 10,500 flats and 3,342 places in the workers' hostels in Jena. Unternehmensarchiv der Carl Zeiss Jena GmbH, Jena (UACZ), VA Nr. 1583, Unterlagen zur Direktion Kultur und Sozialwesen, 20.5.1976.
11. Bouvier, *Die DDR - ein Sozialstaat?*, 264–72.
12. I did not work with Stasi files.
13. GYML, X. 415/128/1, MSZMP Győr-Sopron Megyei Bizottsága. Pártbizottsági ülés jegyzőkönyve, napirendi anyagai. A bérfejlesztés és a különböző bérezési formák bevezetésének hatása a dolgozók helyzetére és a munkaerőmozgásra (a KB november 14–15.-i határozata alapján). 1973. június 28.
14. A bérfejlesztés és a különböző bérezési formák bevezetésének hatása, op. cit. 3–4.
15. Information from the interviews.
16. GYML, X. 415/128/1, MSZMP Győr-Sopron Megyei Bizottsága. Pártbizottsági ülés jegyzőkönyve, napirendi anyagai. Tájékoztató a KB 1970. február 18-19-i, a nők politikai, gazdasági és szociális helyzete megjavítására hozott határozata végrehajtásának tapasztalatairól, 17, 1973. május 4.
17. GYML, X. 415/4/31, MSZMP Győr-Sopron Megyei Bizottsága. Pártbizottsági ülés jegyzőkönyve, napirendi anyagai. A Győr városi V. B. jelentése az üzemi PB alapszervezeteket irányító tevékenységéről. 1975. november 26.
18. According to the interviews, men objected to the equal pay even if their women colleagues had the same qualification and performed the same job as they did. A woman electrician for instance recalled that when she joined a men's brigade in the Vehicle Unit of Rába MVG, who all received special bonuses because of their qualification, the members of the brigade strongly objected to giving the same money to a woman. The brigadier who later married her confirmed the story, adding that at that time he also resented the equal pay.
19. The fourth five-year plan in Hungary (1971–75).
20. Jelentés Győr-Sopron megye munkássága helyzetéről a KB 1974. márciusi állásfoglalása alapján, op. cit.
21. From the contemporary literature see, for instance, J. Berényi. 1974. *Életszínvonal és szociálpolitika*, Budapest: Kossuth Kiadó; E. Jávorka. 1970. *Életszínvonal a mai magyar társadalomban*, Budapest: Kossuth Kiadó; Á. Losonczi. 1977. *Az életmód az időben, a tárgyakban és az értékekben*, Budapest: Gondolat Kiadó. For contemporary statistical analysis of the evaluation of the standard of living see: R. Angelusz, L.G. Nagy and R. Tardos. 1980. *Munkásvélemények az életszínvonalról, a személyes anyagi és az országos gazdasági helyzetről*, Budapest: Tömegkommunikációs Kutatóközpont; R. Angelusz, L.G. Nagy and R. Tardos. 1981. *A megfelelőnek tartott jövedelem*, Budapest: Tömegkommunikációs Kutatóközpont.
22. GYML, X. 415/118/27, MSZMP Magyar Vagon-és Gépgyári Bizottságának anyagai, 1972. április havi információs jelentés.
23. GYML, X. 415/7/14, MSZMP Győr-Sopron Megyei Bizottsága. Pártbizottsági ülés jegyzőkönyve, napirendi anyagai. Az életszínvonal-politikánk értelmezése a gépipari nagyüzemek párttagsága körében, 1. sz. melléklet, 1976. április 27.
24. Az életszínvonal-politikánk értelmezése a gépipari nagyüzemek párttagsága körében, op. cit.
25. Ibid.
26. Ibid.
27. Ibid.
28. The enterprise even had a delegate in the executive committee of the county.

29. For contemporary debates on labour shortage under socialism see e.g.: I. Buda. 1977. 'A munkaerő-gazdálkodás és a bérgazdálkodás időszerű feladatai', *Társadalmi Szemle* 32(5); K. Sz. Falusné. 1969. *Munkabér, ösztönzés, elosztás,* Budapest: Kossuth Könyvkiadó; K. Losonczi. 1973. *A munkaerőmozgásról,* Budapest Kossuth Könyvkiadó; Cs. Makó. 1979. 'Technika – munkásigények – munkakövetelmények I-II', *Ergonómia* 12(3–4); F. Munkácsy, 1976. 'A munkaerőhiány és a munkapiac sajátosságainak összefüggései', *Munkaügyi Szemle* 20(6); F. Munkácsy. 1979. 'Munkaerő-átcsoportosítás tervszerűen, szervezetten', *Munkaügyi Szemle* 23(3); S. Oroszi and J. Veress. 1979. 'Szükségszerű-e a munkaerőhiány a szocialista gazdaságban?' *Közgazdasági Szemle* 26(12); Gy. Pogány. 1982. *Munkaerőgazdálkodás és munkaerő-politika,* Budapest: Közgazdasági és Jogi Könyvkiadó; A. Rácz. 1980. 'Munka szerinti elosztás, ösztönzés', *Társadalmi Szemle* 35(1); T. Sárközy. 1976. 'Felelősség a vállalati vezetésért és gazdálkodásért', *Társadalmi Szemle* 31(3); É. Szeben. 1979. 'A munka szerinti elosztás érvényesítésének néhány problémája a fejlett szocialista társadalom építésének időszakában Magyarországon', manuscript. Budapest; J. Tillmann. 1977. 'Teljesítménykövetelmények és munkaidőalap-kihasználás' *Munkaügyi Szemle* 21(3); J. Tímár. 1977. 'Foglalkoztatáspolitikánkról és munkaerő-gazdálkodásunkról', *Közgazdasági Szemle* 24(2); L. Iványi. 1979. 'A vállalati profitbővítésre és az önellátásra való törekvés hatása a munkaero″helyzetre', *Munkaügyi Szemle* 23(4).
30. GYML, X. 415/3/23, MSZMP Gyo″r-Sopron Megyei Bizottsága. Pártbizottsági ülés jegyzőkönyve, napirendi anyagai. A Magyar Vagon-és Gépgyár vezérigazgatójának beszámolója a KB 1974. december 5.-i határozatáról a minőség, a takarékosság és a munkaerőhelyzetről, 16, 1975. július 22.
31. Ibid., 19.
32. GYML, X. 415/121/1, MSZMP Győr-Sopron Megyei Bizottsága. Pártbizottsági ülés jegyzőkönyve, napirendi anyagai. A vállalatok üzemi és munkaszervezésének korszerűsítésére indított mozgalom feladatairól, 11–14 1972. március 24. See also Katalin Bossányi's interview with the manager: Bossányi, 'Made in Rába'.
33. GYML, X. 415/117/7, MSZMP Győr-Sopron Megyei Bizottsága. Pártbizottsági ülés jegyzőkönyve, napirendi anyagai. A munkaerő-gazdálkodás helyzete és az első félév fő tapasztalatai a megye ipari vállalatainál, 1971, augusztus 5.
34. Ibid. 19.
35. According to the ground-cell information reports many workers thought that the managers received too many premiums.
36. Information from the interviews.
37. A Magyar Vagon-és Gépgyár vezérigazgatójának beszámolója a KB 1974. december 5.-i határozatáról, op. cit., 3.
38. GYML, X. 415/26/29, MSZMP Győr-Sopron Megyei Bizottsága. Pártbizottsági ülés jegyzőkönyve, napirendi anyagai. A Rába Magyar Vagon-és Gépgyár értékesítési, termékszerkezeti, korszerűsítési, termelésfejlesztési és szervezetfejlesztési célkitűzése a VI. ötéves terv időszakában, 1980. november 18.
39. Az életszínvonal-politikánk értelmezése a gépipari nagyüzemek párttagsága körében, op. cit.
40. A közvetlen termelésirányítók helyzete, politikai-szakmai felkészültségük értékelése, op. cit., 2.
41. Ibid., 6.
42. Ibid., 2.
43. Ibid., 5.
44. Ibid.
45. Ibid., 6.
46. GYML, X. 415/12/4, MSZMP Győr-Sopron Megyei Bizottsága. Pártbizottsági ülés jegyzőkönyve, napirendi anyagai. A vállalati belső irányítási és érdekeltségi rendszer fejlesztésének eredményei Győr város könnyűipari vállalatainál, 1984. május 29.

47. GYML, X. 415/12/4, MSZMP Győr-Sopron Megyei Bizottsága. Pártbizottsági ülés jegyzőkönyve, napirendi anyagai. A Sopron városi Pártbizottság Végrehajtó Bizottságának jelentése a munkaidő utáni tevékenységből származó jövedelem növelésének lehetőségeiről, 1983. május 17.

48. Bossányi's interview with Horváth is a good example of this positive image of the profit-able socialist factory (Bossányi, 1986, op. cit.). Bossányi also published articles about the enterprise in *Népszabadság*, the national daily. The county daily *Kisalföld* regularly reported about the economic results of Rába and the international recognition of Rába products (Collection of Rába archive).

49. The profitability of Rába was also frequently emphasized in the factory newspaper *Rába* (Collection of Rába archive). Horváth himself took very seriously the economic criterion. According to his recollection he initiated the closing of the Kispest Tractor Works in spite of the objection of the local party organs: 'After the film many people asked me how I was able to smile. Well, I am in the habit of smiling either at myself or my partner when I have to repeat something twenty times. When we had the great conflict with Kispest, every-body propagated with a big mouth that we have to close the loss-making factories. At the same time, they were making a big sensation out of one case when exactly this happened.' E. Horváth, *Én volnék a Vörös Báró?*, 107.

50. GYML, X. 415/537/2, MSZMP Magyar Vagon-és Gépgyári Bizottságának anyagai. In-formációs jelentés a Motorgyár Pártalapszervezetétől, 1986. július.

51. GYML, X. 415/537/2, MSZMP Magyar Vagon-és Gépgyári Bizottságának anyagai. In-formációs jelentés a Szerszámgépgyár Pártalapszervezetétől, 1986. november.

52. GYML, X. 415/537/2, MSZMP Magyar Vagon-és Gépgyári Bizottságának anyagai. A Vagongyár Pártbizottságának információs jelentése, 1986. október.

53. *Statisztikai évkönyv 1980* (Budapest, Központi Statisztikai Hivatal), 355. The index of real wages increased by 17 per cent between 1970 and 1975 (100%=1970) while only by 4 per cent between 1975 and 1980 (100%=1970). In 1980 the real wage index was lower than in 1979 and the net nominal wage index increased less than the consumer prices.

54. 'Beszélgetés Horváth Edével, a Rába MVG vezérigazgatójával', op. cit.

55. 'Jelenlegi gazdaságirányításunk kritikája', op. cit.

56. For an analysis of the role of working-class culture under socialism see D. Mühlberg. 2002. 'Konnte Arbeiterkultur in der DDR gesellschaftlich hegemonial sein?', *Utopie kreativ* 145.

57. Several interview partners reported about similar careers. Even the appointment of fore-men required a high school certificate. GYML, X. 415/200/3, MSZMP Magyar Vagon-és Gépgyári Bizottságának anyagai. Pártbizottsági ülés jegyzőkönyve, A közvetlen termelés-irányítók helyzete, politikai-szakmai felkészültségük értékelése – az emberi kapcsolatokra gyakorolt hatásuk, 1979. szeptember 21.

58. Az üzemi demokrácia helyzete, az egyszemélyi vezetés érvényesülése és a továbbfejlesztés feladatai, op. cit. 25–26, 1974. március 29.

59. Many retired interview partners reported of a managerial career that they followed after they finished an evening university course in the 1960s or 1970s. Some of them actually said that party membership was a prerequisite.

60. Jelentés Győr-Sopron megye munkássága helyzetéről a KB 1974. márciusi állásfoglalása alapján, op. cit.

61. On the perspectives of working-class youth see: D. Maros. 1976. 'Fiatalok a munkáspályán. Gondolatok az ifjúmunkások társadalmi beilleszkedéséről', *Társadalmi Szemle* 31(3).

62. The social inequality in the Hungarian educational system was discussed by the sociologist Zsuzsa Ferge. There were important differences between the types of secondary schools: training schools did not offer a high school certificate, which was the prerequisite for uni-versity admission. Comprehensive schools did, but they mainly trained technologists. The elite grammar schools, which more or less guaranteed university admission, were mainly attended by the children of the intelligentsia (See: Zs. Ferge. *Az iskolarendszer*). For a more

ethnographic approach on the social inequality of the Hungarian school system see also: K. Dogossy. 1987. *Baj van a gyerekkel*, Budapest: Kossuth Kiadó. The argument of the book is similar to that of P. Willis. 1977. *Learning to Labor: How Working Class Kids Get Working Class Jobs*, Aldershot: Ashgate.

63. GYML, X. 415/134/1, MSZMP Győr-Sopron Megyei Bizottsága. Pártbizottsági ülés jegyzőkönyve, napirendi anyagai. Közművelődésünk helyzete, 1974. július 10.
64. See, for instance, J. Füleki. 1976. 'Mérlegen a közművelődési határozat végrehajtása. Beszélgetés három nagyüzem pártbizottságának titkárával', *Társadalmi Szemle* 31(7).
65. GYML, X. 415/118/27, MSZMP Magyar Vagon-és Gépgyári Bizottságának anyagai, 1972. április havi információs jelentés.
66. A közvetlen termelésirányítók helyzete, politikai-szakmai felkészültségük értékelése, op. cit., 2.
67. Jelentés a munkásművelődés tapasztalatairól, helyzetéről és szerepéről, fejlesztésének feladatairól a Magyar Vagon-és Gépgyárban, op. cit., 1. táblázat, Fizikai dolgozók iskolai végzettsége.
68. Ibid., A szakmunkásképzés adatai 1972–1976.
69. GYML, X. 415/122/6, MSZMP Győr-Sopron Megyei Bizottsága. Pártbizottsági ülés jegyzőkönyve, napirendi anyagai. A Magyar Vagon-és Gépgyár vezérigazgatójának jelentése a termelőkapacitás kihasználásának helyzetéről, 16, 1972. július 18.
70. Jelentés a munkásművelődés tapasztalatairól, helyzetéről és szerepéről, op. cit., A szakmunkásképzés adatai 1972–1976.
71. Jelentés a munkásművelődés tapasztalatairól, helyzetéről és szerepéről, op. cit. 5, 1977. július 6.
72. Ibid.
73. Ibid., Melléklet, Esti, levelező oktatásban résztvevők 1972–1976.
74. GYML, X. 415/200/3, MSZMP Magyar Vagon-és Gépgyári Bizottságának anyagai, Pártbizottsági ülés jegyzőkönyve, A közművelődés helyzete. Az MVG végrehajtó bizottságának jelentése az 1975-ös pártértekezlet után, 12, 1979. december 11.
75. A közművelődés helyzete. Az MVG végrehajtó bizottságának jelentése az 1975-ös pártértekezlet után op. cit., 12.
76. Ibid., 13.
77. GYML, X. 415/204/4/3, MSZMP Magyar Vagon-és Gépgyári Bizottságának anyagai, Pártbizottsági ülés jegyzőkönyve, A vidékről bejáró dolgozóink helyzete, 4, 1980. szeptember 12.
78. Ibid.
79. Ibid., 5.
80. Ibid.
81. Jelentés a munkásművelődés tapasztalatairól, helyzetéről és szerepéről, op. cit.
82. Ibid.
83. Ibid., 2.
84. GYML, X. 415/204/4/2, MSZMP Magyar Vagon-és Gépgyári Bizottságának anyagai, Pártbizottsági ülés jegyzőkönyve, A szocialista munkaverseny és a brigádmunka fejlesztésének feladatai vállalatunknál, 1980. augusztus 29. The cultural activity of the socialist brigades also received a positive evaluation in the interviews.
85. The new building of the theatre was inaugurated in 1978. In 1979 the Győr Ballet was founded, which soon became very popular in the town and also won international recognition.
86. Jelentés a munkásművelődés tapasztalatairól, helyzetéről és szerepéről, op. cit., 4.
87. Ibid., 3–4.
88. A közművelődés helyzete. Az MVG végrehajtó bizottságának jelentése az 1975-ös pártértekezlet után op. cit., 14.
89. Ibid.
90. Jelentés a munkásművelődés tapasztalatairól, helyzetéről és szerepéről, op. cit., 3.

91. A közművelődés helyzete. Az MVG végrehajtó bizottságának jelentése az 1975-ös pártértekezlet után op. cit., 16.
92. The role of socialist brigades in community-building is discussed in a separate chapter.
93. Az életszínvonal-politikánk értelmezése a gépipari nagyüzemek párttagsága körében, op. cit.
94. We can find reflections on the nationally high number of commuters even in the contemporary sociologist literature. See: Bőhm, *Társadalmunk ingázói*; Bőhm, 'A bejáró munkások társadalmi-politikai magatartása'.
95. A vidékről bejáró dolgozóink helyzete, op. cit.
96. GYML, X. 415/197/2, MSZMP Magyar Vagon-és Gépgyári Bizottságának anyagai, Pártbizottsági ülés jegyzőkönyve, Jelentés a vállalati lakásépítési hozzájárulás felhasználásáról, 3, 1978. január 30.
97. GYML, X. 415/200/2, MSZMP Magyar Vagon-és Gépgyári Bizottságának anyagai, Pártbizottsági ülés jegyzőkönyve, Szóbeli tájékoztató vállalatunk dolgozóinak lakáshelyzetéről. A vállalati lakástámogatás felhasználása, 3, 1979. március 21.
98. Jelentés a vállalati lakásépítési hozzájárulás felhasználásáról, op. cit.
99. Szóbeli tájékoztató vállalatunk dolgozóinak lakáshelyzetéről, op. cit., 1.
100. Jelentés a vállalati lakásépítési hozzájárulás felhasználásáról, op. cit., 2.
101. Szóbeli tájékoztató vállalatunk dolgozóinak lakáshelyzetéről, op. cit., 3.
102. Ibid.
103. Ibid., 4.
104. GYML, X. 415/156/1/3, MSZMP Győr-Sopron Megyei Bizottsága. Pártbizottsági ülés jegyzőkönyve, napirendi anyagai. Tájékoztató 'Az ifjúság társadalmi helyzete, a párt feladatai' c. anyag vitájáról, 1984. június 26.
105. GYML, X. 415/236/4, MSZMP Magyar Vagon-és Gépgyári Bizottságának anyagai, Pártbizottsági ülés jegyzőkönyve, Jelentés a KISZ munkájáról, 1, 1986. december 27.
106. GYML, X. 415/528/2, MSZMP Magyar Vagon-és Gépgyári Bizottságának anyagai. Információs jelentés a Szerszámgépgyár Pártalapszervezetétől, 1982. október.
107. GYML, X. 415/533/30, MSZMP Magyar Vagon-és Gépgyári Bizottságának anyagai. Információs jelentés a Futómű Pártalapszervezetétől, 1984. szeptember.
108. GYML, X. 415/534/12, MSZMP Magyar Vagon-és Gépgyári Bizottságának anyagai. A Vagongyár Pártbizottságának információs jelentése, 1985. október.
109. GYML, X. 415/529/8/5, MSZMP Magyar Vagon-és Gépgyári Bizottságának anyagai, A Mosonmagyaróvári Mezőgazdasági Gépgyár (MMG) pártbizottsági ülésének jegyzőkönyve, Jelentés a Rába MMG ifjúságának társadalmi helyzetéről, 1985. október 8.
110. According to the interview partners, the yard of the enterprise and the neighbouring empty estate were full of bicycles during working time.
111. A vidékről bejáró dolgozóink helyzete, op. cit., 1.
112. Ibid.
113. The airport plant was located outside of the town.
114. A vidékről bejáró dolgozóink helyzete, op. cit., 3.
115. Ibid., 2.
116. The name of the state bus company.
117. GYML, X. 415/528/2, MSZMP Magyar Vagon-és Gépgyári Bizottságának anyagai. Információs jelentés a Szerszámgépgyár Pártalapszervezetétől, 1982. június.
118. Bus line between Adyváros and the airport plant.
119. ABC=chain of state food shops. Verseny=competition.
120. GYML, X. 415/534/3, MSZMP Magyar Vagon-és Gépgyári Bizottságának anyagai. A Vagongyár Pártbizottságának információs jelentése, 1984. október.
121. GYML, X. 415/534/5, MSZMP Magyar Vagon-és Gépgyári Bizottságának anyagai. Információs jelentés a T. M. K. Pártalapszervezettől, 1984. április.
122. GYML, X. 415/211/28, MSZMP Magyar Vagon-és Gépgyári Bizottságának anyagai. Információs jelentés a Kovács Pártalapszervezettől, 1982. július.

123. Canteen food also gave rise to political jokes in the Zeiss enterprise.
124. GYML, X. 415/533/30, MSZMP Magyar Vagon-és Gépgyári Bizottságának anyagai. Információs jelentés a Futómű Pártalapszervezetétől, 1984. április.
125. GYML, X. 415/211/33, MSZMP Magyar Vagon-és Gépgyári Bizottságának anyagai. Információs jelentés a Jármű II. Pártalapszervezetétől, 1982. november.
126. GYML, X. 415/211/41, MSZMP Magyar Vagon-és Gépgyári Bizottságának anyagai. A Vagongyár Pártbizottságának információs jelentése, 1982. december.
127. Burawoy, *The Radiant Past*.
128. Information from interviews with former brigadiers.
129. For contemporary literature on socialist brigades see: G. Béky and Z. Zétényi. 1977. 'Szocialista módon dolgozni, tanulni, élni. Helyzetkép a brigádmozgalomról', *Valóság* 20(11); D. Kalocsai. 1978. 'A nagyipari üzemek munkáskollektíváinak társadalmi-politikai aktivitása', *Társadalomtudományi Közlemények* 8(2–3); D. Kalocsai. 1978. 'A szocialista brigádok közösséggé fejlődéséről', *Társadalomtudományi Közlemények* 8(1); E. Sőtér, 'Gondolatok'. From recent literature see: Tóth, *'Puszi Kádár Jánosnak'*.
130. A szocialista munkaverseny és a brigádmunka fejlesztésének feladatai vállalatunknál, op. cit., 3.
131. Ibid., 4.
132. Jegyzőkönyv a Motor Pártalapszervezet 1977. január 26.-i taggyűléséről, op. cit., 5–6.
133. GYML, X. 415/202/3/5, MSZMP Magyar Vagon-és Gépgyári Bizottságának anyagai, Pártbizottsági ülés jegyzőkönyve. A szocialista munkaverseny 1977. évi előkészítésének tapasztalatai, az anyagi-erkölcsi ösztönzés forrásainak további fejlesztése, 14–15, 1977. február 18.
134. A szocialista munkaverseny és a brigádmunka fejlesztésének feladatai vállalatunknál, op. cit., 5.
135. For an interesting study of contrasting the representation of socialist brigades in the contemporary media with postsocialist memories see: E. Zs. Tóth. 2003. 'Egy kitüntetés befogadástörténete: Egy állami díjas női szocialista brigád képe a sajtóban és a tagok emlékezetében', in: Horváth, *Munkástörténet*.
136. Citation from an interview conducted with Éva (55), a Hungarian female production worker in her home in 2003. She was a skilled worker. Since I promised anonymity to all of the interview partners, I use pseudonyms. The age refers to the age of the interview partners at the time of interviewing.
137. The interview was conducted in the weekend house of the interview partner.
138. Citation from an interview conducted with Lajos (62), a former Hungarian brigadier, who represented MVG in the executive committee. He retired as a senior engineer.
139. Citation from an interview conducted with Béla (53), a former Hungarian brigadier in his home in 2003. He was a skilled worker and a shop steward.
140. Citation from an interview conducted with Zsuzsa (49), a Hungarian female production worker in Rába in 2002. She was a skilled worker.
141. GYML, X. 415/12/22, MSZMP Győr-Sopron Megyei Bizottsága. Apparátus iratai. Gazdaságpolitikai osztály, Tájékoztató az MVG Vagon 28-as üzemében végzett vizsgálatokról és a 2 heti jutalom kifizetéséről, 1977. augusztus 16.
142. GYML, X. 415/197/4, MSZMP Magyar Vagon-és Gépgyári Bizottságának anyagai. Jelentés az 1977. évi bérek és jövedelmek alakulásáról, az alkalmazott ösztönző bérrendszerek hatékonyságáról, normakarbantartás végrehajtásának szükségességéről, 1977. június 15.
143. Tájékoztató az MVG Vagon 28-as üzemében végzett vizsgálatokról, op. cit., 2.
144. Ibid., 3.
145. GYML, X. 415/198/7, MSZMP Magyar Vagon-és Gépgyári Bizottságának anyagai. Információs jelentés a Vagon Fémipari Alapszervezettől, 1978. december.
146. GYML, X. 415/198/7, MSZMP Magyar Vagon-és Gépgyári Bizottságának anyagai. Információs jelentés a Vagon Fémipari Alapszervezettől, 1979. május.

147. GYML, X. 415/199/28, MSZMP Magyar Vagon-és Gépgyári Bizottságának anyagai. Információs jelentés a V. J. Kovács Pártalapszervezettől, 1979. július.
148. L. Tóth (ed.). 1984. *Győr-Sopron*, Budapest: Kossuth Kiadó, 107. In an interview Horváth said that the revision found a surplus of 804 employees (Bossányi, 'Made in Rába', 38). The *Rába* newspaper gave a rather one-sided picture (and limited information) of this step. Some characteristic titles are: 'Capacity and quality decide: Only the necessary number of people should be employed for a given job' (2 March 1979), 'We should reinforce a basic economic principle' (16 March 1979), 'The experiences of the revision of the personnel: We have to get the support of the decent employees' (30 March 1979), 'Comments on the revision of labour management' (6 April 1979), 'The revision of the personnel was finished also in Szombathely' (May 25 1979).
149. GYML, X. 415/202/32, MSZMP Magyar Vagon-és Gépgyári Bizottságának anyagai. Információs jelentés az Új Acélöntödéből, 1979. április.
150. Stress is in the original.
151. GYML, X. 415/202/29, MSZMP Magyar Vagon-és Gépgyári Bizottságának anyagai. Információs jelentés a T.M.K. Pártalapszervezettől, 1979. május.
152. The county reports that support this statement are introduced in the following chapter.
153. GYML, X. 415/187/2, MSZMP Győr-Sopron Megyei Bizottsága. Apparátus iratai. A lakossági közhangulatot jellemző főbb tendenciák, 1986. április.
154. GYML, X. 415/187/3, MSZMP Győr-Sopron Megyei Bizottsága. Apparátus iratai. A lakossági közhangulatot jellemző főbb tendenciák, 1986. május.
155. GYML, X. 415/187/4, MSZMP Győr-Sopron Megyei Bizottsága. Apparátus iratai. A lakossági közhangulatot jellemző főbb tendenciák, 1986. június.
156. GYML, X. 415/537/3, MSZMP Magyar Vagon-és Gépgyári Bizottságának anyagai. Információs jelentés a Hátsóhíd Alapszervezetétől, 1986. május.
157. GYML, X. 415/537/2, MSZMP Magyar Vagon-és Gépgyári Bizottságának anyagai. Információs jelentés a Szerszámgépgyár Pártalapszervezetétől, 1986. június.
158. GYML, X. 415/537/5, MSZMP Magyar Vagon-és Gépgyári Bizottságának anyagai. Információs jelentés az Új Acélöntödéből, 1986. október.
159. GYML, X. 415/187/5, MSZMP Győr-Sopron Megyei Bizottsága. Apparátus iratai. A Vagongyár Pártbizottságának információs jelentése, 1986. december.
160. A. Dusza, *A birodalom végnapjai*, 12.
161. Die sich aus den Beschlüssen des 8. Parteitages ergebenden Schlussfolgerungen für die Arbeit der Bezirksparteiorganisationen. op. cit.
162. ThStA Rudolstadt, Bezirksparteiarchiv der SED Gera, IV C-2/3/1/154. Die Sicherung der Versorgung der Bevölkerung im 2. Halbjahr 1974 und über die Verwirklichung der Aufgaben an den Versorgungsplan des Bezirkes zur Verbesserung der Versorgung mit Dienstleistungen und Baureparaturen, besonders in den Zentren der Arbeiterklasse. Sekretariatssitzung, 20 Juni 1974.
163. ThStA Rudolstadt, Bezirksparteiarchiv der SED Gera, IV C-2/6/440. Zur Einführung von Grundlöhnen 21 September 1976.
164. ThStA Rudolstadt, Bezirksparteiarchiv der SED Gera, IV B-2/3/170, Über Erfahrung bei der Qualifizierung der Arbeiterklasse, 25 März 1971.
165. ThStA Rudolstadt, Bezirksparteiarchiv der SED Gera, IV C-2/17/612, Frauenarbeit.
166. UACZ, WB Nr. 487, Abrechnung der Frauenarbeit 1980 nach Schwerpunkten. According to the report the proportion of part-time women workers was 20.8 per cent, which was higher than the average of the GDR (29.5 per cent) but it showed a slightly increasing trend.
167. Frauenarbeit, op. cit.
168. ThStA Rudolstadt, Bezirksparteiarchiv der SED Gera, IV C-2/3/959, Protokoll der Sekretariatssitzung, 29 Juni, 1972, Ergebnisse und Probleme auf den Gebiet der Verbesserung der Arbeits- und Lebensbedingungen der werktätigen Frauen insbesondere der Arbeiterversorgung, der Betreuung der Schichtarbeiter und der Entwicklung des geistig-kulturellen Lebens in den Arbeiterzentren des Bezirkes.

169. ThStA Rudolstadt, Bezirksparteiarchiv der SED Gera, IV C-2/1/15, Protokoll der Sitzung der Bezirksleitung, 8 Januar 1974.

170. ThStA Rudolstadt, Bezirksparteiarchiv der SED Gera, IV C-2/17/612, Probleme die sich aus der Entwicklung der Berufstätigkeit der Frau in der sozialistischen Industrie ergeben. 21 April 1976.

171. ThStA Rudolstadt, Bezirksparteiarchiv der SED Gera, IV C-2/3/66, Protokoll der Sekretariatssitzung, 24 Juli, 1972, Ergebnisse und Probleme bei der Entwicklung der sozialpolitischen Maßnahmen von Partei und Regierung zur Erleichterung des Lebens der berufstätigen Frauen und ihre Auswirkungen auf die Entwicklung der Berufstätigkeit der Frauen im Kombinat.

172. ThStA Rudolstadt, Bezirksparteiarchiv der SED Gera, IV C-2/17/612, Einschätzung der Durchsetzung der Frauenpolitik im VEB Carl Zeiss Jena durch die Leitungen der Gewerkschaft, 28 Juni 1974.

173. Ergebnisse und Probleme bei der Entwicklung der sozialpolitischen Maßnahmen von Partei und Regierung, op. cit.

174. ThStA Rudolstadt, Bezirksparteiarchiv der SED Gera, IV C-2/1/7. Sitzung der Bezirksleitung, 4 Mai 1972.

175. ThStA Rudolstadt, Bezirksparteiarchiv der SED Gera, IV C-2/3/721. Informationsbericht der IKL Zeiss, Februar 1975.

176. ThStA Rudolstadt, Bezirksparteiarchiv der SED Gera, IV B-2/6/489, Die Leitung und Organisation der Produktion im Rahmen der Schichtarbeit. 2 August 1968.

177. ThStA Rudolstadt, Bezirksparteiarchiv der SED Gera, IV C-2/7/612. Frauenarbeit: Aussprache mit Produktionsarbeiterinnen im Papiersaal. 29 Oktober 1976.

178. ThStA Rudolstadt, Bezirksparteiarchiv der SED Gera, IV C-2/6/441. Information über die Arbeiteraussprache in der Dreherei im Stahlwerk Silbitz am 12 Juni 1972.

179. For a similar argument see: Hübner. 1993. 'Balance des Ungleichgewichtes: Zum Verhältnis von Arbeiterinteressen und SED-Herrschaft', *Geschichte und Gesellschaft* 19. The party sought to de-politicize labour demands, and to this end it was willing to offer material concessions to the workers. For a study of labour conflicts in the GDR in the 1950s see: Hübner, *Konsens, Konflikt,* 178–210.

180. This phrase was also used in the Hungarian sources, and it usually meant a vehement protest against the measure in question.

181. ThStA Rudolstadt, Bezirksparteiarchiv der SED Gera, IV C-2/6/440. Information über die Auszahlung der Jahresendprämie 1972 im Bereich der IG Metall.

182. ThStA Rudolstadt, Bezirksparteiarchiv der SED Gera, IV C-2/6/440. Information über die lohnpolitische Probleme in den neuen VEB. 10 April 1973.

183. ThStA Rudolstadt, Bezirksparteiarchiv der SED Gera, IV C-2/6/440. Die Einführung neuer Grundlöhne in Verbindung mit der WAO. 15 September 1975.

184. See the comment: 'Some of the workers believe that socialism has already been realized and now people can have a rest but they should get their rightful reward.' Bericht der IKPKK (Gen. W), op. cit. Welche Probleme sieht der Betriebsleiter?

185. ThStA Rudolstadt, Bezirksparteiarchiv der SED Gera, IV B-2/5/379. Eingabe der Bevölkerung, 2. Halbjahr 1968.

186. ThStA Rudolstadt, Bezirksparteiarchiv der SED Gera, IV B-2/3/255. Informationsbericht, IKL der SED des VEB Carl Zeiss Jena, 12 Juni 1968.

187. Jelentés a párttagság ideológiai nevelésének eredményeiről, problémáiról, a feladatokról, 1972. augusztus 15, op. cit.

188. ThStA Rudolstadt, Bezirksparteiarchiv der SED Gera, IV B-2/1/10, Referat zur Auswertung der 9. Tagung des ZK. Die weiteren Aufgaben der Bezirksparteiorganisationen zur Gestaltung des entwickelten gesellschaftlichen Systems des Sozialismus. Sitzung der Bezirksleitung, 18–19 November 1968.

189. From 1972, for instance, the employees of the state apparatuses received their class category after the occupation that they had before they were sixteen so that they could count among the workers. According to the investigations of Heike Solga the socialist cadre class started to close its ranks in the period (H. Solga. 2001. 'Aspekte der Klassenstruktur in der DDR in den siebziger und achtziger Jahren und die Stellung der Arbeiterklasse' in: Hürtgen, *Der Schein der Stabilität.*

190. ThStA Rudolstadt, Bezirksparteiarchiv der SED Gera, IV C-2/3/721, Informationsbericht des 1. Sekretärs der IKL Zeiss, 12 Mai 1975.

191. ThStA Rudolstadt, Bezirksparteiarchiv der SED Gera, IV D-2/9/1/408, Zur inhaltlichen Fragen der politisch-ideologischen Arbeit die gegenwärtig besonders im Mittelpunkt der Diskussion der Bev0lkerung stehen (Jena-Stadt, Jena-Land, Zeis, Gera-Stadt, Rudolstadt), 5 Mai 1977.

192. ThStA Rudolstadt, Bezirksparteiarchiv der SED Gera, IV D-4/13/76, Informationsbericht von IKL Zeiss, 10 November 1977.

193. Zur inhaltlichen Fragen der politisch-ideologischen Arbeit, op. cit.

194. ThStA Rudolstadt, Bezirksparteiarchiv der SED Gera, IV C-2/3/721, Informationsbericht des 1. Sekretärs der IKL Zeiss, 24 Oktober 1977.

195. Bericht der IKPKK (Bericht, Gen. W). op. cit.

196. For a study on housing programme for workers in the 1960s see: Hübner, *Konsens, Konflikt*, 171–76; under the Honecker era see: Bouvier, *Die DDR – ein Sozialstaat?*, 152–201.

197. UACZ, VA Nr. 3741, Ihre erneute Eingabe vom 24 April 1980, 8 Mai 1980.

198. UACZ, VA Nr. 1583, Unterlagen zur Direktion Kultur und Sozialwesen, 20 Mai 1976.

199. Mühlfriedel, *Carl Zeiss*, 305.

200. Probleme die sich aus der Entwicklung der Berufstätigkeit der Frau in der sozialistischen Industrie ergeben. 21 April 1976, op. cit.

201. AWU=Arbeiterwohnunterkunft (workers' hostel).

202. UACZ, VA Nr. 3453, Eingabe 17.07.1980.

203. It should be added that there were differences among the standards of the workers' hostels because the hostel of Josef-Klose Straße was mentioned negatively in other letters of complaint, too.

204. UACZ, VA Nr. 3741, Eingabe 04.22.1983.

205. Stress is mine.

206. UACZ, VA 933, Eingabe zur schlechten Unterbringung in der AWU, 09.03.1974.

207. UACZ, VA Nr.3742, Eingabe 09.06.1983.

208. UACZ, VA Nr. 3742, Untersuchungsbericht zur Eingabe des Kolln. X, 24.6.1983.

209. UACZ, VA Nr. 3742, Ausspracheprotokoll zur Eingabe der Kolln. X, 20.6.1983.

210. UACZ, VA Nr. 3453, Eingabe 06.12.1980.

211. UACZ, GB Nr. 1569, Eingabe zur unzureichenden Unterkunft in AWH, 21.05.1987.

212. UACZ, VA Nr. 933, Eingabe,04.04.1974.

213. UACZ, VA Nr. 933, 15.05.1974.

214. UACZ, VA Nr. 934, Eingabe, 05.01.1975.

215. UACZ, VA Nr. 934, 29.01.1975.

216. UACZ, VA Nr. 3741, Eingabe 01.04.1980.

217. UACZ, VA Nr. 3741, Eingabe 24.04.1980.

218. UACZ, VA Nr. 3741, Ihre erneute Eingabe vom 24.04.1980, 08. 05.1980.

219. UACZ, VA Nr. 934, Aussprache mit Kollegin R am 4.2.76.

220. UACZ, VA Nr. 3741, Eingabe, 28.02.1983.

221. UACZ, VA Nr. 3741, Untersuchungsbericht zur Eingabe des Gen D, 17.03.1983.

222. UACZ, VA Nr. 4617, Eingabe an den Ministerrat der DDR, 14.03.1983.

223. People could apply for permission to leave the GDR (*Ausreiseantrag*), which would mean the loss of their GDR citizenship.

224. UACZ, VA Nr. 4617, Untersuchungsbericht zur Staatsrat- und Ministerrats – Eingabe in der Wohnungsangelegenheit Frau X, 27.04.1983.

225. UACZ, VA Nr. 3453, Eingabe 23.09.1980.
226. UACZ, VA Nr. 3453, Eingabe 09.04.1980.
227. UACZ, VA Nr. 3455, Eingabe 06.12.1982.
228. Information from the life-history interviews.
229. Citation from an interview conducted with Gisela (48), an East German female production worker in Zeiss in 2002. She was a skilled worker and a shop steward.
230. Citation from an interview conducted with Edith (49), an East German female production worker in her home in 2002. She was a skilled worker.
231. Citation from an interview conducted with Paul (51), a former East German brigadier in Zeiss in 2002. He was a skilled worker.
232. Citation from an interview conducted with Ernst (57), an East German production worker in Zeiss in 2002. He was a skilled worker.
233. UACZ, VA Nr. 5170, Eingabe, 30.03.1987.
234. To address someone as 'du' instead of 'Sie' (speaking on familiar terms).
235. ThStA Rudolstadt, Bezirksparteiarchiv der SED Gera, IV C-4/13/124, Konzeption zu 'Du und die Werk' VEB Carl Zeiss Jena.
236. Fair of the Future Experts. It was organized at the level of the district.
237. ThStA Rudolstadt, Bezirksparteiarchiv der SED Gera, IV C-2/3/126, Sekretariatssitzung vom 29 November 1973, Erfahrungen der IKL/SED des VEB Carel Zeiss Jena bei der ideologischen Leitung, langfristigen Planung und Entwicklung des geistig-kulturellen Lebens in Einheit mit der sozialistischen Rationalisierung und Verbesserung der Arbeits- und Lebensbedingungen.
238. Bericht der IKPKK (Gen. W), op. cit. Welche Probleme sieht der Betriebsleiter?
239. ThStA Rudolstadt, Bezirksparteiarchiv der SED Gera, IV D-2/3/102, Sekretariatssitzung vom 28 September 1978, Wie entwickeln die GO [GO=Grundorganisation, base organization] der IKL Zeiss eine offensivepolitische Massenarbeit in den Partei- und Arbeitskollektiven zur weiteren Vertiefung der sozialistischen Intensivierung, besonders zur Beschleunigung des wissenschaftlich-technischen Fortschritts und der sozialistischen Rationalisierung?
240. On the establishment of socialist brigades, their structure and their role in production see: Hübner, *Konsens, Konflikt*, 212–32. For their role in conflict management see: J. Roesler. 1999. 'Die Rolle des Brigadiers bei der Konfliktregulierung zwischen Arbeitsbrigaden und der Werkleitung', in: Hübner, *Arbeiter in der SBZ – DDR*. For a study of cultural life in the factories see: A. Schumann. 2003. 'Veredlung der Produzenten oder Freizeitpolitik? Betriebliche Kulturarbeit vor 1970', *Postdamer Bulletin für Zeithistorische Studien* 29; A. Schumann. 2005. '"Macht die Betriebe zu Zentren der Kulturarbeit": Gewerkschaftlich organisierte Kulturarbeit in den Industriebetrieben der DDR in den fünfziger Jahren: Sozialhistorisches Novum oder Modifizierung betriebspolitischer Traditionen?' in: Hübner, *Arbeiter im Staatssozialismus.*
241. UACZ, GB Nr. 1205, Brigadebuch, Abrechnung des Brigadeplanes/Kampfprogramms 1984 der Brigade 'Salvador Allende' zur 10. Wiederholverteidigung des Staatstitels 'Kollektiv der sozialistischen Arbeit' am 04.02.1985, 14.00 Uhr.
242. Ibid.
243. Citation from an interview conducted with Karl (51), who was a male production worker in Zeiss and a shop steward. After he lost his job, he participated in a training course. At the time of interviewing he worked for a bank (*Sparkasse*). The interview was conducted in his house in 2003. He said that the bank planned lay-offs, and one of his colleagues with whom he worked on a similar project explicitly told him that he would do everything to keep his job. This might be one explanation for his bitter comment.
244. This is also supported by the findings of W. Schmidt. 1995. 'Metamorphosen des Betriebskollektivs. Zur Transformation der Sozialordnung in ostdeutschen Betrieben', *Soziale Welt* 45(3); W. Schmidt. 1999. *'Jeder hat jetzt mit sich selbst zu tun': Arbeit, Freizeit und politische Orientierungen in Ostdeutschland*, Konstanz: Univ.-Verl.-Konstanz; R. Bittner.

1999. 'Kleine Leute, Bastler, Pfadfinder – Transformationsfiguren. Ethnografische Versuche im Feld des regionalen Strukturwandels', *Berliner Debatte Initial* 10(2).

245. Citation from an interview conducted with Magda (48), an East German female production worker in Zeiss in 2002. She was a skilled worker.

246. Citation from an interview conducted with Anna (60), an East German unemployed woman in her home in 2002. Before 1991, she was a skilled worker in Zeiss.

247. Citation from an interview conducted with Magda (48).

248. Citation from an interview conducted with Chris (57), an East German production worker in Zeiss in 2002. He was a skilled worker.

249. Citation from an interview conducted with Theresa (54), an East German quality controller in her home in 2002.

250. Citation from an interview conducted with Francesca (52), an East German production worker in her home in 2002. She was a skilled worker.

251. Harsch, *Revenge of the Domestic*.

252. For studies of gender in the GDR see Harsch, *Revenge of the Domestic*; Ansorg, 'Ich hab immer von unten Druck gekriegt und von oben'; Merkel. ... *und Du, Frau an der Werkbank*; Schüler, '*Die Spinne*'; Weil, *Herrschaftsanspruch und soziale Wirklichkeit*.

253. The women's commissions were controlled by the party.

254. UACZ, WB Nr. 487, Abrechnung der Frauenarbeit 1980 nach Schwerpunkten, Entwicklung der Berufstätigkeit der Frau.

255. ThStA Rudolstadt, Bezirksparteiarchiv der SED Gera, IV C-4/13/115, Frauenkommission.

256. ThStA Rudolstadt, Bezirksparteiarchiv der SED Gera, IV C-2/17/612, Frauenarbeit.

257. UACZ, VA Nr. 1583, Unterlagen zur Direktion Kultur- und Sozialwesen, 1976.

258. Ibid.

259. UACZ, WB Nr. 487, Abrechnung der Frauenarbeit 1980 nach Schwerpunkten.

260. Informationsbericht des 1. Sekretärs der IKL Zeiss, 12 November 1970, op. cit. Another report estimated that around 1,000 women could not work in the whole district in 1973 because of the lack of places in the nurseries and kindergartens (Frauenarbeit, op. cit.).

261. The proportion of part-time workers among women was considerably higher, 34.1 per cent, in the district. (ThStA Rudolstadt, Bezirksparteiarchiv der SED Gera, IV C-4/13/115, Frauenkommission, op. cit.).

262. On the development of part-time female employment see: A. Rietzschel. 1997. 'Frauenerwerbstätigkeit und Teilzeitarbeit in der DDR, 1957 bis 1970', *Postdamer Bulletin für Zeithistorische Studien* 9.

263. UACZ, WB Nr. 487, Abrechnung der Frauenarbeit 1980 nach Schwerpunkten, Teilzeitbeschäftigung.

264. ThStA Rudolstadt, Bezirksparteiarchiv der SED Gera, IV C-2/17/612, Frauenarbeit, Carl Zeiss Jena, Optik-Betrieb, 21. April 1976.

265. Ibid.

266. Stress is mine.

267. Unterlagen zur Direktion Kultur- und Sozialwesen, op. cit.

268. Citation from an interview conducted with Chris (57).

269. Citation from an interview conducted with Ina (58), an East German quality controller, in her home in 2002.

270. Citation from an interview conducted with Sebastian, an East German production worker in Zeiss in 2002. He was a skilled worker and a shop steward.

271. Citation from an interview conducted with Susan, an East German production worker (58) in Zeiss in 2002. She was a skilled worker.

272. Citation from an interview conducted with Francesca (52).

273. The name of the currency of the GDR.

274. Citation from an interview conducted with Rita (53), a female quality controller, in her home in 2002.
275. *Gleichberechtigt. Die Entwicklung der Frauen und Mädchen im VEB Carl Zeiss Jena*, op. cit., 6.
276. ThStA Rudolstadt, Bezirksparteiarchiv der SED Gera, IV C-4/13/115, Frauenkommission, op. cit.
277. Frauenarbeit, Carl Zeiss Jena, Optik-Betrieb, op. cit.
278. *Gleichberechtigt. Die Entwicklung der Frauen und Mädchen im VEB Carl Zeiss Jena*, op. cit., 7.
279. ThStA Rudolstadt, Bezirksparteiarchiv der SED Gera, IV C-4/13/115, Frauenkommission, op. cit.
280. The classes also provided lasting friendships (I have found two interview partners with the help of one former student).
281. Citation from an interview with Rita (53).
282. *Gleichberechtigt. Die Entwicklung der Frauen und Mädchen im VEB Carl Zeiss Jena*, op. cit., 6.
283. UACZ, WB Nr. 487, Abrechnung der Frauenarbeit 1980 nach Schwerpunkten, Qualifikationsstruktur.
284. The research centre that employed 4,741 people in 1975 was one of the most 'elite' plants with a proportion of 51 per cent of those who obtained a high-school leaving certificate or a degree of higher education. The proportion of skilled workers and direct production managers was 47 per cent (Mühlfriedel, *Carl Zeiss*, 369, 33. Tabelle).
285. UACZ, WB Nr. 564, Referat des Direktors W zum Frauenforum am 8. 11.1984.
286. This was a special type of school in the GDR that was meant to give education after training school. Apart from vocational training it offered a special high-school leaving certificate to the students with which they could apply to technical colleges and universities.
287. ThStA Rudolstadt, Bezirksparteiarchiv der SED Gera, IV C-2/17/612, Frauenarbeit, Einschätzung der Durchsetzung der Frauenpolitik der Partei im VEB Carl Zeiss Jena durch die staatliche Leitung. Wie werden die Frauen politisch-ideologisch befähigt, ihrer Rolle und Verantwortung bei der Durchsetzung der Beschlüsse der 8th Parteitages gerecht zu werden? 28. Juni 1974.
288. Qualifikationsstruktur, op. cit.
289. Referat des Direktors W zum Frauenforum am 8. 11.1984, op. cit.
290. Frauenarbeit, Einschätzung der Durchsetzung der Frauenpolitik der Partei im VEB Carl Zeiss Jena durch die staatliche Leitung, op. cit.
291. Qualifikationsstruktur, op. cit.
292. Abrechnung der Frauenarbeit 1980 nach Schwerpunkten, Frauen in Leitungsfunktionen, op. cit.
293. Frauenarbeit, Einschätzung der Durchsetzung der Frauenpolitik der Partei im VEB Carl Zeiss Jena durch die staatliche Leitung, op. cit.
294. ThStA Rudolstadt, Bezirksparteiarchiv der SED Gera, IV C-4/13/115, Frauenkommission, 1981, op. cit.
295. A separate subchapter discusses the role of women in the party and other mass organizations.
296. UACZ, VA Nr. 3740, Analyse zur Entlohnung und Eingruppierung werktätiger Frauen im Vergleich zu werktätiger Männern im Kombinat VEB Carl Zeiss Jena, 6. September 1979. Verteilung weiblicher Werktätiger auf die einzelnen Lohngruppen im Vergleich zu männlichen Werktätigen.
297. Ibid.
298. Ibid.
299. On 17 June 1953 the East German workers had protested against the higher norms and price increases with an uprising.

300. ThStA, Rudolstadt, Bezirksparteiarchiv der SED Gera. Nr. IV C-2/6/441.

301. ThStA Rudolstadt, Bezirksparteiarchiv der SED Gera, IV D-4/13/76, Informationsbericht von IKL Zeiss, 10 November 1977.

302. Ferge, *Az iskolarendszer.*

303. H. Solga. 1995. *Auf dem Weg in eine klassenlose Gesellschaft? Klassenlagen und Mobilität zwischen Generationen in der DDR.* Berlin: Akademie Verlag.

304. R. Angelusz and R. Tardos. 1995. 'Társadalmi átrétegződés és szociális-politikai identifikáció'. *Szociológiai Szemle 2.*

CHAPTER 3

....

WORKERS AND THE PARTY

While the first and second chapters of the book discussed the rise and fall of welfare dictatorships, the third and the fourth chapters are directly engaged with the relationship between the workers and the 'workers' state'. The third chapter analyses party life from below: it describes the criteria and methods of recruitment, the role of working-class quotas in party building, attending meetings, party discipline, the ways and consequences of losing the membership of the party and the loss of the appeal of the party, which can be nicely documented in the Hungarian case. The fourth chapter compares the memory of the two regimes in the light of the East German and Hungarian interviews and it interrogates the question of how the different political climate of the two countries and the different trajectories of postsocialist transformation impacted on the subjective evaluation of the welfare dictatorships. To avoid repetitions, the conclusions of the third and fourth chapters are incorporated in the concluding chapter of the book.

In socialist regimes the ruling parties were mass organizations, whose membership encompassed a significant part of the adult population. The control of the party over the economic and social life was also maintained through the party organizations, which operated in the workplaces. The party made significant efforts to win the blue-collar workers for the membership: large enterprises such as Rába and Zeiss had their own party committees with a full-time party secretary. Thanks to the surviving party archives, organizational life can be well documented in Hungary in this period. The opposite is true for the East German case study, where the least well documented area of the social and political life of the working class in the Honecker era is the relationship between the party and the workers.[1] The papers of the party organization in the factory were supposed to be transferred to the Rudolstadt archive at intervals of every twenty years, but the change of regimes prevented a transfer in 1991.[2]

The materials were not found in the factory archives either. Since party membership of the party was seen as a sensitive issue, there was very little information in life-history interviews either. (When asked if they were members of the party, people gave an answer, but I rarely heard positive answers.) This explains the limited scope of the East German in comparison with the Hungarian case study.

In the Hungarian case the decreasing appeal of the party became more visible in the 1980s, when the party organizations regularly reported on the problems of recruiting workers in large industry. Despite the efforts to popularize the party among the working class, individualism was claimed to have affected organizational life after the economic reform: functionaries regularly complained that the membership neglected party work, and they were indifferent to political issues. There was a high percentage of workers among those who left the party, which, as the secretary of the county formulated, showed that the membership was not an existential question for them.

An even more serious warning was that discontent also mounted among the grass-roots membership of the party. Particularly valuable sources in this respect are the information reports, which the party organizations regularly collected in order to monitor the political mood of the population. The reports nicely illustrate the process of how the economic criticism of the people developed into a more encompassing criticism of the political regime: people recognized the failure of the standard-of-living policy, and they refused to believe in further promises. In the second half of the 1980s a large part of the population (including the party membership) was reported to be pessimistic about the future prospects, and many questioned the ability of the government to improve the situation. The party's authority declined and the first signs of disintegration manifested themselves: youth refused to join (the membership of the youth organization significantly decreased), recruitment fell, and more and more people requested the termination of their membership. An ever-increasing part of the population sympathized with the call for political reforms. In the light of the information reports it can indeed be argued that the attraction of the party and the system that it represented had decreased long before it lost political power in Hungary, and even those who envisaged a different, democratic socialism supported the reforms.

There is an important difference between the East German and Hungarian case studies that has to be pointed out.[3] In Hungary, ideological discipline within the party was never as rigid as in the GDR, and from the late 1970s onwards, increasing liberalization could be observed that enabled the grass-roots membership to articulate their discontent with the existing economic and political conditions. In this politically more liberal atmosphere it was possible to detect the signs of the increasing unpopularity of the regime among the people, which rendered visible the decline of the system. In the GDR, on the contrary, ideological discipline was maintained practically until the fall of the Honecker regime. On the basis of the surviving party documents of the district, it is unlikely that the materials of the party organization of the Zeiss factory would have been more informative. There is some evidence that ideological life in Jena and the factory was a bit more liberal; at least the leniency of the latter was criticized in district leadership meetings. Given the lack of minute books of factory party meetings, it is difficult to say, however, what this leniency meant in practice and how far the grass-roots members could or did express their opinions in cell meetings. It is still unlikely that any criticism of existing conditions, let alone of the party, would have been recorded if we take into account that a satirical carnival publication almost cost the editor, a physicist, his job – and it was only through the intervention of the chairman of the IKPKK[4] that he 'got off' with a disciplinary transfer.[5] This story explains why it is so difficult, if not impossible, to detect the signs of the decline of the regime in the official party documents.

The policy of intimidation was not, however, successful. It was possible to hide the signs of the decline, but the collapse of the Soviet control over Eastern Europe revealed in stark fashion the unpopularity of the regime. While in the Hungarian case it is possible to distinguish between the 1970s and 1980s (the latter being characterized by gradual marketization and liberalization of the political climate), in the case of the GDR the two decades of the Honecker regime were more uniform in terms of the approach to both economic policy and the practice of political rule. The regime could, however, maintain the silence of the population only with the help of repressive methods; this was true of grass-roots party members also, where ideological discipline was taken even more seriously. By intimidating grass-roots party members, the leadership prevented internal debate, but it also blocked off official channels through which it could have been informed about the true political views of the members. It is remarkable that the party was never mentioned among those GDR institutions that were remembered positively later. The majority of those who contrasted the communality of the GDR with the individualism of the new, capitalist society were not members of the party. Even though it was recognized that there were some committed communists, party membership was usually associated with careerism in the eyes of the majority of my interview partners (including some members of the party). This suggests that its political education – despite, or rather because of the practice of oppression – was not very successful, and the SED[6] was seen rather negatively by many workers even before the collapse of the regime.

The Workers' Party and the Workers in Hungary

Quotas

The Hungarian Socialist Workers' Party (Magyar Szocialista Munkáspárt = MSZMP) was by definition a mass party and a workers' party. In 1986, the party had 883,131 members across the country, which constituted 11.1 per cent of the Hungarian population. The membership of Győr-Sopron county numbered 31,893 in the same year.[7] Throughout the 1980s there was very little fluctuation: in 1981 the membership in the county amounted to 30,808,[8] and in 1983 it numbered 30,800.[9] In 1984, a figure of 31,000 was given for the membership of the party in the county.[10] Despite every effort of the party to increase the percentage of the workers in the membership, between 1975 and 1981 the number of party members in the county increased by 9 per cent while the number of the working-class party members increased by only 6 per cent. In 1981 less than half of the county membership (40.2 per cent) were blue-collar workers, while 10 per cent of all workers were party members (the percentages varied between 6 and 20 per cent in the factories). The majority of the workers admitted after 1975 were skilled workers and foremen. The overwhelming majority of those who left the party during the period were also workers (70 per cent).[11]

Since MSZMP was defined as a workers' party, the party aimed to maintain what it deemed a healthy percentage of the blue-collar workers within its organization through various forms of affirmative action, typically quotas for recruitment. In reports on enrolment, party functionaries freely spoke of the quotas that the party organizations filled and those that they had to 'correct' in the future. Quotas were set for the blue-collar workers, women and youth. These forms of affirmative action often had a contradictory effect because many workers were convinced the need to join the party was only because of the pressure on recruiters to meet the quotas. Their lack of commitment was also reflected in the statistics: the percentage of blue-collar workers was very high among those who left the party after only a short period of membership (65–70 per cent). The most frequent reasons people gave for a voluntary withdrawal were the refusal to pay the party dues, lack of time to participate in the party meetings and ideological disagreement with the party line (this usually meant religious commitment).[12] This shows that in many cases the requirements of admission to the party were not so seriously enforced.

The declining percentage of working-class party members was a particular concern among the party functionaries after the economic reform of 1968. Many thought that the decrease of working-class support was the result of the reform, which people linked with the increase of prices.

The party secretary of MVG argued that the bad political mood of people was reflected in the declining political activity of party members:

> In my view we should indicate that after the Tenth Party Congress[13] the relationship of the party with the masses did not improve to the extent that we had expected after the successful congress. Quite the contrary, our experience is that after the parliamentary and local council elections the political activity of the masses decreased and our relationship to the masses became weaker. Our political work fails to increase the activity to the desired level. I think that we should say it bluntly to the highest party leadership so that they can draw the right conclusions.[14]

The old party workers explained the declining force of political mobilization by referring to the material discontent of workers:

> Concerning people who have dropped out of the party, I fully agree with Comrade Gy., who spoke of the problem of the enrolment of blue-collar workers in that it expresses the political mood of people in an area. I would even go further to argue that it reflects their opinion about the policy of the party. In general employees agree with our political line but workers have a different view of particular issues, for instance, the question of wages and the setting of prices. It influences the local political mood of people. Party membership is not a matter of livelihood to workers, who 'go from one workbench to the other'. When we prepare the candidates for the enrolment, I am not sure that they know their obligations to the party. Suppose we asked party members in MVG, five out of ten would not give a right answer.[15]

The social and material discontent of the workers undoubtedly influenced recruitment. The party organization of Rába MVG reported frankly on the problems of building local organizations:

> In the case of the majority of the new members it is the party organization that initiates the recruitment, and only occasionally the volunteers. These [new members] are primarily young people who are either discharged from the army or apply for membership on the basis of their work in KISZ (Kommunista Ifjúsági Szövetség = the youth organization of the party). There are sometimes problems with the responsibility of the patrons and the supervision of the candidates' work, because out of the new members whom we admitted in 1969–1970, we had to exclude one, strike off four and take party disciplinary action against two. Another problem is that some party secretaries do not consult with the party members and the leaders of other party groups. That's why it happens that instead of the set quotas of workers, they enrol white-collar employees. The efforts of the party leadership to increase the number of blue-collar workers in the party was not successful enough. Although we succeeded in increasing our membership, the percentage of the newly admitted

workers shows only a slight increase (1970: 61.5 per cent, 1972: 62 per cent). In 1971 and the first quarter of 1972 we admitted 170 new members out of which 105 (62.5 per cent) are workers.[16]

The low percentage of working-class party members was criticized at county level, too:

> We fulfilled the enrolment quotas in the county sooner than the national aver-age but the percentage of workers among the new members is 0.5 per cent lower, which is significant in an industrial county. Our experience is that the blue-collar workers are more difficult to win and they leave the party more eas-ily. In the enterprise party committees the intellectuals constitute the majority, and they often encourage the enrolment of the intelligentsia.[17]

A further problem was religious commitment, which was reported to be strong in the county. An information report urged the purge of religious party members: 'In our county there are around five hundred party mem-bers who send their children to Bible classes and regularly participate in church programmes. We should be more consequent to get rid of this influence.'[18] Religious commitment was an obstacle to recruitment as late as the beginning of the 1980s: 'Religiousness is still widespread in the villages. This could not influence the new admissions: many people had to be rejected in the town just for this reason. A further problem is that many of those who moved from the villages to the town only want to be members of the party in the hope of certain advantages.'[19]

The summary report of the new admissions in 1983 also complained about the under-fulfilment of the most important quotas in the county:

> We did not succeed in increasing the percentage of workers among the newly admitted members; on the contrary, there is a decrease mainly in the cities of Győr and Sopron. We could not ensure that of the new admissions in the large enterprises, a majority would be workers (25–28 per cent of the newly admit-ted members are employed in the nineteen large enterprises of the county). We could not – or hardly – hit the target that two-thirds of the new members be young people (aged below thirty). In the past years – because of the weak-ness of the leadership of the party organizations and the political education of the base cells – we could not ensure the significant majority of the workers and the two-thirds majority of youth among the new members mainly in the cities of Győr and Sopron.

The percentage of youth among the party membership of the county de-creased from 12.3 to 8.9 per cent, while nationally it decreased from 12.4 to 10.7 per cent. The ratio of the age group between 18 and 26 decreased from 5.9 to 3.4 per cent in the county.[20] Even though 73.8 per cent of the party members enrolled in 1983 were originally workers, only 44.4 per cent worked in production at the time of their enrolment. The county also failed to reduce the percentage of workers leaving the party: nearly 80 per cent of the drop-outs were workers or peasants of the collective farms. The report stated that in spite of the requirements, *'the number of new admissions in the large enterprises did not increase but it rather showed a decreasing trend in the past years'*.[21]

The decrease in new admissions in the large enterprises was a particularly negative sign because the working class of the large enterprises was the traditional social base of the party. In the city of Győr there were seven enterprise party committees: MVG, Construction Works, Richards Cloth Factory, Cotton Mill, Textile Industry, MÁV (Hungarian Railways) and VOLÁN (state bus company).[22] In 1975, the membership of the enterprise party organizations numbered 4,300 people, which constituted 37.14 per cent of the party membership of the city. The enterprises had eighty base cells, around half of the number of the base cells citywide. The seven large enterprises employed 33,000 people, and 77 per cent of them were blue-collar workers. This meant that the overwhelming majority of the local working class worked in the large enterprises.[23] Since MVG was the largest one of them, it had the largest party organization. In 1975 it had twenty-eight base cells (the base cells of the six other large enterprises in the town varied at between six and eleven) and a full-time party secretary. In 1975 the party membership of MVG in its Győr plants numbered 1,965 people. The overwhelming majority (86 per cent) of the party members were men.[24] In 1983, the party organization of MVG numbered only 1,786 people (while the membership of the county increased during the period). The party organization could not replace those of its members who left: between 1975 and 1980, it admitted 6,412 new members, while 9,573 ceased to be members (the reasons could have been the change of workplace, retirement, death, exclusion or voluntary withdrawal).[25] The party organization admitted that it was difficult to win over young workers:

> It is a problem that few young skilled workers are admitted to the party. Many of them are commuters; after their marriage, the family and the building of the house takes up much of their free time. Their environment accepts that they have no time for political work, only 'after they have got settled'. The reorganization of labour within the enterprise, the conflicts about the dismissals and the wage disputes increased the number of drop-outs. Many people thought that the party did not defend them, therefore they resigned their membership.[26]

There is some evidence that white-collar employees were admitted to fill the ranks of the party: 17 per cent of the employees of MVG in 1983 were members of the party, while the percentage of the party members among the blue-collar workers was 15 per cent. The workers still constituted a majority among the party members: 64 per cent of the membership belonged to the working class. The percentage of youth (below thirty) was around 10 per cent among the party members.[27]

In the second half of the 1980s policies of affirmative action in favour of workers were less and less observed. This was paralleled by the decreasing rate of expansion of the party. In 1980, the rate of increase was 1.8 per cent, in 1982, dropping to 1.5 per cent in 1984, and 1 per cent and in 1986 (0.5 per cent in the country). The main reasons for this were resignations, deaths and a decreasing number of the new admissions.[28] In the county the number of new admissions continually decreased from 1983.

> The enrolment of the workers did not increase according to the requirements. More workers ceased to be members of the party than those who were enrolled. In spite of our efforts we could not significantly improve the building of party organizations in the large enterprises of the county. *New admissions decreased in MVG, the Textile Industry Factory, Graboplast, Rába MMG.*[29] The reasons are closely related to our socio-economic problems, in some places the weakness of the base cells, the indifference of the party members and their failure to set an example to people.[30]

The national data likewise showed a decrease in the percentage of the workers: between 1980 and 1986 the percentage of the workers among the new members decreased by 6 per cent and in 1986 they constituted only 42 per cent of the party membership of the country.[31] This shows that despite the quotas the traditional social basis of the party had started to crumble.

Organizing Women

There were special quotas used to increase the percentage of women in the party and the leadership. The improvement in the situation of women was on the political agenda of the party. The party statistics of the large enterprises in the county in the mid-1970s show that in traditional industries the number of female party members and leaders significantly lagged behind the men.[32] In MVG, 25 per cent of the employees were women while they constituted only 14 per cent of the membership in 1975. Out of the forty-one members of the party committee of MVG only five were women. The percentage of women in the party committees lagged behind also in traditional 'female' industries: in Richards Cloth Factory, 60 per cent of the party members were women but the percentage of women members of the party committee was only 50 per cent. In the Cotton Mill, 35 per cent of the membership and 30 per cent of the party committee were women. In MÁV and Volán the percentage of women party members hardly reached 10 per cent.[33]

A report of 1973 found that even though there were improvements in the situation of women, more effort was needed to assert the policy of equal rights in every field.

> In spite of the increase of the percentage of women in the party, state and social organizations, it is a frequent experience even today that the engagement of women is considered to be a matter of statistics. In these fields many women get no help to improve their skills and leading competence. We consider the preparation and employment of women leaders to be unreasonably slow.[34]

According to the report, the percentage of women in the party committees of the county increased from 10–12 to 20 per cent. A closer look at the statistics shows, however, that women occupied the low-level leading positions, and their activity mainly focused on organizations directly involved in work in local communities: 43 per cent of the members of KISZ, 40 per cent of SZMT (Szakszervezetek Megyei Tanácsa = County Council of the Trade Unions) and 32 per cent of the municipal committees of the People's Front were women. At the same time, women constituted only 17.2 per cent of the full-time party workers in the county. The comments in the report showed that a certain bias continued to exist against women leaders in the county: 'Even though we can meet less open misogynist remarks and backward opinions mainly among the leaders and the leading bodies than in the previous years, in practice they frequently set higher requirements for women than for men, and they sometimes only look for excuses to reject women.' The report stated that there was a low percentage of women in the party apparatus (with the exception of KISZ), in the apparatuses of the councils and among the leaders. It was a further problem that there were not enough women candidates for membership who had the necessary political education. There was an initiative to increase the number female students at party schools: their percentage increased from 5–8 to 20 per cent.[35]

Concerning the construction of party organization among women, the report argued that the party organizations had to concentrate their efforts on recruitment among women workers because they were often disadvantaged:

Even today we can often meet the opinion that the party uses double measures for men and women. This opinion causes much harm to the party because with this we renounce the political mobilization and the communist education of women. We agree that the special situation of women should be considered individually and we should adjust their party work to their situation but this cannot lead to any distinction between the members of the party. This distinction renders many women timid and indifferent. It reveals the weakness of our political work among women that there are still many passive, politically indifferent women. In many places the party and mass organizations simply accept that a significant number of women 'have no time' or 'they are not interested in public affairs'. They often won't even invite these women to the meetings of the enterprise. The behaviour of the majority of the passive women can partly be explained by the fact that their political knowledge and intellectual horizon is lower than the average. The reason is often in the family circumstances, the conservatism of their husbands, their relatives, and their household duties.[36]

Women workers had another disadvantage: their lack of skills. The party mainly sought to win the skilled core of the industrial working class, while even though 35.8 per cent of the workers of the county were women, only 16.5 per cent of them were skilled workers.

The number of skilled workers among women increased but their percentage did not change much. The reasons are the following: there are still attitudes both among men and women that negatively influence the choice of profession. Many parents allow their daughters to go to training schools only in the worst case, and even then they look for jobs in other fields after they finished training. Even today it is a problem that the girls and their parents are interested in fashionable trades. We expect some results from the increase of the number of comprehensive schools[37] but we have to wait for their effect.[38]

In MVG the percentage of women slightly increased in the admissions between 1980 and 1983: out of the 250 new members 50 were women.[39] At the level of the county the percentage of women in the new admissions was 40 per cent between 1983 and 1986 and it even increased to 42 per cent in 1987.[40] There is no data about the percentage of women in the leading bodies. From the report of 1973 it can, however, be concluded that traditional biases against the political activity and role of women continued to exist in the county; and even though the party set quotas for women, attitudes did not change together with the statistics.

Party Life

The forum of the base cells were the party meetings, which members were obliged to attend regularly, at least in principle. In MVG few minute books of the meetings of the base cells survived, but the existing documents suggest that party members often voiced their grievances in these meetings, and there was room for real debate. One example is the critical contribution of the mechanic, which was quoted in the introduction, in which he openly expressed his discontent with his economic situation as opposed to what propaganda said of it. The quoted comments of the former brigadiers likewise suggest that people did not refrain from speaking of problems that they had in production (e.g. the comment that 'in my view, every worker has his own problem but he would not speak of it because it won't be solved anyway. I also had a tool problem, I was promised to get one and I did not get any'[41]). As the contribution of the mechanic shows, criticism sometimes even went beyond to address more general problems with the building of socialism.

From the surviving documents it is, of course, difficult to estimate the political activity of the membership in these meetings or in general. The reports were generally more optimistic than the comments of the party officials. In the discussion of a report on exemplary communist conduct, the first secretary of the county stated bluntly that one had to look for it with a magnifying glass. Although he did not relate his comments to economic reform, his moral criticism well expressed the view of the old party workers that the life of the movement was undermined by the spread of materialism and indifference:

> We can experience passivity also in the party. I don't want to argue about the 5 per cent,[42] but we can multiply it safely by five and even then we are too optimistic. No numbers can express the indifference to party work and political questions. When it comes to a political debate, party members just stand there open-mouthed and they do not stand up to defend the party's standpoint. This question does not even come up in the factories and still we are all satisfied and declare that everything is all right.[43]

A member of the executive committee argued that in his opinion the grass-roots members learned only one-quarter to one-third of the important central decisions. 'The secretaries of the ground cells have to write down or memorize very important tasks at one hearing. Unfortunately, the majority of them are unable to do this.'[44]

In the discussions there was much criticism of the formality of party life and the difficulties of mobilizing party members. Indifference was allegedly characteristic of both the managers and the workers. The party secretary of MVG took the side of the workers in a meeting of the executive committee:

It is difficult to engage the workers in party work but you can look at the workers' militia, which the people have to do after work: most of them are workers. At the same time we write down that it is difficult to convince the workers of the importance of party work. What is written here does not agree with the facts even if a committee of fifty-two people examined it. The other problem: the report discusses the activity of the party membership, the number of party commissions and the ratio of the participants. According to this report it is like sport. We declare that we organized three foot races with 100-100 participants but if the same people showed up at three different times, we will still report that there were 300 participants. We put down that 2,300 people have party commissions but in reality it could be only 1,000 people. We could fold our hands if 85 per cent of the party membership actively participated in the party and mass organization work. I have a feeling that the 85 per cent does not show the reality. You should not think that my hobby horse is the worker policy but we write down that we stroke ninety-seven members off the party list. The majority of them, seventy-something were stroked off for their failure to attend the party events, and sixty-seven of them are workers. At the same time when the leaders don't come because they are busy, nobody asks them: do you want to remain in the party or not? I think that our party organizations counter the workers a bit more assertively.[45]

Allegedly, it was more difficult to recruit commuters because they did not want to stay for the regular party meetings after they finished work. Since the same reason was used to explain their withdrawal from adult education, it may well have expressed the anti-peasant bias of the party functionaries, who thought that the 'village people' were politically less developed than the urban working class. Since the economic reform, commuters were reported to be more materialistic, and interested in their private wealth rather than community life.[46] In the 1980s, the criticism of materialism became more lenient in relation with the growing social inequalities: party functionaries did indeed explain the reluctance of working-class youth to join the party through the increased burdens of establishing an independent household.[47]

The few surviving registers give no information about how often the base cells actually met. With respect to the brigade meetings, the party committee of the factory demonstrated a remarkable lenience when it was recognized that people who performed heavy physical work during the day did not always have time for the common meetings.[48] There is some evidence that the obligations of regular party life were likewise not so seriously enforced; at least the report of the leadership of the enterprise party committees sharply criticized the leadership of MVG in this respect. It was reported that thanks to their lenience, there were party groups in the factory which had not meet for months:

Regarding the monthly party meetings in MVG we saw the problem earlier. We even made a compromise when we thought that Comrade K can solve the problem that we indicated to him. Unfortunately, there was very weak leadership in MVG. Things declined to the point that there were base cells that did not have regular party life. We had to send a comrade from the town committee to reproach the local comrades. We think that this question is solved with the appointment of Comrade L.[49]

The monthly party meetings of the base cells of MVG triggered a debate even in the executive committee of the county. One member of the committee observed that 'it almost looks like a punishment to participate in the party meetings. Where there are problems in the base cells, they should be solved. The party groups should hold a meeting in every month.'[50] Given, however, that Comrade L was nicknamed 'Comrade Simpleton' in the factory, it can be questioned whether he had the authority to significantly improve party life.[51] In 1977 it was reported that the relationship between the party and the mass organizations was good and 50 per cent of the leaders of the mass organizations were members of the party. The report, however, indicated that there was less agreement between the party and the management: 'We still need to develop the political leading activity of the managers. They tend to neglect political work referring to the production tasks.'[52] Even though the manager of MVG was member of the Central Committee between 1970 and 1989 – or perhaps because of it – the interest of production preceded party work.

Losing Members

The high percentage of workers among those who walked out of the party shows that the membership was not an existential question to the workers. They could be persuaded to join but the commitment was often not strong enough to keep them in the party. One could leave the party voluntarily (withdrawal) or upon the initiative of the party (through exclusion or being struck off). Withdrawal usually happened upon retirement or after a change of place-of-work, but people sometimes resigned because they did not have time for party life or they did not want to pay dues. With their withdrawal the workers could also express their disagreement with the ideology of the party (religious commitment), its policy or the policy of the factory (e.g. dismissals in MVG). According to the information reports resignation was frequently a sign of protest (wage disputes, the distribution of premiums, etc.): in the introduced case of the regulation of paid holiday of 1986, many people gave back their trade union cards and refused to pay the trade union or party dues in order to show their disagreement with the measure.[53] Such cases reveal that people expected the defence of labour interests from the party and the mass organizations, and their failure to do so frequently motivated voluntary withdrawals.

Many people decided to resign membership upon retirement, and they constituted a significant group of those whose membership terminated. In 1982, of the drop-outs 23.3 per cent were retired people, in 1984 it was nearly one-third (27.8 per cent)[54] and in 1987 almost the same (27.4 per cent).[55] The high percentage of the retired among the drop-outs shows that the party organization was closely connected with the workplace in the eyes of people. When they finished their active working life, they were unwilling to continue political work in their local party organizations. The most frequent reasons that they gave for their withdrawal were the high party dues and their bad health. A report of 1985 gave the following reasons for the withdrawal of retired people:

> 27.8 per cent of the drop-outs are retired; many of them were engaged in so-cial and political work full of struggles for decades. A significant part of them suffer from chronic health problems by the time they retire. They grow tired, indifferent, passive, which is largely understandable. Of course, this does not justify their complete withdrawal from political and social life. Some of them are offended without due reason.[56]

But there were people who had a reason to be offended. In the executive committee of MVG, the party secretary told of a comrade who performed very good work until his last work day and in the farewell dinner he said that 'I worked here for forty-five years; there is one thing that hurts me that I tell you now. After I was fifty-eight, I did not get a pay increase because they told me I was too old.'[57] The secretary added that this was a justified complaint. The executive committee of MVG was also responsive to the financial problems of the retired. The average pension in the factory was 3,000 Ft, but those who retired earlier often had a very low income. The party due of 100 Ft could, argued that party commit-tee, indeed burden their budget.[58] The grass-roots members would also complain about the lack of attention that they experienced from the lead-ers. In the Rear Bridge Unit, a party member who had worked there for eighteen years noted that during this time nobody asked him if he and his family were well. The questions asked are only 'how long you stay, how many pieces you do, etc.'[59]

The withdrawal of the active workers was an even more sensitive loss to the party because it was usually a direct sign of disagreement or dis-content with its policies. The high percentage of the workers among the drop-outs therefore also reflected the weakness of political work. A reason

for resignation had to be given – even though by 1987 many people refused to give a reason.[60] The party could also initiate the termination of
membership. Exclusion was used as a punishment if a party member seriously and repeatedly offended the community (e.g. by committing criminal offences, or stealing from the property of the collective). Those who
emigrated to the West were also excluded from the party.[61] There was a
less drastic way to leave the party: to become an inactive party member –
those who regularly did not attend the party meetings, did not participate
in party life and did not pay the party dues were struck off. The judgement of the activity of the members could be, of course, subjective. The
party secretary of MVG was probably right to argue that the managers
could find better reasons to miss the party meetings than the workers.[62]
The party reports of MVG likewise complained that the weight of the
management increased at the expense of the party organization: 'In the
past when the party secretary wanted to talk to a manager and asked him
into his room, the manager would grow white with fear about why the
secretary wanted to see him. Today the manager would answer without
hesitation that he does not have time.'[63]

The statistics suggest that the party rarely resorted to purging its members. In 1985, 192 members withdrew from the party, 150 were struck off
and 52 were excluded in the county. Between 1980 and 1984, 699 people
withdrew from the party in the county: 20.2 per cent of them explained
it through family and religious reasons, and 14.3 per cent said that they
could not meet the party requirements.[64] There is some evidence that at
that time the party showed more flexibility on religious issues: a report of
1984 noted that in the villages the parents often expected their children
to marry in church and to christen their grandchildren in exchange for
their financial support.[65]

People were mainly struck off because of the negligence of organizational life or their failure to ask for a transfer to the relevant party organizations upon changing their workplace.[66] It was mentioned in a report
of 1977 that some people would not transfer to the party organization
of the new working place, and thus drop out of the party.[67] This suggests that the workplace was often central to the organization of people.
It would be wrong to assume that the party encouraged the exclusions:
from the 1980s a defensive attitude can be observed in the documents.
The party aimed to keep rather than lose its members. Between 1979 and
1983 the party membership of Rába MMG was reduced from 502 to 411
people: 123 were transferred to other party organizations, 20 were struck
off, 9 withdrew, 3 were excluded, and 7 people died. The organization
admitted 49 new members, and 22 arrived from other party groups. The
balance was still an almost 20 per cent decline in the membership.[68] With

a shrinking membership, it is unlikely that the party organizations looked for reasons to exclude or strike off party members.

The less strict form of punishment was the party reprimand. The party disciplinary proceedings suggest that the main aim was to maintain the moral respectability of the party rather than to reinforce organizational life. Improper conduct and an unorganized family life were likely to be punished with a strong reprimand, but these offences could also lead to exclusion from the party. People who outraged the public with their behaviour received a warning and they risked being excluded from the party. It was, for instance, reported to the party that the new party secretary of a collective farm 'got so drunk after a council meeting that he vomited through the window of the building of the party committee. This was a very bad introduction and it triggered very negative responses in the village.'[69] The case was investigated and the secretary received a strong reprimand. The party also respected – and promoted – settled family life and relations. Adulterers also risked a strong reprimand. This, in turn, often led to denunciations to the party committee by jealous partners.[70] Between 1980 and 1984, 268 party members (among them 180 workers) were excluded from the party in the county (so perhaps it is true that the party organizations countered the workers more assertively). More than one-third (35.7 per cent) were excluded because of offences against socialist property. Indecent private life was the second most frequent reason for exclusion: it amounted to 25.9 per cent of the punishments; 6 per cent were excluded because of negligence of party duties, 5.3 per cent for causing accidents, 4.5 per cent for violating labour discipline and 3 per cent for their failure to meet the ideological requirements of the party (this meant the demonstration of religious commitment, participation in church ceremonies, etc.).[71] The party evidently watched over the moral respectability of the membership, and it adhered to the 'bourgeois' rules of conduct regarding family life. The referees were frequently warned to consider the moral character of the candidates so that they could not bring disgrace to the party with their behaviour.[72] Since most of the members were excluded for offences against socialist property, political education in this sense was not always effective.

Even though the party strove for moral respectability, being a party member was not in itself enough to win social respect. This was true also for the membership: according to a survey of 1972 conducted within the county membership, a tiny minority (3.3 per cent) thought that there was a difference between the Marxists and non-Marxists in their attitude to work, and only half of them thought that there was a difference in political opinions.[73] In 1983 people who were not members of the party rejected political discussion with party members on the basis 'that they would not talk to those who can't do their daily work properly. Some people said that no one asked them when they spoilt the standard of living. Others refused to state their opinion saying that they would not consider it all the same.'[74] In the second half of the 1980s party reports in fact complained of instances of discrimination against the members of the party. With the increasing economic problems of the 1980s (increasing prices, high inflation, and the stagnation of real wages), more and more people raised the question of responsibility: grass-roots members charged the leaders with incompetence, while those who were not members of the party blamed the whole party membership. People would ask why they had to 'pay' the price of the bad decisions of the leaders. It was reported that in the Industrial Tool Factory 'people complained that the leaders again want to shift the responsibility onto the producers. *But the making of the plans and the command of the economy are not done from the machines.*[75] It would be good if the leaders took responsibility for their bad decisions and removed the hair-cracks that had appeared between the party and the people.'[76] Another report noted that 'today it is not rewarding to be a communist. Many people refuse to take the responsibility for the mistakes – this explains the high number of withdrawals.'[77] Ever more people refused to identify themselves with the policy of the party; the increase of resignations was indicative of the political weakening of the regime.

The Failure of the Standard-of-Living Policy

With the help of the information reports it is possible to give a very good documentation of the mounting economic discontent of the population.[78] Since the reports were mostly written by low-level party functionaries, the criticism that they formulated reflected the deteriorating political mood of the grass-roots membership for the regime. It is worth comparing the reports of the early 1970s with those of the late 1970s and 1980s in this respect: while the former mainly addressed local issues that had to be improved, the latter critically reported on the 'general questions' of the social and economic development of the country. In particular two criticisms were stressed: the first was the failure of the standard-of-living policy, which people bitterly experienced as opposed to the government's promises, and the second was the issue of growing material inequalities – again as opposed to the egalitarian ideology that the party propagated. In the light of the information reports these factors effectively undermined the credibility of the government.

The increase of prices, understandably, never had a positive reception among the population. The reports of the late 1970s, however, stressed that the measure was socially unjust because it hit mainly those who lived from wages, while other, wealthier strata who worked in the private sector could compensate for the increase of prices by increasing their prices, too.

> In the past weeks our employees were mainly concerned with the increase of prices. They agreed with some of the items but they found the increase of the price of meat definitely too much. They said that they cannot buy a sandwich from their hourly wage. They also disagreed with the increase of the prices of cars; they said that they had saved for a car for years but with these prices and the increase of the price of petrol they could not afford to buy a car. They thought that the peasants and the self-employed would have no problem to pay this higher price but for an urban worker, who had to work one hour for 1 kg of paprika, it would cause an almost unsolvable problem. They also found the increase of the price of utilities too much.[79]

It was likewise pointed out that the disappointment of the population would increase the number of those who have lost their interest in politics:

> But more importantly, we have to accept that the key to solve this 'more difficult' economic situation is not the increase of prices! Sometimes society can expect restraint from its members if it is demanded by the economic situation, but this cannot be an alternative – because in the long run, modesty will be replaced with the lack of demands – which goes together with 'indifference'. Indifference can be an almost incurable disease of society.[80]

Another informant put it bluntly that economic dissatisfaction was widespread among the party membership:

> It influences the political mood and production that many of our party members and foremen do not understand the objectives of our economic policy. Their economic 'agitation' means that they emphasize only the mistakes together with the discontented people. They blame the higher leaders for our economic difficulties. They are convinced that they have always worked well and efficiently.[81]

That this was not an isolated phenomenon is supported by the minute books of the base-cell meeting of the forge shop on 22 February 1978:

> Indifference is spreading among people. Nothing makes them interested in community and socialist work. The most important for them is economic work: this is what they want to do well. This is the opinion of the blue-collar workers but it is also characteristic of the managers. The older people are tired and the youth believes that it has no perspective. A still tongue makes a wise head, this is what the people think here. They don't even argue, just nod to everything. Political work is a secondary issue here.[82]

The passivity of the party members was likewise criticized in the Industrial Tool Unit: 'Many expect – even among those who finished a political school – to be themselves convinced by somebody else.'[83] The comments, similarly to the quoted contribution of the mechanic, revealed that the failure of the standard-of-living policy had become evident already in the late 1970s, parallel with the recognition that the party had nothing else to offer to the people.

Direct political criticism, which used to be a rare phenomenon, also manifested itself more often throughout the 1980s.[84] People openly started to express their doubts about the credibility of the socialist media, and the informants' comments suggested that many of them, too, shared these doubts – for instance the question of 'why the balance of the foreign trade is getting worse from year to year, our employees ask',[85] or that of 'will they increase the price of petrol?'[86] Officially nothing is said but the increase of the price in the world market makes one worried.[87] The comments likewise revealed that people refused to believe the economic explanations, particularly when the media had previously declared that the oil crisis would not influence the socialist countries.

> It is difficult to understand and even more difficult to bear for a 'simple' worker that the unfavourable changes of the world economy have reached us, too. The workers don't deny that it is necessary to spare reasonably but unreasonable sparing triggers antipathy only. The unduly high increase of prices and the stagnation of the standard of living reinforce a climate of insecurity. Those who live from their wages will never afford to buy a flat, which costs 500–800,000 Ft. The number of shortage goods increased, which means a big problem for the consumers and higher profits for private traders.[88]

Informants clearly expressed that people refused to believe that the economic problems were only temporary: 'In our opinion, our leaders, who declare even today that we can preserve the standard of living of the 1970s, themselves do not think it seriously.'[89]

An even stronger argument was that failure of the standard-of-living policy mainly affected the industrial working class as the largest social group, which lived from the state sector. Throughout the 1980s it was frequently stressed that they were the main losers of the state's attempt to reduce expenditures, while the state could not control the incomes of those who worked in the private sector. Growing material inequalities did not only trigger envy but they also revealed that the 'building of socialism' was limited to the propagation of socialist ideology. In the light of the information reports, scepticism towards the regime increased among the workers. They found it ever more ridiculous to believe that they were

the beneficiaries of the economic policy of the state; the real beneficiaries, in their eyes, were the managers, the high functionaries and those
who worked in the private sector. Informants often consciously refused to
write more 'nuanced' reports: 'There is no positive change in the prices
and transport so the people's opinions (which we have reported earlier)
have not changed, either. I request the acceptance of our information
report!'[90] The informant elaborated his position in another report:

> In the training courses we received many instructions concerning the structure
> of information reports. It is, however, difficult or impossible to satisfy these
> demands if people fail to react to events according to the given criteria. It was
> often criticized that information reports are limited to complaints about the
> provision with consumer goods and public transport. If we do not want to
> forge the reports (and we certainly don't), we can only write about the things
> that really concern people. These are the increase of prices, the provision with
> consumer goods, transport and the 'preservation' of the standard of living.
> We cannot write new things about them because the circumstances have not
> changed; or better to say, they have deteriorated after the increase of the price
> of fuel. I request the acceptance of our information report![91]

According to the reports, workers often directly contrasted their economic situation with that of the wealthier social strata. Such comparisons
evidently reflected the workers' mounting social discontent:

> The pay increases are not proportionate to the increase of the prices, so the
> majority of the employees experience a gradual decline in their standard of liv-
> ing. This applies only to the people who live from their work and wages and
> not to the speculators – and there are many of them, unfortunately. According
> to the report of the OTP the savings of the people in the bank have increased,
> despite the price increases. Whose savings have increased, and how many of
> them earned their money with honest work?[92]

The informant argued prices had constantly increased since 1973, which
made it more difficult for industrial workers to earn their living.[93] In a
base-cell meeting party members argued that the increase of the prices hit
most the urban industrial working class because they could only rely on
the wages that they earned in the factory: 'They are not satisfied with the
reasoning of the price increases. They refuse to understand the necessity
of these measures.'[94] Similar reports from other plants suggest that dissatisfaction and pessimism were widespread among the workers: people
did not understand why they were expected to make sacrifices in the interest of the country while others – as they perceived – prospered at their
expense: 'The most important topic among the workers is invariably the

standard of living. They complain that prices have changed without an announcement. The newspapers and the TV always talk about the savings of the people, how much they increased, but no one investigates how much money the workers have in the bank.'[95] In the Industrial Tool Unit the workers also complained about the decline of the standard of living:

> Our statistical office always publishes data about the savings of the population, and then they can argue that people can afford to pay the higher prices. Our workers say that if someone investigated who were the lucky ones, who had money in the bank, one would find very few Rába workers among them.[96]

The visible material differences between the social groups urged many to question social justice. Few people believed that the rich earned their money by honest means; at least in the light of the information reports people spoke of non-productive work with disapproval. A report of the ideological training of the party membership concluded that the workers did not feel that their situation improved in spite of overtime:

> In their judgement the basis of distribution is not the work that one performs. They think that the money goes to the non-productive sphere, and that the working class, which produces the national income, receives an ever-decreasing share. An 'upper class', which is not affected by the economic situation of the country, has emerged. The economic restrictions reduce only the income of the people who work in the over-regulated industry. They are worried about the expansion of the private sector, which will broaden this upper class.[97]

The reference to solidarity was rejected with the reasoning that social justice has disappeared from society:

> In a TV-interview it was argued that our economic situation and the standard of living won't improve in the near future. According to the interview, there is a group which does not notice the economic situation, another where the standard of living stagnates, and a third, largest group, where it declines (which affects the majority of the employees). Question: why can't all the strata share the burdens equally? For example, while one builds a villa, another has a problem to buy one kilo of meat.[98]

People also argued that not everybody could find work in the private sector, which thus only increased existing inequalities:

> It is a general opinion that today the urban workers have a problem to make ends meet. We don't think that this can be explained with the increase of the demands. Everybody who wants to achieve something – whether a car, family house or the support of the children and we are back to the flat problem

(parental support!) – needs an extra income. An opportunity[99] is needed to participate in the private economy.[100]

It was also pointed out that the high incomes that could be earned in the private sector rendered people more responsive to the capitalist ideology: 'Here we have a political question: if the proportion between the state and private economy further shifts, which will be more dominant in the consciousness of a worker: where he goes to work or where he earns the money?!'[101]

The economic dissatisfaction of the working class was linked with the argument that their social and political role also declined. It was disputable even in the light of the reforms of the 1970s whether the workers regarded themselves as members of the ruling class; in the 1980s, however, there was an increasing complaint that instead of a solid integration into the socialist middle class, they found themselves at the bottom of the social ladder. The growing material differences rendered painfully evident this social decline:

> Unfortunately, price increases continue in 1983, too. The monthly wage of an average worker – without overtime – is 4,500 Ft. As compared to this, engineers earn 6,500–7,000 Ft a month. We don't think that this big difference is justified. It seems that the leading role of the working class is manifest only by the workbenches but it plays no role in the distribution of the incomes.[102]

The party membership of the Vehicle Unit criticized that everything was explained through the economic situation of the country, which became more important than the leading role of the party: 'They therefore do not experience the leading role of the party', the report concluded.[103] The unequal chances of young people to buy flats were likewise repeatedly stressed: the children of working-class families were reported to belong to the disadvantaged groups.[104] But workers had to cut back their demands in other fields of life, too, which reinforced their bitterness against the more fortunate social groups, who had enough means to finance their luxuries. According to an extraordinary information report of the forge shop, the workers were very surprised to hear that the price of petrol increased while it went down in the world market:

> The question is who are the most affected by the price increase? Those who have a higher income will have no problem to drive in the future. For the low-income groups the car is often the only means of entertainment. According to the employees these groups are the working class, the retired and the big families.[105]

In the Industrial Tool Unit people wondered 'how high the prices can be increased'.[106] Holiday trips also started to be regarded as a luxury; people particularly complained of the increasing prices of the holiday resorts at Lake Balaton, which were also frequented by foreign tourists:

> There is no cheap accommodation or catering; for instance, one week of camping costs 1,000 Ft. The prices in the restaurants are beyond the means of a simple Hungarian worker. The private shopkeepers perhaps exploit this because their prices are dishonestly high. A pancake costs 6–8 Ft, the maize 10–15 Ft and the fruit costs two to three times more than in Győr. The local councils should do something against these unfair profits![107]

The mounting discontent of people was manifest in their political opinions, too. The information reports of the 1980s speak of the gradual deterioration of the political mood: the criticism that the economic situation of the industrial working class deteriorated was followed by openly critical political comments:

> The constant price increases negatively influence the public mood. In our opinion, the workers are not enlightened enough to regard this process as natural. Particularly if we take into account that the only 'effect' of the world market on our country is the increase of the prices; we can never experience its opposite effect. The workers say that according to our leaders the prices of our products are going down in the world market, but nevertheless, they continue to increase in Hungary.[108]

Price increases were reported to strongly influence the mood of the employees of the Energy Unit because 'they feel that they cannot preserve their former standard of living'.[109] According to the informant of the Motor Unit 'the public mood of the majority of the workers is deteriorating from day to day. They relate this to the ever greater and varied taxes, price increases and the attempt of the state to put the public burden on the working class.'[110] The discussions with the party members concluded that it irritated the workers that while their standard of living declined, there were more opportunities for the 'speculators' and self-employed to get rich. This contributed to the passivity of the membership.[111]

It was argued that after the economic reform, there was a relatively sharp criticism of the managers; political criticism, however, remained a taboo. This changed strikingly in the 1980s: in the light of the information reports, people openly questioned the credibility of their leaders and the official media: 'We do not understand why we can't know how much debt the Hungarian state has while they tell us the debts of Poland and Romania. Why can we know only the military expenses of the USA and not that of Hungary?'[112] It was also criticized that the state leaders were actually afraid of the people, and they enjoyed unjustified privileges:

> It can be safely argued that people were outraged by the exaggerated security measures concerning the Austrian visit of György Lázár in a private train. This is not only the opinion of the grass-roots membership but also that of those who had to wait 30–45 minutes because of the closed bridges. People criticize this sterile isolation of the leaders during the visits of other state leaders, too. A state leader should have more confidence in the people even if it implies some risks.[113]

It was also reported that people refused to believe the reasons that the leaders and the media gave for the restrictive measures, and they blamed the leadership for the wrong economic policy of the country even though they suffered the least from it. The following comment shows how 'far' people went in political criticism: 'Today the Hungarian people work very hard in Europe and they still get nowhere. Our socialist way of life means that everybody works himself to death and achieves nothing while society goes to the dogs.'[114] The 'Hungarian lifestyle' was evidently associated with too much work and low pay: 'Our employees find it remarkable that with respect to the health condition of the middle-aged, we are among the last in Europe. According to our employees, it is not only the result of the 'unhealthy' Hungarian 'cuisine' but also that of too much work.'[115]

The quotations well illustrate the process of how the regime increasingly lost working-class support. People recognized that while the state failed to improve the standard of living of the industrial working class, its economic policy opened new opportunities for other social groups, which lived significantly better than the workers. The situation of the 1980s was in some aspects similar to the reception of the economic reform of 1968 when growing social differences were criticized strongly. There were, however, two important differences: first, at that time the state still had reserves to appease the working class; and second, there was still space for a social dialogue. The reports of the 1980s reflect that the increasing gap between the policy and ideology of the party effectively undermined the credibility of the regime. This deeply rooted disappointment rendered it unlikely that the majority of the workers would have accepted the party as a conversation partner; and, contrary to the era of the new economic mechanism, the party in fact made no noticeable attempt to start a dialogue with the workers.

'Would you call the capitalists back?'

In the 1980s the decreasing appeal of the party became more visible. Functionaries reported of the increasing problems of recruitment, in particular the diminished appeal of the party for young people. The executive committee of MVG reported that young people attached too much importance to material things upon leaving school, and if the party failed to organize them in their twenties, 'it is very difficult to persuade them when they are thirty'. It was, however, added that materialism was characteristic of older people, too: 'today people count too much; for example, a blue-collar worker would pay his car tax from party dues'. That indeed some workers or candidates would make this point is supported by the awkward defence of the workers: 'We have to say that these people are not at all against the system but it is the consequence of exaggerated materialism that has become characteristic of society.'[116] A concrete case was mentioned that threw bad light on the party: a direct production manager, who was a candidate, declared that he did not want to be a party member.[117]

The party organizations were apparently aware of the 'difficult political situation' and the decreasing appeal of the party membership. The executive committee of Rába MMG openly spoke of interest in relation to the membership, and recommended that the party should make the membership attractive to people, which implied that it was not attractive enough. The membership of the party organization of Rába MMG had decreased by 20 per cent between 1979 and 1983.

> The party members are the same people as everybody else. The individuals always have an interest and if we want to increase the attraction of the party, we should tell people where it brings advantages. We have to be 'cunning' to win the new party members. We have to make the party attractive to the individuals and the collective.[118]

One member of the executive committee proposed it be more lenient with its requirements:

> Besides showing to the individuals that their interest and ambition can be realized in the party, we could increase the attraction of the membership if we accepted the party members together with all their faults and lapses on condition that they do not violate the party regulation ... It is very dangerous what natural selection means. It means the reduction of the party membership. We can afford it only if there are sufficient new candidates.[119]

Other speakers openly admitted that this was not the case. The members complained that it was difficult to win over working-class youth for the party:

We had a negative experience with the political education of the young skilled workers. They do not know the basic concepts and it is very difficult to involve them in political work. We experience an increasing materialism. Young people are unwilling to undertake a task that has no financial benefit. They find their wages too low and then they run to their second workplace where they would undertake any work. They need more money because they established a family, started building a house, etc.[120]

It was also reported from MVG that people thought that a young couple has to work so much to establish their life that they hardly have time to undertake social and political tasks.[121] In 1987 the party members in Rába MMG complained that youth is passive, that they do not feel the honour of work, and the materialistic attitude is developed already in primary school.[122]

The members of party committees usually explained the withdrawal of youth through increasing materialism. There is some evidence, though, that it was not the only, nor the most important reason; it indicated the declining prestige of the membership and political work. A report on the influence of KISZ in Győr frankly stated that young people were 'in general not indifferent; they are interested in the issues that directly influence their life. Passivity means a distance from the official organizations.'[123] In 1987 the party committee of Rába MMG reported a radical decline of the interest in the mass organizations. Only 12.4 per cent of the youth of the factory (below thirty) were members of KISZ, whose membership had decreased by more than 50 per cent since 1985: 'The figures show the indifference and the lack of interest of the youth and the continued decline of the influence of KISZ.'[124] Since KISZ was the youth organization of the party, its decreasing membership indicated the problem of the new enrolments.

Given the closeness of prosperous, capitalist Austria, it was very difficult to argue that socialism offered a higher standard of living to its subjects than did capitalism. One member of the executive committee of Rába MMG mentioned the cases of two party leaders in Mosonmagyaróvár who emigrated to the West.[125] There is some evidence that the reformers' news of the bad economic situation of the country confused part of the grass-roots membership:

We were very surprised to hear the justification of the increase of the price of petrol (22 April, *Hírháttér – Behind the News*). For years we have told to people that one should not compare the Western prices with ours because it gives an unrealistic picture. Now the chairman of the price office does this on TV. What can we say to the argument that 'we have to increase the price of petrol because it costs 10 schillings in Austria, which is 22 Ft'? If we take this into account, an Austrian worker can buy 1,000 litres of petrol from his wage while his Hungarian counterpart can buy only 200 litres. Why should one make such comparisons? After this how can we argue that the prices are incomparable? People understand that the prices will increase but they don't want to be treated as fools. It is more and more difficult to make a living with honest work![126]

Rába MMG reported that the Austrian standard of living was envied by workers:

The more courageous (and the least informed) even question the superiority of the socialist system over capitalism. These arguments are supported by the transitional economic difficulties. Because of the deficiencies of our propaganda, they do not judge the situation according to the decisive role of socialist property, the power of the proletariat, and social redistribution. The overrating of the economic and technological achievements of capitalism renders it more difficult to realistically evaluate our situation.[127]

In the second half of the 1980s the decline of the regime evidently accelerated; in the various reports both the economic and social problems received an ever-greater emphasis. The reasons for the declining social support of the party and the government were well summarized in the county report of 1986:

The decrease of the real wages of the workers and the employees increases the sensitivity of the population. They frequently mention the social injustices, which seem to be known to everybody and still nothing happens. There are opinions that the dependence of the employees becomes stronger and the will of a narrow stratum (those with property) is realized. Moral judgement does not correspond to the rules of law and private business, and incomes are uncontrollable. There is an ever-decreasing number of people who have the moral right to call anybody to account.[128]

More and more people demanded the punishment of the responsible leaders, which showed the declining authority of the party:

Our economic problems should be discussed more frankly. People want to know who got the country into this situation. The leadership is largely to be blame for this. Why don't they take the responsibility? There is much cunning in this country, ever more people are making illegal profits. How long will it go on like this? There is much expectation for the programme of the government but people would like to hear a clear speech. Not that one leader says this and the other leader says that.[129]

The lack of confidence in the leadership manifested itself in many other information reports:

> Our employees are displeased with the fact that the leaders relieve themselves from the responsibility referring to the unpredictably and unfavourably changed circumstances. Comrade Gáspár admitted in his recent TV-speech that the leadership was not always truthful to the public. Many people ask: how can we believe the official declarations after this? The mood of our employees is not optimistic, to put it mildly. They do not see the beginning of the real development and they say that they are afraid of the future. Neither can the leadership guarantee the success of the development.[130]

The workers of the Gear Unit doubted that the leadership that let the conditions deteriorate to this point would be able to make a tangible progress.[131] These were not sporadic manifestations of social discontent; according to a county report of 1987 the process of disintegration irresistibly continued, and the party possessed an ever-decreasing authority while distrust in the government increased:

> Even though the population understood the decrease of the standard of living from the planned increases of the prices, in practice they refuse to accept it. The concrete announcements receive negative comments and the drastic increase of the prices of some products triggers repulsion. People think that the 15 per cent increase of the prices is too high as compared to the strict regulation of the wages. The permanent increase of the prices has tested the patience of people in the last two to three months. There is no trust because the government has not done anything against the uncontrollable increase of the prices. People are afraid that it will trigger a spiral of inflation, which renders it impossible to plan the future. Some people believe that since the acceptance of the September programme of the government there have been no substantial results. ... The decrease of the real wages of the workers and employees increases the sensitivity of the population. People more frequently mention the social injustices, which everybody knows but there are no efficient measures against them, for instance getting income without work. Some people think that people are becoming more dependent, the will of a small minority (the wealthy) is enforced, and the incomes in the private sector are uncontrollable.[132]

The diminished appeal of the party was manifest in statistics, too. In 1987 – for the first time in the examined period – the enrolments failed to balance the reduction of the membership, and the party membership decreased by 1.3 per cent in the country. The decreasing trend could be observed in the county, too: on 1 January 1988 the membership numbered 31,862 – which was 445 less than one year before. Those who resigned their membership were more willing to give their political discontent as a reason. In 1986, it was only three people in the county who justified their withdrawal with political reasons while in 1987 thirty-five people said that they did not agree with the policy of the party.[133] The number of people who resigned their membership also showed an increasing trend: 192 people withdrew from the party in 1985, then 241 in 1986 and in 504 in 1987 (half of them workers).[134] In the beginning of 1988, discussions with party members revealed that many of them thought that the leading role and the authority of the party weakened and so did public confidence in it. It was a general opinion that the party failed to call to account the leaders who were responsible for bad decisions and that the development was slow. The grass-roots members expected more personal changes. But the most important criticism was that the leading role of the party was only manifest in the possession of power, it reacted slowly to the changes and lacked initiative:

> They see the weakening of the leading role of the party in the decrease of the trust in the party leadership, the declining authority of the local party organs, the insulting comments of people who are not members of the party and the difficulties of the party building. Party members think that the failure to explain the economic and social processes of the past years confused the membership and hindered their emotional identification with the party. The difference between the taught concept of socialism and today's reality causes a conflict for some of the membership.[135]

From 1987 the 'value' of party membership radically deflated. In 1985 the industry of the county admitted 350 new members; in 1988 the increase was only 124. The loss of the membership of the county significantly exceeded that of the previous year with the withdrawal of 2,051 people. Thus, the number of those who resigned the membership quadrupled in one year.[136] In the first three quarters of 1989, as many as 2,372 people resigned their membership in the county, and 542 gave the reason that they did not agree with the policy of the party. In Győr 1,194 people withdrew from the party, 241 for political disagreement. In Sopron, these numbers were 598 and 156 respectively.[137]

According to party reports, the economic policy of the reformers failed to win popularity; in fact, the population identified reform with increasing restriction. The discussions with grass-roots party members concluded that the conflict between its reformist and conservative wings impacted negatively on the political mood of the membership: a significant number of them were sceptical about the economic policy of the party and their future prospects:

In the past quarter of the year public opinion deteriorated to an unprecedented degree for the regime. The more hopeful mood after the national party meeting quickly disappeared because the execution of the former decisions had no palpable impact on the economy (change of production profile, the improvement of the balance). The population felt that the distance between ideas and practice was increasing. From the government programme only the decline of the standard of living, the price increases, the taxation and the inflation were realized. The majority of people identify reform with these negative phenomena. They think that instead of stabilization, only social injustice and tension are increasing, which approaches a crisis. This lack of any prospects irritates people and it increases their insecurity. Apart from the lack of economic prospects, the government, unfortunately, broke its past promises and took contradictory measures with which it generated inflation and lost the confidence of people. The loss of trust did not spare the party either because it seems that the economic reform was driven to a political level and now the people blame the party for the lack of perspective.[138]

The report from Sopron also argued the case that the old leadership had lost credibility and social support:

Party members ask: how does the government want to realize this ambitious programme if it loses the trust of the membership? We are frequently told what we have done wrong but the reasons are not discussed. It is not the working class who should be blamed. They have been working hard up to now. It is not their fault that they produced non-marketable goods; there was no structural change and a large part of the budget was spent on the subvention of state enterprises! Did we not have scholars, economists and respected experts who could have called attention to the problems? And if they did, why did their opinions receive no consideration? Is it not the party or the government or both to be blamed in the first place?[139]

An even more important question was how the grass-roots members responded to the announced reform of the party and its call to democratize. Few base-cell materials survive from this period, but they suggest that the majority of the population did not comprehend the accelerated political crisis of the regime. The system of democratic centralism was criticized but at that time the reform of the party was not linked with the reform of the whole political system:

People expect a change in the work style of the party that would testify to a more direct knowledge and representation of the problems of simple people, and strengthen their security and trust in the party. Many people think that the present political system does not even represent the democratic values that could be realized within the framework of this system.[140]

The demand to democratize the party rapidly developed into a more radical demand to increase political participation of the whole of society. In the political debates of how to transform the political system the intellectuals were the main actors. Even though some voices can be documented in the period that spoke of the necessity of the workers' political representation in the new system, it seems that the majority of the population was unprepared for the rapid and radical political change to come. Among the few documents that expressed concern about the future role of the working class, one can mention the discussion of the reform of the political system among the base organizations of MVG. The party organization of the Industrial Tool Factory did indeed anticipate a situation in which the social decline of the working class became inevitable:

> We do not see unambiguously if the legalized multi-party system means a real economic opportunity for every Hungarian citizen or gives an opportunity for a very extreme situation: impoverished workers or unemployed on the one hand, and rich proprietors, bankers, speculators, etc. on the other hand. The rightful claims of the decent citizens of the Hungarian nation, including the right to work, should be fully considered, because if not, then long-term chaos and not decent, productive work will be characteristic of the Hungarian economy.[141]

From the New Foundry the following was reported: 'Life has created the conditions for the change of property relations and the establishment of the plurality of the parties. This does not depend on the will or objection of the people's democracy. ... The mixed property relations already exist; this is no longer a political question. The functioning of the system can still be, however, determined.'[142] Another party organization argued that the party had to initiate a substantial renewal otherwise people would desert the party in the election.[143]

While, in 1989, there were some East European intellectuals who still argued for a democratic socialism based on workers control, other groups, including many of the MSZMP reformers, were calling for a 'third way' between capitalism and socialism, and some for the creation of a social democracy based on a mixed economy and strong trade unions, even though it was also widely expected that the working class would either resist any attempt to restore capitalism or even support a reformist collectivist alternative. On the basis of the surviving documents it is difficult to say what kind of social and political alternatives were discussed among the workers. The opinion that there was a need for the political representation of working-class interests in the new system was voiced in the county conference of the party on 10 June 1989, which was held in the congress hall of MVG. The contribution is interesting not only because the speaker criticized increasing populism and the practice of formulating demands in the 'name of the working class' without considering their real interests, but also because it shows that there were supporters of democratic social-ism among the workers, who demanded a political change but considered it equally important to ensure the social rights of people:

> Today in this country uninvited speakers agitate, act and demand in the name of the working class and the nation. I am a worker. In my place no one should make declarations, let alone demands. It would be good if people understood that in the past forty years we have learnt to think and work for ourselves, and not robots but thinking people stand by the machines. And one more thing: we learnt to appreciate and respect the intellectuals who serve social progress with their work and knowledge and they recognize us, workers as partners in their work. It does not move me if someone declares himself to be pro-labour even if he has a leading position. According to us a leader is pro-labour if he demands work from everybody, provides for decent conditions and performs his task in the market. The workers want no favours but work and livelihood ... I would like to mention how the Minister of Finance explained the restrictions: 'The achievement of the country has not increased!' Whose achievement has not in-creased? That of the workers, the institutions, the budget or the whole of society within the existing bad structure? I think the latter is true and we should not blame each other. Because it is not a good perspective that if something is good, we did it and there are plenty of applicants and if something is wrong, then we blame the executors, mainly the workers and the peasants. What kind of society do we want? Democratic. Socialist. I think that we want a society where every-body receives a fair share of the reward from what he produced. We want a so-ciety where a worker receives a real share of the political power that he deserves on the basis of his work. For us the socialist direction means a development built on communal democracy. It is incomprehensible to me that some smart, nation-ally recognized politicians, who declare themselves to be reformers, do not even dare to speak of socialism as a possible way of development. We, however, think that this is the real reform task. We would like to participate in its realization, in our own way – of course, only if the party also accepts and does not reject us.[144]

It is remarkable that the speaker spoke of a possibility of a reformed party finding a new social basis that was not the working class (and in the origi-nal text a strong expression is used for being rejected). This shows that the workers who did not give up socialist demands felt that the first cracks were appearing between the party and the working class.

Within the ruling party, however, this was very much a minority view. The 'hard facts' (the massive decrease of the membership) show that the general political mood was not pro-socialist. Even though there was a political move to attack the regime in the name of the working class, it was, nevertheless, true that the regime was not popular among the workers, which was also recognized by the manager of Rába in the quoted interview that he gave in the summer of 1989.[145] In the interview the manager admitted that the workers had good reason to feel deceived because many of the regime's promises (including socialist proprietorship) remained unfulfilled. It was perhaps symbolic that the interview was published on the same page as the readers' answers to the timely question of '*Would you call the capitalists back?*'[146]

It is a theoretical question why a leftist alternative failed to attract the majority of the working class. In the light of the information reports it can be argued that it reflected a deeply rooted dissatisfaction with socialism, the signs of which were visible throughout the 1980s. The party's policy towards the working class, which was strongly propagated after the economic reform of 1968, failed to achieve real results, and in the 1980s the party made no more attempt to fill the socialist ideology with a new content. Even the term 'working class' disappeared from the rhetoric of the party. As is evident from their mounting social discontent, workers believed that they had to pay the price for the wrong economic policy while those who worked in the private sector enjoyed a much higher standard of living than did the working class. The party and its ideology thus increasingly lost the support of the workers: as the abundant criticisms show, people were conscious of the political decline of the regime.

This political climate was not very favourable for socialist alternatives. The consistent persecution of any leftism other than official Marxism rendered the regime closed to the left and open to the right – which was evident from the reform discussions of the 1980s as reformers increasingly saw 'more market' as panacea for the economic problems of the country. There is no evidence from the interviews that alternative concepts (such as self-management) were known to the majority of the workers. The failure of the party to respond to the political criticism of the working class after the economic reform of 1968 deprived people of further illusions: the improvement of enterprise democracy was limited to theoretical discussions, which could do little to challenge established power relations in the factory. In the light of the information reports, the party 'successfully' discredited the socialist ideology in the eyes of many people. At the time of the political crisis of the regime it was unrealistic to expect that after the decades of the welfare dictatorship, which replaced working-class consciousness with an orientation towards consumerism, they would have been responsive to a new, leftist political programme. As shopping tourism demonstrated, the appeal of the full supermarkets of neighbouring Austria was greater than any political ideology. In the era of the first economic reform there may have been a chance to renew the social settlement between the working class and the party; in the 1980s neither of the two parties demonstrated a willingness to restart the dialogue.

The SED and the Workers

The IKPO of Zeiss in Numbers

The available figures show that the party was much larger in the Zeiss factory than in the Hungarian Rába. While in the latter around 10 per cent of the workforce were members of the party, in the Zeiss factory in 1967 this proportion was 20.2 per cent, then 20.7 per cent in 1975,[147] and by 1982 every fourth employee was a member of the party, at least according to reports written by the leadership.[148] In 1967, the factory party organization consisted of 23 base organizations, 28 departmental organizations (APO)[149] and 289 party groups. In 1970 there were 13 base organizations, 56 departmental organizations (APO) and 397 party groups in the IKPO of Zeiss.[150] There was not much change in the figures throughout the 1980s: in 1982 the factory party organization was divided into 30 base organizations, 135 departmental organizations and 572 party groups,[151] while in 1988 the relevant figures were 32, 152 and 605 respectively.[152]

In contrast to the Hungarian situation, the party membership in the Zeiss factory shows a constant increase over the period: in 1967 there were 3,121 members of the party and 413 candidates, in 1975 there were 4,730 members,[153] in 1982 it had risen to 7,360 members and candidates,[154] in 1984 it was 7,600,[155] and in 1988 an information report gave a figure of 8,394 members.[156] The first secretary of the factory party organization spoke of 'more than eight thousand communists' in a speech of 1987 in front of the party leadership of the district.[157] Meanwhile the total workforce increased significantly, too, but the percentage of them who were party members also rose: in 1967, every fifth employee was a member of the party,[158] while throughout the 1980s every fourth member belonged to the organization.[159] We do not know about the generational composition of party membership in the 1980s but the comment that there were 193 youth brigades and youth collectives in the factory in 1982[160] suggests that the decline of the prestige of the party among young people was not as marked in the GDR as in Hungary, where reports throughout the 1980s increasingly complained of a problem of recruitment and of the declining appeal of the youth organization of the party, the KISZ. While in Hungary the decrease in party membership was characteristic of the last years prior to the collapse of the regime, in the GDR it seems that the loss of appeal of the party became manifest only with the change of regime. In fact, the first time when the statement 'there are people who want to resign their party membership' appeared in official reports was the summer of 1989,[161] and this step required courage even at that time.[162]

The surviving statistics of the factory party organization show that the affirmative action, in order to maintain the proportion of members who were working-class, quotas were observed in the GDR the same way as in Hungary. In 1967 in the IKPO of Zeiss, the proportion of workers among the membership was 54.7 per cent, that of the intelligentsia 20.3 per cent, that of the white-collar workers 23.8 per cent and that of the students 1.2 per cent. The majority of the members (56 per cent) joined the party between 1959 and 1967; of these, 27.5 per cent were between 31 and 40 years old, 20.6 per cent were between 26 and 30 years old, 16.7 per cent between 41 and 50 years old, 16.3 per cent between 51 and 60 years old, and 13.2 per cent were below 25 (the remaining 5.7 per cent were older than 60). In terms of education, 13.7 per cent of party members had finished comprehensive school with a high-school leaving certificate, and 6.6 per cent were university or college graduates. In the light of these figures, the intelligentsia and those with technical-school training were overrepresented among the membership, a fact that shows education was often linked with the membership: 27.8 per cent of those with only technical training and 32.9 per cent of the *Fachschulkader* and graduates were members of the party (19.2 per cent of workers were members). Among the youth, 12 per cent of 18 to 25 year olds were members of the party. In 1970, of the total membership, 51.3 per cent were workers, while 29.1 per cent belonged to the intelligentsia and 18.7 per cent were other white-collar workers. The average age of the membership was 38.1 years. In 1975, records show that 20.7 percent of workers were party members, 29.5 percent members of the intelligentsia, and 8.7 per cent young people.[163] It seems that the party paid close attention to these percentages, as in 1977 similar figures were reported: 51 per cent of the membership were workers, and 20.7 per cent of the workers belonged to the organization. The proportion of the under-30s in the party was 29.4 per cent, which was much better than the district average (20.4 per cent). It was, however, noted that some plants contained higher proportions of members than others: in the research centre, for instance, only 13.3 per cent of employees were members of the party and their proportion was also low in the base organization of the electro-technology unit.[164] The fact that the percentage of members as a proportion of all employees was at its lowest in the 'elite' plants was not flattering to the party at any rate, even though it may well have changed throughout the 1980s.

There is not much data about recruitment during the period, but it can be assumed that if every fourth employee was a member of the party, the requirements could not have been very seriously enforced. Just like the Hungarian party secretary, who said that in MVG five out of ten members were unaware of their obligations to the party,[165] a report in 1968 complained of the mechanical way in which members were accepted into the party: '*There are cases when the economic functionaries and party sec-*

retaries, contrary to the instructions of the leadership, instead of helping the candidates, fill out the enrolment forms themselves so that the candidates only need to sign them.[166] In this way they exerted a moral pressure on the candidates, which had a negative effect on their future political development.

> It was also a widespread practice to not inform, or at best, to only partially inform candidates for membership of the basic questions of party policy, and members' rights and obligations. The violation of the principles of the party during recruitment, and the harmful practice of 'candidates at any price' could also be explained by the fact that the base organizations, in their attempts to increase the proportion of workers in the party, forgot to consider each application on a case-by-case basis and to respect the rules. The result was a high proportion of workers among those excluded from the party or struck off.

The document also criticized the selection of candidates for full membership, arguing that there were workers enrolled who were neither professionally nor privately respected by their fellow workers and that the party admitted even candidates who 'disagreed with basic questions of the policy of our party'. In many cases there was no interview with candidates before acceptance, even though 'during the personal discussion one can check whether the candidate has faith in the party, or whether he really thinks that he is part of the collective'.[167] On the basis of this document, the policy of the SED towards working-class members shows much similarity with the practice of the MSZMP in Hungary. Both parties sought to win over 'respectable' working class to set an example to other workers. The East German officials encountered the same difficulties of party organization among the workers as did the Hungarians; most notably, the refusal of many workers to join the party. It is remarkable that the document mentioned and criticized the practice of 'forcing' candidates to join the party by handing out forms to them that had already been filled in. This and the information that the party admitted 'ideologically unreliable' candidates suggest that in the GDR, just as in Hungary, 'worker comrades' were frequently pressured to join the party simply in order to fulfil centrally stipulated targets.

Women in the Party

The proportion of women in the factory party organization was lower than that of men: in 1970, around 40 per cent of the employees were women[168] and they constituted only 20 per cent of the membership.[169] In Rába MVG the proportion of women was 25 per cent in the factory and 14 per cent among party members.[170] In 1977, the proportion female party members stood at 26 per cent[171] in the Zeiss factory, but it was still lower than the district average (36.4 per cent); and 40 per cent of female members in the factory were blue-collar workers.[172]

Despite administrative measures that promoted women leaders, the 1977 figures show that the proportion of female members was still low, particularly among those in high-ranking positions. Around 20 per cent of district party secretaries were women, and they only made up 13 per cent of district secretariat members. Around one-quarter of employees of the party apparatuses and one-fifth of teachers in party schools were women. There had, however, been a marked increase in the percentage of women among leaders of the base organizations; from 21 per cent to 33.8 per cent between 1975 and 1977. It seems that the public role of women also increased: in the plenums of the party leadership of the district the proportion of women was 30 per cent, while in the plenums of the district their average was 38 per cent. In the Zeiss factory 26.1 per cent of the party leaders of the factory organization and 17 per cent of the party secretaries were women.[173]

Just as in Hungary, women were mainly active in the youth organization – the FDJ[174] – and the trade union committees, which had less power. In the Zeiss factory, women made up 54 per cent of FDJ members, against a district average of 51 per cent. In the districts' trade union committees the proportion of women varied at between 43 per cent and 55 per cent (among the chairpersons it varied between 27 and 45 per cent). The proportion of women was also high (42 per cent) among the members of the *Konfliktkommission* (even though among the chairpersons it was only 22 per cent). The highest proportions of women were found among the committees in charge of the social education of children (71.6 per cent), social insurance (61.9 per cent), social policy (54 per cent) and organized holidays (51.8 per cent).[175] This suggests a continued association of women with community work, which at the same time negatively affected their opportunities to get promoted to leading positions. An information report from the Zeiss factory commented in 1973 that even though 905 women finished comprehensive school with a high-school leaving certificate, or obtained a college or university degree, only 15 of them achieved a position commensurate with their education level.[176] As in 1977 it was stated that the majority of women leaders held low-ranking positions,[177] it seems that gender inequalities continued to structure the political careers of men and women.

Party Life

Since none of the minute books of party meetings survived from the period, it is difficult to reconstruct grass-roots party life. Documents from an
enquiry conducted in 1969 into party life in the instrument plant suggest
that there were similar problems with the regular party meetings to those
encountered in Hungary at that time. This holds for the base-cell meetings; according to a report of 1976 the attendance of the meetings of the
party leadership of the factory was 84.9 per cent.[178] An East German report from 1968 lists further deficiencies with ideological training that un-
derlines the similarities with Hungary: 'With respect to most of the party
commissions, the candidates don't have to report on their fulfilment of
tasks. In this way the candidate is not trained to actively participate in
the execution of the decisions of the party, but he only learns that he
does not need to take seriously responsibility and discipline in the party.'
Furthermore, the report stated that the large factories did not have a concrete picture of the Marxist–Leninist education of candidates, and they
enrolled candidates who lacked basic training. In some places managers
prevented candidates from attending courses, and they lacked support
from the party organizations. According to a report, low attendance of
local courses was at a 'frightening' level: out of the 207 invited candidates
less than half turned up, 92 attended a course in Pößneck (only 20 out of
the invited 160 came from Lobeda, and 8 out of the invited 40 from the
town of Jena).[179] In 1977, the Zeiss factory reported that 31.2 per cent
of the membership visited a party school for more than three months and
the proportion was even higher (43.5 per cent) among the *Fachsculkader*,
and the college or university graduates.[180] This, at any rate, shows that
ideological training was taken more seriously in Honecker's GDR than in
Kádár's Hungary at the time.

Even though there is little information on the forms and methods of
political education in the surviving documents, a 1974 report showed
that the distribution of Marxist–Leninist literature was also taken more
seriously in the GDR than in Hungary. In the district there were 594
shop assistants who dealt with its distribution, and 146 of them (24 per
cent) worked in the industrial plants themselves. This did not mean that
political literature reached every factory evenly: booksellers could only
supply 85 plants, out of a total of 250, with political literature, and the
government, as the report critically commented, was reluctant to increase
the number of booksellers. Out of the district's 577 municipalities only
50 were served. The base organizations also contracted the shops to fa-
cilitate the distribution of political literature. There is no further information about the type of literature that was supported in this way, but

there is some evidence that the contracts mainly helped the distribution of propaganda materials[181] since the report mentioned that in the first half of 1974 there were 2,165 copies of the publication entitled *Methodik der politischen Bildung* (The Methodology of Political Education) sold in the factories.[182]

Although the 'liberalism' of the Zeiss party organization was criticized by the district leadership, in the light of the albeit fragmentary information about party life, not only was this liberalism very limited as compared to the situation in Hungary, but deviation from the party line was much more strictly punished in the GDR. There were people who objected to the formality of elections by refusing to vote. For this reason, there were campaigns organized before the elections to mobilize people: in 1971, for instance, turnout was 25–30 per cent in the elections, while it increased to 52 per cent in 1974.[183] Criticism of the elections was regarded as 'ideological deviation': in 1977, it was reported that 'young comrades' from Zeiss and the town of Gera complained that the candidates on the ballot paper had all been selected before the elections.[184] The party reports mention another case that shows that criticism in this respect had serious consequences: Comrade F, who was a designer in the research centre of VEB Carl Zeiss and a member of the party, was removed from his position as chairperson of the National Front[185] in the electoral district of Winzerla because in the working group that prepared the elections, he:

> constantly objected to the resolutions and tasks of the group so that the city councillor of internal affairs, Comrade K, always had to warn him of the leading role of the party. When the working group was informed that the proposals for the electoral committees would be changed, he declared that he would not accept commands and that he would not assist in any show – 'we want here democratic elections and not a circus'. *When he went as far as to protest against the top candidates who were selected in a public meeting of the nominations committee, he was relieved of his position because he declared that he would not work as a chairperson from 31 March 1979.*[186]

During the interview with Comrade F, he gave back his membership card, declaring that he would resign his membership. This was not accepted and he was informed that he would be disciplined. Comrade F declared that he 'would no longer participate in any discussion and for him the matter is settled'.[187] The case confirms that the party preferred to exclude those who threatened to resign their membership. It is likewise remarkable that even in this case, when Comrade F publicly criticized the candidates of the party, it was emphasized that he was relieved of his post upon his request – not because he would have been, nor indeed was, removed anyway. This shows that officials themselves did not want to recognize explicitly the degree to which repression was used to maintain the rule of the party. Comrade F undoubtedly showed considerable courage when he refused to play his part in this 'show'; but this ideological climate also explains why there were so few openly discontented grass-roots members in the GDR, compared to Kádár's Hungary.

Another field where the members of the party in the Zeiss factory were too lenient with the 'class enemy' was in work with the *Antragsteller*.[188] In 1984 an inquiry was conducted in the instrument plant (which at the time had five thousand employees) because twenty-five of them applied for permission to leave the GDR. The purpose of the inquiry was to supervise targeted political work to convince these people to withdraw their applications to leave the GDR. The inquiry concluded that political work in this respect was 'totally inadequate' and that many employees were reluctant to contradict the *Antragsteller* because they supported the view that the state should let them leave if they wished. Others even argued that there would be fewer *Antragsteller* if the supply of consumer goods were better. In many places the colleagues refused to enter into political debate with the *Antragsteller*, because they were good workers:

> The colleagues direct the discussions to the liberal position that 'we would not have expected this from this person' instead of evaluating their actions as a betrayal of our state and siding with the class enemy ... It is not easy to contradict the *Antragsteller*, because the majority of them do not have a provocative attitude. Among many, there is almost human sympathy for them, because as Comrade E said, our people are too liberal in small communities. A section of the comrades believe that the existing problems of the supply of consumer goods hinder our policy.[189]

There were concrete examples mentioned of how far political work was neglected in this respect: one *Antragsteller*, for instance, argued that even were he to withdraw his application, he would always be discriminated against in the GDR – his colleagues should have explained to him that this was not true – while another *Antragsteller* was asked to undertake extra shifts, even though she wanted to participate in the movement '*Mach mit!*' during that time. Her colleagues failed to argue that she was interested in the social life of the GDR.[190] An inquiry in the milling shop found that the channels for exchanging information worked unevenly: it took four days for the manager to be told that an employee who was transferred to his plant 'because of security reasons' was actually an *Antragsteller*. When asked, the manager and the party secretary did not know in which brigade he worked. There was an 'offensive' discussion with the party group of the mill shop but the report suggests that the attitude to the *Antragsteller* was rather liberal, because one comrade declared during the interview that there would be less *Antragsteller* if there was a better supply of goods, and he himself had to walk his legs off until he could buy the parts for his car.[191]

The political attitudes of many grass-roots members did not differ much from those who were outside the party, and if they had been allowed, they would have criticized economic policy in similar terms to the Hungarian grass-roots membership. Many East German workers who were members of the party also expressed their discontent with the supply of consumer goods and their human sympathy for the stigmatized 'class enemy', if only in a very restrained manner. Conflict between the managers and workers frequently manifested itself as one between the party leaders and the grass-roots members. On the basis of the minute books of the 1969 inquiry in the instrument plant, many grass-roots members thought that workers' opinions did not matter much in party meetings and that leaders enforced their will anyway. A similar conflict can be documented in the model building workshop in 1971, which was examined by the IKPKK. According to one member of the leadership of the base organization to which the party group of the workshop belonged, the main problem was that there were two camps within the party group: 'the two direct production managers have a common opinion and the comrades who work on the machines have a different view. The main reason is that the organizer of the party group and the manager of the workshop is the same person.' According to this information, base-cell meetings were irregular, grass-roots members did not know the topics of discussion beforehand, and nobody did anything on their own initiative. In the meetings the leaders presented the lists of annual premiums and their evaluation of socialist labour competition, which could be discussed, but could not be changed. On the concrete question of whether the tasks given by the party leadership of the base organization represented the party line, the speaker – not surprisingly – gave a positive answer, but he added that '*the colleagues and the comrades do not agree with the way these tasks are communicated or the methods used to implement the party line*'.[192] An interview with a young worker confirmed this view. He commented that even though the workers often contradicted the direct production managers, their opinions did not count. He also had a conflict with one of the direct production managers over a proposal of improvement that he made to the manager of the plant, but since his wage depended on the direct production manager, he would be afraid to criticize him in the future.[193]

Even these fragmentary sources show that grass-roots party life was often highly formalized, just as in Hungary, and that it is at best doubtful how far the party could train committed communists, let alone politically educate the masses. Taking into account the frequently voiced criticism that there would be fewer people who would want to leave the GDR if the supply of goods were better, it seems that the propaganda of the party was less effective in the 1980s like in Hungary even if people in the GDR were more careful not to criticize the policy of the party openly. On the basis of the documents it would be difficult to reconstruct the atmosphere of party meetings; it can be assumed, however, that people also formulated criticism at least in the base-cell meetings, but in the light of likely retaliation it is unlikely that they would have openly discussed their discontent with the socialist state.

Losing Members

There are no overall figures for the Zeiss factory for the numbers excluded from the party, or who were struck off. The discussion, however, of disciplinary procedures suggests that the party sought to keep its loss of members to a minimum. One exception was conflict over the Soviet intervention in Czechoslovakia, when disciplinary action was taken against 139 members district-wide who opposed the official line; this figure included 32 managers.[194] The report introduced two cases that show that the party did indeed 'fight' for members, where the individuals concerned were good workers, yet, on the other hand, many grass-roots members lacked ideological commitment to the party, just like in Hungary. One worker in VEB Carl Zeiss Jena, Comrade Z,

> despite his 20-year-long membership, does not have close contacts with our party. He wanted to resign his membership because he could not reconcile his religious faith with Marxism. Since he is a very good worker – he is one of the best innovators in his workshop – he was persuaded to withdraw his resignation. Only after he made unclear statements concerning the events in Czechoslovakia was he eventually struck off.

Another case was that of an electrical engineer who claimed that

> he was forced to join the party in the army. He has totally fake ideas about the party and he makes ideologically unclear statements, for instance, that 'our media has not informed people truthfully' and therefore he listened to the Western media. Concerning the Czechoslovakian events he therefore did not accept our measures.[195]

The year 1968 was clearly important politically, for the Zeiss factory party organization compiled a report on the political education of its mem-

bership, and the 'deviations from the official line' that emerged in relation to events in Czechoslovakia. The report did not give statistics, but
it introduced individual cases. A foundry worker was expelled from the
party because he compared the Soviet intervention in Czechoslovakia to
Hitler's occupation of the country, and he said that the Czechoslovak
comrades at the Moscow conference only obeyed commands. The following case sheds some light on the 'everyday' methods of repression
and the degree of political control over society: it was reported that a
55-year-old woman worker protested against the military support that
the socialist countries gave to the Soviet Union in a workers' bus, and
her comrades that were riding the bus informed her base organization.
In another case a brigadier and another comrade visited a Czech family
before the intervention, where the husband, who had just been released
from prison, told them that 'at last we have socialism and real freedom',
and therefore they refused to sign a form indicating their agreement with
the Soviet Union's 'friendly help'. These workers were, however, eventually persuaded of their mistake. One candidate-member who worked in
the tool factory and was promoted to study engineering had, however, to
be expelled because he declared that he would like to keep his personal
freedom and he could not subordinate himself to party discipline. This
candidate-member had already made critical comments concerning the
Exquisit shops.[196]

The Soviet intervention in Czechoslovakia opened conditions in the
GDR to criticism, too. According to an analysis of the 'hostile manifestations' concerning the Czechoslovak events, people made formal comparisons of prices and wages between East and West Germany; they argued
that the East German media was either not objective, or lied utterly; and,
from this, they concluded that there was limited freedom of speech and
of the press in the GDR, and that those who made 'hostile' statements
in public or tried to 'heckle' the others usually watched or listened to
Western television or radio.[197] Attacks on the state order were criminally
punishable; but these cases show that even members of the party, who
were excluded in 1968, criticized the limited freedom of the press and the
lack of democracy within the party.

An analysis of the 'hostile manifestations' among district party members between 1973 and 1976 likewise shows that the relationship to West
Germany was at the centre of political education. One party member was,
for instance, excluded because he argued that the 'borders are not necessary because there are also Germans living there, they speak the same
language and we are the same nation. The wall in Berlin should be removed.' The report regretfully commented that the comrade concerned
was a likeable man. Another member was relieved of his post as party

secretary because he was a philatelist and he refused to break his contacts with Western people who had the same hobby.[198] The report commented that because of this refusal his request to study in the Soviet Union could be reconsidered. A woman worker who was a party member continued a 'hostile discussion' in public with a candidate because her husband had been sentenced for *Republikflucht*,[199] and she compared the penal authorities of the GDR to the fascist concentration camps. An old comrade who joined the party in 1930 was excluded because he 'praised above all the conditions in West Germany, he defended the social democratic position and he said that he always felt like a "little follower". His organization formerly tolerated these comments because he was an old comrade.'[200]

A report from the Zeiss factory likewise shows that the party tolerated much less open criticism in the GDR than in Hungary. In 1977, six people wanted to resign their membership in the micro plant after only a short period in the party. The investigation revealed that the people concerned spoke out against party policy in party meetings, but the party leadership was too liberal and demanded no explanation. The report also mentioned the case of a skilled worker who had commented that

> the theory of Marxism–Leninism is good but the practice of the party and the government is not in line with the theory. The high functionaries have been detached from the people and in the GDR there are differences between the classes – look at the Intershop, Exquisit and Delikat shops. People are not correctly informed about the economic situation, and those who tell the truth are silenced. Even Marx and Engels would turn in their graves if they had seen our policy.

The skilled worker made these comments in a party meeting and 'some comrades nodded because he referred to existing holes in the supply of goods. He had authority in his party group, because he had been a member of the party since 1945, and he had held leading party functions until 1960.' Despite his merits, the skilled worker was expelled from the party.[201]

Criticism of the party was frequently linked to resignations from the party. One member of the IKPO of the Zeiss factory, who was, allegedly, the first to be 'openly opportunist', resigned his membership arguing that the party disappointed the masses. During the interview it turned out that 'in his view the party should be separated from the economy and that it should be more open and democratic like the Western parties'. The 'opportunist' member was not given the opportunity to resign, but was simply expelled.[202] In 1980 in the Göschwitz plant, two people submitted resignation letters: a direct production manager declared that he was not happy to represent party policy, and a worker in the tool factory announced that he was ashamed to be a party member and could not support the party line.[203]

This shows that the party took political criticism much more seriously in the GDR than in Hungary, and that criticism of the party among the grass-roots membership was punished more severely. One party member was disciplined because his son was brought to trial because of truculence. This suggests that the organization was also expected to control the lives of the individuals to a higher degree than in Hungary. In court it was revealed that Comrade S had allowed his son to watch Western television programmes, and

> as father he started to explain this position with the words: 'Comrade Honecker explained his attitude to watching Western TV in detail at the Ninth Party Congress ...' The public prosecutor interrupted him because he could not let anybody distort the party line in this way. Comrade S and his party group did not recognize that there is no coexistence in the ideological field. Instead of confronting Comrade S with his mistake, his party group felt sorry for him because of the troubles that he has with his son and they wanted to see the 'human' side of the problem only. This means that in their view, when it comes to a fight against the bourgeois ideology and its manifestations in our country, 'humanity' precedes party discipline and the political education of members. The party group took this approach because they didn't understand the role of criticism and self-criticism in our development, and they lack confidence in our party and state organs. Therefore they refused to take disciplinary action against Comrade S. As they did not understand the information that they received and they doubted the facts, they let Comrade S influence them negatively against the public prosecutor. The views and attitude of the members of the group display the influence of social democracy ... We see the main reasons of this liberal attitude of the party group in the following. There was no strong political leadership in the group, therefore they could not correctly evaluate the political–ideological conditions. Community life was mixed with companionship, and therefore political education was neglected in the group.

After the discussion with the members of the IKPKK, the party group 'recognized' its mistake: the organizer of the group received a reprimand and Comrade S a strong reprimand.[204]

The role of the IKPKK was, however, not only to punish people, but also to demonstrate that members could expect due process from the party. In one case, for instance, the IKPKK conducted an inquiry concerning the case of a trainee who was an FDJ secretary and a candidate-member. After he had problems in his dormitory, he gave notice in the factory and his candidacy was terminated. The inquiry found that the case had the following antecedents: there was a meeting in the dormitory where the FDJ secretary criticized the relationship between the trainees and the teachers, and demanded that trainees should be treated differently. This created a difficult situation for the candidate-member in the dormitory, which finally led him to give notice in his workplace; but as the inquiry stated 'his exclusion from the party was wrong because only the facts and not the reasons for his behaviour were taken into consideration. He tried to solve his problems alone because he lost his trust in the collective.' It was therefore decided that the trainee should be readmitted as a candidate-member.[205] There was also an investigation of the living conditions of trainees, which concluded that many of them, mainly those who came from the northern territories, were disappointed, because they thought that the factory consciously deceived the trainees with their advertisements:

> Many trainees see that young skilled workers who lived in dormitories come to the AWU where the discipline is too strict; for example, a colleague who lives in the AWU cannot have his own radio, neither can he hang a picture on the wall of his room,[206] that is to say that young people feel like they are in prison and they want to have their own home, or at least a small room that they can call their own. Therefore we should examine whether the regulations in the AWU are right in the long run, and perhaps it would be better to build more apartments.[207]

It seems that the case of the FDJ secretary shed light on more general problems concerning the training and future perspectives of young skilled workers.[208]

The IKPKK could mitigate punishment, but on the other hand it also reveals that offences against party discipline could very easily end the political careers of party members. In 1978 a political 'case' was created after a satirical carnival newspaper was published by a department of the research centre that received the title of the 'collective of socialist work'. The publication included 'provocative' articles like one bearing the title 'Conversation in the Pub', which 'highly distorts the work of the academic-technical personnel of the VEB Carl Zeiss Jena and practically describes them as idlers', while from the Zeiss-Alphabet one could learn that 'B = brothel, the last institution that Zeiss still misses; C = chattering, the main content of the meetings of the leadership; S = stupidity, the precondition of employment in our enterprise; S as *Scheinwerfer*[209] = too thin for reading, too thick for toilet paper.' The leader of the research centre immediately recommended that the main editor of the publication, Comrade J, who was a physicist, should be expelled from the party and dismissed from his job. The IKPKK chairperson, however, took the side of the physicist: he 'got off' with a strong reprimand and was transferred to model building where 'he should prove himself worthy of the confidence of the party because he violated political watchfulness at a time when the class enemy increased its activity in the field of ideology'. The report stressed that it was the IKPKK chairperson who intervened on behalf of the physicist and apart from him two colleagues who were graduates, one of them was a group leader, were also transferred because of their involvement in the case of the carnival publication.[210] This gives one example of how the system created 'enemies' and it also reveals why it would have been naive to expect that discontent at the grass roots would be expressed in public forums.

The End of Silence

The rigid ideological discipline of the party was maintained until the very end. Thus, in sharp contrast to the Hungarian case where it was possible to trace the mounting discontent of the population in the information reports, in the GDR the party succeeded in suppressing criticism with repression. This, however, also meant that the party itself had no adequate information on the political mood of the grass-roots membership.[211] Even party reports from 1989 are silent on the evident discontent of the population – in the beginning of 1989 the factory party organization proved its political watchfulness by informing the responsible comrades that on the day of Soviet cinema, five films were presented that, according to the audience, did not depict the Soviet Union in a positive light; 'on the contrary, it seems that the state has violated the law, and anti-Semitism and alcoholism have become predominant in society. Therefore we ask the responsible comrades not to present films like these in the future.'[212] Political vigilance worked efficiently until the last months of the regime: in October 1989 the chief manager of Zeiss reported of a handwritten leaflet to Minister Meier that was found on the staircase of one of the plants: 'The day before yesterday Poland, today Czechoslovakia, tomorrow Hungary? How far does the opportunism of East German citizens extend?'[213] The brigade named after Salvador Allende held out – at least according to the testimony of the diary of the brigade:

> In spite of the 'mass flight' experienced in the last days and the massive increase in the number of those who want to leave the GDR, we cannot let our country be defamed. We are whole-heartedly determined to protest against such attempts. Everybody needs to recognize that without the GDR there would have been no peace or peaceful coexistence of nations in Europe for forty-five years. We, the citizens of the GDR, can only be proud of it.[214]

Some signs of crisis could, however, be detected in the information reports in summer 1989. In July, 'events such as the elections in Poland and
Hungary, and the strikes and violent conflicts in the Soviet Union, are
evaluated as the weakening of the socialist system.' Further, many party
groups represented the opinion that the results of the GDR were too
optimistically evaluated by the leadership, and the daily selection of the
shops contradicted this evaluation. The report added – for the first time –
that party members wanted to resign.[215] According to an autumn report,
20 members of the IKPO of Zeiss resigned their membership in September, and 18 in October. A further 321 people announced their intention
to leave the party in November. These figures are still very low compared
to the Hungarian 'mass flight' from the party, but they did indicate a
weakening of the regime. The October report also admitted that 'there
are often not enough arguments to satisfy the employees or to show them
the right solutions to the problems that they describe – for instance, the
increases in prices (technical articles), long waiting times for repairs and
services, missing spare parts for cars, long waiting times in health care.'[216]
A report of 23 October 1989 informed of a 'public letter' that hung on
the noticeboard of various departments in the Zeiss factory that attacked
the leading role of the SED, called for the dissolution of party cells in
the factory, and the separation of the party from the economy. It also demanded 'bourgeois democracy, a socialist market economy, free elections,
and the right to strike and to demonstrate'. According to the report, the
factory party leadership immediately took the initiative to 'clarify the letter in discussions with the involved collectives'.[217] It seemed that such an
approach survived until the last days of the regime.

   The 'transition' was so quick that a few months later an official letter
informed employees that a warrant had been issued for the arrest of the
feared chief manager, who was charged with fraud. According to the letter, the whereabouts of the manager were unknown; he allegedly escaped
to Munich.[218] It is worth recalling his last speech in front of the district
party leadership on 2 November 1989:

> As I see it in Jena, finally a 'hard core' was left from the fifteen thousand dem-
> onstrators, who were drunk and shouted slogans like 'Every communist pig to
> the wall!' and the usual insults concerning our state, and security organs and
> many other things, after which I cannot believe that they would demonstrate
> for this country, for socialism and for the republic. And personally, I would
> like to add that we should try to win over the positive forces who, as Comrade
> Krenz said, accept the constitution of the GDR, socialist state power and who
> are ready to make socialism better. But we cannot allow irresponsible elements
> to question everything that has happened here, that we have done for this
> country in the past forty years, without any consequences.[219]

The speech of the chief manager well illustrated how deeply the East German party functionaries were indoctrinated by their own propaganda and how far they distanced themselves from the 'masses'. Many East German workers claimed that they had participated at the demonstrations and they were proud of it, without making any reference to insulting slogans such as 'Every communist pig to the wall!' Some said that they demonstrated for a better socialism, and they thought that West Germany would take over some of the socialist achievements which they were proud of (working women, state institutions of childcare, education and polyclinics). However, none of them said that they regretted that the *Wende* came, and the overwhelming majority declared themselves to be happy with the German unification.

The surviving East German sources of grass-roots party life essentially demonstrate a lack of any dialogue between the workers and the party. Even though the party did indeed attempt to provide material and social security for the workers, not only were they effectively excluded from control over the means of production, but they could not even express their opinions of party policy towards the working class. While Hungarian sources rendered visible the mounting social and political discontent among the population in the 1980s, silence in the GDR was essentially broken by the mass flight of the population that revealed a regime that was not popular even among those in whose name it exercised power. It remains a question of how far the East German economic reform – had it continued – could have triggered a process of liberalization, but it is certain that under Honecker this process was effectively blocked. The result of the long process of the workers' alienation from the system was that in 1989 the regime could no longer address the working class because the workers themselves did not accept the party as a conversation partner.

Notes

1. For a study of the party control over the factories see: T. Reichel. 2001. 'Die "durchherrschte Arbeitsgesellschaft": Zu den Herrschaftsstrukturen und Machtverhältnissen in DDR-Betrieben', in: Hürtgen, *Der Schein der Stabilität*.
2. Information from the colleagues of the Rudolstadt archive.
3. On East German society, see in particular Fulbrook, *Anatomy of a Dictatorship*; Maier, *Dissolution*; Lindenberger, *Herrschaft und Eigensinn*; Hürtgen, *Der Schein der Stabilität*.
4. Industriekreis-Parteikontrollkommission (control committee of the party organization of the factory).
5. ThStA, Rudolstadt, Bezirksparteiarchiv der SED Gera. Nr. IV D-4/13/85, IKPKK Informationsberichte, 17.2.1978.
6. Sozialistische Einheitspartei Deutschlands (Socialist Unity Party of Germany – the ruling party of the GDR).
7. GYML, X. 415/186/4, MSZMP Győr-Sopron Megyei Bizottsága. Apparátus iratai. Tájékoztató az 1986. évi tagfelvételekről és a pártból való kikerülésekről.

8. GYML, X. 415/32/10, MSZMP Győr-Sopron Megyei Bizottsága. Pártbizottsági ülés jegyzőkönyve, napirendi anyagai. A párt tömegbefolyása, szervezettsége, a pártépítő munka tapasztalatai a munkások körében, 1982. február 9.

9. GYML, X. 415/36/1, MSZMP Győr-Sopron Megyei Bizottsága. Pártbizottsági ülés jegyzőkönyve, napirendi anyagai. A pártonkívüliekkel folytatott beszélgetések tapasztalatai, javaslat a további feladatokra, 1983. április 5.

10. László Tóth, op. cit., 70.

11. A párt tömegbefolyása, szervezettsége, a pártépítő munka tapasztalatai a munkások körében, op. cit.

12. GYML, X. 415/48/2, MSZMP Győr-Sopron Megyei Bizottsága. Apparátus iratai. Jelentés a tagkönyvcsere munkálataival kapcsolatos számszerű adatokról, 1976, július 6. Of those whose membership terminated, 70 per cent were blue-collar workers, 28 per cent referred to family reasons (religion), 20 per cent could not participate in party life and 22 per cent referred to old age and sickness. In 1985, of those whose membership terminated, 70 per cent were blue-collar workers. The main reason for the withdrawal was their refusal to fulfil their party duties (GYML, X. 415/194/5, MSZMP Győr-Sopron Megyei Bizottsága. Apparátus iratai. Szóbeli tájékoztató az 1985. évi tagfelvételek alakulásáról, 1986. március 4).

13. The Tenth Congress of MSZMP was held on 23–28 November 1970.

14. Feljegyzés 'A párt tömegkapcsolata, a pártszervezetek és tömegszervezetek, tömegmozgalmak politikai vitája' című vita anyagáról, op. cit., 2.

15. GYML, X. 415/117/8, MSZMP Győr-Sopron Megyei Bizottsága. Pártbizottsági ülés jegyzőkönyve, napirendi anyagai. Jelentés a 10. kongresszus óta felvett párttagok szociális összetételéről, valamint a pártból kikerültek összetételéről és okairól, 9, 1971. október 13.

16. GYML, X. 415/124/14, MSZMP Győr-Sopron Megyei Bizottsága. Pártbizottsági ülés jegyzőkönyve, napirendi anyagai. Jelentés a Vagongyári Pártbizottság párttaggá nevelési munkájáról. 1972. március 30.

17. GYML, X. 415/4/31, MSZMP Győr-Sopron Megyei Bizottsága. Pártbizottsági ülés jegyzőkönyve, napirendi anyagai. A Győr városi VB jelentése az üzemi pártbizottságok alapszervezeteket irányító tevékenységéről. 1975. november 26.

18. GYML, X. 415/132/54, MSZMP Győr-Sopron Megyei Bizottsága. Apparátus iratai. Havi összefoglaló jelentések a kül- és belpolitikai eseményekről, a lakosság hangulatáról, 3. 1973. február.

19. GYML, X. 415/156/2/4, MSZMP Győr-Sopron Megyei Bizottsága. Pártbizottsági ülés jegyzőkönyve, napirendi anyagai. Tájékoztató az 1984. 1. félévi tagfelvételek összetételének alakulásáról. 1984. szeptember 4.

20. GYML, X. 415/37, MSZMP Győr-Sopron Megyei Bizottsága. Pártbizottsági ülés jegyzőkönyve, napirendi anyagai. Jelentés az MSZMP Politikai Bizottsága 1983. jún. 21-i határozata alapján a tagfelvételi munkáról, a párt összetételének alakulásáról, a további feladatokról a megyében. 1983. október 4.

21. GYML, X. 415/37, MSZMP Győr-Sopron Megyei Bizottsága. Pártbizottsági ülés jegyzőkönyve, napirendi anyagai. Jelentés a tagfelvételi munkáról. 1983. december 13. Stress is mine.

22. On the role of enterprise party organizations see e.g. J. Balogh. 1977. 'A vállalat gazdasági és politikai funkcióinak kapcsolata', *Társadalmi Szemle* 32(12); S. Borbély. 1976. 'A pártszervezetek gazdaságirányító és -ellenőrző munkájáról', *Társadalmi Szemle* 31(6).

23. A Győr városi VB jelentése az üzemi pártbizottságok alapszervezeteket irányító tevékenységéről, op. cit.

24. Ibid., melléklet.

25. GYML, X. 415/25/13, MSZMP Győr-Sopron Megyei Bizottsága. Pártbizottsági ülés jegyzőkönyve, napirendi anyagai. Kimutatás a megye területén lévő nagyvállalatok párttagfelvételének alakulásáról 1975–1979 között. MVG győri telephelyén be-és kilépők száma. 1980. március 14.

26. A párt tömegbefolyása, szervezettsége, a pártépítő munka tapasztalatai a munkások körében, op. cit.

27. GYML, X. 415/532/2/2, MSZMP Magyar Vagon-és Gépgyári Bizottságának anyagai, Pártbizottsági ülés jegyzőkönyve. Tájékoztató az 1983. évi párttaggá nevelés, a párttag felvételek tapasztalatairól, 1984. február 2.

28. Tájékoztató az 1986. évi tagfelvételekről és a pártból való kikerülésekről, op. cit.

29. Stress is mine.

30. GYML, X. 415/224/4, MSZMP Gyo″r-Sopron Megyei Bizottsága. Pártbizottsági ülés jegyzőkönyve, napirendi anyagai. Szóbeli tájékoztató az 1987. évi tagfelvételek alakulásáról a Megyei Párt-végrehajtó Bizottság 1983. december 13-i határozata alapján, 1988. február 23.

31. Tájékoztató az 1986. évi tagfelvételekről és a pártból való kikerülésekről, op. cit.

32. Full female employment was strongly supported by the party as a means of female emancipation. Since the equal division of labour proved to be more difficult to realize within the family, in practice this often meant double work for the women in the workplace and in the 'second shift' of the household. From the contemporary literature see: Zs. Ferge. 1976. 'A nők a munkában és a családban', *Társadalmi Szemle* 31(6). For a study of working women in Hungary see: Fodor, *Working Difference*; Tóth, *'Puszi Kádár Jánosnak'*.

33. A Győr városi VB jelentése az üzemi pártbizottságok alapszervezeteket irányító tevékenységéről, op. cit.

34. Tájékoztató a KB 1970. február 18-19-i, a nők politikai, gazdasági és szociális helyzete megjavítására hozott határozata végrehajtásának tapasztalatairól, op. cit., 2.

35. Ibid., 4–5.

36. Ibid., 7.

37. Comprehensive schools also gave a high school certificate.

38. Tájékoztató a KB 1970. február 18-19-i, a nők politikai, gazdasági és szociális helyzete megjavítására hozott határozata végrehajtásának tapasztalatairól, op. cit., 18.

39. Tájékoztató az 1983. évi párttaggá nevelés, a párttag felvételek tapasztalatairól, op. cit.

40. Szóbeli tájékoztató az 1987. évi tag alakulásáról a Megyei Párt-végrehajtó Bizottság 1983. december 13-i határozata alapján, op. cit.

41. Jegyzőkönyv a Motor Pártalapszervezet 1977. január 26.-i taggyűléséről, op. cit., 5–6.

42. The report states that the passive party members constitute 4–5 per cent of the total membership that belongs under the party committee of Győr town (104 base cells with a membership of 9,804 people).

43. A Győr városi Párt-végrehajtó Bizottság jelentése a pártszervezeti fegyelem, a kommunista munkamorál, magatartás, életmód helyzetéről, op. cit., 18–19.

44. Jelentés a 10. kongresszus óta felvett párttagok szociális összetételéről, valamint a pártból kikerültek összetételéről és okairól, op. cit.

45. A Győr városi Párt-végrehajtó Bizottság jelentése a pártszervezeti fegyelem, a kommunista munkamorál, magatartás, életmód helyzetéről, op. cit., 14–15.

46. A vidékről bejáró dolgozóinak helyzete, op. cit., 5.

47. Jelentés a KISZ munkájáról, op. cit., 1.

48. A szocialista munkaverseny és a brigádmunka fejlesztésének feladatai vállalatunknál, op. cit., 5.

49. A Győr városi VB jelentése az üzemi pártbizottságok alapszervezeteket irányító tevékenységéről, op. cit.

50. Ibid.

51. Information from the interviews with the workers of the factory.

52. GYML, X. 415/195/1, MSZMP Magyar Vagon-és Gépgyári Bizottságának anyagai. Jelentés a tömegszervezetek pártirányításáról a Vagon gyáregység és az Irodák III pártalapszervezeteknél, 1977. május.

53. GYML, X. 415/187/2, MSZMP Győr-Sopron Megyei Bizottsága. Apparátus iratai. A lakossági közhangulatot jellemző főbb tendenciák, 1986. április.
54. GYML, X. 415/161/2/4, MSZMP Győr-Sopron Megyei Bizottsága. Pártbizottsági ülés jegyzőkönyve, napirendi anyagai. A pártból kikerülés elemzése és az abból adódó feladatok. 1985. június 28.
55. Szóbeli tájékoztató az 1987. évi tagfelvételek alakulásáról a Megyei Párt-végrehajtó Bizottság 1983. december 13-i határozata alapján, op. cit.
56. A pártból kikerülés elemzése és az abból adódó feladatok, op. cit., 5.
57. GYML, X. 415/203/2/7, MSZMP Magyar Vagon-és Gépgyári Bizottságának anyagai. Pártbizottsági ülés jegyzo"könyve. A párttagok körében végzett politikai nevelo"munka és a párttagokkal való foglalkozás tapasztalatai, 5. 1980. november 28.
58. Ibid., 6.
59. GYML, X. 415/203/2/5, MSZMP Magyar Vagon-és Gépgyári Bizottságának anyagai. Pártbizottsági ülés jegyzőkönyve. Az emberi kapcsolatok alakulásának tapasztalatai. Politikai feladatok a zavartalan munkahelyi légkör elősegítésére, 4. 1980. május 22.
60. Szóbeli tájékoztató az 1987. évi tagfelvételek alakulásáról a Megyei Párt-végrehajtó Bizottság 1983. december 13-i határozata alapján, op. cit.
61. The immigration of the leaders caused an even greater loss of prestige to the party. In Mosonmagyaróvár, for instance, the immigration of the party secretary of the base organization of the Water Works and his wife, who was also a member of the party, was discussed also in the party organization of Rába MMG. GYML, X. 415/529/1/2, MSZMP Magyar Vagon-és Gépgyári Bizottságának anyagai. A Mosonmagyaróvári Mezőgazdasági Gépgyár (MMG) pártbizottsági ülésének jegyzőkönyve. A párttaggá nevelés és a pártépítő munka tapasztalatai a Rába MMG-ben. 1984. május 3.
62. A Győr városi Párt-végrehajtó Bizottság jelentése a pártszervezeti fegyelem, a kommunista munkamorál, magatartás, életmód helyzetéről, op. cit.
63. A párttagok körében végzett politikai nevelőmunka és a párttagokkal való foglalkozás tapasztalatai, op. cit.
64. Szóbeli tájékoztató az 1985. évi tagfelvételek alakulásáról, op. cit.
65. GYML, X. 415/237, MSZMP Győr-Sopron Megyei Bizottsága. Pártbizottsági ülés jegyzőkönyve, napirendi anyagai. Tájékoztató az 1983-as pártfegyelmi eljárásokról. 1984. március 5.
66. Szóbeli tájékoztató az 1985. évi tagfelvételek alakulásáról, op. cit.
67. GYML, X. 415/195/1, MSZMP Magyar Vagon-és Gépgyári Bizottságának anyagai. Pártbizottsági ülés jegyzőkönyve, napirendi anyagai. A tagkönyvcserével kapcsolatos elbeszélgetések és taggyűlések tapasztalatai. 1977. január 26.
68. A párttaggá nevelés és a pártépítő munka tapasztalatai a Rába MMG-ben, op. cit.
69. GYML, X. 415/47/36, MSZMP Győr-Sopron Megyei Bizottsága. Apparátus iratai. Dolgozók által tett bejelentések, panaszok, 1975.
70. Ibid. A woman, for instance, denounced her divorced husband (a party member) for making anti-party comments; the investigation, however, stated that she denounced him out of revenge.
71. A pártból kikerülés elemzése és az abból adódó feladatok, op. cit.
72. A párttagok körében végzett politikai nevelőmunka és a párttagokkal való foglalkozás tapasztalatai, op. cit.; GYML, X. 415/161/2/5, MSZMP Győr-Sopron Megyei Bizottsága. Pártbizottsági ülés jegyzőkönyve, napirendi anyagai. A párttaggá nevelő munka tapasztalatai a munkások és az ifjúság körében a Politikai Bizottság 1983. június 21-i és a Megyei Párt-végrehajtó Bizottság 1983. december 13-i határozata alapján. 1985. október 16.
73. GYML, X. 415/122/6, MSZMP Győr-Sopron Megyei Bizottsága. Pártbizottsági ülés jegyzőkönyve, napirendi anyagai. Jelentés a párttagság körében végzett ideológiai nevelőmunkáról, 1-5. melléklet. 1972. augusztus 15.

74. GYML, X. 415/36, MSZMP Győr-Sopron Megyei Bizottsága. Pártbizottsági ülés jegyzőkönyve, napirendi anyagai. A pártonkívüliekkel folytatott beszélgetések tapasztalatai, javaslat a további feladatokra. 1983. április 5.
75. Stress is mine.
76. GYML, X. 415/537/2, MSZMP Magyar Vagon-és Gépgyári Bizottságának anyagai. Információs jelentés a Szerszámgépgyár Pártalapszervezetétől, 1986. május.
77. GYML, X. 415/235, MSZMP Győr-Sopron Megyei Bizottsága. Apparátus iratai. A lakossági közhangulatot jellemző főbb tendenciák, Sopron, 1987. december.
78. There were also national surveys conducted on the subjective evaluation of the standard of living. See: Angelusz, *Munkásvélemények az életszínvonalról*; Angelusz, *A megfelelőnek tartott jövedelem.*
79. Információs jelentés a Vagon Fémipari Alapszervezettől, 1979. május, op. cit.
80. GYML, X. 415/199/28, MSZMP Magyar Vagon-és Gépgyári Bizottságának anyagai. Információs jelentés a Kovács Pártalapszervezettől. 1979. szeptember.
81. GYML, X. 415/202/32, MSZMP Magyar Vagon-és Gépgyári Bizottságának anyagai. Információs jelentés az Új Acélöntödéből, 1979. május.
82. GYML, X. 415/199/28, MSZMP Magyar Vagon-és Gépgyári Bizottságának anyagai. Jegyzőkönyv a Kovács II. üzem MSZMP alapszervezetének taggyűléséről. 1978. február 22.
83. GYML, X. 415/199/12, MSZMP Magyar Vagon-és Gépgyári Bizottságának anyagai. Információs jelentés a Szerszámgépgyár Pártalapszervezetétől, 1979. február.
84. This statement is supported by the findings of the oral history project of Szalai: *Beszélgetések a gazdasági reformról.*
85. GYML, X. 415/206/12, MSZMP Magyar Vagon-és Gépgyári Bizottságának anyagai. Információs jelentés a Szerelde Pártalapszervezetétől, 1980. február.
86. Stress is in the original.
87. Információs jelentés a T. M. K. Pártalapszervezettől, 1979. május, op. cit.
88. GYML, X. 415/206/28, MSZMP Magyar Vagon-és Gépgyári Bizottságának anyagai. Információs jelentés az Új Acélöntödéből, 1980. július.
89. GYML, X. 415/206/28, MSZMP Magyar Vagon-és Gépgyári Bizottságának anyagai. Információs jelentés az Új Acélöntödéből, 1980. március.
90. GYML, X. 415/211/38, MSZMP Magyar Vagon-és Gépgyári Bizottságának anyagai. Információs jelentés az Új Acélöntödéből, 1982. február.
91. GYML, X. 415/211/38, MSZMP Magyar Vagon-és Gépgyári Bizottságának anyagai. Információs jelentés az Új Acélöntödéből, 1982. április.
92. GYML, X. 415/211/4, MSZMP Magyar Vagon-és Gépgyári Bizottságának anyagai. Információs jelentés a Technológia Pártalapszervezetétől, 1982. február.
93. Ibid.
94. Jegyzőkönyv a Szerszámgépgyár Egység Pártalapszervezetének 1983. februári taggyűléséről, op. cit.
95. GYML, X. 415/212/15, MSZMP Magyar Vagon-és Gépgyári Bizottságának anyagai. Információs jelentés a Kovács Pártalapszervezettől. 1982. november-december.
96. GYML, X. 415/528/2, MSZMP Magyar Vagon-és Gépgyári Bizottságának anyagai. Információs jelentés a Szerszámgépgyár Pártalapszervezetétől, 1982. március.
97. GYML, X. 415/210/3, MSZMP Magyar Vagon-és Gépgyári Bizottságának anyagai. Pártbizottsági ülés jegyzőkönyve. Jelentés a párttagok körében végzett politikai nevelőmunkáról, 2. 1982. október 14.
98. GYML, X. 415/211/33, Magyar Szocialista Munkáspárt (MSZMP) Magyar Vagon-és Gépgyári Végrehajtó Bizottságának anyagai. Információs jelentés a Jármű II. Pártalapszervezettől, 1982. november.
99. Stress is in the original.
100. GYML, X. 415/212/5, MSZMP Magyar Vagon-és Gépgyári Bizottságának anyagai. Információs jelentés a Motor Pártalapszervezettől. 1982. február.

101. Ibid.
102. GYML, X. 415/528/1, MSZMP Magyar Vagon-és Gépgyári Bizottságának anyagai. Információs jelentés a Hátsóhíd Alapszervezetétől, 1983. január.
103. Információs jelentés a Jármű II. Pártalapszervezettől, 1982. november, op. cit.
104. A Vagongyár Pártbizottságának információs jelentése, 1985. október, op. cit.
105. GYML, X. 415/211/28, MSZMP Magyar Vagon-és Gépgyári Bizottságának anyagai. Rendkívüli információs jelentés a Kovács Pártalapszervezettől, 1982. december.
106. GYML, X. 415/528/13, Magyar Szocialista Munkáspárt (MSZMP) Magyar Vagon-és Gépgyári Végrehajtó Bizottságának anyagai. Információs jelentés a Szerszámgépgyár Pártalapszervezetétől. 1983. április.
107. GYML, X. 415/528/1, MSZMP Magyar Vagon-és Gépgyári Bizottságának anyagai. Információs jelentés a Hátsóhíd Alapszervezetétől, 1983. augusztus.
108. GYML, X. 415/537/1, MSZMP Magyar Vagon-és Gépgyári Bizottságának anyagai. Információs jelentés a Jármű Pártalapszervezetétől, 1985. november-december.
109. GYML, X. 415/211/39, MSZMP Magyar Vagon-és Gépgyári Bizottságának anyagai. Információs jelentés az Energetikától. 1982. október.
110. GYML, X. 415/537/16, MSZMP Magyar Vagon-és Gépgyári Bizottságának anyagai. Információs jelentés a Motor Pártalapszervezettől. 1986. október.
111. GYML, X. 415/536/11, MSZMP Magyar Vagon-és Gépgyári Bizottságának anyagai. A párttagok körében végzett politikai nevelőmunka feladatai. 1985. október.
112. GYML, X. 415/208/35, MSZMP Magyar Vagon-és Gépgyári Bizottságának anyagai. Információs jelentés a Motor Pártalapszervezettől. 1981. november.
113. GYML, X. 415/211/33, Magyar Szocialista Munkáspárt (MSZMP) Magyar Vagon-és Gépgyári Végrehajtó Bizottságának anyagai. Információs jelentés a Jármű II. Pártalapszervezettől, 1982. szeptember.
114. GYML, X. 415/236/8, MSZMP Magyar Vagon-és Gépgyári Bizottságának anyagai. Információs jelentés az MVG KISZ szervezetétől. 1986. december.
115. GYML, X. 415/231/5, MSZMP Győr-Sopron Megyei Bizottsága. Apparátus iratai. A lakossági közhangulatot jellemző főbb tendenciák. 1987. január.
116. A párttagok körében végzett politikai nevelőmunka és a párttagokkal való foglalkozás tapasztalatai, op. cit., 5.
117. Ibid., 6.
118. A párttaggá nevelés és a pártépítő munka tapasztalatai a Rába MMG-ben, op. cit., 5.
119. Ibid., 5
120. Ibid., 6.
121. Jelentés a KISZ munkájáról, op. cit. In 1984, the workers said that a flat cost 10–15 times more than their annual income. GYML, X. 415/533/30, MSZMP Magyar Vagon-és Gépgyári Bizottságának anyagai. Információs jelentés a Futómű Pártvezetőségétől, 1984. szeptember.
122. GYML, X. 415/529/14/3, MSZMP Magyar Vagon-és Gépgyári Bizottságának anyagai. Pártbizottsági ülés jegyzőkönyve. Jelentés a gyár ifjúsága társadalmi helyzetének javítására tett intézkedésekről. 1987. november 19.
123. Jelentés a KISZ munkájáról, op. cit.
124. Jelentés a gyár ifjúsága társadalmi helyzetének javítására tett intézkedésekről, op. cit.
125. A párttaggá nevelés és a pártépítő munka tapasztalatai a Rába MMG-ben, op. cit.
126. GYML, X. 415/234, MSZMP Győr-Sopron Megyei Bizottsága. Apparátus iratai. A lakossági közhangulatot jellemző főbb tendenciák. 1986. december.
127. GYML, X. 415/529/2/3, MSZMP Magyar Vagon-és Gépgyári Bizottságának anyagai. A Mosonmagyaróvári Mezőgazdasági Gépgyár (MMG) pártbizottsági ülésének jegyzőkönyve. Az ideológiai munka és az agit. prop. feladatai, 2. 1985. július 16.
128. GYML, X. 415/232/4, MSZMP Győr-Sopron Megyei Bizottsága. Apparátus iratai. A lakossági közhangulatot jellemző főbb tendenciák. 1986. november.

129. GYML, X. 415/538/1, MSZMP Magyar Vagon-és Gépgyári Bizottságának anyagai. Információs jelentés a Motor Pártalapszervezettől. 1987. április.

130. GYML, X. 415/538/3, MSZMP Magyar Vagon-és Gépgyári Bizottságának anyagai. Információs jelentés a Szerszámgépgyár Pártalapszervezetétől. 1987. szeptember.

131. GYML, X. 415/538/6, MSZMP Magyar Vagon-és Gépgyári Bizottságának anyagai. Információs jelentés a Futómű Pártvezetőségétől. 1987. május.

132. A lakossági közhangulatot jellemző főbb tendenciák, Sopron, 1987. december, op. cit.

133. Szóbeli tájékoztató az 1987. évi tagfelvételek alakulásáról a Megyei Párt-végrehajtó Bizottság 1983. december 13-i határozata alapján, op. cit.

134. Ibid.

135. GYML, X. 415/220/4, MSZMP Győr-Sopron Megyei Bizottsága. Apparátus iratai. A párttagkönyvcserével kapcsolatos elbeszélgetések tapasztalatai. 1988. március 28.

136. GYML, X. 415/238, MSZMP Győr-Sopron Megyei Bizottsága. Apparátus iratai. Párttagság összetétele 1988. decemberi állapot szerint.

137. GYML, X. 415/238, MSZMP Győr-Sopron Megyei Bizottsága. Apparátus iratai. Háromnegyedévi összesítők 1989.

138. GYML, X. 415/234/3, MSZMP Győr-Sopron Megyei Bizottsága. Apparátus iratai. A lakossági közhangulatot jellemző főbb tendenciák. 1988. szeptember.

139. Ibid.

140. GYML, X. 415/526/3/1, MSZMP Magyar Vagon-és Gépgyári Bizottságának anyagai. A politikai nevelőmunka tapasztalatai, az agitáció, propaganda és tájékoztatás fejlesztésének feladatai. 1988. február 2.

141. GyML, X. 415/526/4/3, AZ MVG Pártbizottságának iratai. Pártbizottsági ülés jegyzőkönyve. Állásfoglalás az MSZMP KB 1989. február 10-11-i, 'A politikai rendszer reformjának néhány időszerű kérdéséről szóló állásfoglalás' tervezetéről, 3. 1988. március 2.

142. Ibid., 13.

143. Ibid., 3.

144. GyML, X. 415/226/1, MSZMP Győr-Sopron Megyei Bizottsága iratai. Megyei Pártértekezlet anyaga, 6-7. 1989. június 10. Rába MVG Kongresszusi terem. The conference was held in the Congress Hall of the factory.

145. 'Beszélgetés Horváth Edével, a Rába MVG vezérigazgatójával', op. cit.

146. 'Visszahívná a kapitalistákat?', *Tér-kép*, 1989. június 1.

147. ThStA, Rudolstadt, Bezirksparteiarchiv der SED Gera. Nr. IV B-4/13/96, Statistik.

148. ThStA, Rudolstadt, Bezirksparteiarchiv der SED Gera. Nr. IV E-2/3/49, Protokoll der Sekretariatssitzung, Wie ist es der IKL des Veb Carl Zeiss Jena gelungen, in den Arbeitskollektiven und besonders in den Jugendbrigaden der Produktionsbetriebe und der produktionsvorbereitenden Bereiche einen aktiven Kern von Kommunisten herauszubilden, den Parteieinfluß auf die Entwicklung vom Wissenschaft und Technik zu stärken und erfolgreich den Kampf um Spitzenleistungen zu führen? 23 September 1982.

149. Abteilungsparteiorganisation.

150. IKPO: Industriekreisparteiorganisation (the party organization of the factory). The source of data is Statistik, op. cit.

151. Protokoll der Sekretariatssitzung, 23 September 1982, op. cit.

152. ThStA, Rudolstadt, Bezirksparteiarchiv der SED Gera. Nr. A. 9258, Informationsbericht, Jena, 8 Juli 1988.

153. Statistik, op. cit.

154. Protokoll der Sekretariatssitzung, 23 September 1982, op. cit.

155. ThStA, Rudolstadt, Bezirksparteiarchiv der SED Gera. Nr. IV-E/2/3/97, Protokoll der Sekretariatssitzung, Standpunkt der IKL der SED des VEB Carl Zeiss Jena zu den Ergebnissen und Erfahrungen der Parteiarbeit bei der Befähigung und Erziehung der Kommunisten zur Meisterung der Aufgaben in ihrer Einheit vom Wort um Tat, 13 September 1984.

156. Informationsbericht, Jena, 8 Juli 1988, op. cit.
157. ThStA, Rudolstadt, Bezirksparteiarchiv der SED Gera. Nr. A. 9970, Sitzung der Bezirksleitung, 11 Februar 1987.
158. Statistik, op. cit.
159. Protokoll der Sekretariatssitzung, 23 September 1982, op. cit.; Sitzung der Bezirksleitung, 11 Februar 1987, op. cit.
160. Protokoll der Sekretariatssitzung, 23 September 1982.
161. ThStA, Rudolstadt, Bezirksparteiarchiv der SED Gera. Nr. A. 9938/2, Informationsberichte, Carl Zeiss Jena, 26 Juli 1989.
162. According to some interview partners, those who announced this intention were either agitated to stay in the party or they were excluded from the organization.
163. Statistik, op. cit.
164. ThStA, Rudolstadt, Bezirksparteiarchiv der SED Gera. Nr. IV-D/2/5/300, Information über die Entwicklung der Mitgliederbewegung, 10 Mai 1977.
165. Jelentés a 10. kongresszus óta felvett párttagok szociális összetételéről, valamint a pártból kikerültek összetételéről és okairól, op. cit.
166. Stress is mine.
167. ThStA, Rudolstadt, Bezirksparteiarchiv der SED Gera. Nr. IV-B/2/4/290, Bezirksparteikontrollkommission, Gewinnung von Kandidaten, 12 November 1968.
168. *Gleichberechtigt. Die Entwicklung der Frauen und Mädchen im VEB Carl Zeiss Jena*, op. cit. 4.
169. Statistik, op. cit.
170. *A Győr városi VB jelentése az üzemi pártbizottságok alapszervezeteket irányító tevékenységéről*.
171. The proportion of women among the party members also varied among the individual plants. According to a report of 1977, even though the optical plant had a high proportion of female workforce, only 11.3 per cent of the women were members of the party. Information über die Entwicklung der Mitgliederbewegung, op. cit.
172. ThStA, Rudolstadt, Bezirksparteiarchiv der SED Gera. Nr. IV-D/2/17/508, Analyse der gegenwärtigen Ergebnisse bei der Entwicklung und den Einsatz von Genossinnen in Parteifunktionen.
173. Ibid.
174. Freie Deutsche Jugend (Free German Youth).
175. Analyse der gegenwärtigen Ergebnisse bei der Entwicklung und den Einsatz von Genossinnen in Parteifunktionen, op. cit.
176. ThStA, Rudolstadt, Bezirksparteiarchiv der SED Gera. Nr. IV-C/2/3/720, Informationsberichte, Carl Zeiss Jena, 10 August 1973.
177. Analyse der gegenwärtigen Ergebnisse bei der Entwicklung und den Einsatz von Genossinnen in Parteifunktionen, op. cit.
178. ThStA, Rudolstadt, Bezirksparteiarchiv der SED Gera. Nr. IV-C/2/5/337, Information über einige Probleme der Parteiarbeit, 24 März 1976.
179. Gewinnung von Kandidaten, 12 November 1968, op. cit.
180. Information über die Entwicklung der Mitgliederbewegung, 10 Mai 1977, op. cit.
181. On the basis of party literature that some interview partners gave me as a present, it is, however, unlikely that these publications were widely read in the factories.
182. ThStA, Rudolstadt, Bezirksparteiarchiv der SED Gera. Nr. IV-C/2/3/162, Protokoll der Sekretariatssitzung, Ergebnisse bei der Propagierung und den Vertrieb marxistisch-leninistischer Literatur und der Entwicklung des gesellschaftlichen Literaturvertriebes in Bezirk Gera, 29 August 1974.
183. ThStA, Rudolstadt, Bezirksparteiarchiv der SED Gera. Nr. IV-C/2/3/152, Protokoll der Sekretariatssitzung, Einschätzung der Ergebnisse der Wahlbewegung, 30 Mai 1974.
184. Zur inhaltlichen Fragen der politisch-ideologischen Arbeit die gegenwärtig besonders im Mittelpunkt der Diskussion der Bevölkerung stehen, op. cit.

185. *Nationale Front* was the popular front of the political parties and mass organizations in the GDR. Formally, the GDR was a multi-party system, but in practice the elections and the selection of the candidates were controlled by the SED.
186. Stress is mine.
187. ThStA, Rudolstadt, Bezirksparteiarchiv der SED Gera. Nr. IV-D/4/13/85, IKPKK, Informationsberichte, 16 April 1979.
188. People who officially asked for a permanent permit to leave the GDR (this involved the loss of GDR citizenship).
189. ThStA, Rudolstadt, Bezirksparteiarchiv der SED Gera. Nr. IV-E/2/4/255, Bericht über die Untersuchung der BPKK (Bezirksparteikontrollkommission) und der IKPKK Carl Zeiss Jena in den GO (Grundorganisation) des Betriebes Wissenschaftlichen Gerätebau des VEB Carl Zeiss Jena (G-Betrieb) zur Wirksamkeit der politisch-ideologischen Arbeit bei der Zurückdrängung der rechtswidrigen Anträge auf Übersiedlung in das nichtsozialistischen Ausland, 24 April 1984.
190. According to the given statistics, 35 Zeiss employees applied for the permission to leave the GDR in 1980, 31 in 1981, 37 in 1982 and 120 in 1983. In 1980, 63 per cent of the *Antragsteller* were workers. Bericht über die Untersuchung der BPKK, op. cit.
191. Ibid, Niederschrift über die Aussprache mit Genossen J, Parteigruppenorganisator in der Fräserei im Beisein des APO-Sekretärs Genossen H am 04.04.1984.
192. Stress is mine.
193. ThStA, Rudolstadt, Bezirksparteiarchiv der SED Gera. Nr. IV-B/4/13/83, Untersuchung in der APO/ZGss – Parteigruppe Modelltischlerei, 27 September 1971.
194. According to the report there were very few comrades among these 139 who had already made critical comments concerning the Hungarian 'events' of 1956 and the building of the 'anti-fascist wall of defence' of 1961.
195. ThStA, Rudolstadt, Bezirksparteiarchiv der SED Gera. Nr. IV-B/2/4/290, Bezirksparteikontrollkommission, Einschätzung über die im Bezirk aufgetretene Erscheinungen und Auseinandersetzungen mit Genossen im Zusammenhang mit den Ereignissen in der CSSR, 12 November 1968.
196. ThStA, Rudolstadt, Bezirksparteiarchiv der SED Gera. Nr. IV-B/2/4/297, Einschätzung zur parteierzieherischen Maßnahmen in den Grundorganisationen der IKPO des VEB Carl Zeiss Jena im Zusammenhang mit der Entwicklung in der CSSR und der sozialistischen Waffenhilfe am 21.8.1968. 8. Oktober 1968.
197. ThStA, Rudolstadt, Bezirksparteiarchiv der SED Gera. Nr. IV-B/2/3/72, Protokoll der Sekretariatssitzung, Bericht zum Stand der Durchsetzung und Wirksamkeit der Rechtsprechung im Bezirk auf der Grundlage der neuen Gesetzeswerke zur sozialistischen Strafrecht insbesondere die sich daraus ergebenden politisch-ideologische Probleme, 5 Dezember 1968.
198. One interview partner told a similar story; he had the hobby of rearing carrier pigeons.
199. Attempt to leave the GDR illegally.
200. ThStA, Rudolstadt, Bezirksparteiarchiv der SED Gera. Nr. IV-C/2/4/303, Feindliche Handlungen von Mitgliedern und Kandidaten der Partei (1973–1976).
201. ThStA, Rudolstadt, Bezirksparteiarchiv der SED Gera. Nr. IV-D/2/4/242, Bezirksparteikontrollkommission, 4 Januar 1978.
202. ThStA, Rudolstadt, Bezirksparteiarchiv der SED Gera. Nr. IV-D/4/13/85, IKPKK, Informationsberichte, 8 März 1979.
203. Ibid., 19 November 1980.
204. ThStA, Rudolstadt, Bezirksparteiarchiv der SED Gera. Nr. IV-B/4/13/83, Bericht der IKPKK, 1 Oktober 1973.
205. ThStA, Rudolstadt, Bezirksparteiarchiv der SED Gera. Nr. IV-B/4/13/80, Bericht der IKPKK, 19 September 1969.
206. See the complaints of young skilled workers concerning this type of accommodation in the section *From Hostels to Flats*.

207. ThStA, Rudolstadt, Bezirksparteiarchiv der SED Gera. Nr. IV-B/4/13/80, Bericht der IKPKK, Argumente der Lehrlinge im Bereich des FB, 25 Januar 1970.

208. It seems that impertinence was also frequently counted among the 'hostile' manifestations because one teacher spoke of the 'negative political attitude' of a trainee who was rebuked for the bad quality of his work to which he replied 'now what are the other 20–30 per cent of the employees doing here?' ThStA, Rudolstadt, Bezirksparteiarchiv der SED Gera. Nr. IV-C/2/1/5, Protokoll der Sitzung der Bezirksleitung der SED Gera, 4 Januar 1972.

209. The title of the newspaper of the factory.

210. IKPKK Informationsberichte, 17.2.1978, op. cit.

211. I base this statement on the party reports of the factory and the district; I have not studied Stasi files.

212. UACZ, VA Nr. 4447, Information über die Bearbeitung der Eingabe der Gewerkschafts-gruppe 'Dr. Richard Sorge' aus dem Betrieb Entwicklung wissenschaftlich-technischer Ausrüstungen, 5.1.1989.

213. UACZ, VA Nr. 4722, Fallmeldung, 4.10.1989.

214. UACZ, GB Nr. 1209, Brigadebuch, op. cit. 7 Oktober, 40. Jahrestag der Gründung unserer DDR.

215. ThStA, Rudolstadt, Bezirksparteiarchiv der SED Gera. A 9938/2, Informationsberichte, Carl Zeiss Jena, 26 Juli 1989.

216. ThStA, Rudolstadt, Bezirksparteiarchiv der SED Gera. A 9635, Informationsberichte, 19 Oktober 1989.

217. ThStA, Rudolstadt, Bezirksparteiarchiv der SED Gera. A 9807, Informationsberichte, 23 Oktober 1989.

218. UACZ, VA Nr. 4743, 13.2.1990.

219. ThStA, Rudolstadt, Bezirksparteiarchiv der SED Gera. Nr. A 9981, Sitzung der Bezirkslei-tung Gera von 02.11.1989.

CHAPTER 4

CONTRASTING THE MEMORY OF THE KÁDÁR AND HONECKER REGIMES

The immediate experience of the change of regimes was different in the two countries. In East Germany mass demonstrations indicated the collapse of the legitimation of the Honecker regime, while in Hungary MSZMP agreed with the opposition about the organization of democratic elections. As we have seen in the above chapters, the East German political climate was much more repressive than Kádár's Hungary. The following citation comes from an interview that I conducted in an unusual 'terrain' in East Germany with a Zeiss worker (*Zeissianer*), who had been imprisoned in the Honecker era for his oppositionist political activity. In the summer of 1989 he left the GDR, and he found new employment in Munich as a transport worker. After suffering an injury he lost his job and he failed to find a new one. At the time of interviewing he lived in a hostel for homeless people. This is how he recalled the socialist past in the light of his experience in the new, capitalist society:

We were fifty people in the [oppositionist] group. We did not do big things: we published some posters and a journal in which we wrote that there is political repression in the GDR. In 1982 they [the party] took the case very seriously – I was arrested and I spent six months in prison. When I was released, the organization had already been dissolved. There was no point in continuing. I did not have any problem in the factory, I earned good money. What I did not like was that I could not have my own opinion. You could not say openly what you thought because there was a constant spying on you, even in the pub or within the factory. They [the party] declared everything to be anti-state activity and subversion. 'You [the party] made a mistake' – this was impossible to say. 'The party decides everything, without the party the grass does not grow and people can't breathe' – this was the general attitude. People wanted to think for themselves, make suggestions, better things – but no one listened. 'The party is always right, you should not think, you should just do your work.' They wanted to deprive people of their ability to think. People should just do their work and leave the serious things to the leadership. I don't see a change in this. Those who are at the top don't want people to think. *Today I don't see a really big difference between the two systems, socialism and capitalism.*[1]

Jan's life-history is not a typical East German working-class career. The citation, however, reflects a crucial difference between the subjective evaluations of the two welfare dictatorships. In East Germany, no one, including Jan, who lost his job and his home in the new regime, wanted Honecker's state back. In the Hungarian interviews we meet a more ambiguous picture: the desire for greater social and material equality triggers a longing for a strong state, order and an autocratic government, which is expected to restore national pride, protect Hungarian industry and increase the standard of living of the working people – the latter being the most attractive 'catchword' of the Kádár regime.[2]

To explain the different evaluations of the change of regimes and the new democracies it is important to point out structural differences between the two countries, which shaped the experience of the change of regimes. While the East German average wages were still lower – 70–72 per cent of the West German average – in 2004 and 2008 the German GDP per capita was higher than the EU average by 16 per cent, while the Hungarian GDP per capita was 63 per cent of the EU average in 2004 and 64 per cent in 2008.[3] If we define the poor as people who live at a consumption level that is half of the EU average, then nearly three-quarters of the Hungarian population can be considered to be poor.[4] Although the East German unemployment rate was higher than the Hungarian at the time of interviewing (20 per cent, while in Hungary it only exceeded 10 per cent in 2009), the employment rate is very low in Hungary: in 2009 for example, 71 per cent of the population of 15–64 year-olds were employed in Germany, but this was only 55 per cent in Hungary. Ferge estimates that one million jobs were lost in Hungary as a result of economic restructuring, while according to the calculation of Mark Pittaway there were 23 per cent fewer jobs in Hungary in 2008 than in 1989.[5] According to the estimate of Ferge (2010), 45–50 per cent of the Hungarian population belongs to the losers of the change of regimes, 30–35 per cent experienced no change in their situation, and 20–25 per cent belongs to the winners. It is worth pointing out that poverty seems to be a 'durable' condition in Hungary: according to a panel survey with three thousand respondents, the majority (60 per cent) of those who were poor in 1992 were in the same situation fifteen years later, and only 7 per cent had improved their conditions.[6] These data suggest that Hungarian society is becoming more closed socially.

These differences were visible in the life-history interviews, too. On the basis of the interviews I distinguished between three dimensions of postsocialist experience: (1) the world of labour, (2) subjective evaluation of the standard of living and the level of integration into consumer society, and (3) interpersonal relations. The first dimension is divided into two different types of experience: half of the interviewees in both groups could experience transition in the factory, while the other half lost their jobs or were sent to early retirement. The transition to post-Fordism was an essentially different experience in the two countries.[7] The Rába workers unanimously constructed 'narratives of decline' about the postsocialist history of their factory: the managers decreased production, the new proprietors refused to invest in innovation or the technical development of the factory, and they made profit by selling the valuable estates of Rába and laying off workers who had worked there for the many years since the plants had been built by the legendary communist manager, Ede Horváth. Many workers argued that the proprietors intentionally destroyed production in order to make a profit from the selling of the estates. Workers' grievances were frequently translated into full-fledged conspiracy theories as we will see below.

Szalai distinguishes between the workers of the multinational sector and those of the domestic sector. The latter are described as poorly paid, badly exploited '*bricoleurs*', who are often informally employed and they live from one day to the next.[8] By using this model, the Rába workers unmistakably identified themselves with the '*bricoleurs*' of the domestic sector. They associated (post)industrial development with the multinational enterprises, which destroyed the former prides of domestic industry, enticed their best workers and forced an unfair competition upon the impoverished national companies. Here are the views of two Rába workers:

Because you can see that in the West the state protects the national enterprises. But look at the Wagon Factory.[9] It was a profitable enterprise and now I think that there is a will to destroy it so that it can't be a competitor. I can see through these practices. Győr had famous textile factories, all of them were sold to the competitor [Western] firms, and they were all closed or destroyed otherwise. I can mention Richards, where my wife worked, Graboplast, they were all famous and serious enterprises and all of them were destroyed. This is what I don't understand in this change of regimes: how the state could allow this. I don't say that it should support an enterprise which operates at a loss, but if it sees a perspective in an enterprise … – because we should observe our own interests, and we should not entrust ourselves to the mercy of the West. Because here is this Audi, which is exempt from taxation. If the Wagon Factory could spend the same money on development, it would not be in this bad situation. There has been no innovation here since the change of regimes because the high taxes kill this factory.[10]

My younger son works in Audi. They only exploit the Hungarians there. They make them work harder in comparison to us. But if I compare how much they pay there [in Germany] with how much he gets, then they are exploited, no doubt. They did not come here to benefit the Hungarians but to make a profit for themselves because our workforce is cheaper. It should not have been allowed that Hungarians are exploited to that extent. The politicians point to each other instead of preventing the selling of the whole country.[11]

The above citations nicely illustrate how the workers' grievances are translated into an ethnical-populist discourse, in which the 'multinational' (Western) capital identified with the 'traitor' domestic elite destroys Hungarian industry, thereby becoming responsible for the misery of the workers, who lose the secure existence which was guaranteed under the Kádár regime. To stress the decline, many workers explicitly contrasted the glorious era of Rába under Ede Horváth, when Rába exported its products to the COMECON countries and the United States, and enjoyed wide press and media coverage as a successful socialist company with the 'lean years' of the 1990s:

In the old times it was an honour to work in the Wagon Factory. I was so proud when my father first brought me here at the age of eighteen, and that I am going to work in the famous Wagon Factory ... and now here I am [sigh]. And if they give me notice, I don't know what I will do. Distributing newspapers, cleaning offices or flats ... sadly, there is nothing else. And this is so frightening! In addition, I married late, my daughter has just started secondary school and my son will go to university next year. If we were only the two of us, my husband and me, it would not be so bad. But I have to support them, and both of them are excellent students, which is my biggest problem because both will go to university because I cannot let them go to work after secondary school. ... Back then there was no such insecurity as we have today. I did not have to worry about whether they need me for work today or not. The Wagon Factory was an elite company, the neighbours were envious of us: 'it was easy for you, you were well off, you got very good money in the Wagon Factory'. The value of the wages was much higher back then. There were no such differences between workers and managers. The chief manager earned six times as much as a skilled worker. But today the differences are much, much greater. If only we could see the signs of progress. But unfortunately, there are none.[12]

The Hungarian workers unanimously argued that the history of their factory was one of decline after 1989, which they blamed on the management at the local level, and on the multinational companies and the state's failure to protect successful enterprises at the national level. Post-Fordist innovation and development was represented by Audi, which they experienced as the humiliation of their company: Audi, in fact, bought the giant hall, which Ede Horváth had built with the purpose of bringing the production of motor cars back to Győr. Rába workers recalled bitterly that under Ede Horváth Rába was the main sponsor of the town: it built a stadium, and it could boast about a football team, a house of culture, a well-equipped library, an orchestra, a choir and a dance group. After the change of regimes Audi became the main sponsor of Győr, which Rába workers held to be the unjust consequence of tax exemption (which they blamed on the government).

The Zeiss experience differed from the 'narratives of decline' characteristic of the Rába workers. The company implemented massive lay-offs: the chairman of the enterprise council (*Betriebsrat*) estimated that around sixteen thousand people lost their jobs in the first few years after the *Wende*. The company mainly lost the young workforce because young skilled workers were expected to find new jobs in West Germany more easily than middle-aged family men. In 1995 a further six hundred workers had to be given notice.[13] The Zeiss picture was, however, more ambiguous than the Hungarian experience. Workers in fact had positive experiences with the post-Fordist model of production because the new proprietor, the West German Zeiss, modernized the plants, bought new machines and technology and made significant investments in the town of Jena. Workers reported improving working conditions (competitive salaries, the installation of air conditioning, new bathrooms and canteens, and flexible working hours). They noted, however, that they had to work under greater stress and tension than in the old production regime:

> Requirements are persistently increasing: you have to be flexible and serve more jobs at the same time. In the GDR it was different. We had work but we had to do the same job every day, so you had a certain routine. Today everything is faster, tenser and more hectic. It is difficult to compete with young people even if you have thirty years of work experience. In the GDR we received enormous orders and we produced for stock. Today we work for orders, and if the customers order something, they want to get it today or yesterday. Today you get more tired than in the GDR albeit we also worked hard back then.[14]

The 'narratives of decline' are essentially missing from the East German interviews. The workers, including a former party secretary who told me that he continued to hold himself to be a communist, did not mention such cases of corruption or the deception of the people in relation to privatization as the Hungarians. Instead, the East Germans explained the massive lay-offs through the collapse of the COMECON market and the rise in the price of production:

Our boss told us to beware: 'now everybody is celebrating, we are opening the borders and we will have the Western currency because everyone wants to go to Western shops, but I warn you: once we have the Western currency, you will all lose your jobs.' No one believed him although we should have done – just a simple calculation. We all produced for the Eastern markets and when we started to calculate in Western currency, no one could afford to buy our products. But the boss was right: we could not sell our products; there were lots of losses and we had to stop production. In these times people lose their jobs.[15]

Unemployment was unmistakably the most negative experience that the East German interviewees had to face after the change of regimes. In contrast, this was a far less palpable fear and experience in Győr.[16] The Hungarian interviewees thought that whoever wants to work can find 'something' in Győr; indeed, anti-Roma attitudes were often justified with the reasoning that Roma people, who live from social security and child-care allowance, could find employment if they really wanted to work. For the East German workers privatization was not associated with corruption, the decline of the company or the rise of a Western rival firm such as Audi in Győr. Unemployment was, however, a constant source of tension and fear which all interviewees had to face either personally or through the fate of their relatives/partners/children. Long-term unemployment meant not only exclusion from the respected world of labour but also social isolation, which often led to severe psychological problems. Some interviewees even spoke of the clinical treatment and eventual suicide of their male partners, who were long-term unemployed.

I could tell you many examples ... there is a very close one, unfortunately, in my family. I got divorced and I had a new partner. We had a good life but then the problems started. He ran his own business, he was his own master. The company went bankrupt and I understand somewhere what it meant for him – he lost everything that he had built and worked for. He could not cope with the *Wende*. He had three suicide attempts, and even today ... he has to attend a clinic [sigh] ... I am slowly learning to what extent a man is able to just give up ... I don't know how to say this ... he just sits at home the whole day and he stares into space, he does not do anything, he has no motivation. I know that it is very hard to sit at home but somehow I feel that he does not really try ... Of course, it must be harder for a man.[17]

After the *Wende*, my husband became self-employed. We moved to Hamburg but his business was not successful and he had to declare bankruptcy. My husband could not cope with the change of regimes. He became completely passive – depression. I tried everything but I could not help him. I don't blame myself. I wanted to return to Jena, I had all my friends here. He stayed in Hamburg, we met a couple of times and he said that he would move back to Jena but he died one-and-a-half years ago. No, it was not depression [later: he committed suicide]. It was not his fault ... he could not find his place after the bankruptcy.[18]

As the above two citations show, the worst aspect of unemployment was not the material decline (although this was, too, mentioned) but the loss of face in front of people, which had very negative psychological consequences. The interviewees, who were affected by long-term unemployment, would often mention that their working relatives/friends/acquaintances refused to believe that they could not find work, and some even held them to be lazy people, who live on social benefits. Many voluntarily chose to lock themselves away in order to spare the regretful comments. Those who agreed to give me an interview all said that they made a conscious effort not to fall into this trap: they used existing networks that were formed in the GDR or joined other communities (e.g. one female production worker did voluntary work for the trade union) and self-help groups (the son of one of the interviewees, who found no regular employment for many years, joined a group of unemployed people who exchanged services).

In the second dimension (subjective evaluation of the standard of living) we can also observe striking differences between the two groups. The overwhelming majority of the German interviewees reported improvement in their material conditions: those who had work spoke of material prosperity, which allowed them to build family houses, buy new cars and spend their vacations in exotic foreign countries, while the unemployed positively mentioned the improvement of services and the supply of consumer goods. The Hungarian interviewees, on the contrary, held their material situation to be the continuation of the 'narratives of decline': they all reported stagnation or the decline of their standard of living, which they considered to be the most painful experience of the change of regimes. The Kádár regime was calculable: even though the urban skilled workers admitted that the regime held no great perspectives, there were realistic goals for them: an urban flat or a family house in the country, a car, a weekend plot and regular holidays. The new regime offered them no such perspectives; even those who said that they could maintain their former standard of living claimed that they no longer have to support their children, but that if they had to they would have to content themselves with a poorer quality of life. Those who had school-age children spoke bitterly of the rise of the new material inequalities:

I don't want the Kádár regime back even though I did have a much better life back then. I could spend my holidays abroad, at the beaches of Yugoslavia and

Bulgaria. I had a very active social life. I could go everywhere, to concerts, cinema and theatre ... I think that [the change of regimes] benefited only a narrow group of people: managers, economists and lawyers. My sister works as an accountant and she makes a lot of money. I am not envious but I don't think that such differences in the wages are justified. Perhaps people were not very rich in the Kádár regime, but real misery was also rare. ... And I am really afraid that this will affect my children ... Both are clever [and] I am so proud when their names are listed among the excellent students. My son studies in an elite high school and the parents of his classmates are all managers, lawyers and bankers. My children are not demanding and they fully understand that we can't afford as much as others. But I really feel guilty because they are left out of so many things ... When there is a school excursion and we pick up my son, I always tell my husband: leave the car at the back of the car park so that the other children won't see that we have such an old car.[19]

In the mirror of the Hungarian interviews, the loss of material security was a dominant experience of the change of regimes. In the research the overwhelming majority of the workers reported that they lived worse now than they had in the past. In order to make ends meet, many interviewees had to renounce such 'luxuries' as travelling, eating out in restaurants (let alone expensive ones) and maintaining a car. People who lived in single income households, were in a particularly bad financial situation. They reported to have experienced the most radical decline:

My husband is an alcoholic. Our problems started when he lost his job because the state farm was closed and he could find no other job because he has no education. He felt very desperate; he started going to the pub, and then he went more and more frequently ... the only reason for this was that he lost his job because before that he was a very good man, he did everything for his family, he worked overtime and he built this house with his own hands. And he never drank before. We never had any serious arguments, he loved his children, and ... I can only tell you that he was a very, very good man [she cries]. I am different, I am a fighter but now I am so much scared of what will happen to us. What will happen if I lose my job? I told my daughter-in-law yesterday that I am so much afraid of the future. If I can't buy my medicine, I can't work. If I can't pay the bills, we will accumulate debts. If we are indebted, they [the creditors] will sell our house. Why did I work then so hard in all my life? So that this damned government should make us homeless? They have no right to dispossess me and chase me out of my own house! Why can't I pay my bills? Because our wages are so low that it is impossible to make ends meet! Medgyessy[20] should try to make a living from 52,000 HUF![21]

The above story cannot be considered as an exceptional case. I interviewed a female skilled worker who got divorced, and she provided for her three children from one wage in the Kádár regime until she met her second husband. At the time of interviewing she lived on disability pension. Her second husband was a technician in Rába and they raised one common child. After her illness, the family sold their urban flat and they moved to a nearby village, in the hope that life would be cheaper there:

> In Győr we lived in a condominium; heating was very expensive, and we thought that it would be cheaper to live in the country. We spent all our savings, and now we literally live from one wage to the next, believe it or not. We support only one child, we spend only on the basic necessities and here we are, because the wage is so low. My husband earns 100,000 HUF but after taxation he brings 70,000 home including the child-care allowance. And he is a leading technician. In the 1980s we lived much better and we had to support four children back then. We fed them, they went to school, and we could still maintain a car, buy a TV, video, other things. But now we can buy nothing. *I think that the Kádár regime was much better for us than this system.*[22] Because it gave something also to the poor. There were not such great differences between people. Today, one to one-and-a-half million people live in real misery in Hungary.[23]

While the Hungarian interviewees unanimously held the working class to be the main loser of the change of regimes, the East Germans would rather criticize the crystallization of social hierarchies in the new regime. The unemployed mentioned that they were 'second-class' consumers in the German society because they could afford considerably less than their acquaintances with a job. However, while in Hungary many workers continued to measure the success of the government against the standard of living, the East Germans expressed no wish for a return of the Honecker regime. Not even Jan, who lost his job and his home in the new regime, considered 'the workers' state' a viable alternative. In the East German case we can observe a gradual shift towards post-materialistic values: the unemployed Dora could have found a job in Hamburg but she decided to live in Jena because of the proximity of her friends; many workers called attention to the new, environment-friendly technologies which cleared the air of the town; many explicitly criticized consumption for consumption's sake and some participated in self-help groups or did some other forms of voluntary work. In Hungary, the workers explicitly complained of the loss of existing networks; no one mentioned voluntary work; and many Hungarian rural female workers expressed an explicit wish for the return of the Kádár regime, when their families had a safer and often better life. In the Hungarian case material values continued to dominate political thinking. Since they saw no alternative value system to consumerism, the feeling of deprivation and frustration was prevalent among the interviewees.

The perceived lack of social integration takes us to the third dimension (interpersonal relations). Here we can find a common criticism of a capitalist society, which can be explained through the shared experience in a system, which advocated more egalitarianism. Interviewees in both groups reported negative changes in interpersonal relations: working-class communities are destroyed as a result of lay-offs and a fierce competition for jobs, people at the workplace are individualized and atomized, solidarity declines and everybody is focused only on himself/herself. People consciously reduce private contacts because they are afraid to open themselves up and display their weaknesses, which others can use against them. German interviews used military terms to express the intensification of competition: they spoke of lonely fighters (*Einzelkämpfer*), two-third society (*Zwei-Drittel Gesellschaft*)[24] and racing society (*Ellbogengesellschaft*). Interviewees in both groups recalled the collegiality and intensive community life under socialism with a sense of loss:

> In the past we regularly held festive occasions in the housing estates when neighbours sat together and had a chat. Today no one wants something like that. They don't want to sit together and discuss their things because they might reveal something that benefits the others. Today everybody is scared of *sharing his ideas, things or troubles with the others* because it might put him in a disadvantageous position.[25] In my opinion today the regime does not want real communities at the workplace or anywhere else. Below a certain level they don't even want really close contacts between people.[26]

While the Hungarians typically argued that their deteriorating material situation forced them to reduce social contacts (they could no longer afford restaurants, parties and common holidays),[27] the East Germans explained the disintegration of the old communities through the fierce competition characteristic of the new regime. They argued that technological development renders part of society redundant, which creates a sharper competition for jobs than they experienced in the old regime. This results in an extensive individualization in society, the loss of the old collegial, communitarian spirit and more intensive fighting against the rivals at the workplace, the reduction of private contacts among colleagues, secrecy (to prevent others benefiting from individual knowledge) and atomization. Workers in both groups stressed that under the socialist regime people related differently to each other: communities were stronger and interpersonal relations were less directed towards profit-making, social advancement or material interest. More people were willing to work voluntarily and freely for the community than under the new regime. The disintegration of workplace communities was thus an equally negative experience for both groups – it is not accidental that this was the dimension which triggered the most similar criticism of the new regime.

The Hungarians would typically speak of the material decline of the middle class (in which they counted themselves) while the East Germans criticized the growing social gap between the privileged part of the middle class (professors, doctors, lawyers and managers) and the production workers. Many explicitly recalled the more egalitarian climate of the GDR with a sense of loss:

> Today the [occupational] hierarchy is a lot more visible than in the GDR but this is clear. In the past the regime promoted egalitarianism that people should stick together, they should always be in a community and a blue-collar worker should be respected as much as an engineer. Today they advocate exactly the opposite: that there should be greater and greater differences among people, sharing is wrong and the only thing that matters is how much you have – my horse, my house, my wine cellar and so on. Now, what do you think will happen? Of course, there will be great differences! In the past a young engineer made as much money as we did. We did more if we had black work. We worked for doctors and professors, and they were happy that we did the job because there were no service companies. Today these people constitute a separate caste and I have to tell you: you can meet more and more young engineers and managers who look down on production workers. Some even don't greet me when they see my dress although they are much younger than my age. I can't stand this arrogance. In the GDR there were no such differences. I don't care about whatever career he makes but it is very annoying if someone treats you like that.[28]

It should be noted, however, that the East German workers had no objection to a working-class career for their children. They were only concerned about the requirement that it should be a profession or a trade, which gives them work. The Hungarians, on the contrary, considered working-class life to be utterly hopeless; those who wanted to secure the future of their children all intended to send them to college. They unanimously agreed that a worker cannot make a normal living in Hungary. They bitterly recalled that they could all save enough money to buy their own homes under the Kádár regime; they saw no chance for their children to acquire a flat without parental or grandparental help in the new regime.

As the above comparison shows, the structural differences between the two countries essentially shaped the everyday experience of postsocialist change. The peripheral experience of post-Fordism in Hungary was reflected in the workers' construction of the 'narratives of decline', which blame the failure of catching-up development on external factors, and frequently follow the logic of conspiracy theories. The essentially similar critique of the new regime developed in the third dimension, however, suggests that the workers had a shared human experience under social- ism, which they recalled with a sense of loss. This experience was voiced similarly by the workers of the two groups, albeit their fears differed: Hungarians were mainly afraid of the material decline while the East Ger- mans' greatest fear was unemployment. This experience, however, did not discredit the new regime in the eyes of the East German workers as much as was the case in Hungary. Hungarian interviewees had no direct experience of the change of the political regime: none participated in demonstrations, and many maintained a distance from 1989:

> It was not important for me to have a say in politics. I don't want to embellish the truth but for me these [free elections] were not so important. If I want to be honest, I had my secure existence, I lived my life and we raised our chil- dren. I achieved everything, which was possible *at my level.*[29] For me it was not the most important in what kind of issues I should have a say. I worked twelve hours a day. I also worked during the weekends. This is my honest answer to you.[30]

While the East Germans identified themselves with the *Wende* (either be- cause they did not like Honecker's dictatorship or because they supported German unification or both) the Hungarians did not feel that it was *their* change of regimes. For the majority, it was the 'business' of the elite, and as disappointment grew with the worsening of their material situation, so did people lose trust in the democratic institutions, which were believed to breed corruption, the rule of the rich over the poor, and dishonest and deceitful practices with which everybody associated privatization:

> I don't know what people profited from 1989. I had a more relaxed life under socialism, and I think that the majority of Hungarian people lived better under the Kádár regime [than they live today]. When this democracy came in, they sold everything that was movable in this country. I think that it is a horrible sin to privatize hospitals, the electronic and gas industries, the ambulance because the new proprietors will rob the working people of all their savings and prop- erty. We learnt this in the Party school and it is true. Today's Hungary is ruled by plundering capitalism. There are no regulations, no law and no respect for morality. Everybody steals as much as he can.[31]

> Whatever is privatized becomes more expensive. And I don't think that they [private companies] will pay high taxes. State funds disappear somewhere … For instance in Rába. When they privatized the company, they gave some shares to the workers. What can a poor man do? He will sell his shares to the managers at a low price. This is how it worked. In this country everybody stole only for himself. Take the limited companies. Everyone earns only the minimal

wage – on paper. And they laugh at those who are registered normally because they earn a lot more money, which is not taxed. They are young and they don't mind how this [practice] will affect their pension.[32]

Those who harboured left-wing sympathies were strongly opposed to privatization. However, those, who declared themselves to be 'committed' anti-communists had an equally negative opinion of privatization and the working of capitalism – the only exception being that they blamed the malfunctioning of Hungarian capitalism on the communist functionaries, who in their opinion continued to govern the country:

> It was the dream of my youth to be self-employed, in today's term: entrepreneur. But I hate this new term because it can be applied to practically anything today. No one respects individual skills or good craftsmanship. If I have money, I can open a restaurant, a beauty salon or a pharmacy. But it does not mean that I know something of the trade or the profession. If you have money, you don't need to know anything and you just employ people who know the business. But I would never equate this with the entrepreneurs of the past, who mastered their profession. I think that entrepreneurship underwent a huge dilution. Those who work hard are downgraded in this system. The only thing that matters is how you can sell things – no one is interested in the quality. It is a very superficial system, with very superficial values, this is my opinion.[33]

Hungarian nationalism was also evoked in this respect:[34]

> I have a firm trust in Hungarian youth because they study, they go abroad and sooner or later they will also found their own companies. They [the communists] were in a favourable situation after 1989 but they lack the moral standing and education and I am sure that our young men will take over their places.[35]

Ost develops the argument that in Poland the liberal intellectuals betrayed the alliance with the working class, which had been formed in the Solidarity movement, and in response the disappointed workers chose to vote for the right or the extreme right, which promised them the restoration of national pride and the protection of the interests of the 'little man'.[36] In the Hungarian case we cannot speak of an alliance between the workers and the intellectuals after 1956; my research concludes that workers were not familiar with concepts of self-governance or self-management developed by left-wing intellectuals, who were critical of state socialism, and many interviewees did not consider free parliamentary elections as something that were very important for their life or their identity.[37] The corruption, which they directly experienced with privatization, greatly undermined the credibility of democratic institutions and market economy, which instead of the promised and expected prosperity only gave them a stagnating or outright declining standard of living and the experience of a sharpening material inequality between the workers and the new, bourgeois classes (managers, bankers, lawyers, doctors and businessmen – in other words, those who can be seen as the winners of the change of regimes). Like their Polish counterparts, many Hungarian workers were susceptible to nationalistic-populist 'catchwords', which operate with a concrete enemy picture: 'foreign', exploiting capital, multinational enterprises, which take the profit out of the country, etc. The feeling of *ressentiment* was intensified by the 'conspicuous consumption' of the new elite, which rendered their own impoverishment all the more visible. The reason this was possible was because the weakness of the state found many receptive ears: workers argued that a strong government was needed which would take a firm stance against global capital.

Thus, Hungarian workers expressed strong doubts about the change of regimes and the newly established democracy that many did not feel to be theirs. These doubts, however, failed to translate into a criticism of capitalism. Instead, workers spoke of a special, Hungarian model of capitalism, where the government acts as a mediator between the interests of multinational and domestic companies, and between the interests of the workers and capitalists. There are a number of reasons why the Hungarian political left failed to profit from the workers' disillusionment with 'actually existing' capitalism. Apart from the aforementioned differences between the German and Hungarian working-class mentalities, it is worth pointing out the absence of an anti-capitalist, left-wing public in Hungary; even committed left-wing voters argued that none of the political parties represented labour interests. The spectacular exclusion of the working class from the Hungarian political arena and the weakness of the trade union movement strengthened the faith in a strong state and government: workers thought that the state stands above classes, and that therefore it would do something for the 'little man'.

It cannot be said that the East Germans were not critical of the new democracy. They, however, made no difference (as did the Hungarians) between Western capitalism, globalization and 'national' capitalism. Neither did they hold the uniformly rejected Honecker regime to be a special East German path towards modernity. They counted such institutions and social practices to be the positive heritage of the GDR, which can be easily incorporated into the new left-wing ideologies: socially responsible thinking, the strengthening of communities, more social solidarity and the increase of reciprocity in social life. This East German 'identity' – if we understand it as open towards communitarian values and less consumption-oriented than the more materialistic West – can be easily reconciled with a post-materialistic value system, which stands in direct opposition to the materialistic Honecker regime. Therefore many interviewees declared themselves to 'be in agreement' (*einverstanden*) with such political 'catchwords' as environmental consciousness, sustainable development and greater social responsibility. The East Germans did not criticize globalization; on the contrary, many workers thought that the multinational companies established new jobs, and they brought capital and innovation to Jena. They had a positive attitude towards the multiculturalism of university life and they spoke positively of the appearance of foreign students in Jena;[38] some criticized only the *Deutschrussen* (ethnic Germans, who lived in the ex-Soviet Union, and were given German citizenship).[39] Anti-Fascist education played an important role in the political and social thinking of this age group: they all argued that war is the most horrible experience, one that humankind should avoid at any price (the overwhelming majority were born after the Second World War), and even the committed anti-communists refused to compare the Nazi dictatorship with the Honecker regime because the former was held to be a lot more monstrous. There was one man among the interviewees, who recalled memories of the Nazi period:

> Contemporary propaganda glorified heroes and it exploited that the Germans were so stupid that they believed in the cult of heroes. The most beautiful death, they said, is that of the soldier's death. I remember [similar] news, which the newspapers reported: 'we regret to say that our son, Michael or Helmuth died for the people and for the *Führer*'. Sure, he died in the war but not for the people or for the *Führer* – but because of the war. And there was the uniform – I don't say that the women were proud that their husbands died but many Germans were infatuated with the uniform. If he [the man] was an officer, he could have any woman he wanted because they were so much infatuated with his decorations. Privates counted for nothing; but an officer – he was already somebody in Germany … Women stayed alone, they worked and they raised their children without a man. But the same happened in Russia. At the very end, none was proud that their husband or their father died for the people and the *Führer*. It was a horrible and unjust war, which Germany started and she was punished for it. We started the war – Hitler – but many Germans also wanted this war because they wanted to rob and they wanted to govern the whole world in a German fashion. We were the first to bomb England and then the English aeroplanes returned and destroyed our cities. This was the punishment. But Germany started the war.[40]

Opinions of West Germany varied across the interviewed group, but in general the East Germans were more conscious of the nature of peripheral capitalism than the Hungarians. Many admitted that before the *Wende* they felt inferior to West Germans because they were strongly influenced by the stereotypical representation of capitalism (Western workers are more educated, more creative, more diligent and more motivated than the Eastern workers of the state-owned enterprises, who were held to be less disciplined and 'brainwashed' in the West).[41] The postsocialist years modified these stereotypes as East Germans grew more critical of capitalism: they said that albeit their technology was not as advanced as the West German, their skills were comparable, and in fact they had to be more creative than the West Germans because of the technological deficiencies (one example that they mentioned: if a machine went wrong, they had to be able to fix it while the West Germans called a maintenance man). The majority were sceptical of the prospects of catching up with West Germany: they estimated that levelling would take at least twenty to thirty years. While they were familiar with the terms *Wessi/Ossi*,[42] they argued that this distinction would disappear in their children's generation:

> There are some typical East German products, which many people miss – certain food brands and the like – but it has got nothing to do with quality, people are just used to them. And they are in demand only in the new provinces (*neue Bundesländer* – the former GDR) ... In the EU every country becomes a market and all member states seek to sell their own products. This does not mean that people have to live worse but they have to find other means of living if they can't sell a given product. We will have no more such [planned] economy as the GDR was, where some giant enterprises supply the whole domestic market, and I fully agree with this. I don't feel any constraint to buy only domestic products.[43]

> In the GDR the worker was at the same [social] level as his boss. I can't imagine that a *Wessi* [boss] can be the same. I had an aunt who immigrated to West Germany at a young age, and she married a West German man. She saw everything differently, she looked down on us. She was not interested in our things, if something was *Ossi*, for her it was not good enough. She sent us a package, which she filled with pudding powder and secondhand clothes because they are good enough for the poor *Ossis*. So I did not even want to hear of this aunt. After the *Wende* we also went to the West, and we met simple people similar to us – it was totally different, they were friendly and they did not look down on us. We exchanged presents, and we slept at their place – in short, it was a totally different relationship than with this aunt.[44]

As the above story shows, the feeling of inferiority was often nourished by humiliating experiences with West Germans. The interview partners, however, all argued that German unification benefited the 'nation' and that their children would not know of the intensive propaganda campaign that the two German states led against the social order of the 'other' Germany. Women workers recalled stories when the West Germans thought that the East German children only learnt communist rallying songs in the kindergarten and that they were indoctrinated at a very young age. One reason why many East Germans identified with post-materialistic values was rooted in this feeling of inferiority: they sought to show to the 'West' that there were things which the East Germans did better than the West Germans, albeit their achievements went unrecognized. Women's policy, education and the health-care system ranked high in the list of the institutions which were mentioned positively. Mothers unanimously argued that their children received more attention in the East German school system than after the *Wende*. They also mentioned that the teachers in the GDR system paid attention to the individual needs of the children, and they invested more time and energy in the education of those whose school grades were lower than the average. Many of my female interview partners participated in a special form of education: *Frauensonderklasse* (women's school). They positively recalled that they met women who were in a similar situation: working mothers with small children. The networks that were established in the *Frauensonderklasse* continued to be important for the women, although most of them lost their jobs in Zeiss.

The last issue that I would like to examine is the subjective evaluation of labour interest representation after the change of regimes. The Hungarians were unanimously pessimistic in this respect: in Rába several trade unions operated, which fragmented the membership, and were considered to be incompetent and powerless even by the interviewed shop stewards. In Zeiss the chairperson of the enterprise council was of the opinion that labour interest representation works effectively in large companies such as Zeiss, but small and medium-sized firms often (informally) ban trade union membership, and workers will not protest because they want to keep their jobs. This is how he evaluated the Honecker regime in retrospect:

> The GDR was a worker and peasant state. Workers got certain things and they were free to study. They got more opportunities to study than the children of engineers and officers. And there was a certain community culture in the factories. They sought to show that people are equal so the enterprise hierarchy was less visible. There were no differences in the social interactions between people: you could talk to everybody in the same way regardless of whether someone was a worker, a foreman or a manager. People who were socialized in this system find it harder to accept that the managers get detached from the production workers ... For me the decisive question is what chance a man has in his life, how he can influence his own personal development. And in my opinion in this new regime a man has more chance.[45]

The above citation reflects a crucial difference between the East German and Hungarian evaluations of the change of regime. Even the homeless Jan would have agreed with the chairperson of the enterprise council of Zeiss in that a man has more chance in the new system than in the old one. The Hungarians, on the contrary, felt that even the limited goals that they could attain under the Kádár regime (a flat, a house, a weekend plot and regular holidays) were taken away from them by the new regime.

The results help us to explain the ambiguous evaluation of the Kádár regime. The vision of greater social and material equality is confused with a longing for a strong state, order and an autocratic government, which we can observe in many interviews. While the German interviewees identified with the *Wende* and not even the unemployed wanted Honecker' state back, only few Hungarians thought that they profited from the change of regimes and the newly established democracy. Thanks to their negative experiences, which triggered the above described 'narratives of decline', the majority were opposed to 'Western' capitalism, and they thought that a stronger state and a distinctive Hungarian path towards modernity would offer a panacea for the sores of peripheral development. While East Germany's greater success of integration into the capitalist world economy was accompanied with a change of mentality and the appearance of post-materialistic values, in Hungary nationalism seemed to be the only alternative to a capitalism, which disappointed and effectively impoverished many people.

Notes

1. Citation from an interview conducted with Jan (52), an East German male production worker in a hostel for homeless people in Jena in 2004. He had been a skilled worker in Zeiss until 1989; at the time of interviewing he was unemployed.
2. For an early discussion of my Hungarian case study see: E. Bartha. 2003. 'Munkások a munkásállam után. A változás etnográfiája egy volt szocialista "mintagyárban"', in D. Némedi (ed.), *Kötőjelek*. Az Eötvös Loránd Tudományegyetem Szociológiai Doktori Iskolájának Évkönyve, Budapest: ELTE Szociológiai és Szociálpolitikai Intézet.
3. http://epp.eurostat.ec.europa.eu/tgm/table.do?tab=table&init=1&plugin=1&language=en&pcode=tsieb010
4. Zs. Ferge. 2011. 'A magyarországi szegénységről', *Info-Társadalom-Tudomány*, 54.
5. M. Pittaway. 2011. 'A magyar munkásság és a rendszerváltás', *Múltunk* 1.
6. Ferge, *Társadalmi áramlatok*, 165–67.
7. For an influential left-wing criticism of post-Fordism see: L. Boltanski and E. Chiapello. 2005. *The New Spirit of Capitalism*, London: Verso Books. From the Hungarian literature see: Somlai, *Társas és társadalmi*.
8. Szalai, 'Tulajdonviszonyok'.
9. The local name of Rába.

10. Citation from an interview conducted with Péter (49), a Hungarian male production worker in Rába in 2002. He was a skilled worker and a shop steward.
11. Citation from an interview conducted with Brigitta (51), a Hungarian female production worker in Rába in 2002. She was a skilled worker.
12. Citation from an interview conducted with Judit (50), a Hungarian female production worker in Rába in 2002. She was a skilled worker, who had finished secondary school.
13. Information from an interview conducted with Thorsten (52), the chairperson of the enterprise council in Zeiss in 2003. He was a production worker before 1989, and a member of the Church opposition. He received a religious education, for which he was negatively discriminated at school, and was rejected admission to an art school which he wanted to attend. One of his sisters emigrated to West Germany, which rendered him even more suspicious in the eyes of the authorities. After the *Wende* he became actively involved in the reorganization of the trade union.
14. Citation from an interview conducted with Gisela (48), an East German female production worker in Zeiss in 2003. She was a skilled worker.
15. Citation from an interview conducted with Vera (53), an East German female production worker in Zeiss in 2003. She was a skilled worker.
16. Official unemployment was less than 5 per cent in Győr at the time of interviewing, while it was twice as high in Jena.
17. Citation from an interview conducted with Gisela (48), an East German female production worker in Zeiss in 2003. She was a skilled worker.
18. Citation from an interview conducted with Dora (56), an unemployed mother in her flat in 2004. She started her career as a skilled production worker in Zeiss; she got a university place as an economist-engineer, which she could do in parallel to her work. Zeiss supported adult education by offering free learning days for the workers. Dora's husband was also engaged in adult learning, and both became engineers in the company. In West Germany, however, the degrees of the 'Marxist schools' were not always good references; in addition, those, who finished these schools were often held to be 'indoctrinated' communists.
19. Citation from an interview conducted with Judit (50), a Hungarian female production worker in Rába in 2002.
20. Péter Medgyessy, Hungarian Prime Minister between 2002 and 2004.
21. Citation from an interview conducted with Flóra (53), a Hungarian unskilled female production worker, in her house in 2004. She started working in Rába as an unskilled worker; later, on the urge of her husband, she joined the cooperative farm and she raised pigs and cows for extra income. At the time of interviewing she worked as an unskilled production worker in a packing factory.
22. Stress is mine.
23. Citation from an interview conducted with Éva (54), a Hungarian skilled female production worker, in her house in 2004.
24. The two-third society refers to a society where two thirds of the population belongs to the middle or upper classes. In Germany it was argued that the two thirds would mean the employed while one third is condemned to live from social and unemployment benefits and/or black work. In Hungary the interviewees did not use this term; however, the citations suggest that they would have agreed with the concept of the reverse two-third society developed for postsocialist Eastern Europe: that two thirds of society fell out of the middle class.
25. Stress is mine.
26. Citation from an interview conducted with Karl (51).
27. Utasi conducted a nationwide survey in Hungary, from which she concluded that the poorer classes can only count on their immediate families and that

the social trust is very low in Hungary. See: Á. Utasi. 2008. *Éltető kapcsolatok: A kapcsolatok hatása a szubjektív életminőségre*, Budapest, Új Mandátum.

28. Citation from an interview conducted with Jörg (57), an East German male production worker in Zeiss in 2003. He was a skilled worker.
29. Stress is mine.
30. Citation from an interview conducted with Péter (49), a Hungarian male production worker in Rába in 2002.
31. Citation from an interview conducted with Tibor (67), a retired male manager, in his house in 2004. He started his career as a skilled worker in Rába and he obtained his degree in adult education.
32. Citation from an interview conducted with Éva (54), a Hungarian skilled female production worker, in her house in 2004.
33. Citation from an interview conducted with Miklós (51), a male self-employed plumber, in his house in 2004. He started his career as a skilled worker in Rába, and he also spent two years in the Soviet Union as a guest worker, which was a good 'business' because the workers earned very well. As he proudly said, he could thank this only to his good work because he was never a member of the party, and he disliked communists (his father was a peasant, whose land was nationalized and he never forgave the communists for this). Miklós became self-employed in 1981; in the 1990s he expanded his business but he could not bear the stress, and after an operation he gave up his business and accepted a job as a maintenance man. He also worked black to secure a 'normal' income.
34. For a collection of studies which discuss the increasing appeal of right-wing, neo-nationalistic ideologies see: D. Kalb and G. Halmai (eds). 2011. *Headlines of Nationalism, Subtexts of Class*, Oxford and New York: Berghahn Books.
35. Citation from an interview conducted with István (56), a male caretaker, in his house in 2004. István started his career as a skilled worker in Rába, and he was offered a college place but then they found out that he attended a Church school and he had to interrupt his studies. He added that 'he was lucky' because at that time 'they' (the communists) could change his world-view. After 1989, the Church helped him to find a job.
36. D. Ost. 2005. *The Defeat of Solidarity: Anger and Politics in Postcommunist Europe*, Ithaca, NY: Cornell University Press.
37. These findings are in line with Haraszti's study of the Red Star Tractor Factory (*Vörös Csillag Traktorgyár*). Workers would explicitly tell him that he will not be long in the factory because he is educated, which reveals a perceived social distance between the workers and the intellectuals. The Red Star Tractor Factory belonged to Rába for a while; Ede Horváth recalled his fight with the 'Budapest people', whom he wanted to discipline, but the workers self-consciously resisted: the district party secretary was invited to attend a meeting where the workers told the manager their grievances and they demanded remedies. Horváth recalled the case as evidence that the interests of economic efficiency, which he advocated, were sacrificed to political interests, which the district party secretary represented, who wanted to pacify the angry workers. Horváth, *Én volnék a Vörös Báró?*
38. Jena has a famous university, Friedrich-Schiller-Universität, which accepted many ERASMUS exchange students and other students from all over the world.
39. The East German interview partners all knew prior to the interview that they would talk to a Hungarian citizen. Therefore, those, who held strongly nationalistic views were unlikely to have participated in the research.
40. Citation from an interview conducted with Ernst (75), a retired male skilled production worker, in the club of Zeiss pensioners in 2003. He held himself to be a social democrat, and was strongly anti-communist (he called them social

Fascists). The only reason he did not leave Jena after the Second World War was his attachment to his mother and his birthplace. Ernst was satisfied with his pension, and he proudly recalled that after the *Wende* he could travel to Las Vegas.

41. Concerning this topic, some interview partners explicitly told me that they would not give an interview to a West German researcher because of the mutual stereotypes. In this respect, it was an advantage that I also came from a socialist country; furthermore, Hungary was held to be a 'friendly' and politically 'liberal' country, where East Germans could meet their West German relatives. The 'liberalism' of the Hungarian Communist Party was observed by the SED functionaries as well.

42. Pejorative distinction between the West and East Germans.

43. Citation from an interview conducted with Peter (58), a male skilled production worker in Zeiss in 2003. Peter was strongly opposed to communists; he said that he was given a college place after he started working in Zeiss but he interrupted his studies because he was pressurized to join the party.

44. Citation from an interview conducted with Martha (52), a female accountant, in her house in 2003. Martha started her career as a skilled production worker in Zeiss, then she finished a training course and she continued working in Zeiss as an accountant. She lost her job in 1991, and she tried several small jobs (call centres, selling books, raising fish, selling *Tupperware* and packing). She said that her main motivation was not money – her husband earned well but she wanted to be in company. Eventually, she got a job as an accountant in the firm where her husband worked.

45. Information from an interview conducted with Thorsten (52), the chairperson of the enterprise council in Zeiss in 2003.

SQUARING THE CIRCLE?
The End of the Welfare Dictatorships in the GDR and Hungary

The book has discussed the rise and fall of the welfare dictatorships in three main chapters: in the formative period when political reforms and a compromise with the working class were still on the agenda of the party in both countries, in the 'flourishing' period of the 1970s when the standard-of-living policy provided for the political stability of both regimes, and the declining phase of the 1980s; and the third chapter investigated the relationship between the working class and the political power. The Hungarian case study illustrated the process which triggered the social crisis of the welfare dictatorships as the failure of the standard-of-living policy undermined the legitimacy of the ruling regime. Lastly, in the fourth chapter, we compared how the workers of the two countries evaluated the welfare dictatorships in retrospect. The similar chronology of the welfare dictatorships suggests that in spite of the differences in the political climate and the trajectory of economic reforms in the two countries, there is a greater similarity between the two regimes than what is assumed in the national literature of these two countries, which tend to underline the specificity of the East German or the Hungarian regime. The comparative study of the party's policy towards labour in both countries, however, showed that there were essential similarities between the functioning of the two regimes and the accommodation of working-class demands. The relationship between the party and the working class likewise followed a similar trajectory in the two countries. These similarities explain the lack of political activity of the working class during the reign of the welfare dictatorships and after the collapse of these regimes.

The book interrogated the question of why the East European socialist regimes, which claimed to reign in the name of the working class, had lost the political support of the workers. I sought to show that the period of economic reforms of the 1960s was crucial for the formation of a social settlement between the ruling Communist parties and the working class. The party refused to change the power structure; instead, it offered economic concessions to the workers. Financing these concessions took the regimes beyond their economic means, and this provided the background to the collapse in the authority of the regime during the 1980s. The chapters of the book followed the history of the welfare dictatorships in a chronological order. In the elaboration of the conclusions I will use a thematic order to discuss three main issues. These are: (1) the similarities in the party's policy towards the working class in the two countries, (2) the development of the relationship between the working class and the Communist parties, and (3) the evaluation of the results of the welfare dictatorships in the GDR and Hungary, and the political balance of the two regimes in the eyes of their working classes. The three themes are, of course, interrelated but I seek to avoid repetitions.

The history of welfare dictatorships started in the 1960s. The possibilities of extensive industrialization were exhausted; this was reflected not only in the social dissatisfaction of industrial workers (this is a euphemistic formulation since dissatisfaction triggered a revolution in Hungary!) but also in the deteriorating economic indexes (and these were officially published data). Both countries experimented with the reform of their planned economies (they were not the only ones in the region) in order to increase the efficiency of socialist economy. The restoration of capitalism was, of course, not on the political agenda; the reforms were in fact far even from the establishment of a socialist market economy. The East Germans thought that if they gave greater independence to the enterprises, this would result in a 'quasi-capitalist' competition among them, which could substitute for free market. Hungarian reformers developed an enterprise reform along the same lines. Nonetheless, in its original, radical form the Hungarian reform sought to extend the private sector, thus giving further concessions to capitalism. A socialist market economy could, however, only be a bold dream, even in Hungary.

What did the reform policy communicate towards the working class? They probably understood little of the great objectives. The great majority only saw that the managers demanded more and better quality work from them, while the government sought to decrease real wages.[1] Furthermore, in the Hungarian case workers had to witness the enrichment of other social classes (managers and peasants), which added fuel to their anti-reformist mood. The 'dogmatic' communists could easily exploit the general dissatisfaction of industrial workers in both countries. True, reformers also promised to increase the welfare of the population, but only after the reform policy would bear fruit. Workers, however – understandably – refused to wait for the better future. They rather demanded the immediate 'realization' of socialism.

The negative social reception of the reform largely determined the party's policy towards the working class in both countries. The new social message of the party was simple and it sounded very encouraging after the 'lean years' of the Stalinist era. As we have seen, the Hungarian standard-of-living policy can be easily matched with the unity of economic and social policy in Honecker's GDR. Both sought to win over the working class for the party through the increase of consumption. I go a step further: both the Kádár and the Honecker regimes based their legitimacy on the general improvement of the standard of living of the population and the establishment of a strong, socialist 'middle class'. Of course, the idea was not to promote *some* members of the industrial working class; the Communist parties promised social advancement to *all* industrial workers. Under 'advancement' the majority of workers meant the improvement of their material conditions. After the failure of the reform, both governments took several measures to emphasize this new policy and demonstrate the advantages of welfare dictatorships. Workers' wages were increased in both countries, and further improvements were on the agenda. Honecker cut back structural investments that his predecessor, Ulbricht, had urged, and he increased the targets of consumer goods (let us recall: in the reform era, workers complained that there were not enough goods in the shops and Professor Hager, a member of the Political Committee, declared in front of the local party leadership that the most important task of the communists was to satisfy consumer needs in the district). There was also an important advancement in the field of social policy: several measures were taken to improve the situation of working women and families. And one should not forget about the flat policy: the acquisition of one's own home became a realistic objective for workers in both countries (the East Germans based this on state redistribution while the Hungarians mobilized private initiative and family resources).

While this new, consumption-driven legitimacy was successful at the beginning because it increased the popularity of welfare dictatorships and effectively prevented the formation of a leftist working-class opposition, it had in store at least as many political dangers as it could solve. Firstly, we saw that workers were not fully satisfied with the standard-of-living policy even at the time when they could get the most of it. In the subsequent years the failure of the standard-of-living policy seriously undermined the regime's legitimacy and the popularity of the party and government in Hungary (as we have seen, in the 1980s dissatisfaction was mounting even among party members). The credibility of the welfare state of the GDR was damaged by the fact that it could not compete with the West

German levels of consumption, which were strongly propagated in the Western media. Further, the state could only finance this policy through further credits from West Germany. In exchange, they had to give ideological concessions (e.g. the introduction of *Reiseantrag*, which enabled East Germans to leave the GDR).[2] An even greater problem was that they could not convince their citizens: they could profit more from the welfare dictatorship than from the West German capitalism, and if we take the 'summary of criteria' – as they called it – then socialism provides for the people better than the rival world system. As we have seen from the last public speech of the chief manager of Zeiss, leading executives may well have truly believed that this was the case. However, no one asked for the political opinions of workers under Honecker; more precisely, whoever spoke of the problems of socialism was stigmatized as an 'opportunist' and was excluded from the party. That dissatisfaction still existed even among party members can be demonstrated by the fact that in the autumn of 1989 several party groups reported to the factory party committee that the supply of goods in the shops 'failed to match with the declarations of the leaders'.[3] It is obvious that this was not a new phenomenon (the former party reports usually gave a long list of the 'current difficulties', which prevented the satisfactory supply of certain consumer goods). We have every reason to believe that in the 1980s East German workers were also dissatisfied with the party's policy towards the working class, just like their Hungarian counterparts; nonetheless, they remained silent because of the massive political repression.

In the second part of the book I stressed that the party's policy towards the working class had certain positive elements. I argued that the party was forced to take into account the demands of industrial workers, and the welfare dictatorship itself can be regarded as the result of a compromise between the party and the working class. If, however, we would like to explain the ultimate and spectacular failure of this policy,[4] we need to focus on the negative aspects, namely on the question: what was *not* achieved through this compromise?[5] The most important contradiction was that while the party sought to win over the political support of the working class with the help of a new consumption policy, its leaders were unable to break with the old, dogmatic left in their propaganda and organizing methods.[6] They could not build capitalism in a Soviet-controlled Eastern Europe; but they also regarded an opening towards the new left as unthinkable both for external and internal reasons. The contradiction was thus left unresolved: 'time stood still' both in the movement and the communist ideology.[7] The old political slogans remained (however, they became so meaningless that in Hungary the majority of youth maintained a distance from the party),[8] and the party revived some of the progressive

goals of the old labour movement (community building, workers' education). While the latter, however, sought to emancipate workers culturally
and politically, the party's intention was to depoliticize the working class,
encouraging them to turn towards the social and private spheres rather
than towards the political one. The documented conflicts between the
brigade leaders and the managers suggest that the party had no intention
of increasing the workers' role in the decision-making process.[9] The self-
governing and self-organizing ideas of the new left were absolutely excluded as alternatives: socialist communities in both the GDR and Hungary were organized by the state from above.[10]

This 'consumerist turn' of the party has, however, gradually changed the
social significance of the working class. Even in the dogmatic GDR it was
reported that the 'new privileged class' consisted of people who possessed
Western currency. Workers were ranked as 'ordinary consumers', who had
to content themselves with the Eastern products that they could buy in the
ordinary shops.[11] The 'working class' became an empty category since many
executives remained members of the working class (they were classified according to the workplace that they had at the beginning of their career),[12]
and as we have seen, engineers also frequently asked: who is regarded as a
worker after all in the GDR? In Hungary in the reform era, workers complained that other social classes – who did not work as hard as they the workers did, and consequently did not deserve the better wages – had a better
life than the working class. In the 1980s they again felt that the government
wanted industrial workers to pay the price for the new reforms. All these – in
the eyes of the public – inevitably downgraded the social status of the working class. The party leadership of both countries lacked the political will to
face the question: how can one 'modernize' not only the inefficient industrial sector but also the relationship between the workers and the Communist parties? The leading Hungarian economists were under the spell of private economy, while the East Germans were preoccupied with the question
of the 'adequate and satisfactory' supply of the population with consumer
goods. The elites of both countries lost sight of the 'actually existing' working class. There is a sad irony in the fact that in this book I have consistently
discussed the party's policy towards the working class while in the reports of
the 1980s we can, indeed, rarely meet even the term 'worker'! This is particularly striking in the East German documents, where the 'working class'
never appears as a concrete social group; it only serves as an abstract point of
reference. With the exhaustion of the resources of the welfare dictatorships,
the party had no more relevant social message to the working class.[13]

The consistent persecution of any leftism other than official Marxism
was another important consequence of the establishment of welfare dictatorships.[14] Fearing that a leftist critique of the regime would endanger the

tacit compromise with the working class, the party used hash retaliation against left-wing intellectuals, but also against workers, who criticized the rise of new inequalities. We have seen that in East Germany, critics of the Exquisit shops and Intershops were ruthlessly expelled from the party even if they were 'old' comrades or they enjoyed authority in their party organizations. In the Hungarian case the party gradually gave up its ideological positions throughout the 1980s: as the information reports show, the old communist slogans were discredited even in the eyes of the party membership.[15] The East Germans were compelled to continue the ideological battle with West Germany but the rivalry with the strongest European economy discredited any effort to convince the people of the superiority of socialism. Western unemployment was a permanent slogan of the socialist propaganda, but as informants complained, workers argued that the unemployment benefit in the West was higher than the East German wages, while the West Germans could all the more convincingly boast about their supermarkets full of goods and the newest auto models (whereas the East German had to wait long years for a car). True, the Western new left criticized consumer society and its materialistic values. Nonetheless, the party strictly excluded concepts of self-organization and self-management from any public discussion. Community life, as we have seen, was organized from above; and even though it did give communal experience to the workers, the political role of these communities was insignificant – in line with the party's intention to eliminate competing power structures.

Thus, the welfare dictatorship *necessarily* formed a political consciousness, which was open towards capitalism. From the perspective of the regime, the standard-of-living policy was successful in both countries because it prevented the formation of an active working-class opposition upon the model of Solidarity. Left-wing intellectuals – lacking access to the public sphere and mass support – did not pose a serious threat to the rule of the party. However, the legitimacy of the welfare dictatorships was fragile because it was not based on a strong, export-driven economy (as Ulbricht planned and hoped for) but on the 'doctored' results of an inefficient plan economy – and on the credits, which led to the severe indebtedness of both countries and the threat of a state bankruptcy.[16]

At the end of the 1970s the signs of the crisis of the welfare dictatorships were already visible in Hungary. The government sought to overcome the growing economic troubles by further extending the private sector and the market. Since they could not increase the wages in the state sector, they allowed the population (including industrial workers) to acquire an additional income in the growing private sector. Extra work, of course, had its harmful social consequences: society became more individualistic, the general health condition of the population (mainly that

of men) deteriorated and people had less time for socialization and rec-
reation.[17] The opening of these new opportunities, nonetheless, further
decreased the political activity of workers: after finishing work, people
had no time for 'normal' social activity, let alone for political organization. As we have seen from the reports, even older workers sympathized
with young people, who had no time for the party because 'they had to
establish first their own homes'. For Hungary, we can argue that further
marketization met the 'full understanding the population'. If we think of
the answers to the question 'Would you call the capitalists back?' and the
reports on the public mood, we can state that capitalism hammered on
open doors in Hungary.[18]

In the GDR, foreign loans enabled Honecker to continue his welfare
policy until the end of the 1980s (although we should not forget about the
political repression, which forced many people to hide their true opinion
about the regime!). The population felt the economic troubles later than
the Hungarian people did – but the practice of watching West German
television programmes (*Westfernsehen*) rendered visible the gap between
Eastern and Western standards of living that was increasing, rather than decreasing. While in the 1970s people were happy to acquire a flat on newly
built housing estates, in the 1980s there was much less hope that the state
would 'catch up' with Western levels of consumption. The capitalist products that could be bought for Western currency or in special shops (Intershops, Exquisit and Delicat shops) likewise reinforced perceptions of the
economic superiority of capitalism. Young people in the 1980s did not see
the kind of future in the system that their parents' generation had.[19]

The policy described above determined the relationship between the
party and the working class; therefore, it is not surprising that we can
observe several similarities. The reform era in both cases marked an important phase in the history of this relationship. It can be easily demonstrated
that the political opinions of industrial workers were not indifferent to the
party leaders since their strong criticism and the mounting social dissatisfaction of the working class were important factors in the failure of the
reform. In a somewhat paradoxical way, this was the last time when there
was a social dialogue between the workers and the party, and both sides
considered it important to find a political compromise. In the Hungarian case – apart from addressing the problem of increasing materialism
and individualism in society – there were also attempts among workers to
criticize enterprise democracy and existing management practices. In the
GDR, workers mainly complained of the contradictions of the NES, but
there were also signs of a more far-reaching criticism of the system (e.g. the
distance between the leaders and the grass-roots members of the party). In
both cases, the party showed a marked interest in working-class opinions

and it even demonstrated a willingness to consider their demands. Judged by the high number of comments, at that time at least part of the working class held the party to be a workers' party, and they believed that it would be able to renew its social settlement with the people.

The dialogue between the party and the working class ended, however, in failure in both countries. Both regimes thought that the satisfaction of consumers' demands would render it unnecessary to renegotiate the terms of its tacit agreement with the workers. The re-hardening of the political line in the 1970s effectively blocked the channels of communication between the party and the working class.[20] Real workers practically disappeared from the party documents in the GDR, while in Hungary in the 1980s, when the political climate became more liberal, the working class was taken even less seriously as a social category. Fearing to upset consolidated, socialist society in the GDR, and interested in pro-market rather than leftist alternatives in Hungary, ruling parties showed little interest in restarting social dialogue; and as the events of 1989 showed, neither did the workers believe that the party could have carried through reform. As for the party, even though its leaders failed to admit, the welfare dictatorship implied a consumerist turn – and in this sense, it was a concession to capitalism. The ideological victory of the dogmatists was therefore illusory, and in the long run it inevitably led to the loss of the credibility of the official communist ideology among the workers.

I have demonstrated this process – the growing distance between the workers and the Communist parties – in the third chapter of the book, in the light of the local party materials (and we could reasonably assume that the local party officials were far from the national politics, thus, the observed similarities indeed express similar experiences in the two countries). Workers – and this was stressed in several documents in both cases! – had no interest in joining the party; even in the politically more repressive GDR the party organizers had to accept that many workers refused candidacy with the reasoning that they 'had no time for party life'. Thus, administrative measures were used in both cases to maintain an 'adequate' working-class proportion in the party: they recruited people who did not have a strong Marxist conviction, were religious or did not show much enthusiasm towards the party (in the East German case, as we have seen, there were even instances when the managers completed the membership forms for the workers). The result was that workers constituted the largest group (60–70 per cent) of those whose party membership was terminated because they 'neglected party life' (they did not pay party dues, or failed to attend party meetings).

Based on the available sources and the interviews that I conducted with workers in both countries, it is unlikely that party life indeed gave the workers a communal experience, a feeling of 'belonging together'. In the Hungarian case we saw that in the 1980s few people joined the party out of true communist conviction, and the great majority of working-class youth kept a conscious distance from the party and the movement. The East German documents give us little information about the political conviction of the party members; but it is by no means surprising if we consider that everybody who criticized the official line of the party – the leftist critique, for instance the criticism of the Intershops was even less tolerated than the complaints about the shortage of consumer goods – was excluded from the party, even if the bold critic was an 'old' comrade or held a leading position in the party group. Given that the party members had to consider carefully what they said publicly at the party meetings, it is unlikely that they remembered these events as communal gatherings. At the great national festive occasions (which were abundant in the GDR) representation was even more important: thus, we can only read speeches where the population 'fully and enthusiastically' supports the official line of the party, they are very happy to participate in the heroic struggle of the party for the 'regular and satisfactory supply of consumer goods',[21] and in general, they do their best to 'prove themselves worthy of the confidence of the party'. All these could not really reinforce the impression of the workers that they belong to a freely chosen political community.

German interviewees also pointed out the difference in the level of tolerance in the GDR and Hungary: they remembered Hungary as a 'Western' country. I have already cited a report of 1964, where the East German delegates who visited Hungary complained about the 'lenient' and 'too informal' working style of the Hungarian party groups, and they critically observed that 'they had not seen enough posters and other forms of visual agitation in the factories and at the universities'.[22] The information reports of the Honecker era completely lack any real information on the political mood of the population in comparison to the Hungarian sources. Only the sharpening criticism of the supply of the population with consumer goods displays the crisis of the regime: in 1988, for instance, we can read a very critical report of the supply of cars and bicycles, where the informant openly complained about the bad quality of Dacia and Lada cars, and he added that there was a shortage of Wartburg cars and bicycles in the country. Such open criticism was, however, indicative of the social crisis of the regime.[23]

In the third part of the book we examined in detail, to what extent workers regarded the party as a political community. In the Hungarian case we can hear several complaints even in the reform era that the party fails to represent the interests of industrial workers, and that the labour movement was undermined by the rush for money and the increasing social inequalities, which alienated people from the party. The welfare dictatorships and the standard-of-living policy increased the popularity of the party in the short run, but at the price that this policy oriented people towards consumerism. Already in the 1970s we can read several complaints that workers had no time for party or community life, they were becoming indifferent, the old comrades were growing tired of political work, and young people were not attracted by the movement.[24] In the 1980s lower-level officials criticized not the spread of materialism and individualism but the fact that workers could hardly keep their former standard of living even if they undertook extra work. We have already observed that the Hungarian Communist Party, whose reformers lived under the spell of 'more market', gradually gave up its ideological positions. The state party as a political community started to disintegrate well before the actual political collapse of the Kádár regime.

In the GDR we can only make guesses regarding how the party membership related to the regime under Honecker. The widespread habit of *Westfernsehen* and the argument that people who could buy in the Intershops formed a privileged class in the GDR at best calls into question the assumption that all party members would have been so 'dogmatic' as it is stated in the reports. Shortage of certain consumer goods was mentioned even in official political documents; for instance, some party members thought that there would be less *Antragsteller* if there were more goods in the shops, or another party member complained that he had to run his legs off until he could buy the required parts for his car. It is also not accidental that when the base organizations – eventually – sent negative reports about the public mood of people to the factory party committee, they criticized that the supply of consumer goods contradicted the optimistic declarations of the party leaders.[25] Everybody could be convinced of the shortage of consumer goods even prior to 1989; but the repressive political climate prevented the formation of a clear picture about the size of the camp which rejected the Honecker regime. Angelusz referred to this phenomenon as the 'double opinion climate' since the hiding of the true opinions of the people concealed the fact from the regime how much it had lost the support of the population.[26] Biermann's last public speech nicely demonstrates how far the SED leaders were indoctrinated by their own propaganda. The regime suffered a decisive political defeat at the moment when the opening of the Hungarian borders and the mass escape of the citizens to the West dispelled the illusion that the 'masses' backed the Honecker regime. In the interviews workers saw no direct relationship between party membership and political conviction; nonetheless, there were many instances when workers regarded those who joined the party as 'careerists'. Many interview partners said that for this reason they refused candidacy, or they chose to undertake positions in the brigade or the trade union, where less power was concentrated. Neither the surviving archival documents nor the interviews give evidence that the East German workers held the SED to be a political community.

While it can be safely argued that both the MSZMP and SED lost the political support of the working class before 1989, it is a more difficult task to compare the political balance and heritage of the two regimes. In the Hungarian case the market reforms introduced in the 1960s bore fruits in the 1980s when the incomes from the private sector compensated for the stagnation of real wages. The careful political liberalization went in parallel with the political liberalization, which, as we have seen, strongly influenced party life. While the Hungarian party membership could already openly criticize the government's policy at public forums in the second half of the 1980s, the East German party members had to wait with criticism until the last days of the Honecker regime. The examples that I introduced in the third chapter of the book, nicely illustrate why East German citizens regarded Hungary as a 'free' country. The East German interview partners happily recalled the holidays that they had spent in Hungary even ten to fifteen years after the collapse of socialism.

This leads us to the discussion of an important difference between the two regimes. Hungarian reformers of the 1980s already envisaged a socialist market economy; whereas Honecker, on the contrary, nationalized existing private companies in the 1970s. Both regimes supported community life; however, as we have seen, work in the private sector increasingly absorbed Hungarians. Thus, they had less time for communal life; it is not accidental that already in the 1960s party organizers complained that people grew more individualistic and the communal spirit declined. The East Germans, on the contrary, maintained the model of collectivist socialism until the end of the Honecker regime. We can argue that while in Hungary the private sector compensated for the stagnating industrial wages, in the GDR intensive community life offered a 'substitute' for the missing consumer goods and services. This can be understood literally since communal network and the strong social solidarity gave practical aid under the conditions of general shortage: people exchanged services and goods through these private networks.[27] In the Hungarian case individualization meant that people concentrated their efforts on family-based farms or businesses, while in the East German collectivist model people relied on the strong communities at the workplace and in the neighbourhood to secure the 'adequate and satisfactory' supply of consumer goods of their households.

When I discussed community life, I frequently mentioned – and supported by several citations from the interviews – that both the East German and Hungarian interview partners recalled the former socialist communities with a sense of loss.[28] They frequently contrasted the communal values of socialism with the egoism, ruthlessness and 'pushing' demanded by the new regime, which goes hand in hand with a drastic decline in social solidarity (the Germans spoke of *Ellbogengesellschaft* and *Einzelkämpfer*). This positive evaluation of socialist communities was independent of how people judged the successes and failures of actually existing socialism. It can be explained through the shared community experience under socialism that workers in both countries were responsive to a community-based, anti-capitalist criticism.[29]

Before we would draw our own balance, it is worth taking a look at how the workers themselves evaluated the achievements of the Kádár and Honecker regimes. We need to stress that the difference between the political climates of the two countries was reflected also in the workers' memories of the two regimes. Although it cannot be said that the socialist system left only negative memories behind in East Germany – in fact, most of the interview partners said that the school system, health care system and child care institutions were better, and the state gave more support to the working mothers than after 1989 – no one wanted to return to Honecker's GDR. Most of the interview partners said that they were happy that the *Wende* had come. Many people did, however, also express a disappointment with the new, capitalist regime: it was the members of the younger age groups in particular (people between forty and fifty) who argued that they went to the street for a different society in 1989. They believed that in the united Germany there would be more social justice, and ordinary people would have more say in the issues that affected their country. The new political system received a rather negative evaluation: most workers thought that there was only formal democracy in Germany, and that politics was decided by economics. Interview partners typically argued that the politicians who sat in parliament had lost touch with the reality of ordinary peoples' lives, a comment on planned reforms that cut welfare benefits. Although they held Honecker's GDR to be a dictatorship, all of them, including those who said that they were opponents of the socialist system, objected to the equation of the GDR with the Nazi regime.

Even if we take into account that workers' experiences of postsocialist transformation was different in the two countries, the Kádár regime received a more ambiguous evaluation in the Hungarian interviews than the Honecker regime did in the GDR context. While people argued that there were many positive features of the socialist system (full employment, and social security), it was typically skilled urban workers who told me that material security did not compensate them for limited political freedom. Many of my interview partners who lived in the villages, however, reported a marked decline of their standard of living, and they claimed that they would have preferred to live in Kádár's Hungary. There were more female interview partners than men who would have liked to have the previous regime back. Regardless of how the socialist system was seen, the change of regime was felt to be a period in which society was cheated. It was commonly believed that privatization benefited the old elite and that ordinary people received nothing of 'peoples' property'. Many workers argued that foreign companies only bought local firms to close them and eliminate business rivals, and they were only interested in acquiring the Hungarian markets. They would blame the old elite for selling off national property. Although a majority of my interview partners considered the collapse of the Kádár regime to be inevitable, they thought that political power was appropriated by a narrow group of people who could capitalize on their connections. The change of regime is thus related with exclusion and dispossession. Interestingly, these negative experiences did not challenge capitalism as such: most of my interview partners argued that something went wrong with the implementation of capitalism in Hungary and they typically expected the state to intervene and protect them from the harmful effects of globalization.[30]

If we would like to draw a balance on the grounds of the above, we have to stress: the policy of the party towards the working class failed socially and it essentially did so before the political collapse of the two regimes. We can regard the Kádár regime politically more successful in as much as it created a better, more 'liveable' (and likeable) socialism. In the light of the life-history interviews the massive ideological repression of the Honecker era essentially proved counter-productive, because not even those who identified themselves as socialists (or even communists) wanted his regime back, and neither did those who – after years of unemployment – could have counted themselves among the losers of the change of regime.[31] The limited contacts between East Germans and Hungarians also suggest that it is not true that material security offered sufficient compensation for a lack of political freedom: even though East German workers enjoyed a higher standard of living than the Hungarians, the evaluation of the Kádár regime shows an ambiguous picture not only in Hungary; the East German interview partners who had visited socialist Hungary also remembered it as a 'Western' country – which, on the basis of the relative economic achievement of the GDR can only be explained through the experience of greater freedom.

In the introduction of the book I raised two questions: (1) Why was there no working-class opposition to the regime in the GDR and Hungary? and (2) Why did the working class remain passive in 1989? The book has attempted to show that the establishment of the welfare dictatorships created a social and political context which integrated the working class into the regime but at the same time oriented the people towards consumerism.

After the end of the reform era of the 1960s a tacit political compromise was concluded between the party and the working class. The party refused to share political power with the working class, and it also consistently rejected concepts of self-organization and self-management, which could have offered a 'third road' between state socialism and capitalism. Instead, it offered concessions to the workers in the material sphere in the form of the standard-of-living policy. The original emancipating goals of the old left were replaced by the increase of consumption levels of the population 'at any price'. In the 1970s, at the peak of the standard-of-living policy, the welfare dictatorships achieved certain popularity.[32] This legitimacy was, however, essentially fragile because it was based on the satisfaction of consumer needs for which the planned economies were ill prepared.

The welfare dictatorships effectively prevented the formation of a strong working-class opposition to the regime like the example of Solidarity in Poland. Workers' attention focused on the establishment of their own homes and the acquisition of durable consumer goods – all these gave satisfaction to people, who experienced prosperity after the 'lean years' of their childhood. More and more people grew disinterested in politics – but the party itself had no intention of reviving the old spirit of the movement.[33] In Hungary the market reforms and second jobs provided for the de-politicization of the working class, while in the GDR harsh retaliation threatened anybody who criticized the line of the party.

And now we arrived at the point why this policy was risky for the regime. The most obvious reason is that it deluded not only the workers but also those who were in power. In the 1980s everybody – including the Western observers – thought that the two regimes were socially consolidated since the narrow groups of oppositionist intellectuals posed no serious danger to the party. Nonetheless, beyond the surface the social and economic basis of the welfare dictatorships was crumbling throughout the 1980s. The competition with the West European market economies pushed their planned economies beyond their limits, which resulted in the huge indebtedness of both regimes. The tacit political compromise with the working class rendered it impossible to cut back the old, traditional industries, which at the time produced ever greater losses.[34] All these greatly burdened the economies of both countries and undermined the basis of the social compromise, which ensured their legitimacy.

Thus, the consumerist turn of the party and the collapse of state socialism can be seen as interrelated events. The welfare dictatorships effectively de-politicized industrial workers, who regarded themselves as consumers rather than as members of a revolutionary class. After they were disappointed in 'actually existing' socialism, they placed a renewed hope for 'catching up' with the consumption levels of the advanced Western countries under capitalism. In Hungary there were visible signs of the loss of credit of socialist ideology even in the eyes of the party membership. The East Germans consistently 'enforced' the party line in public but they had to use repressive methods to silence people. The result was that few dared address the contradictions between ideology and the political practice of welfare dictatorships (and those who did were excluded from the party or had to content themselves with worse jobs). While Hungarian party members could openly criticize the policy of the party in the 1980s, in the GDR, as we have seen, a 'political action' was created out of a harmless carnival publication, which cost the jobs of the authors.

The welfare dictatorships were therefore open to the right but closed to the left as left-wing critics were accused of undermining the compromise between the party and the working class and thereby threatening the political stability of the regime. Workers felt alienated from the party, which failed to fulfil the promise that they would live at the same material level as did their Western counterparts. Paradoxically, when workers 'chose' capitalism in 1989, they only followed the internal logic of the development of welfare dictatorships. To what extent workers were 'indoctrinated' by consumerism is nicely illustrated by the answers to the question of 'Would you call the capitalists back?' or the naïve belief that a market economy would create a more just (and equal!) society. The fact that after forty years of socialism people believed that there is more equality under capitalism, well illustrates to what extent socialist ideology lost credit in the eyes of the working people. This loss of credit (because in the euphoria of 1989 people dismissed *every* anti-capitalist critique as 'communist propaganda') largely contributed to the easy triumph of neoliberal capitalism in Eastern Europe, and the lack of labour resistance. Thus, the welfare dictatorships – albeit unintentionally – did a great service to the capitalist 'class enemy'.

Throughout the chapters we have seen that in spite of the similarities between the labour policies of the SED and MSZP towards the working class, the differences of the industrial development of the two countries could not be levelled. The large group of Hungarian worker-peasants, who were engaged in both industrial and agricultural activities, lived in the countryside and maintained the culture and mentality of the peasantry, cannot be found in the GDR. The educational statistics of the two large factories likewise reflect that the Hungarian workers finished fewer classes than the East Germans in spite of all cultivating efforts of the party. The women's policy of the party was also more efficient in the GDR than in Hungary – both in the light of the statistics of women's education and the life-history interviews.

These differences between the two countries deepened after the change of regimes, when East Germany was united with the leading industrial power of Europe while Hungary experienced a more peripheral develop-ment. The East German and Hungarian working-class experiences of the change of regimes therefore substantially differed. Suffice it to mention that while the 'premature' welfare state was dismantled in Hungary, East Germany adopted the welfare system of West Germany, which counted as a 'role model' for an advanced capitalist welfare state. Employment policy after 1989 also differed in the two countries: the Germans used 'active' means (e.g. re-education, state-financed courses and jobs) while the Hungarians mainly relied on 'passive' methods (e.g. early retirement, disability pension and severance pay).[35]

The structural differences in the position of the two countries in the global world economy were reflected in the life-history interviews. The overwhelming majority of the German interviewees experienced improve-ment in their material conditions: those, who had work, spoke of material prosperity; the unemployed spoke of the marked improvement in services and the supply of consumer goods. The Hungarian interviewees, on the contrary, experienced the stagnation or the decline of their standard of living; for them this was the most painful experience of systemic change. The Kádár regime was calculable: even though the workers agreed that the regime did not offer them great perspectives, they could still achieve something: a flat, a house, a car, a weekend plot. All interviewees held the working class to be the loser of the systemic change. While the Germans complained of the crystallization of social hierarchies in the new regime, for the Hungarians the material decline was the most frequent source of complaint. While in the eyes of the German interviewees the social securi-ty that was guaranteed to all GDR citizens did not sugarcoat Honecker's state, many Hungarian workers continued to measure the achievement of a government against the standard of living. Thus, many rural women workers expressed an explicit wish for the return of the Kádár regime, when their families had a safer and often better life. In the Hungarian case material values continued to dominate political thinking. Since the major-ity of the workers thought that they could satisfy their consumer needs at a higher level in the old system than in the new one, and there was no alternative value system in the public other than consumerism, the feel-ing of deprivation and frustration was prevalent among the interviewees. Thus, materialistic values continued to dominate the political thinking of the Hungarian workers while in East Germany we can observe the spread of post-materialistic values.

The fourth chapter of the book examined two questions: the situa-tion of labour under the two regimes and the evaluation of the newly established democracies. The German interviewees considered the skilled working class to be part and parcel of the middle class and they refused to consider university education as a sole means of social advancement.[36] Many of them did not necessarily prefer university education to a good vocation for their children. This group vividly remembered the egalitarian society of the GDR, where managers, engineers and scientists did not constitute a privileged group as under the new regime. Many of them reported left-wing, some even communist, sympathies. In Hungary, however, all interviewees listed the workers among the losers of the change of regimes. Contrary to the German workers, all Hungarian interviewees reported a decreasing standard of living and the necessity to spend their savings. Workers were frustrated by the fact that they could hardly make ends meet even though they had a regular job. The majority saw the situation of the middle class (where they counted themselves) to be deteriorating. Those, who could provide for their children, wanted them to get a university degree rather than get vocational training. Many workers preserved left-wing sympathies; but they all stressed that in Hungary none of the parties did anything to improve the situation of the working class.

The second question is how the workers evaluated the two regimes in the light of the aforementioned experiences. The German picture is clear: none of the interviewees regretted the collapse of Honecker's regime, including former party members, engineers, managers, accountants and draftsmen, who experienced short- or long-term unemployment under the new regime. In general, the interviewees thought that Honecker's dictatorship was doomed to failure. Although they were strongly opposed to a comparison between Nazism and Honecker's dictatorship (anti-fascism – perhaps as a result of education – was characteristic of this age group) the workers excluded the opportunity of a new, communist dictatorship. The degree of opposition to Honecker's state is indicated by the fact that not even the long-term unemployed wanted the GDR back.

Capitalism, however, received a more ambiguous evaluation from the German workers. Although they experienced the positive side of post-Fordism, they also observed many of its drawbacks, most notably structural unemployment and excessive individualization, which endangers social life. Both the workers and the unemployed criticized consumer society; they expressed a strong concern for the environment (humankind endangers its future if it carelessly exploits and destroys environment for the sake of greater profit) and they expressed a preference for a self-sustaining development.

Hungarian opinions significantly differed from the German views. The German interviewees identified with the opposition; many participated at the mass demonstrations and they thought that the people had an active role in the demise of communism. Most Hungarians identified neither with the opposition nor with the communists. They felt a strong *ressentiment* towards the groups, which benefited from systemic change and the people's property: the former *nomenklatura*, the intellectuals and the new propertied class. Privatization received a uniformly negative judgement: workers thought that the managers 'stole' the factory (they were either bribed to sell the plants at preferential prices or they bought them themselves). Workers had a strong distrust of multinational companies, which were believed to have destroyed Hungarian enterprises, and which were seen as possible rivals. In addition, they took the profit that they made in Hungary out of the country and exploited the local workforce. It is therefore not surprising that the majority were opposed to Western capitalism, from which they experienced only the drawbacks: production declined, the factory laid off four-fifths of its pre-1989 personnel, the enterprise lost its former prestige (which was stressed by Audi buying up the large hall that Rába built) and the Rába workers experienced a material decline. The feeling of *ressentiment* was intensified by the 'conspicuous consumption' of the new elite: many complained that under socialism the social distance between the workers and the managers had been much less marked than under the new regime.

Thus, Hungarian workers expressed strong doubts about systemic change and the new democracy. These doubts, however, failed to translate into a criticism of capitalism.[37] Instead, workers spoke of a special, Hungarian model of capitalism, where the government acts as a mediator between the interests of multinational and domestic companies and between the interests of workers and capitalists. There are a number of reasons why the Hungarian political left failed to profit from the workers' disillusionment with 'actually existing' capitalism. Apart from the aforementioned differences between the German and Hungarian working-class mentalities, it is worth pointing out the absence of an anti-capitalist, left-wing public in Hungary; even committed left-wing voters argued that none of the political parties represented labour interests. The spectacular exclusion of the working class from Hungarian politics and the weakness of the trade union movement strengthened the faith in a strong state and government: workers thought that the state stands above classes, and it would do something for the 'little man'.

The results help us to explain the ambiguous evaluation of the Kádár regime. The vision of greater social and material equality is confused with a longing for a strong state, order and an autocratic government, which we can observe in many interviews. While the German interviewees identified with the *Wende* and not even the unemployed wanted Honecker' state back, only few Hungarians thought that they profited from systemic change and the new democracy. Thanks to their negative experiences under the new regime, the majority were opposed to Western capitalism and they thought that a stronger state and a special Hungarian road to capitalism would offer a panacea for peripheral development. Thus, East Germany's greater success of integration into the capitalist world economy was accompanied by a change of mentality, which is less characteristic of Hungary.

By undertaking a comparative study of the welfare dictatorships that developed in the GDR and Hungary under Honecker and Kádár, this book offers a historical explanation of why the workers did not defend the workers' state in countries where there had been no open working-class protest against the ruling regimes since the 1960s. Taking this argument a step further, it argues that factory histories can offer a new perspective on the turning point of 1989 by focusing on what made the socialist regimes weak internally, rather than concentrating on opposition activists, or political elites. While the party in both countries consistently refused to seek a political compromise with the working class, both types of welfare dictatorships – the reformist and collectivist – offered economic concessions in exchange for political passivity. Since the continuation of the standard-of-living policy increasingly collided with economic performance in both countries, the party's refusal to renegotiate the terms of agreement with the working class left the regime much weaker socially than both its leaders and the Western advocates of post-totalitarian theories of the Communist state assumed. The book argued that under the given historical conditions the Kádár regime created a more liveable and likeable socialism than Honecker's variant of socialism, where repression was used much more extensively than in Hungary. There was, however, one basic similarity in the politics of repression, which was applied in both countries: fearing upsetting the compromise with the working class, the regime did not tolerate any leftism other than official socialism, and consistently used harsh retaliation against leftist critics of the welfare dictatorships, who pointed out that the regime reinforced materialistic values and oriented working-class consciousness towards consumerism.

This experience contributed to the illusion of generalized welfare and the high consumption levels that capitalism could generate for them. Despite the more painful experience of transformation in Hungary, idealized views of capitalism persisted, leading to a desire for national capitalism as opposed to the bleak realities of globalization on the eastern periphery of the European Union.[38] In East Germany, the anti-capitalist ideology of the party that was rather ineffective under the Honecker regime seemed to have a greater appeal after the regime's collapse: my interview partners mostly blamed the regular functioning of the capitalist system for what they saw as negative social phenomena such as growing inequalities, egoism and social insecurity. The newly established democracy also received a more negative evaluation in Hungary than in East Germany. The ambiguous evaluation of the Kádár regime suggests that many Hungarians would reconcile themselves to an authoritarian regime in exchange for a more secure and calculable life. It seems that it is not only the memory of the collectivist and reformist models of the welfare dictatorships that differ but they also had a different impact on the development of workers' political attitudes after 1989.

It is, however, important to point out essentially common human experiences of the change of regimes. It needs to be stressed that the interviewees in both groups were pessimistic about the situation of the trade union and labour movements. The Hungarian workers explained the absence of working-class protests through the closing of large industrial enterprises and the disintegration of the trade union movement. The German interviewees argued that at the workplace everyone is a lonely fighter, who is only interested in how to keep his or her job (even at the expense of others). Workers in both groups thought that the labour movement was weakened and disoriented under the new regime. They did not expect significant social changes in the near future; however, in the micro-world of everyday human interactions they expressed a longing for a more intensive community life than what is available for the lonely fighters.

Notes

1. Large industry was state-owned industry.
2. On the condition that they lose their East German citizenship.
3. See the section in chapter 3 entitled *The End of Silence*.
4. I refer back to the question put in the introduction: why did workers refuse to defend the workers' state?
5. The question of why workers refrained from independent class action after 1989 has rarely been addressed in the otherwise rich literature on state socialism. In the introduction I referred to Linda Fuller, who argued that the East German workers felt alienated from the intelligentsia. See: Fuller, *Where was the Working Class?*. This book, however, attempted to prove that working-class interests were to a large extent accommodated by the welfare dictatorships. The analysis of the labour policy of the party therefore offers a historical explanation for workers' integration into the regime and their eventual refusal to defend the workers' state. Földes gave a good outline of the labour policy of the party after the 1956 revolution and he also argued that this policy should be taken seriously. Földes, *Hatalom és mozgalom*.
6. For the spread of hypocrisy in society see in particular the section in chapter 1 entitled *The Appearance of the New Rich*.
7. On the impact of 1968 on Eastern Europe and in particular on Hungary see: E. Balázs, Gy. Földes and P. Konok (eds). 2009. *A moderntől a posztmodernig: 1968. Tanulmányok*, Budapest: Napvilág; E. Bartha and T. Krausz (eds). 2008. *1968. Kelet-Európa és a világ*, Budapest: L'Harmattan Kiadó.
8. The decreasing appeal of the party is vividly demonstrated in the section entitled *'Would you call the capitalists back?'*.
9. Community life was rather offered as a substitute for real political participation.

10. As we have seen in the fourth part of the book, even though community-building was heavily supported 'from above', workers recalled that they used to participate in an intensive community life under socialism.
11. Criticism of the 'materialism' of the Honecker regime was harshly retaliated. See the sections entitled *New Inequalities?* and *Losing Members*.
12. Let us recall: working-class origins meant positive discrimination at the entrance exam to higher education. For Hungary, Ferge demonstrated that educational inequalities were characteristic of the Hungary of the 1960s (and later they increased further). Ferge, *Az iskolarendszer*. Solga shows that the educational mobility in the GDR also declined. See: Solga, *Auf dem Weg in eine klassenlose Gesellschaft?*
13. Burawoy's fieldwork nicely demonstrated how far Hungarian workers became disillusioned with official socialism. See: Burawoy, *The Radiant Past*.
14. It is worth recalling the cases of Domaschk and Haraszti, which demonstrate that both regimes were equally hostile to any left-wing criticism of the 'establishment'.
15. The information reports cited in the section entitled *The Failure of the Standard-of-Living Policy* are particularly illuminating in this respect and they show to what extent society became materialistic.
16. See Steiner, *Von Plan zu Plan*; Kopstein, *The Politics of Economic Decline in East Germany*; Földes, *Az eladósodás politikai története*.
17. See: Szalai, *Beszélgetések a gazdasági reformról*.
18. For a similar argument see: Szalai, 'Tulajdonviszonyok'.
19. I base this argument on the interviews that I conducted with East German workers between 2002 and 2005. Schüler found a similar difference between the attitudes of older and younger generations of female textile workers. See: A. Schüler. 1999. 'Mächtige Mütter und unwillige Töchter', in Hübner, *Arbeiter in der SBZ – DDR*.
20. See also: Földes, *Hatalom és mozgalom*.
21. The never-ending fight for the supply of the population with consumer goods itself demonstrates the consumerist turn of the welfare dictatorships disguised in the GDR as the 'unity of the economic and social policy'.
22. Bundesarchiv, Stiftung Archiv der Parteien und Massenorganisationen der DDR, DDR DY 30/IV A 2/5.
23. Bundesarchiv, Stiftung Archiv der Parteien und Massenorganisationen der DDR, DDR DY 34/14298. Information zur Versorgung der Bevölkerung mit Fahrzeugen und Fahrrädern durch die VEB IFA Betriebe.
24. It can be argued that such complaints were 'typical' of low-level party functionaries. It is, however, worth noting that in the 1980s we can mainly read negative criticisms in the local information reports. The contrast is all the more sharp if we compare these reports with the East German documents.
25. See the section entitled *The End of Silence*.
26. R. Angelusz. 2000. *A láthatóság görbe tükrei: Társadalomoptikai tanulmányok*. Budapest: Új Mandátum Könyvkiadó.
27. Pickles observed, however, that such practices were revived in many postsocialist regions (mainly in the former Soviet Union) where economic hardships persisted after the change of regimes. Pickles, *Theorising Transition*.
28. See in particular the East German and Hungarian chapters on the socialist brigade movement. In the East German case, I also found strong women's networks, which were supported by the women's policy of the party (for instance, *Frauensonderklasse*).
29. See in particular chapter 4: *Contrasting the Memory of the Kádár and Honecker Regimes*.

30. On the increasing appeal of right-wing, nationalistic ideologies see: Kalb, *Headlines of Nationalism*.

31. It is worth recalling here the story of Jan, who was homeless at the time of the interviewing and had been imprisoned in the 1980s for political reasons in the GDR. Even though he said that he would not fight against such a system, not even his experience of the new society could embellish the memory of the Honecker regime.

32. See: Angelusz, *Munkásvélemények*.

33. Földes gave a programme of how to revitalize the movement. See: Földes, *Hatalom és mozgalom*. However, as events of 1989 showed, the working class no longer opted for a new movement led by the same party.

34. Hungarian reformists warned that such a step would cause massive unemployment, which would be detrimental for the regime.

35. Ferge gives a good analysis of 'what went wrong' in Hungarian social policy after the change of regimes. See: Ferge, *Társadalmi áramlatok*.

36. It is worth recalling that a comparative study in the early 1990s found that in West Germany more people would identify themselves with the middle class than in East Germany and Hungary, where people would rather consider themselves workers. This shows that the workers' state had some lasting impact on the generation of blue-collar workers, who were socialized under socialism. See: Angelusz, 'Társadalmi átrétegződés'.

37. These findings support Ferguson's conclusions. Ferguson, *Expectations of Modernity*.

38. It could be a topic for a new book to interrogate the question of why 'catching-up development' is such a persistent myth in the East European semiperiphery. In Hungary, Erzsébet Szalai and Tamás Krausz can be mentioned as the most consistent critics of 'catching-up development'. Disillusionment with 'catching-up development' in Eastern Europe is often exploited by right-wing political parties, which operate with strong anti-Western, anti-European Union rhetorics. See: Kalb, *Headlines of Nationalism*.

REFERENCES

1. Primary Sources (published)

Autorenkollektiv der Geschichtskommission der IKL/SED Kombinat VEB Carl Zeiss Jena. 1988. *40 Jahre in Volkes Hand: Aus der Chronik des Kombinates VEB Carl Zeiss JENA, Teil 1: 1948 bis 1970*, Jena: Carl Zeiss-Stiftung Jena.

Dusza, A. 2003. *A birodalom végnapjai, Így láttam Horváth Edét*. Győr: X-Meditor Kft.

Frauenkommission der Industriekreisleitung der SED des BEB Carl Zeiss Jena. 1975. *Gleichberechtigt. Die Entwicklung der Frauen und Mädchen im VEB Carl Zeiss Jena*, Weimar: Carl Zeiss Jena.

Horváth, E. 1990. *Én volnék a Vörös Báró?*, Pécs: Szikra Nyomda.

Industriegewerkschaft Metall für die Bundesrepublik Deutschland, Verwaltungsstelle Jena/Saalfeld. 1995. *Geschäftsbericht 1993 bis 1995*. Jena.

Lenski, K. And U. Kulisch. 2001. *Thüringer Archiv für Zeitgeschichte 'Matthias Domaschk': Übersicht zu den erschlossenen Sammlungen & Dokumenten*. Jena.

Rába. A Magyar Vagon- és Gépgyár Pártbizottságának hetilapja. [The weekly of the party committee of the MVG]. 20. évfolyamtól (1968) a 41.-ig (1989).

Der Scheinwerfer. Betriebs-Zeitung der Belegschaft des VEB Carl Zeiss Jena. Jahrgänge 20 (1968) bis 41 (1989).

Tér-kép. Független nyugat-magyarországi hetilap. 1/18. 1989. június 1.

2. Secondary Sources

Adam, J. 1999. *Social Costs of Transformation to a Market Economy in Postsocialist Countries*, London: Macmillan.

Akgöz, G. 2012. *Many Voices of a Turkish State Factory: Working at Bakırköy Cloth Factory, 1932–1950*, Ph.D., University of Amsterdam.

Akszentievics, Gy. 1977. 'Ki hogyan érdekelt az üzemi demokrácia gyakorlásában?', *Társadalmi Szemle* 32(10), 94–99.

Amsden, A.H., J. Kochanowicz and L. Taylor. 1994. *The Market Meets its Match: Restructuring the Economies of Eastern Europe*, Cambridge, MA: Harvard University Press.

Andics, J. and T. Rozgonyi. 1979. 'A vállalati konfliktusok és a hatékonyság', *Társadalmi Szemle* 34(5), 48–59.

Andor. L. 2010. *Eltévedt éllovas: Siker és kudarc a rendszerváltó gazdaságpolitikában*, Budapest: Napvilág Kiadó.

Angelusz, R. 2000. *A láthatóság görbe tükrei: Társadalomoptikai tanulmányok*, Budapest: Új Mandátum Könyvkiadó.

Angelusz, R., L.G. Nagy and R. Tardos. 1980. *Munkásvélemények az életszínvonalról, a személyes anyagi és az országos gazdasági helyzetről*, Budapest: Tömegkommunikációs Kutatóközpont.

Angelusz, R., L.G. Nagy and R. Tardos, 1981. *A megfelelőnek tartott jövedelem*, Budapest: Tömegkommunikációs Kutatóközpont.

Angelusz, R. and R. Tardos. 1995, 'Társadalmi átrétegződés és szociális-politikai identifikáció', *Szociológiai Szemle* 2.

Ansorg, L. 1999. '"Ich hab immer von unten Druck gekriegt und von oben": Weibliche Leitungskader und Arbeiterinnen in einem DDR-Textilbetrieb. Eine Studie zum Innenleben der DDR-Industrie', *Archiv für Sozialgeschichte* 39, 123–65.

Auerbach, F. 1919. *Ernst Abbe: sein Leben und Wirken*, Leipzig: Akad.-Verlag.

Auerbach, F. 1925. *Das Zeisswerk und die Carl-Zeiss-Stiftung in Jena: ihre wissenschaftliche, technische und soziale Entwicklung und Bedeutung*, Jena: Fischer.

Bahro, R. 1977. *Die Alternative: zur Kritik des realexistierenden Sozialismus*, Cologne: Europäische Verlaganstalt.

Balázs, E., Gy. Földes and P. Konok (eds). 2009. *A moderntől a posztmodernig: 1968. Tanulmányok*, Budapest: Napvilág.

Balogh, J. 1977. 'A vállalat gazdasági és politikai funkcióinak kapcsolata', *Társadalmi Szemle* 32(12), 67–70.

Bartha, E. 2003. 'Munkások a munkásállam után. A változás etnográfiája egy volt szocialista "mintagyárban"', in D. Némedi (ed.), *Kötőjelek. Az Eötvös Loránd Tudományegyetem Szociológiai Doktori Iskolájának Évkönyve*, Budapest: ELTE Szociológiai és Szociálpolitikai Intézet, 117–47.

Bartha, E. 2005. 'The Disloyal "Ruling Class": The Conflict between Ideology and Experience in Hungary', in P. Hübner, C. Kleßmann and K. Tenfelde (eds). *Arbeiter im Staatssozialismus – ideologischer Anspruch und soziale Wirklichkeit. Die DDR im ostmitteleuropäischen Vergleich*, Cologne: Böhlau Verlag, 141–62.

Bartha, E. 2010. 'Transition, Transformation, "Postsocialism". Theorizing Systemic Change in Eastern Europe', in K. Csaplár-Degovics, M. Mitrovits and Cs. Zahorán (eds). *After Twenty Years: Reasons and Consequences of the Transformation in Central and Eastern Europe*, Berlin: Osteuropa-Zentrum and Terra Recognita Foundation, 13–34.

Bartha, E. and T. Krausz (eds). 2008. *1968. Kelet-Európa és a világ*, Budapest: L'Harmattan Kiadó.

Bartha, E. and T. Krausz (eds). 2011. *Háború és nemzeti önismeret: 70 éve támadta meg a náci Németország a Szovjetuniót*, Budapest: Komáromi Nyomda és Kiadó.

Bauer, T. 1975. 'A vállalatok ellentmondásos helyzete az új mechanizmusban', *Közgazdasági Szemle* 22(6), 725–35.

Bedau, K.-D., 1993. *Untersuchungen zur Einkommensverteilung und –umverteilung in der DDR 1988 nach Haushaltsgruppen und Einkommengrößenklassen auf der methodischen Grundlage der Verteilungsrechnung des Deutschen Instituts für Wirtschaftsforschung*, Beiträge zur Strukturforschung, Heft 143.

Béky, G. And Z. Zétényi. 1977. 'Szocialista módon dolgozni, tanulni, élni. Helyzetkép a brigádmozgalomról', *Valóság* 20(11), 53–63.

Belwe, K. 1989. 'Sozialstruktur und gesellshcaftlicher Wandel in der DDR', in W. Weidenfeld and H. Zimmermann (eds), *Deutschland-Handbuch. Eine doppelte Bilanz 1949–1989*, Bonn: Landeszentrale für politische Bildung, 125–43.

Belwe, K. 1990. *Entwicklung der Intelligenz innerhalb der Sozialstruktur der DDR in den Jahren 1978 bis 1989 – eine Literaturanalyse*, Bonn: Gesamtdeutsches Institut.

Bence, Gy. and J. Kis [Mark Rakovski]. 1983. *A szovjet típusú társadalom marxista szemmel*, Paris: Magyar Füzetek.

Bence, Gy., J. Kis and Gy. Márkus. 1992. *Hogyan lehetséges kritikai gazdaságtan?*, Budapest: T-Twins.

Berend, T.I. 1990. *Hungarian Economic Reforms 1953–1988*, Cambridge and New York: Cambridge University Press.

Berend, T.I. and Gy. Ránki. 1974. *Gazdaság és társadalom. Tanulmányok hazánk és Kelet-Európa XIX-XX. századi történetéről*, Budapest: Magvető.

Berend, T.I. and Gy. Ránki. 1985. *The Hungarian Economy in the 20th Century*, London: Croom Helm.

Berényi, J. 1974. *Életszínvonal és szociálpolitika*, Budapest: Kossuth Kiadó.

Bessel, R. and R. Jessen (eds). 1996. *Die Grenzen der Diktatur: Staat und Gesellschaft in der DDR*, Göttingen: Vandenhoeck & Ruprecht.

Beyme, K. 1996. *Transition to Democracy in Eastern Europe*, London: Macmillan.

Bittner, R. 1998. *Kolonien des Eigensinns. Ethnographie einer ostdeutschen Industrieregion*, Frankfurt and New York: Campus Verlag.

Bittner, R. 1999. 'Kleine Leute, Bastler, Pfadfinder – Transformationsfiguren. Ethnografische Versuche im Feld des regionalen Strukturwandels', *Berliner Debatte Initial* 10(2), 18–28.

Bittner, R. 2000. 'Rund um die Uhr – ostdeutscher Arbeiteralltag im Kraftwerk Elbe', *Zeitschrift für Volkskunde* 96, 203–17.

Bittner, R. 2001. 'Der kleine Mann – Paradoxien und Ambivalenzen einer ostdeutschen Arbeiterfigur vor und nach der Wende' in R. Hürtgen and T. Reichel (eds), *Der Schein der Stabilität: DDR-Betriebsalltag in der Ära Honecker*, Berlin: Metropol-Verlag, 217–28.

Boltanski, L. and E. Chiapello. 2005. *The New Spirit of Capitalism*, London: Verso Books.

Borbély, S. 1976. 'A pártszervezetek gazdaságirányító és -ellenőrző munkájáról', *Társadalmi Szemle* 31(6), 3–16.

Bossányi, K. 1978. 'A versenyképesség stratégiája. Beszélgetés Horváth Edével, a Rába vezérigazgatójával', *Társadalmi Szemle* 33(11), 51–59.

Bossányi, K. 1986. 'Made in Rába', in: I. Matkó (ed.), *Ipari Közelképek*, Budapest: Ipari és Kereskedelmi Minisztérium Kiadása, 27-42.

Bouvier, B. 2002. *Die DDR- ein Sozialstaat? Sozialpolitik in der Ära Honecker*, Bonn: Dietz.

Bozóki, A. (ed.). 2000. *A rendszerváltás forgatókönyve: kerekasztal-tárgyalások 1989-ben: alkotmányos forradalom: tanulmányok*, Budapest: Új Mandátum Könyvkiadó.

Bőhm, A. and L. Pál. 1979. 'A bejáró munkások társadalmi-politikai magatartása', *Társadalmi Szemle* 34(10), 50–58.

Bőhm, A. and L. Pál. 1985. *Társadalmunk ingázói – az ingázók társadalma*, Budapest: Kossuth Kiadó.

Bródy, A. 1983. 'A gazdasági mechanizmus bírálatának három hulláma', *Közgazdasági Szemle* 30(7–8), 802–7.

Bryant, C.G.A. and E. Mokrzycki. 1994. *The New Great Transformation? Change and Continuity in East Central Europe*, London: Routledge.

Buda, I. 1977. 'A munkaerő-gazdálkodás és a bérgazdálkodás időszerű feladatai', *Társadalmi Szemle* 32(5), 38–48.

Burawoy, M. 1985. *The Politics of Production: Factory Regimes under Capitalism and Socialism*, London: Verso.

Burawoy, M. and J. Lukács. 1992. *The Radiant Past: Ideology and Reality in Hungary's Road to Capitalism*, Chicago and London: The University of Chicago Press.

Burawoy, M. and K. Verdery (eds). 1999. *Uncertain Transition: Ethnographies of Change in the Postsocialist World*, Lanham: Rowman & Littlefield Publishers.

Burawoy, M. 2000. 'Introduction: Reaching for the Global' in Burawoy (ed.), *Global Ethnography: Forces, Connections, and Imaginations in a Postmodern World*, Berkeley and Los Angeles: University of California Press, 1–38.

Búza, M. 1977. 'Az üzemi demokrácia érvényesítése: a gazdasági vezetők kötelessége', *Társadalmi Szemle* 32(9), 67–71.

Casals [Pavel Campenau]. 1980. *The Syncretic Society*, White Plains, NY: M.E. Sharpe.

Cornelsen, D. 1988. 'Die Wirtschaft der DDR in der Honecker-Ära', in G.-J. Glaeßner (ed.), *Die DDR in der Ära Honecker*, Opladen: Westdeutscher Verlag, 357–70.

Csizmadia, E. (ed.). 1995. *A magyar demokratikus ellenzék 1968–1988*, Budapest: TTwins.

Dániel, A. 1979. *Karambol*, Budapest: Móra.

Deutscher. I. 1949. *Stalin: A Political Biography*, New York: Oxford University Press.

Djilas, M. 1983. *The New Class: An Analysis of the Communist System*, San Diego: Harcourt Brace Jovanovich.

Dogossy, K. 1987. *Baj van a gyerekkel*, Budapest: Kossuth Kiadó.

Egerszegi, Cs. 1977. 'Termelési tanácskozás és üzemi demokrácia', *Társadalmi Szemle* 32(9), 81–85.

Erbe, G. 1982. *Arbeiterklasse und Intelligenz in der DDR. Soziale Annäherung von Produktionsarbeiterschaft und wissenschaftlich-technischer Intelligenz im Industriebetrieb?*, Opladen: Westdeutscher Verlag.

Esche, P.G. 1963. *Ernst Abbe*, Leipzig: Teubner.

Esche, P.G. 1966. *Carl Zeiss: Leben und Werk*, Jena: Wartburg-Verlag.

Evans, R.J. 1990. *Proletarians and Politics: Socialism, Protest and the Working Class in Germany before the First World War*, New York: St. Martin's Press.

Evans, T.M.S. and D. Handelmann (eds). 2006. *The Manchester School: Practice and Ethnographic Praxis in Anthropology*, New York and Oxford: Berghahn Books.

Falusné, Sz. K. 1969. *Munkabér, ösztönzés, elosztás*, Budapest: Kossuth Könyvkiadó.

Faulenbach, B., A. Leo and K. Weberskirch. 1994. 'Die "Wende" 1989/90 aus der Sicht von Stahlarbeitern in Henningsdorf und Dortmund', *Jahrbuch Arbeit, Bildung, Kultur* 12, 167–201.

Faulenbach, B., A. Leo and K. Weberskirch. 2000. *Zweierlei Geschichte. Lebensgeschichte und Geschichtsbewusstsein von Arbeiternehmern in West -und Ostdeutschland*, Essen: Klartext-Verlag.

Fehér, J. 1977. 'Diósgyőri munkások az üzemi demokráciáról', *Társadalmi Szemle* 32(11), 76–80.

Feitl, I. 1989. 'A magyar munkástanácsok és az önigazgatás 1956-ban', *Eszmélet* 2, 42–52.

Feitl, I. 2005. 'Parlamentarizmus és önigazgatás az 1956-os forradalomban', *Múltunk* 2, 231–43.

Feitl, I. (ed.). 2009. *Budapest az 1960-as években*, Budapest: Napvilág.

Fejtő, F. 1991. *A népi demokráciák története*, 2. volume, Budapest: Magvető.

Ferenczi, I. 1977. 'Az üzemi demokrácia: fokozott társadalmi ellenőrzés', *Társadalmi Szemle* 32(12), 72–74.

Ferge, Zs. 1969. *Társadalmuk rétegződése: Elvek és tények*, Budapest: Közgazdasági és Jogi Könyvkiadó.

Ferge, Zs. 1976. 'A nők a munkában és a családban', *Társadalmi Szemle* 31(6), 40–50.

Ferge, Zs. 1976. *Az iskolarendszer és az iskolai tudás társadalmi meghatározottsága*, Budapest: Akadémiai Kiadó.

Ferge, Zs. 1979. *A Society in the Making: Hungarian Social and Societal Policy, 1945–1975*, Harmondsworth: Penguin.

Ferge, Zs. 2001. 'A magyarországi szegénységről', *Info-Társadalom-Tudomány* 54.

Ferge, Zs. 2010. *Társadalmi áramlatok és egyéni szerepek*, Budapest: Napvilág Kiadó.

Ferguson, J. 1999. *Expectations of Modernity: Myths and Meanings of Urban Life on the Zambian Copperbelt*, Berkeley and Los Angeles: University of California Press.

Fodor, É. 2003. *Working Difference: Women's Working Lives in Hungary and Austria 1945–1995*, Durham, NC: Duke University Press.

Folkmayer, T. 1978. 'Üzemi demokrácia és tervezés', *Társadalmi Szemle* 33(4), 95–97.

Földes, Gy. 1989. *Hatalom és mozgalom 1956–1989*, Budapest: Reform Könyvkiadó and Kossuth Könyvkiadó.

Földes. Gy. 1993. 'A Kádár-rendszer és a munkásság', *Eszmélet* 19.

Földes, Gy. 1995. *Az eladósodás politikai története 1957–1986*, Budapest: Gondolat.

Fulbrook, M. 1995. *Anatomy of a Dictatorship: Inside the GDR, 1949–1989*, New York: Oxford University Press.

Fuller, L. 1999. *Where Was the Working Class? Revolution in Eastern Germany*, Urbana, Chicago: University of Illinois Press.

Füleki, J. 1976. 'Mérlegen: a közművelődési határozat végrehajtása. Beszélgetés három nagyüzem pártbizottságának titkárával', *Társadalmi Szemle* 31(7), 86–93.

Gábor, R.I. and P. Galasi. 1981. *A "második" gazdaság: Tények és hipotézisek*, Budapest: Közgazdasági és Jogi Könyvkiadó.

Gati, C. 2006. *Failed Illusions: Moscow, Washington, Budapest and the 1956 Hungarian Revolt*, Stanford: Stanford University Press.

Gergely, Gy. 1979. 'Hogyan látják a munkások üzemi gondjainkat és tennivalóinkat?', *Társadalmi Szemle* 34(9), 41–47.

Gerth, K. 2005. *Ernst Abbe: 1840–1905; Wissenschaftler, Unternehmer, Socialreformer*, Jena: Bussert-Stadeler.

Geyer, M. and S. Fitzpatrick. 2009. *Beyond Totalitarianism: Stalinism and Nazism Compared*, New York: Cambridge University Press.

Glaeßner, G.-J. (ed.). 1988. *Die DDR in der Ära Honecker*, Opladen: Westdeutscher Verlag.

Gleason, A. 1995. *Totalitarianism: The Inner History of the Cold War*, New York: Oxford University Press.

Gowan, P. 1995. 'Neo-liberal Theory and Practice for Eastern Europe', *New Left Review* 213, 317–43.

Haney, L. 2002. *Inventing the Needy: Gender and the Politics of Welfare in Hungary*, Berkeley: University of California Press.

Hann, C. (ed.). 2002. *Postsocialism: Ideals, Ideologies and Practices in Eurasia*. London: Routledge.

Haraszti, M. 1977. *A Worker in a Workers' State*, New York: Penguin.

Harsch, D. 2007. *Revenge of the Domestic: Women, the Family, and Communism in the German Democratic Republic*, Princeton: Princeton University Press.

Haupt, H.G. (ed.). 2004. *Aufbruch in die Zukunft: die 1960er Jahre zwischen Planungseuphorie und kulturellem Wandel: DDR, ČSSR und Bundesrepublik Deutschland im Vergleich*, Weilerswist: Velbrück-Wissenschaft.

Hegedüs, A. 1989. *Élet egy eszme árnyékában*, Budapest: Bethlen Gábor Könyvkiadó.

Hermann, A. 1992. *Carl Zeiss: die abenteuerliche Geschichte einer deutschen Firma*, Munich: Piper.

Heumos, P. 2010. 'Workers under Communist Rule: Research in the Former Socialist Countries of Eastern-Central and South-Eastern Europe and in the Federal Republic of Germany', *International Review of Social History* 55.

Héthy, L. 1977. 'Bérvita az építkezésen (Az érdékérvényesítési képesség problémája)', *Valóság* 20(11), 76–88.

Héthy, L. 1977. 'Hogyan látjuk ma az üzemi demokráciát?', *Társadalmi Szemle* 32(9), 64–66.

Héthy, L. 1978. 'Az üzemi demokrácia fejlesztésének útján (Az eszmecsere befejezéséhez)', *Társadalmi Szemle* 33(6), 52–64.

Héthy, L. 1979. 'A gazdasági munka pártirányítása és az érdekegyeztetés', *Társadalmi Szemle* 34(2), 26–35.

Héthy, L. 1980. *Az üzemi demokrácia és a munkások*, Budapest: Kossuth Kiadó.

Héthy, L. 1983. *Vállalatirányítás és demokrácia. Az üzemi demokrácia szociológiai koncepciója és fejlesztésének lehetőségei szervezeti- társadalmi viszonyainkban*, Budapest: Közgazdasági és Jogi Könyvkiadó.

Héthy, L. and Cs. Makó. 1972. 'Az automatizáció és az ipari munkások. Beszámoló egy nemzetközi kutatási program menetéről', *Szociológia* 2, 262–73.

Héthy, L. and Cs. Makó. 1972. 'Work Performance, Interests, Powers and Environment: The Case of Cyclical Slowdowns in a Hungarian Factory', *The Sociological Review Monograph* 17, 123–50.

Héthy, L. and Cs. Makó. 1972. *Munkásmagatartások és a gazdasági szervezet*, Budapest: Akadémiai Kiadó.

Héthy, L. and Cs. Makó. 1975. *Az automatizáció és a munkástudat*, Budapest: az MTA Szociológiai Kutató Intézet Kiadványa.

Héthy, L. and Cs. Makó. 1976. 'A munkások perspektívái és a szocialista vállalat', *Társadalmi Szemle* 31(1), 53–63.

Héthy, L. and Cs. Makó. 1978. *Munkások, érdekek, érdekegyeztetés*, Budapest: Gondolat Kiadó.

Horányi, L. 1976. 'Megalapozott teljesítménykövetelmények és a termelő kapacitás kihasználása (Beszélgetés a Magyar Vagon- és Gépgyárban)', *Társadalmi Szemle* 31(7), 66–72.

Horváth, L. 1977. 'Üzemi demokrácia és vállalati stratégia', *Társadalmi Szemle* 32(9), 72–77.

Horváth, S. 2004. *A kapu és a határ: mindennapi Sztálinváros*, Budapest: MTA Történettudományi Intézete.

Horváth, S. 2005. 'Remaking Working-Class Life in Hungary's First Socialist City', *Journal of International Labor and Working-Class History* 68, 24–46.

Horváth S. 2012. *Két emelet boldogság. Mindennapi szociálpolitika Budapesten a Kádár-korszakban*, Budapest: Napvilág Kiadó.

Horváth, S., L. Pethő and E. Zs. Tóth (eds). 2003. *Munkástörténet – munkásantropológia. Tanulmányok*, Budapest: Napvilág Kiadó.

Horváth, S. (ed.). 2008. *Mindennapok Rákosi és Kádár korában*, Budapest: Nyitott Könyvműhely.

Hübner, P. 1993. 'Balance des Ungleichgewichtes: Zum Verhältnis von Arbeiterinteressen und SED-Herrschaft', *Geschichte und Gesellschaft* 19, 15–28.

Hübner, P. 1995. *Konsens, Konflikt und Kompromiß: Soziale Arbeiterinteressen und Sozialpolitik in der SBZ/DDR 1945–1970*, Berlin: Akademie Verlag.

Hübner, P. and K. Tenfelde (eds). 1999. *Arbeiter in der SBZ – DDR*, Essen: Klartext-Verlag.

Hübner, P. 1999. 'Durch Planung zur Improvisation: Zur Geschichte des Leitungspersonals in der staatlichen Industrie der DDR', *Archiv für Sozialgeschichte* 39, 197–233.

Hübner, P., C. Kleßmann and K. Tenfelde (eds). 2005. *Arbeiter im Staatssozialismus: ideologischer Anspruch und soziale Wirklichkeit*, Cologne: Böhlau.

Hürtgen, R. and T. Reichel (eds). 2001. *Der Schein der Stabilität: DDR-Betriebsalltag in der Ära Honecker*, Berlin: Metropol-Verlag.

Iványi, L. 1979. 'A vállalati profitbővítésre és az önellátásra való törekvés hatása a munkaerőhelyzetre', *Munkaügyi Szemle* 23(4), 1–6.

Jarausch, K.H. 1999. 'Die gescheiterte Gesellschaft. Überlegungen zu einer Sozialgeschichte der DDR', *Archiv für Sozialgeschichte* 39, 1–17.

Jarausch, K.H. and M. Sabrow (eds). 1999. *Der Weg in den Untergang. Der innere Zerfall der DDR*, Göttingen: Vandenhoeck und Ruprecht.

Jávorka, E. 1970. *Életszínvonal a mai társadalomban*, Budapest: Kossuth Kiadó.

Joas, H. and M. Kohli (eds). 1993. *Der Zusammenbruch der DDR. Soziologische Analyse*, Frankfurt am Main: Suhrkamp Verlag.

Kaelble, H., J. Kocka and H. Zwahr (eds). 1994. *Sozialgeschichte der DDR*, Stuttgart: Klett-Cotta.

Kalb, D. 1997. *Expanding Class: Power and Everyday Politics in Industrial Communities, the Netherlands, 1850–1950*, Durham and London: Duke University Press.

Kalb D. and G. Halmai (eds). 2011. *Headlines of Nationalism, Subtexts of Class*, Oxford and New York: Berghahn Books.

Kalocsai, D. 1978. 'A nagyipari üzemek munkáskollektíváinak társadalmi-politikai aktivitása', *Társadalomtudományi Közlemények* 8(2–3), 199–205.

Kalocsai, D. 1978. 'A szocialista brigádok közösséggé fejlődéséről', *Társadalomtudományi Közlemények* 8(1), 10–26.

Katona, I. 1976. 'Eszmecsere a párttagokkal', *Társadalmi Szemle* 31(2), 15–25.

Katznelson, I. and A.R. Zolberg (eds). 1986. *Working-Class Formation: Nineteenth-Century Patterns in Western Europe and the United States*, Princeton: Princeton University Press.

Kaufmann, M. 1990. 'Arbeitseinkommen in der DDR', *Leistung und Lohn*, Nr. 223/224, Sonderheft DDR, 3–20.

Kemény, I. 1972. 'A magyar munkásság rétegződése', *Szociológia* 1, 36–48.

Kemény, I. 1990. *Velünk nevelkedett a gép: Magyar munkások a hetvenes évek elején*, Budapest: Művelődéskutató Intézet.

Kemény, I and B. Lomax (eds). 1986. *Magyar munkástanácsok 1956-ban: Dokumentumok*, Paris: Magyar Füzetek.

Kenney, P. 1997. *Rebuilding Poland: Workers and Communists 1945–1950*, Ithaca, NY: Cornell University Press.

Keren, M. 1978. 'The Rise and Fall of the New Economic System', in: L.H. Legters (ed.), *The German Democratic Republic: A Developed Socialist Society*, Boulder, CO: Westview Press, 61–84.

Kleßmann, C. 2007. *Arbeiter im Arbeiterstaat im 'Arbeiterstaat' DDR: Deutsche Traditionen, sowjetisches Modell, westdeutsches Magnetfeld 1945 bis 1971*, Bonn: Dietz.

Kleßmann, C. (ed.). 2001. *The Divided Past: Rewriting Post-War German History*, New York: Berg Press.

Kochanowicz, J. 1997. 'Incomplete Demise: Reflections on the Welfare State in Poland after Communism', *Social Research* 64(4), 1445–69.

Kocka, J. 1979. 'Stand – Klasse – Organisation. Strukturen sozialer Ungleichheit in Deutschland vom späten 18. bis zum frühen 20. Jahrhundert im Aufriß', in H.U. Wehler (ed.), *Klassen in der europäischen Sozialgeschichte*, Göttingen: Vandenhoeck & Ruprecht, 137–65.

Kocka, J. 1983. *Lohnarbeit und Klassenbildung. Arbeiter und Arbeiterbewegung in Deutschland 1800–1875*, Berlin and Bonn: Dietz Verlag.

Kocka, J. (ed.). 1983. *Europäische Arbeiterbewegungen im 19. Jahrhundert: Deutschland, Österreich, England, und Frankreich im Vergleich*, Göttingen: Vandenhoeck & Ruprecht.

Kocka, J. (ed.). 1993. *Historische DDR-Forschung: Aufsätze und Studien*, Berlin: Akademie Verlag.

Kocka, J. (ed.). 1994. *Von der Arbeiterbewegung zum modernen Sozialstaat: Festschrift für Gerhard A. Ritter zum 65. Geburtstag*, Munich: Saur.

Kocka, J. and M. Sabrow (eds). 1994. *Die DDR als Geschichte: Fragen-Hypothese-Perspektive*, Berlin: Akademie Verlag.

Kohut, T. 2008. '"Erkölcsi téren ma már a szállókon rend van". Mindennapi élet a szocialista korszak munkásszállásain', *Korall* 32(9).

Kolosi, T. 1987. *Tagolt társadalom. Struktúra, rétegződés, egyenlőtlenség Magyarországon*, Budapest: Gondolat Kiadó.

Konrád, Gy. and I. Szelényi. 1979. *The Intellectuals on the Road to Class Power*, New York: Harcourt Brace Jovanovich.

Kopstein, J. 1997. *The Politics of Economic Decline in East Germany 1945–1989*, Chapel Hill, NC: University of North Carolina Press.

Kornai, J. 1957. *A gazdasági vezetés túlzott központosítása*, Budapest: Közgazdasági és Jogi Könyvkiadó.

Kornai, J. 1980. *A hiány*, Budapest: Közgazdasági és Jogi Könyvkiadó.

Kotkin. S. 1995. *Magnetic Mountain: Stalinism as a Civilization*, Berkeley: University of California Press.

Kovács, J.M. (ed.). 1994. *Transition to Capitalism? The Communist Legacy in Eastern Europe*, London: Transaction Publishers.

Krause, P. and J. Schwarze. 1990. 'Die Einkommensstichprobe in Arbeiter- und Angestelltenhaushalten der DDR vom August 1988 – Erhebungskonzeption und Datenbankzugriff', Diskussionspapier Nr. 11. Berlin: Deutsches Institut für Wirtschaftsforschung.

Krausz, T. 1991. *Pártviták és történettudomány: Viták 'az orosz fejlődés' sajátosságairól, különös tekintettel az 1920-as évekre*, Budapest: Akadémiai Kiadó.

Krausz, T. 1996. *Szovjet thermidor: A sztálini fordulat szellemi előzményei 1917–1928*, Budapest: Napvilág Kiadó.

Krausz, T. 2006. 'Az 1956-os munkástanácsokról', *Eszmélet* 72, 32–38.

Krausz, T. 2007. 'Perestroika and the Redistribution of Property in the Soviet Union: Political Perspectives and Historical Evidence', *Contemporary Politics* 13(1).

Krejci, J. 1976. *Social Structure in Divided Germany*, London: Croom Helm.

Kuczynski, J. 1967. *Die Geschichte der Lage der Arbeiter unter dem Kapitalismus*, Berlin: Akademie Verlag.

Kürti, L. 2002. *Youth and the State in Hungary: Capitalism, Communism and Class*, London: Pluto Press.

Laatz, H. 1990. *Klassenstruktur und soziales Verhalten. Zur Entstehung der empirischen Sozialstrukturforschung in der DDR*, Cologne: Verlag Wissenschaft und Politik.

Laba, R. 1991. *The Roots of Solidarity: A Political Sociology of Poland's Working-Class Democratization*, Princeton: Princeton University Press.

Laky, T. 1982. *Érdekviszonyok a vállalati döntésekben*, Budapest: Közgazdasági és Jogi Könyvkiadó.

Lampland, M. 1995. *The Object of Labor: Commodification in Socialist Hungary*, Chicago and London: University of Chicago Press.

Legters, L.H. (ed.). 1978. *The German Democratic Republic: A Developed Socialist Society*, Boulder, CO: Westview Press.

Leptin, G. 1968. 'Das "Neue ökonomische System" Mitteldeutschlands', in K.C. Thalheim and H.H. Höhmann (eds), *Wirtschaftsreformen in Osteuropa*, Cologne: Verl. Wissenschaft und Politik, 100–30.

Lewin, M. 1985. *The Making of the Soviet System: Essays in the Social History of Interwar Russia*, London: Methuen.

Linden, M. 2007. *Western Marxism and the Soviet Union: A Survey of Critical Theory and Debates since 1917*, Leiden: Brill.

Linden, M. 2008. *Workers of the World: Essays toward a Global Labor History*, Leiden and Boston: Brill

Lindenberger, T. (ed.). 1990. *Herrschaft und Eigensinn in der Diktatur: Studien zur Gesellschaftsgeschichte der DDR*, Cologne: Böhlau.

Litván, Gy. (ed.). 1974. *Magyar munkásszociográfiák 1888–1945*, Budapest: Kossuth Kiadó.

Lomax, B. 1989. *Magyarország 1956*, Budapest: Aura.

Losonczi, Á. 1977. *Az életmód az időben, a tárgyakban és az értékekben*, Budapest: Gondolat Kiadó.

Losonczi, K. 1973. *A munkaerőmozgásról*, Budapest: Kossuth Könyvkiadó.

Lukács, Gy. 1985. *Demokratisierung heute und morgen*. Budapest: Akadémiai Kiadó.

A Magyar Szocialista Munkáspárt határozatai és dokumentumai 1963–1966. 1978. Az MSZMP Központi Bizottságának Párttörténeti Intézete. Budapest: Kossuth Kiadó.

A Magyar Szocialista Munkáspárt határozatai és dokumentumai 1971–1975. 1978. Az MSZMP Központi Bizottságának Párttörténeti Intézete. Budapest: Kossuth Kiadó.

Maier. C. 1997. *Dissolution: The Crisis of Communism and the End of East Germany*, Princeton: Princeton University Press.

Majtényi, Gy. 2009. *K-vonal. Uralmi elit és luxus a szocializmusban*, Budapest: Nyitott Könyvműhely.

Makó, Cs. 1977. 'Az érdekegyeztetés és a cselekvési egység az üzemben. Az üzemi demokrácia fejlesztésének kérdéséhez', *Társadalmi Szemle* 32(5), 58–67.

Makó, Cs. 1979. 'Részvétel: a feladat átalakítása vagy a hatalmi viszonyok átalakítása', *Valóság* 22(4), 14–24.

Makó, Cs. 1979. 'Technika – munkásigények – munkakövetelmények', *Ergonómia* 12(3–4), 190–97.

Manz, G. 1965. 'Tapasztalatok a népgazdasági tervezés és irányítás új rendszeréről az NDK-ban', *Közgazdasági Szemle* 12(2), 176–88.

Marle, Gy. 1978. 'Az üzemi demokrácia és a termelés', *Társadalmi Szemle* 33(3), 69–75.

Maros, D. 1976. 'Fiatalok a munkáspályán. Gondolatok az ifjúmunkások társadalmi beilleszkedéséről', *Társadalmi Szemle* 31(3), 51–58.

Marosi, J. 1977. 'Nem csak a gazdasági vezetők dolga ...', *Társadalmi Szemle* 32(12), 70–72.

Merkel, I. 1990. *... und Du, Frau an der Werkbank: die DDR in der 50er Jahren*, Berlin: Elefanten Press.

Merkel, I. 1999. *Utopie und Bedürfnis: die Geschichte der Konsumkultur in der DDR*, Cologne: Böhlau.

Merkel, I. (ed.). 2000. *'Wir sind doch nicht die Meckerecke der Nation': Briefe an das Fernsehen der DDR*, Berlin: Schwarzkopf & Schwarzkopf.

Meuschel, S. 1993. 'Überlegungen zu einer Herrschafts- und Gesellschaftsgeschichte der DDR', *Geschichte und Gesellschaft* 19(1), 5–14.

Mód, A. 1974. 'Munkásismeretek, munkástörekvések, üzemi demokrácia (Kutatási tapasztalatok)', *Társadalmi Szemle* 29(11), 53–63.

Munkácsy, F. 1976. 'A munkaerőhiány és a munkapiac sajátosságainak összefüggései', *Munkaügyi Szemle* 20(6), 1–5.

Munkácsy, F. 1979. 'Munkaerő-átcsoportosítás tervszerűen, szervezetten', *Munkaügyi Szemle* 23(3), 1–5.

Murphy, K.J. 2005. *Revolution and Counterrevolution: Class Struggle in a Moscow Metal Factory*, New York: Berghahn Books.

Mühlberg, D. 2002. 'Konnte Arbeiterkultur in der DDR gesellschaftlich hegemonial sein?', *Utopie kreativ* 145, 965–76.

Mühlfriedel, W. (ed.). 1996. *Carl Zeiss: Die Geschichte eines Unternehmens*, Weimar: Böhlau.

Mühlfriedel, W. and E. Hellmuth. 2004. *Carl Zeiss in Jena 1945–1990*, Cologne: Weimar, Vienna: Böhlau.

Nemitz, E. 1988. *Junge Produktionsarbeiter und Lehrlinge in der DDR. Eine empirische Untersuchung über Jugendliche in volkseigenen Betrieben des Bauwesens*, Koblenz: Verlag Siegfried Bublies.

Neumann, P. 2002. 'Betriebliche Sozialpolitik im VEB Carl Zeiss Jena 1948 bis 1953', M.A., Jena: Friedrich-Schiller-Universität.

Neumann, P. 2000 '"... bisher nicht Gedachtes denken ...": Zur Bedeutung der Prognostik im Neuen Ökonomischen System. Das Beispiel des VEB Carl Zeiss Jena', manuscript, Jena: Friedrich-Schiller-Universität.

Niethammer, L., A. Plato and D. Wierling. 1991. *Die volkseigene Erfahrung: eine Archäologie des Lebens in der Industrieprovinz der DDR*, Berlin: Rowohlt-Berlin-Verlag.

Nyers, R. 1968. *Gazdaságpolitikánk és a gazdasági mechanizmus reformja*. Budapest: Kossuth Kiadó.

Oroszi, S. and J. Veress. 1979. 'Szükségszerű-e a munkaerőhiány a szocialista gazdaságban?', *Közgazdasági Szemle* 26(12), 1462–73.

Ost, D. 1990. *Solidarity and the Politics of Anti-politics: Opposition and Reform in Poland since 1968*, Philadelphia: Temple University Press.

Ost, D. 2005. *The Defeat of Solidarity: Anger and Politics in Postcommunist Europe*, Ithaca, NY: Cornell University Press.

Pappné, R.J. and L. Tüü. 1968. 'A kis-és középüzemek szerepéről', *Gazdaság* 2(2), 12–25.

Parkin, F. (ed.). 1974. *The Social Analysis of Class Structure*, London: Tavistock.

Pető. 1992. *A munkások életkörülményei Magyarországon az 1950-es években*, manuscript, Budapest: Eötvös Loránd University.

Pickles, J. and A. Smith. 1998. *Theorising Transition: The Political Economy of Postcommunist Transformations*, London and New York: Routledge.

Pierstorff, J. 1905. *Ernst Abbe als Sozialpolitiker*, Munich: Allgemeine Zeitung.

Pittaway, M. 1998. 'Industrial Workers, Socialist Industrialisation and the State in Hungary, 1948–1958', Ph.D., University of Liverpool.

Pittaway, M. 2002. 'The Reproduction of Hierarchy: Skill, Working-Class Culture and the State in Early Socialist Hungary', *The Journal of Modern History* 74, 737–69.

Pittaway, M. 2004. *Eastern Europe 1939–2000*, London: Hodder Arnold.

Pittaway, M. 2005. 'Accommodation and the Limits of Economic Reform: Industrial Workers during the Making and Unmaking of Kádár's Hungary', in P. Hübner, C. Kleßmann and K. Tenfelde (eds), *Arbeiter im Staatssozialismus – ideologischer Anspruch und soziale Wirklichkeit. Die DDR im ostmitteleuropäischen Vergleich*, 453–71.

Pittaway, M. 2006. 'A magyar forradalom új megközelítésben: az ipari munkásság, a szocializmus széthullása és rekonstrukciója, 1953–1958', *Eszmélet* 72, 11–31.

Pittaway. M. 2011. 'A magyar munkásság és a rendszerváltás', *Múltunk* 1.

Pittaway, M. 2012. *The Workers' State: Industrial Labour and the Making of Socialist Hungary, 1944–1958*, Pittsburgh, PA: Pittsburgh University Press.

Pogány, Gy. 1982. *Munkaerő-gazdálkodás és munkaerő-politika*, Budapest: Közgazdasági és Jogi Könyvkiadó.

Pollack, D. 1998. 'Die konstitutive Widersprüchlichkeit der DDR Oder War die DDR-Gesellschaft homogen?', *Geschichte und Gesellschaft* 24(1), 110–31.

Rácz, A. 1980. 'Munka szerinti elosztás, ösztönzés', *Társadalmi Szemle* 35(1), 81–89.

Radice, H. 1998. 'A feltámadt kapitalizmus: Kelet-Közép-Európa a "globalizáció" fényében', in T. Krausz (ed.), *Rendszerváltás és társadalomkritika*, Budapest: Napvilág, 194–209.

Rainer, M.J. 2011. *Bevezetés a kádárizmusba*, Budapest: L'Harmattan.

Ránki, Gy. 1983. *Mozgásterek, kényszerpályák. Válogatott tanulmányok*, Budapest: Magvető.

Reichel, T. 2001. 'Die "durchherrschte Arbeitsgesellschaft": Zu den Herrschaftsstrukturen und Machtverhältnissen in DDR-Betrieben', in: R. Hürtgen and T. Reichel (eds), *Der Schein der Stabilität: DDR-Betriebsalltag in der Ära Honecker*, 85–110.

Rézler, Gy. 1938. *A magyar nagyipari munkásosztály kialakulása, 1867–1914*, Budapest: Rekord.

Richter, J., H. Förster and U. Lakemann. 1997. *Stalinstadt-Eisenhüttenstadt: von der Utopie zur Gegenwart: Wandel industrieller, regionaler und sozialer Strukturen in Eisenhüttenstadt*, Marburg: Schüren.

Rietzschel, A. 1997. 'Frauenerwerbstätigkeit und Teilzeitarbeit in der DDR, 1957 bis 1970', *Potsdam Bulletin* 9, 34–42.

Ritter, G.A. 1976. *Arbeiterbewegung, Parteien und Parlamentarismus. Aufsätze zur Deutschen Sozial- und Verfassungsgeschichte des 19. und 20. Jahrhunderts: Beiträge zur Geschichte des 19. und 20. Jahrhunderts*, Göttingen: Vandenhoeck & Ruprecht.

Ritter, G.A. 1989. *Der Sozialstaat: Entstehung und Entwicklung im internationalen Vergleich*, Munich: Oldenbourg.

Ritter, G.A. (ed.). 1990. *Der Aufstieg der deutschen Arbeiterbewegung: Sozialdemokratie und Freie Gewerkschaften im Parteiensystem und Sozialmilieu des Kaiserreichs*, Munich: Oldenbourg.

Ritter, G.A. and K. Tenfelde. 1992. *Arbeiter im Deutschen Kaiserreich 1871 bis 1914*, Bonn: Dietz.

Roberts, G. 2006. *Stalin's Wars: From World War to Cold War, 1939–1953*, New Haven, CT: Yale University Press.

Roesler, J. 1999. 'Die Rolle des Brigadiers bei der Konfliktregulierung zwischen Arbeitsbrigaden und der Werkleitung', in: P. Hübner and K. Tenfelde (eds), *Arbeiter in der SBZ – DDR*, 413–38.

Rohr, M. 1940. *Ernst Abbe*, Jena: Fischer.

RónaTas, Á. 1997. *The Great Surprise of the Small Transformation: The Demise of Communism and the Rise of the Private Sector in Hungary*, Ann Arbor: University of Michigan.

Rózsa, J. 1978. 'Napjaink kérdése: az üzemi demokrácia', *Társadalmi Szemle* 33(2), 79–84.

Sárközy, T. 1976. 'Felelősség a vállalati vezetésért és gazdálkodásért', *Társadalmi Szemle* 31(3), 67–76.

Sas Judit, H. 1995. *Szubjektív történelem 1980–1994*, Budapest: MTA Szociológiai Intézet.

Sas Judit, H. 2003. *Közelmúlt. Rendszerváltások, családtörténetek*, Budapest: Új Mandátum Kiadó.

Schmidt, W. 1995. 'Metamorphosen des Betriebskollektivs. Zur Transformation der Sozialordnung in ostdeutschen Betrieben', *Soziale Welt* 45(3), 305–25.

Schmidt, W. 1999. *Jeder hat jetzt mit sich selbst zu tun': Arbeit, Freizeit und politische Orientierungen in Ostdeutschland*, Konstanz: Univ.-Verl.-Konstanz.

Schumann, A. 2003. 'Veredlung der Produzenten oder Freizeitpolitik? Betriebliche Kulturarbeit vor 1970', *Postdamer Bulletin für Zeithistorische Studien* 29, 73–78.

Schumann, A. 2005. '"Macht die Betriebe zu Zentren der Kulturarbeit": Gewerkschaftlich organisierte Kulturarbeit in den Industriebetrieben der DDR in den fünfziger Jahren: Sozialhistorisches Novum oder Modifizierung betriebspolitischer Traditionen?', in: P. Hübner, C. Kleßmann and K. Tenfelde (eds), *Arbeiter im Staatssozialismus – ideologischer Anspruch und soziale Wirklichkeit. Die DDR im ostmitteleuropäischen Vergleich*, 271–89.

Schumann, W. et al. 1962. *Carl Zeiss Jena, einst und jetzt*, Berlin: Rütten and Loening.

Schüler, A. 1999. 'Mächtige Mütter und unwillige Töchter', in P. Hübner and K. Tenfelde (eds), *Arbeiter in der SBZ – DDR*, 709–40.

Schüler, A. 2001. *'Die Spinne': die Erfahrungsgeschichte weiblicher Industriearbeit im VEB Leipziger Baumwollspinnerei*, Leipzig: Leipziger-Univ.-Verl.

Schweitzer, I. 1982. *A vállalatnagyság*, Budapest: Közgazdasági és Jogi Könyvkiadó.

Šik, O. 1967. *Plan and Market under Socialism*, White Plains, NY: International Arts and Sciences Press.

Simonyi, Á. 1977. 'Munkásrészvétel üzemi bérezési döntésekben (Kutatói tapasztalatok a Magyar Vagon és Gépgyárban)', *Társadalmi Szemle* 32(10), 99–101.

Simonyi, Á. 1978. 'Mukahelyi demokrácia és nyilvánosság', *Társadalmi Szemle* 33(1), 59–67.

Sipos, P. 1988. *Legális és illegális munkásmozgalom, 1919–1944*, Budapest: Gondolat.

Solga, H. 1995. *Auf dem Weg in eine klassenlose Gesellschaft? Klassenlagen und Mobilität zwischen Generationen in der DDR*, Berlin: Akademie Verlag.

Solga, H. 2001. 'Aspekte der Klassenstruktur in der DDR in den siebziger und achtziger Jahren und die Stellung der Arbeiterklasse', in: R. Hürtgen and T. Reichel (eds), *Der Schein der Stabilität: DDR-Betriebsalltag in der Ära Honecker*, 35–52.

Somlai, P. 2008. *Társas és társadalmi. Válogatott tanulmányok*, Budapest, Napvilág Kiadó.

Sőtér, E. 1977. 'Gondolatok a szocialista brigádmozgalomról', *Társadalmi Szemle* 32(4), 9–16.

Statisztikai évkönyv 1980. Központi Statisztikai Hivatal, 1981. Budapest: Statisztikai Kiadó.

Steiner, A. 1990. 'Abkehr vom NÖS. Die wirtschaftlichen Entscheidungen 1967/68 – Ausgangspunkt der Krisenprozesse 1969/70?' in: J. Černy (ed.), *Brüche, Krisen, Wendepunkte: Neubefragungen von DDR-Geschichte*, Leipzig: Urania-Verl, 247–53.

Steiner, A. 1999. *Die DDR-Wirtschaftsreform der sechziger Jahre: Konflikt zwischen Effizienz- und Machtkalkül*, Berlin: Akademie-Verlag.

Steiner, A. 2004. *Von Plan zu Plan: eine Wirtschaftsgeschichte der DDR*, Munich: Dt. Vrl.-Anst.

Stephan, H. and E. Wiedemann. 1990. 'Lohnstruktur und Lohndifferenzierung in der DDR. Ergebnisse der Lohndatenerfassung vom September 1988', *Mittelungen aus der Arbeitsmarkt und Berufsforschung* 23, 550–62.

Swain, N. 1992. *Hungary: The Rise and Fall of Feasible Socialism*, London and New York: Verso.

Sz. Bíró, Z. 2003. 'Politikatörténeti vázlat a késői Szovjetunióról', in: T. Krausz and Sz. Z. Bíró (eds), *Peresztrojka és tulajdonáthelyezés. Tanulmányok és dokumentumok a rendszerváltozás történetéből a Szovjetunióban (1985–1991)*, 11–51.

Szalai, E. 1986. *Beszélgetések a gazdasági reformról*, Budapest: Pénzügykutató Intézet Kiadványai.

Szalai, E. 1989. *Gazdasági mechanizmus, reformtörekvések és nagyvállalati érdekek*, Budapest: Közgazdasági és Jogi Könyvkiadó.

Szalai, E. 2004. 'Tulajdonviszonyok, társadalomszerkezet és munkásság', *Kritika* 33(9), 2–6.

Szeben, É. 1979. *A munka szerinti elosztás érvényesítésének néhány problémája a fejlett szocialista társadalom építésének időszakában Magyarországon*, manuscript, Budapest.

Szelényi, I. 1990. *Új osztály, állam, politika*, Budapest: Európa Kiadó.

Szelényi, I. and Gy. Konrád. 1969. *Az új lakótelepek szociológiai problémái*, Budapest: Akadémiai Kiadó.

Tabiczky, Z. 1977. *A Magyar Vagon- és Gépgyár története*, 1–2 vols, Győr: Rába.

Tenfelde, K. (ed.). 1991. *Arbeiter im 20. Jahrhundert*. Stuttgart: Klett-Cotta.

Thurston. R. 1996. *Life and Terror in Stalin's Russia*, New Haven, CT: Yale University Press.

Tillmann, J. 1977. 'Teljesítménykövetelmények és munkaidőalap-kihasználás', *Munkaügyi Szemle* 21(3), 14–18.

Tímár, J. 1977. 'Foglalkoztatáspolitikánkról és munkaerő-gazdálkodásunkról', *Közgazdasági Szemle* 24(2), 129–50.

Tischler, J. 2005. 'A "győri csata – 1965"', *Beszélő* 10(5), 63–67.

Tóth, E. Zs. 1999. 'A Csepel Vas- és Fémművek munkástanácsainak története (1956– 1957)', *Múltunk* 4, 163–98.

Tóth, E. Zs. 2003. 'Egy kitüntetés befogadástörténete. Egy állami díjas női szocialista brigád képe a sajtóban és a tagok emlékezetében', in S. Horváth, L. Pethő and E. Zs. Tóth (eds). *Munkástörténet – munkásantropológia. Tanulmányok*, 126–39.

Tóth, E. Zs. 2007. *'Puszi Kádár Jánosnak': Munkásnők élete a Kádár-korszakban mikrotörténeti megközelítésben*, Budapest: Napvilág.

Tóth. E. Zs. 2010. *Kádár leányai: Nők a szocialista időszakban*, Budapest: Nyitott Könyvműhely.

Tóth, L. (ed.). 1984. *Győr-Sopron*, Budapest: Kossuth Kiadó.

Tóth, P.P. (ed.). 2011. *Válogatás Rézler Gyula 1932 és 1999 között megjelent írásaiból*, Budapest: Gondolat Kiadó.

Touraine, A. et al. 1983. *Solidarity: The Analysis of a Social Movement, Poland 1980–1981*, Cambridge: Cambridge University Press.

Tőkés, R.L. 1996. *Hungary's Negotiated Revolution: Economic Reform, Social Change, and Political Succession, 1957–1990*, New York: Cambridge University Press.

Trotsky, L. (1937) 1972. *The Revolution Betrayed: What is the Soviet Union and Where is it Going?* New York: (Doubleday, Doran and Co.) Pathfinder Press.

Tütő, L. 1993. 'A szocialista ellenzékiség történetéből – az 1971-es Kemény-per', *Eszmélet* 5(3).

Tütő, L. 2006. '1956 mint nyelvi probléma', *Eszmélet* 72, 5–10.

Utasi, Á. 2008. *Éltető kapcsolatok: A kapcsolatok hatása a szubjektív életminőségre*, Budapest: Új Mandátum.

Vester, M., M. Hofmann and I. Zierke (eds). 1995. *Soziale Milieus in Ostdeutschland. Gesellschaftliche Strukturen zwischen Zerfall und Neubildung*, Cologne: Bund-Verlag.

Vitkovics, P. 1978. 'Az üzemi demokrácia és a pártszervezet munkája', *Társadalmi Szemle* 33(1), 67–69.

Voszka, É. 1988. *Reform és átszervezés a 80-as években*, Budapest: Közgazdasági és Jogi Könyvkiadó.

Wallerstein, I. 1974. *The Modern World System I: Capitalist Agriculture and the Origins of the European World Economy in the Sixteenth Century*, New York: Academic Press.

Weidenfeld, W. and H. Zimmermann (eds). 1989. *Deutschland-Handbuch. Eine doppelte Bilanz 1949–1989*, Bonn: Landeszentrale für politische Bildung.

Weil, F. 2000. *Herrschaftsanspruch und soziale Wirklichkeit: zwei sachsische Betriebe in der DDR wahrend der Honecker Aera*, Cologne: Böhlau.

Weiß, J. 2003. 'Die namenlose Gesellschaft. Identitätsprobleme der Bevölkerung Ostdeutschlands', in S. Beetz, U. Jacob and A. Sterbling (eds), *Soziologie über die Grenzen. Festschrift für Prof. Dr. Dr. h. c. Bálint Balla zum 75. Geburtstag*, Hamburg: Krämer, 487–94.

Welskopp, T. 1993. 'Von der verhinderten Heldengeschichte des Proletariats zur vergleichenden Sozialgeschichte der Arbeiterschaft – Perspektiven der Arbeitergeschichtsschreibung in den 1990er Jahren', *1999 Zeitschrift für Sozialgeschichte des 20. und 21. Jahrhunderts* 3, 34–53.

Welskopp, T. 1994. *Arbeit und Macht im Hüttenwerk. Arbeits- und industrielle in der deutschen und amerikanischen Eisen- und Stahlindustrie von den 1860er bis zu den 1930er Jahren*, Bonn: Dietz.

Welskopp, T., 1996. 'Der Betrieb als soziales Handlungsfeld. Neuere Forschungsansätze in der Industrie- und Arbeitergeschichte', *Geschichte und Gesellschaft* 22, 117–42.

William, H.A. 1967. *Carl Zeiss: 1816–1888*, Munich: Bruckmann.

Willis, P.E. 1977. *Learning to Labor: How Working-Class Kids Get Working Class Jobs*, Aldershot: Ashgate.

INDEX

Abbe, Ernst 65–6
Adam, J. 32–3n87
adult education 124, 126–7, 130
adultery
    condemnation as petit-bourgeois 57
    denunciation of 232
Ady Endre Community House 131
affirmative action, politics of 224
Akgöz, G. 30n64
Akszentievics, Gy. 25–6n37
Amsden, A.H., Kochanowicz, J. and Taylor,
    L. 32–3n87
Andics, J. and Rozgonyi, T. 25–6n37
Andor, L. 32–3n87, 33n88
Angelusz, R. 269n78, 306, 317n26,
    318n32, 318n36
Angelusz, R. and Tardos, R. 216n304
Angelusz, R., Nagy, L.G. and Tardos, R.
    204n21
annual bonuses, distribution of 156
annual premium payments in Hungary 119
Ansorg, L. 29–30n60
anti-fascist education in GDR 290
anti-management attitudes in Hungary
    144–5
anti-peasant feelings at Rába MVG 50–51
anti-reformist attitudes 93
anti-socialism in political mood 248–9
Antragsteller (applicants – for permission to
    leave GDR) 256–7, 273n190, 306
Auerbach, F. 102–3n111
Austria
    capitalism in, closeness of 60–61
    standard of living in, problem of 242–3
authoritarianism of management in GDR
    171, 178
autonomy of enterprises, improvements in
    37–8, 40–41
AWU *see* workers' hostels

Bahro, R. 26–7n39
Balázs, E., Földes, Gy. and Konok, P. 316n7
Balogh, J. 266n22
Bartha, E. and Krausz, T. 24n19, 316n7
Bartha, Eszter 23n11, 30n67, 102n110,
    293n2
base-cell meetings 138
    MSZMP 234, 236
    SED 254, 257–8
Bauer, T. 98n14
Bedau, K.-D. 204n8
Beetz, S., Jacob, U. and Sterbling, A. 32n83
Behrens, Fritz 97n7
Béky, G. and Zétényi, Z. 209n129
Belwe, K. 32n82
Benary, Arne 97n7
Bence, Gy. and Kis, J. 26–7n39
Bence, Gy., Kis, J. and Márkus, Gy 26–7n39
Berend, T.I. 98n14
Berend, T.I. and Ránki, Gy. 33n89
Berényi, J. 204n21
Berlin, workers' demonstrations in (1953) 5
Bessel, R. and Jessen, R. 29–30n60
Beyme, Klaus von 23n11
Biermann, Wolfgang 68–9, 70, 103n130, 306
Bíró, Sz.Z. 31n74
Bittner, R. 29–30n60, 214n244
Böhm, A. and Pál, L. 101n69, 208n94
Bokros, Lajos 33n88
Boltanski, L. and Chiapello, E. 293n7
Borbély, S. 266n22
Bossányi, K. 22n4, 99n45, 100n46, 206n48,
    210n148
Bouvier, B. 27n43, 204n9, 204n11
Bozóki, A. 22n1
Brezhnev, Leonid I. 67
'*bricoleurs*' in Hungary 278
Bruszt, László 32–3n87
Bryant, C.G.A. and Mokrzycki, E. 32n86